THE CANADA-ISRAEL NEXUS

THE CANADA-ISRAEL NEXUS

Eric Walberg

CLARITY PRESS

© 2017 Eric Walberg
ISBN: 9780997896565
EBOOK ISBN: 9780998694702

In-house editor: Diana G. Collier
Cover: R. Jordan P. Santos
Top photo "First Nations Trek" by Fred Chartrand, with permission from Canadian Press.

ALL RIGHTS RESERVED: Except for purposes of review, this book may not be copied, or stored in any information retrieval system, in whole or in part, without permission in writing from the publishers.

Library of Congress Cataloging-in-Publication Data

Names: Walberg, Eric, author.
Title: The Canada-Israel nexus / by Eric Walberg.
Description: Atlanta, GA : Clarity Press, Inc., [2017] | Includes bibliographical references and index.
Identifiers: LCCN 2017031096 (print) | LCCN 2017031797 (ebook) | ISBN
 9780998694702 | ISBN 9780997896565 (alk. paper)
Subjects: LCSH: Canada--Foreign relations--Israel. | Israel--Foreign relations--Canada. | Canada--Ethnic relations. | Israel--Ethnic relations.
Classification: LCC F1029.5.I7 (ebook) | LCC F1029.5.I7 W35 2017 (print) |
 DDC 327.7105694--dc23
LC record available at https://lccn.loc.gov/2017031096

Clarity Press, Inc.
2625 Piedmont Rd. NE, Ste. 56
Atlanta, GA. 30324 , USA
http://www.claritypress.com

TABLE OF CONTENTS

Preface / 9

Introduction
Definitions / 12

PART ONE:
BIRTH OF TWO NATIONS

Chapter 1
Creating Canada
    Geopolitics: Great Game I (up to 1945) / 37
    European Settler Colonies in North America / 38
    The American Dispossession of Native Nations / 40
    Indigenous Dispossession, Canada-Style / 41
    Assimilations, Treaties / 48

Chapter 2
Creating Israel
    Great Game II (1945-1991) / 57
    A European Settler Colony in Palestine / 58
    The Dispossession of the Palestinians / 61
    Jews and Empires / 65
    Other 'Others' / 67
    Conundrum of Jewish nationalism and democracy / 69

Chapter 3
The Seeds of a New Empire
    Hard Power / 76
    Soft Power / 79
    Yiddishkeit as US-Canadian-Israeli Culture / 85

Chapter 4
The Enemy of My Friend Is My Enemy
 US-Canada-Israel vs Soviet Union / 105
 Iran, Egypt / 108
 Palestinian Resistance / 112
 Perpetual War / 116
 Violations of International Norms / 119

PART TWO:
CANADA: ISRAEL'S "BEST FRIEND"

Chapter 5
Jews in Canadian History
 Introduction / 125
 17th-19th Centuries: Golden Age for Jews in Canada /127
 Early 20th Century: Mass Immigration and Assimilation / 130
 Israel as an Escape Clause for Unwanted Refugees / 145
 Post-WWII: Resurgent Identity / 148
 Israel as the 'Promised Land' / 150
 Quebec's 'Jewish Problem' / 154
 The Formation of Jewish/ Zionist Organizations / 156
 Tagging the Early "Antisemites" / 162
  Goldwin Smith
  United Church
  Reben Slonim

Chapter 6
Entrenching a Canadian Pro-Israel Foreign Policy
 From Pearson to Chretien / 186
 Harper / 194
  UN Embroglio / 196
  Kicking Out Iran / 198
  Terrorism from Harperism / 202
 Justin Trudeau: Harper-lite / 205
 Cultural battles / 208
  Israel in Canada: Promised lands / 208

The Power of the Jewish Lobby in Canada / 215
    Wealth, Mining, Media / 215
  Dual Loyalty / 216
    When Dual Loyalty Got the Wink and the Nod / 218

PART THREE:
ANTI SEMITISM WACK-A-MOLE

Chapter 7
The Lone Rangers
  Keegstra, Zundel, Topham / 240
  More Foot Shooting / 256
  The Lone Rangers' Tontos / 260
  Investigating the Conspiracies / 267
  The Unknown Holocaust / 281

Chapter 8
Native Nations/Canada and Palestine/Israel
  Land and Resource Rights / 299
  Israeli/ Zionist Soft/ Hard Power with First Nations / 312
  Native Political Resurgence / 321

Chapter 9
The New Anti Semites: Tarring Anti-Zionism
  Secular Activists / 332
  Jewish, Muslim activism / 343
  From Canadian Jew to Jewish Canadian / 344
  Deconstructing Jewishness / 346
  South Africa and Israel / 351
  Afterword / 352

Bibliography / 358

PREFACE

Why Canada?

Canada and Israel were cut from the same cloth: British white settler colonies[1] that dispossessed and killed natives to steal their lands. While there were stark differences—in the size of the colonies, their geopolitics, their historical period, and in the degree of ruthlessness exercised by the mother country and its settlers—both are offspring of British imperialism.

Canada and Israel have many historical similarities, and Jews have come to Canada in the hundreds of thousands and prospered. The Canadian government under Conservative Prime Minister Stephen Harper (2006–2016) reached a level of worship of things Israeli and Jewish unprecedented in Israel's short history, officially referring to Canada as "Israel's best friend". More than any country except the US and Palau, Canada supports Israeli violations of international law at the UN. Canadian Jews support the obliteration of Palestinian villages famously in Canada Park, an Israeli national park stretching over 700 acres, extending into the West Bank,[2] with donations amounting to hundreds of millions of dollars to the 'charity' the Jewish National Fund. Harper's swan song was the creation (and funding while in office) of a bird sanctuary in Israel, which the Israelis were thoughtful enough to call the Stephen Harper Bird Sanctuary.[3]

In *The End of the Peace Process: Oslo and After,* Edward Said worried that there is "the strong possibility that Palestinians will be Red Indianized forever, that Israel's Jews cannot tolerate our present status either as angry religious terrorists or as compliant Red Indians."[4]

As a weak postmodern nation (i.e., with no independent foreign policy), then famous as a peace-keeper, Canada offered a perfect foil as Israel carried out some of its worst atrocities in Gaza.[5] While the shameful Harper period seems to be at an end, the inhumane siege of

Gaza continues, and Canada applauds, as if it were virtually an outpost of Israel. At the same time, Canada has become a haven for disaffected Israelis, looking for a more promising land than Eretz Israel.[6] So this work is a case study in the way Zionism, Jews and Israel impinge on an otherwise law-abiding nation. It is also a study in contrasting relations with colonial natives.

The problem that a state of Israel might create was foreseen from the start, and addressed publicly by statesmen after WWII, when the form in which a homeland/refuge for Jews was being debated. In Canada, only the United Church spoke out to protest the creation of a Jewish state. Prime Minister Mackenzie King was as usual a fence-sitter, glad to be freed of too many Jewish refugees. But he was shocked by the brutality of the 'war of liberation' of the Jews in 1948, and put off official recognition of the new state. As a seasoned politician with no particular interest in Jewish affairs, he saw trouble coming. When he retired, however, his heirs turned out to be enthusiastic Zionists. There was no public Jewish Canadian voice that was opposed to Israel, outside of the Communist Party, which was barely legal at that point, without much influence, and crippled by Cold War hysteria. The writing was on the wall.

In the US, Einstein represented the most famous Jewish voice rejecting a racially based state, but he and a few others who spoke out were drowned in the euphoria of the novel idea embraced by the more than 2 million American Jews, who were already an important factor in American life. No strong voice was willing to articulate and work to prevent the obvious: a racial state means a racist state, which was the cause of WWII, launched by the 'Aryan' racial state Germany. To found a Jewish state on the same principle was surely a recipe for disaster. In the dozens of books written about Canada and Israel—virtually all by Zionists, whether Jewish or Gentile—this issue is never addressed.

'The Zionists won.' There has been no public debate about the legitimacy of Israel as racially-based state, despite the fact that international law rejects this. That is why it is so important for the Zionists to force Palestinians to recognize not just the state of Israel (which they did at Oslo in 1993), but Israel as a *Jewish* state. It seems that in this instance, only the Arabs understand international law.

The history of Jews in Canada, and Canada in Israel, is fascinating in itself. We in Canada watch with horror the daily news, as if it were the war in Vietnam continuing, as Israel ruthlessly persecutes a people who have no effective means of self-defense. It is instructive to watch a speeded-up version of what our forefathers did to Canadian natives over the past four centuries, though Israel has no time or interest in the niceties of British-style colonialism, so we get the uncensored, much more brutal version.

There are many twists and turns in the struggle of the Zionists to press their case, and the efforts of those, be they sophisticated intellectuals or simply high school teachers or farmers, to fight to bring the truth to light. "The only thing that will have to go in the transition to a non-racist, truly democratic state in Israel/Palestine is the Zionist dream. But what is so terrible about that? Better to call Zionism a delusion than a dream."[7]

Endnotes

1. Only white British colonists could aspire to dominion status with all its perks. While using white is an anachronism, it is appropriate here, as British policy at the time was blatantly racist and white was treated as a race. White is still a category in the US census.
2. See https://en.wikipedia.org/wiki/Canada_Park
3. "Canadian legend Chapter IV: Goodbye Canada, Hello Harperland", *ericwalberg.com*, January 1, 2016.
4. Edward Said, *The End of the Peace Process: Oslo and after*, Vintage, 2001, 50.
5. Gaza War (2008–09), also known as Operation Cast Lead, 2012 conflict, also known as Operation Pillar of Defense, 2014 Israel–Gaza conflict, also known as Operation Protective Edge.
6. The Land of Israel is the traditional Jewish name for an area of indefinite geographical extension in the Southern Levant, appropriately, as Israel's borders keep expanding. In the words of Humpty Dumpty, "a word means precisely what I intend it to mean." Lewis Carroll, *Through the Looking Glass* (1871).
7. Joel Kovel, *Overcoming Zionism: Creating a Single Democratic State in Israel/Palestine*, Pluto Press, 2007, 208.

| Introduction |

DEFINITIONS

Let's face it: the Zionists won.
Or have they?

Just when it looks like the Palestinian cause is hopeless, suddenly things can turn upside down. As this book was about to go to press, the UN Economic and Social Commission for Western Asia (ESCWA) issued a report in March 2017 calling Israel an apartheid state.[1] The report recalled the UN resolution of 1975 calling Zionism "a form of racism and racial discrimination", which was revoked in 1991 under US pressure.

Since most of the world's states have signed the Convention Against Apartheid, they are now obliged to act to punish instances of apartheid. Recommendations from the report include calls for:

- governments to "support boycott, divestment and sanctions activities".
- a comprehensive investigation by the International Criminal Court (ICC) of the situation in Israel. ICC Prosecutor Fatou Bensouda had already opened an investigation on Israel's 2014 bombing of Gaza and on the illegal settlements in the West Bank.
- 'criminal prosecutions of Israeli officials demonstrably connected with the practices of apartheid against the Palestinian people'. Former Israeli Foreign Minister Tzipi Livni cancelled a trip to Brussels in 2017 when she was alerted that the prosecutors there might arrest her using the principle of universal jurisdiction.

Despite the slow-motion 9/11 in Gaza since 2012 (almost 5,000 killed), Obama could still fly to Jerusalem at the drop of a kippah to Shimon Peres's funeral in 2016 and piously state, "My friend Shimon

Peres showed us that justice and hope are at the heart of the Zionist idea." True, Peres too had won the Nobel Peace Prize,[2] but he was responsible for the cynical massacre at Qana only two years later,[3] and he had effectively supported illegal settlement building in Galilee, both "at the heart of the Zionist idea".

The intent of Zionists since they burst on the scene at the first Zionist Congress in 1897[4] was to force all Jews—kicking and screaming, if necessary—into populating the "Holy Lands". Oh, and expelling all Christian and Muslim Arabs who had actually lived there peacefully with their Jewish neighbors up to that time.

Obama's words cannot hide reality. Neither can Zionists convince anyone that Israel is "the only democracy in the Middle East" or that it is a "Jewish *and* democratic state".

The "Nationality" Sleight of Hand

As yet, the state of Israel has no constitution. A constitutional committee was set up in 1949, but almost 70 years later, whatever rights there are for *Arab Israelis* are trumped by *Jewish Israeli*[5] rights. Palestinians make up 20% of the population of Israel, 60% of overall population including the occupied territories, and those who reside in the occupied territories, have no rights as citizens at all. A constitution implies equal rights for all the nation's citizens. The latest attempt to formalize a constitution was in 2011 with the Basic Law proposal: Israel as the Nation-State of the Jewish People, but that effort is stalled. Israel's passport states the holder's nationality is Israeli. **Nationality** is the *relationship* between a person and the political state to which he belongs or is affiliated. **Ethnicity** is the *identification* of a person with a particular racial, cultural, or religious group. The biblical use of 'nation' implies race, but that is now considered unscientific, not conforming to any biological, anthropological or genetic criteria.

Thus, to be a democratic nation, **Israeli** must be the *nationality* of Israel, with the Israeli state composed of *ethnicities* with equal rights. 'Jewish' is not even considered a distinct ethnicity anymore, at least according to the US census. Most countries' census have adjusted to use some combination of place of birth, native tongue, and ethnicity, discarding 'race' altogether—including Canada. Nationality in most cases more or less conforms to ethnicity, but if it differs, nationality trumps ethnicity as a signifier.[6] Given that there is an Israeli passport with the designation Israeli in the nationality box, that logically means there must be an Israeli nationality. But this is only a convenience, *pro tem*. The real nationality is at the state registry, with the label 'Jewish' or 'non-Jewish', which appears only in your records and determines your civil rights.

As of 2005, ethnicity is not printed on Identity Cards either; a line of eight asterisks appears instead. Sounds good. But the registry knows everyone's ethnicity *and* their respective civil rights. Some major violations of civil rights result from this:

- A non-Jew can't obtain citizenship unless married to a Jewish spouse who is a native Israeli. They must marry abroad or the non-Jewish spouse must convert under the supervision of the Orthodox rabbinate, very difficult. Palestinians who marry Israeli citizens cannot immigrate to join their spouses in Israel.
- Non-Jews, even relatives of Israelis, are not automatically allowed to immigrate to Israel, blocking relatives of Palestinian citizens from returning to join their families. No one can run for office while advocating Israel as "a state of all of its people"; in order to participate, s/he must accept Israel as a Jewish state only.
- The only Arabs who can be Israeli citizens are those born in Israel, i.e., the descendants of those Arabs who were not expelled in 1948 and 1967.
- Many services and privileges are granted only to veterans, which means only Jews.[7]
- Land rights are weighted heavily against non-Jews. The Jewish National Fund directly or indirectly controls 93% of the land in Israel, chartered to benefit Jews exclusively. The law claims that Arabs have equal rights, but only Jews are offered land for settlement, Jews do not have land confiscated as do Arabs, and disputes mostly go against Arabs.[8]
- Adalah–Legal Center for Arab Minority Rights in Israel documents laws and bills enacted from 2010–16 which further dispossess and exclude Arab citizens from the land and privilege Jewish citizens in the allocation of state resources; turn Arab Israeli citizenship from a right into a conditional privilege; undermine Arab political participation.

Forward-looking Israelis have since the 1950s petitioned to be assigned an Israeli nationality and are denied. In the latest decision in October 2013, the Israeli Supreme Court again denied the request to recognize Israeli as a nationality. It gave several essential reasons for supporting a specific Jewish nationality over a general Israeli nationality:

- Since a person cannot have two nationalities, this change would compel Jewish citizens of Israel to choose between being Israeli and Jewish. Most Israeli Jews would be forced into an impossible predicament, seeing themselves as both Jewish and Israeli.
- If the nationality of Jewish citizens of Israel were to be classified as Israeli, the implication would be that Judaism is not a nationality for them but is solely a religion. This idea is antithetical to the fundamental doctrine of Zionism and its main thinkers, from Herzl to Ben-Gurion, who saw Zionism as the national movement of the Jewish people.
- If the nationality of Jewish Israelis is defined as Israeli rather than Jewish, then the national bond which binds together Jews in Israel and Jews in the Diaspora would be severed.[9]

The judges ruled citizenship and nationality in Israel should be considered entirely separate categories, as they have been since Israel's founding in 1948. All Israelis have Israeli citizenship, but none enjoys Israeli nationality (despite the passport). "From this simple deception, Israel has been able to gerrymander its population by excluding Palestinian refugees from their land and homes while allowing millions of Jews from around the world to immigrate. ... Israel has not one but two citizenship laws: the famous Law of Return of 1950 gives every Jew in the world the right to come to Israel and instantly receive citizenship; the much less known Citizenship Law, passed two years later, confers citizenship, in very restricted circumstances, to non-Jews."[10]

It is ironic that the only countries following international norms with respect to Israel are the Arab states that refuse to recognize Israeli passports, which claim a nationality that doesn't exist according to the Israeli Supreme Court itself. That is why Israeli governments feel it is so important to get these Arab countries and the stateless Palestinians to recognize Israel as a Jewish state. That would supposedly legitimize Israel without worrying about declaring an Israeli nationality for all

Israelis, Jew or Arab. But that is why it is impossible to do, as that would automatically validate Israel's *de facto* dispossession of its non-Jewish citizens. Unlike Canada with the native peoples, the Israelis are not seeking Arab assimilation into Judaism, but don't want to assimilate them as Israelis with full citizenship. Were it not for the international acceptance of the duplicity of the Israeli passports, the Israeli Arabs would *de facto* be stateless. One can only marvel that Israel managed this confidence trick with most of the non-Arab world.

Palestinians would then be ripe to be further dispossessed or even expelled, now in accordance with international precedent (rather than international law). The West violated international law by recognizing Israel, accepting without question its claim as a Jewish state. Modern Israel came into existence on May 14, 1948 as the homeland for the Jewish people. It was also defined in its declaration of independence as a "Jewish state", a term that appeared in the United Nations partition decision of 1947 as well. The related term "Jewish and democratic state" dates from 1992 legislation by the Israeli Knesset, attempting to appear to comply with international norms. The requirement from 1948 onward was to recognize Israel as a normal state, abiding by international norms, without a formal demand on Israel's part for recognition as a "Jewish state", which is not an international norm. A clever deceit, but the Arabs saw through it. The latter became an issue only after the Oslo Accord in 1993, where the PLO recognized Israel as a normal state, but when asked to do so as a "Jewish state", rightly balked. Israel 'forgot' to demand this from Jordan. "Why didn't they present this demand to Jordan or Egypt when they signed a peace agreement with them?" PLO chair Mahmoud Abbas asked the Arab League when they too refused.[11]

The implication is that Israeli nationality is 'Jewish', denying Arabs their right to exist as persons right from the start. At present, Arab Israelis can have passports, but the passport has no legal standing within Israel, and is only accepted by other countries as a legal pretense to allow the holder to travel abroad. Even Israeli Jews with "Israeli" stamped in their passports are living a lie, a lie which is accepted by the West.[12]

The contradiction in attempting to craft a democratic state based on the Jewish race is epitomized in the Kahane amendment[13] to the Basic Law in 1985, which forbids "negation of the existence of the State of Israel as the state of the Jewish people, negation of the democratic character of the State, incitement to racism." But limiting democracy to 'Jews only' is by definition both undemocratic and racist. Most Israeli

Jews (79%) don't see the contradiction, agreeing that Jews deserve preferential treatment in Israel. They do not see an inherent contradiction between a Jewish homeland and a functioning democracy providing equality before the law for non-Jews.[14]

The US census effectively undermines Israel's claim as a Jewish state. As '**races**', the US census shows White/ Black/ Asian/ Native/ Polynesian.[15] For **ethnic** subdivisions, there is no Jewish ethnicity. Jews are considered members of some other ethnicity (European, Russian, Moroccan, etc.). Jewish is only a religious category and the census doesn't do religion since the 1950s (a blowback from Nazism).

Ergo, a Jewish state can only be a *religious* state a la Iran/ Saudi Arabia,[16] presumably with the titular head of state a chief rabbi. If the majority is secular, then just a normal, secular state called 'Israel' makes much better sense in international law, where all ethnicities have equal rights, and the various confessions either abide by a generally agreed legal system or operate legally according to their religious laws. Iran uses the former, Israel the latter, already admitting it is a religious state in line with Saudi Arabia, but still falling short of the 'equal rights' bit.

Worse yet for Zionism, the US Census Bureau tested a new race category in 2015, "Middle East-North Africa" or MENA, in response to more than three decades of lobbying by Arab American organizations for a designation that better represents them.[17] Nineteen ethnicity options will be offered under the MENA designation, among them **Israeli** and **Palestinian**, as well as Egyptian, Syrian, Lebanese, Turkish, Iranian, Moroccan and Algerian. Even Sudanese and Somali are being considered.

This does not please Rabbi Avi Shafran, a spokesman for Agudath Israel of America, "While Judaism is a religion, the Jewish people is a people. Peoplehood, at least Jewish peoplehood, transcends ethnicity and race."[18] Judaism in its Zionist form (which includes reform Judaism) is a return to its tribal tradition, unlike, say, Christianity or most Hasidic sects such as Satmar, where 'we are all human before God'. Some, but far from all, **Diaspora** Jews want to maintain this special identity and still "want to be fully integrated into broader society and don't want the distinctiveness to come at a price," Marc Stern, general counsel to the American Jewish Committee explains.[19] I.e., "to have their cake and eat it."

The 2011 Canadian census did not ask about religious affiliation but a survey sent to a subset of the population did. Canada has counted people by ethnic origin since 1765 and place of birth from 1871. The options for ethnicity in the 2006 Canadian census were various kinds of European Canadian, Aboriginal Canadian, and various non-white or non-European groups known officially as "visible minorities". The 2011 Canadian census discarded race and ethnicity entirely. As in the US, Jewish is only a religious category.

So the Zionist dream of a *Jewish* state was built on sand, and is still, 70 years after declaring independence, and fighting to gain international acceptance. Not a shred of "justice and hope" in sight, not even for Zionists. Almost all Jews wanted no part of this a century ago, when Zionism's founding father Herzl launched the Zionist Organization. Many Jews and non-Jews have continued to resist this "idea", though until recently, Jews were cowed, too polite to protest, worried they would be perceived as traitors to their 'race', and be cast out of the tribe.

Any people who recognize the problem, especially Jews, are hounded as "antisemites", the Jewish ones as "traitors" or "self-hating Jews". Why this hysteria, 70 years after the state came into being? How will normality ever be established? In researching the history of Canada and the Zionist project, you find unremitting slander, the creation of ever growing mechanisms and institutions to defend the indefensible, avoiding the underlying catch-22.

The majority of Jews today are of European heritage, and everyone in the world knows they suffered terribly in the 1933–45 period of Nazism in Europe, the direct result of the imperial order, where Jews had prospered despite—and because of—their apartness. Herzl's dream was a fantasy in 1897. With the Balfour letter it was still just a vague promise of refuge. Nothing about a Jewish state.

Just as "postmodern" can refer to coups and refugees, it can describe states. Canada is a postmodern state, one that looks like it has evolved into a nationality (Canadian), but it has only limited national sovereignty, its foreign policies determined by US fiat. Harper's pact with Israel signed in 2008, policed by our very own Israeli military adviser,[20] makes that a US-Israeli fiat.

First, who is a Jew? It is difficult to pin down Judaism. Is it a religion, a race, a tribe, an ethnicity, in its Zionist guise—a political ideology? Most Jews, especially Israelis, are secular, many are atheists. There is no such thing as a 'race', except the human race. As people from almost all corners of the earth, Jews form no clear ethnicity. In *Overcoming Zionism: Creating a Single Democratic State in Israel/ Palestine,* Joel Kovel describes Judaism as a tribal, political ideology built on the 'apartness' of ancient lore, "a leap of negative logic":[21] 'I am not a Christian or a Muslim.' As in Morton Weinfeld's *Like everyone else ... but different* (2001).

Apart from the apartness of the Jew, the difficulty of defining who is a Jew and what Jewishness is requires navigating other loaded terminology, including not only "anti-Semite" or "**antisemite**",[22] "the Holocaust", and by implication "Holocaust deniers". By using these loaded terms, debate about the real issues underlying them is clouded. Here "**anti-Jewish**"[23] is used to refer to racial bigotry towards Jews, as anti-Semite is a misnomer which was popularized in the 19th century, when all Jews were (mistakenly) called Semites. Semitic really just refers to the non-Indo-European language group comprising Hebrew, Arabic, Amharic (Ethiopian) and Assyrian—not ethnicities. Arab Jews (Mizrahi) speak Arabic and use Hebrew for prayers, and were thus the only Jewish Semites until Hebrew was revived as a *lingua franca* in Israel, making all Israelis Semites. They descended from local Jewish communities of the Middle East from biblical times into modern era.[24] Most Jews are European since at least the 17th century, and in the Diaspora, are not **Semitic**. Emma Lazarus, who penned the sonnet "The New Colossus" (1883, "Give me your tired, your poor, Your huddled masses," engraved on the Statue of Liberty), wrote a book of poetry *Songs of a Semite* (1882), yet was a Yiddish-speaker, not a speaker of Hebrew, a 'Semite'.

So the term is unnecessarily confusing; in fact, downright wrong, as it is the Palestinians in the stand-off in Israel who are the Semitic speakers, and the Jewish immigrants (except for the Mizrahi) are European, speakers of Yiddish, from the ghettoes of Russia and Poland, and the elite Ashkenazi Jews of Germany. The Schwartzes and Finkelsteins are best described ethnically as east European and Russian Jews, formerly Yiddish speakers. Canadian rabbi Reuben Slonim (see Chapter 5) was convinced of this by Hebrew University professor S.D. Goitein: "Semite was coined to denote a language, not a race. There are racial differences within the Jewish group and within the Arab group. No historic record exists of any Semitic race. There are anti-Semites, but no Semites."[25] "Anti-Semite" from the start was used as a slur, a targeted accusation of racism, which itself is unscientific, more accurately "bigotry" or simply "prejudice", inasmuch as racism implies different races, which itself is a vague term, since there is only the human race.[26]

Neither "anti-Semitic" nor "racist" have any place in a serious analysis of matters Jewish. Jewish denotes both hereditary and social origins, as with any ethnos grouping. But Judaism has always thrived on hostility to its claim of chosenness, which manifests today in Israel's willful violation of international law, refusal to disclose the existence of its nuclear arsenal, etc. 'Anti-Semite' is bandied about daily in both popular media and academia, the subject of institutes and conferences, the tragedy of a 'nation' build on negation. A Jewish joke defines "antisemite" as 'anyone a Jew doesn't like.'

In its Hellenistic period, from the 4th century BC to the 2nd century AD, Judaism was a proselytizing religion. It became insular in the face of the hegemony of arch-rival Christianity in the 4th century, discouraging conversions. The Jews achieved a more or less established negationist position in both the Christian and Muslim worlds until the 19th century, but faced much more victimization in Christian Europe, though there was never any attempt by the Christian establishment from the 4th century to kill all those who remained Jews. They took on the role of outcast, betrayer and murderer in Christian society, living proof of the enemies of Christ, who needed to be constantly forgiven (i.e., not killed), tolerated, but could be loved only by admitting their error and embracing Christianity.

There was hope with the Enlightenment that the lingering tribalism might change. Writers such as Voltaire criticized both Christianity and Judaism for their superstitions, calling for liberation from all superstition. Jewish separateness was especially problematic. The French revolution promised equality and brotherhood, but this implied an end to self-imposed racial exclusivity.

The rest is history, so to speak, all tracing itself back to the crucifixion legend. In 1965, as part of the **Vatican II** council, the Catholic Church published *Nostra Aetate*, arguing that modern-day Jews could not be held accountable for Jesus' crucifixion and that not all Jews alive at the time of the crucifixion were guilty of the crime. Neither the Old nor New Testaments condone the concept of 'blood libel'. "Fathers shall not be put to death because of their children, nor shall children be put to death because of their fathers. Each one shall be put to death for his own sin."[27] It seemed reason finally reigned on Jewish matters.

This blood-curse cum chosen people led to an extreme form under the Nazis, when Jews were labeled subhuman as a race. Jewish priests in the Middle Ages wrote much the same about Gentiles, as passages in the Talmud and statements by some current Israeli religious leaders in reference to Palestinians make clear. The actual treatment by

Israel of Palestinians follows the logic, if not the same inhumanity, of the Nazis.[28]

'Antisemite' looks like its days of value as a silver bullet for Zionists are numbered. In July 2016, Jared Kushner, Trump's (Orthodox) son-in-law and orchestrator of Trump's win, wrote an open letter in the *New York Observer* (which he owns) addressing the controversy around a tweet from the Trump campaign containing allegedly antisemitic imagery. In the letter, Kushner wrote, "In my opinion, accusations like 'racist' and 'anti-Semite' are being thrown around with a carelessness that risks rendering these words meaningless."

What is **Zionism**? But before that, what is **Zion**, an inspiration for Zionists and non-Zionists alike? Zion is a place name often used as a synonym for Jerusalem.[29] The word is first found in 2 Samuel 5:7 which dates from 540 BC, and refers there to a specific mountain near Jerusalem (Mount Zion), on which a fortress stood which David allegedly conquered.[30] The term Tzion came to designate the area of Jerusalem where the fortress stood, and later became a metonym for Solomon's Temple in Jerusalem, the city of Jerusalem itself, and "the World to Come", the Jewish understanding of the hereafter. In the Kabbalah, a more esoteric reference is made to Tzion being the spiritual point from which reality emerges, located in the Holy of Holies of the First, Second and Third Temples.

Judaism's tribalism (and its offspring Zionism) suffers from what Alfred Whitehead called "misplaced concreteness", where abstract belief is treated as if it were a concrete real event or physical entity. It's fine in literature as metonymy, where a reified abstraction is intended as a figure of speech, and actually understood as such,[31] but the use of reification in logical reasoning or rhetoric is misleading and in this case, disastrous. God is not on a hilltop requiring you to steal the property and build a replica of a mythical temple to fulfill a "covenant" with him. Yahweh told Abraham: "In you, all the families of the earth shall be blessed."[32] Claiming that the covenant was a promise of virtually the entire Middle East as real estate in perpetuity (Deuternomony 11:24-25) is misplaced concreteness taken to the level of world war. This fascination of Jews with Palestine was used by the imperialists, first the British and after 1948, the Americans, to set up their military outpost to control this strategic location.

Now, to **Zionism**. Zionism is a nationalist political movement of Jews and Jewish culture that supports what it views as the re-establishment of a Jewish homeland in the territory it defines as the historic Land of Israel. It emerged in the late 19th century in central and eastern Europe as a national revival movement. In Jewish history, where myth has always transcended fact,[33] Jews see themselves as in exile everywhere, and everywhere in search of the Promised Land, for that magical 'see you next year in Jerusalem' moment.[34]

1948 seemed to be that moment, though the stone and mortar Jerusalem remained tantalizingly out of reach, with only vague Zionist promises of good intent for a peaceful settlement with the occupied native Palestinians standing in the way. A settlement could have been forced on the wayward young nation if the international will had been there. It wasn't. Instead, a nation was born of violence and murder, whose birth is celebrated as an act of God. Not a good sign for a future peace.

The current occupation nightmare came to fruition as a baldly imperialist operation of its own in 1967, called by Israelis the Third Arab-Israeli War after the First (1948) and Second (1956) or, more popularly, the **Six-Day War**, boasting how short it was. For the losers—Egyptians, Syrians and Jordanians—it was three years of war, the **War of Attrition** (*Harb al-Istinzaf*) involved fighting between Israel and Egypt, Jordan, PLO and their allies from 1967 to 1970. A nightmare that wore out Egyptian President Abdel Nasser, who died in 1970, his (and Egypt's) heart broken.

That period will long be reflected on, by Jew and Gentile alike, as the fatal turning point-of-no-return for the transformation of the Middle East into an Israeli mini-empire, whose 'motherlands' are many. Occupying all of Palestine allowed the "Zionist idea" to be realized by the now accelerated act of theft, with settlements popping up like sturdy, unwanted weeds in the desert, almost monthly.[35] Since gas has been discovered offshore, this extends the empire into the Mediterranean. The only fly in the ointment was the war with Egypt in 1973, forcing Israel to give back the Sinai to Egypt in exchange for Egypt accepting a vassal role in the new empire.

Mention should be made of "**revionist Zionism**", or "political Zionism", developed originally by Ze'ev Jabotinsky in the 1920s, an extreme form of Zionism at the time, which today is called **neo-Zionism**. Originally Jabotinsky advocated increased cooperation with Britain on transforming the entire Mandate for Palestine territory, including Palestine itself and Transjordan, into a sovereign Jewish state, loyal to the British Empire. To this end, Jabotinsky advocated mass Jewish immigration from Europe. But Britain was a shadow of its former might, still trying to balance its relations with the Arabs, and resisted this open fulfillment of the MacKinder scheme for the global British Empire. The British Empire was already past its 'due date'. Up to 1933, the national-messianist wing of Revisionism, led by Abba Ahimeir, was inspired by the fascist movement of Benito Mussolini. Fascism, like Zionism, was a return to the roots of the national culture and the historical past. The revionists, the 'good' fascists, became the backbone of the new Likud Party in 1977.

Jabotinsky then advocated a "revision" of the **"practical Zionism"** of David Ben-Gurion and Chaim Weizmann, with the open aim of using terror tactics against the British and Palestinians, forcing the British to leave and allowing the Zionists to seize territory to create a Jewish state, admitting that mass expulsion of Palestinians was necessary. This is precisely what happened by 1948, and this extreme form of Zionism became the implicit norm. Menachim Begin was a discipline of Jabotinsky. He signed the Camp David Accords (1978) with Egypt that supposedly referred to the "legitimate rights of the Palestinians", which clause was never acted on. In any case, Begin insisted that the Hebrew version referred only to "the Arabs of Eretz Yisrael" and not to "Palestinians", implying that there would never be a sovereign Palestinian state.

Spiritual Zionism is an interpretation of Zion as a spiritual realm, not a physical place in Israel/Palestine or anywhere else. The Mission of the Jews is the main justification of the survival of the Jews (i.e. the religion), to be "priests and a holy nation", which is a purely religious vocation.[36] Ultra-Orthodox groups such as Satmar and Neturei Karta are spiritual Zionists, against the formation of a concrete state by the actions of humans because they believe that the Messiah or God should be instrumental in its creation. Christians are in a sense spiritual Zionists who accept Jesus as the messiah.

Finally, there is **post-Zionism**, the belief that Zionism has fulfilled its ideological mission with the creation of the modern State of Israel in 1948, and that Zionist ideology should therefore be considered at an end. Hannah Arendt wrote *Eichmann on Trial* as a *"cura posterior,* delayed cure of a pain that weighted upon her as a Jew, a former Zionist, and a former German," convinced that like other 19th century nationalisms, Zionism had already outlived the conditions from which it emerged and ran the risk of becoming, as Arendt once put it, a "living ghost amid the ruins of our times."[37]

An activist response is **anti-Zionism**, seeking an overcoming of Zionism through active struggle,[38] contending that it is impossible to have both a Jewish state and a democracy, and that Israel should become a state of all its citizens. It contends that there are other places, such as North America, where Jews are safer. It sees Zionism as an "artificial nationalism", binding together completely different ethnic groups — Ashkenazi, Russian, Mizrahi, Sephardi, Arab, and many competing Jewish religious groups (ultra-Orthodox, Hasid), along with the majority of Jews who are secular. It posits the need for a real nationalism, Israeli, multi-cultural, multi-ethnic, under a secular state. From this perspective, it is not 'antisemitism' that is the disease, but Zionism.

WWII and post-WWII terms

The Nazis sought to implement a "**Final Solution** to the Jewish Question" (*die Endlösung der Judenfrage*), pursuing an agenda whose alleged intent was to exterminate all Jews in Europe, formally approved in 1942 at the Wannsee Conference, though the only expression used there was "land transfer", with no explicit reference to mass killing. Most historians insist that this was subterfuge, that the Nazis were using euphemisms to cover up their worst crimes.

Whatever the original 'solution' was, there is no doubt that tens of millions of innocent civilians were killed from 1939 to 1945, many of them Jewish. The Hebrew *shoah* (means calamity, destruction, with "na" as prefix "the *shoah*") is the term used by Israeli Jews, less so by non-Israeli Jews, to refer to the mass murder of Jews in WWII. Coincidentally, the Palestinians and Egyptians use the same word in Arabic, "calamity, catastrophe", to refer to the 1948 and 1967 wars (***nakba*** for 1948, and ***naksa*** for 1967).

One of the thorny issues, which Zionists began to raise when "**the Holocaust**" became a popular cultural symbol in the 1970s, is whether Jews now have a monopoly on the use of the capital H version. The Armenians protest; it was Churchill who first coined the expression "the Armenian holocaust" in the 1920s.[39] In 1933, "holocaust" was first associated with the Nazis after a major book burning. Writers in English from 1945 used the term in relation to events such as the fire-bombing of Dresden or Hiroshima, the famines in Bengal and Vietnam in 1944, or the effects of a nuclear war.

There was no mention of a specifically Jewish holocaust till much later after World War II. In the 1930s, the term was used to refer not only to the Armenian tragedy, but to WWI and the approaching WWII, the Stalinist purges, the Japanese mass bombings of China, and already in reference to the campaign against Jews in Germany. A short geneology of the word includes:

- "For the first time since last September Japanese aeroplanes again raided Canton ... Although the damage exceeds September's holocaust, the death toll was somewhat less ..." (*Palestine Post*, May 29, 1938.)
- A *Times Literary Supplement* editorial, August 26, 1939, warned of an impending "holocaust" of Jews in Nazi Germany.
- Israeli English use of "holocaust" in its sense of the Jewish catastrophe was disseminated to the US after the Eichmann trial in 1961.[40]
- In the early 1960s the most common referent of "holocaust" in the US was nuclear war.
- Increasingly in the 1970s the *shoah* "holocaust" was capitalized[41] and it was no longer necessary to include Nazi as a signifier.
- Also in the 1970s, Yad Vashem officially defined the "h/ Holocaust" as starting in 1933.
- Originally references were also made to five million *non-Jewish* victims of "the Holocaust".[42] This five million figure seems to have been pulled out of the air. But that usage faded away. Roma, gays and the disabled, let alone communists, don't have much of a place in the "Holocaust" agenda.

This refashioning of the word, with its religious origins (burnt sacrifice), left not only Armenians, but Ukrainians unhappy, as they want to use "the Ukrainian Holocaust" (Holodomor) to refer to the communist collectivizations and resulting starvation in the 1930s. Both want the capital H, now that the Jews had insisted on it. One-up-manship, and who can blame them? As with everything taken too far, the debate becomes a farce.

And what about the many other 20th century mass murders? The fire-bombing of Dresden, the colonial-induced famines in Bengal and Vietnam in 1944, the mass killings in Cambodia? Hiroshima? Not to mention the native peoples of the entire planet, especially the Americas and Africa, and the African slave trade's Middle Passage.

Yom HaShoah was inaugurated in Israel in 1953, and is

commemorated by secular Israelis on the 27th of Nisan, which is eight days before Israeli Independence Day (late April, early May).[43] Holocaust Memorial Day is celebrated in all western countries with candle-lit vigils and many other versions of this 'remembrance day'.[44] There are Holocaust museums in many countries now. Hollywood continues to turn out Holocaust movies. Many schools in the West have Holocaust studies. The very capitalization of the word and its use to refer only to Jewish deaths as opposed to the term "'Nazi holocaust' referring to all Nazi victims, indicates how our thinking is being manipulated."[45] International Holocaust Remembrance Day, January 27, is the UN memorial day, designated by the United Nations General Assembly resolution 60/7 in 2005.

So, here, *shoah* or 'mass murder of the Jews in WWII' is used, and the official term "the Holocaust" when quoting. This is not a trivial matter. Even Zionists are not of one mind on its use. The Hebrew word *shoah* is widely accepted, even preferred due to the theological connotation of the word "holocaust". The American historian Walter Laqueur (whose parents died in the *shoah*) has argued that the term Holocaust is a "singularly inappropriate" term for the genocide of the Jews as it implies a burnt offering to God. "It was not the intention of the Nazis to make a sacrifice of this kind, and the position of the Jews was not that of a ritual victim."[46] The Israeli historian Saul Friedländer wrote in 1987 of "the growing centrality of the Shoah for Jewish communities in the Diaspora," and that "the Shoah is almost becoming a symbol of identification, for better or for worse, whether because of the weakening of the bond of religion or because of the lesser salience of Zionism and Israel as an identification element."[47]

The preferred use of "the Holocaust" in English in fact subtly *emphasizes* the religious connotation, putting Jewish suffering above that of the Nazis' other victims, the Armenians etc. Jews have protested even the lower-case use of "holocaust" in reference to the non-Jewish victims of the Nazis or the Armenians.

But the atrocities being committed every day by the self-proclaimed secular Zionists suggest they are in opposition to God. Orthodox Jews such as Neturei Karta make this claim against Zionism. Arguing along these lines, they are convinced Zionism must fail, since it can only be described in religious terms as man disobeying God, taking on the role of God.[48]

But we can make the same argument without resorting to religion, the Masons or the Illuminati: the Zionist project is satanic in a metaphorical sense, arising out of addiction to literal Old Testament memes, and flying in the face of morality and ethics. It will be resisted by all who are not part of it, by all who are awakened to it and reject it. A belief in the Masonic or Luciferian origins of our current nightmare is not necessary, and can be a hindrance to effective resistance, leaving opponents feeling helpless in the face of otherworldly powers seemingly governing our lives.

In a sense, use of "the Holocaust" has a mystical connotation, and is avoided here. The *shoah* is less loaded, 'politically correct' in the best sense of that term, and is used here in special reference to the mass murder of Jews (as opposed to Roma, homosexuals, disabled, communists) by the Nazis.

Then there's **"Holocaust denier"**, the new version of the slander, 'your mother wears army boots.' No one, not even the notorious Keegstra or Zundel, denied that an extraordinary number of Jews died in WWII at the hands of the Nazis. They were so incensed by the creepy quasi-religious subtext behind the capital H that they ignored what evidence there was, convinced that Israel's penchant for lies applies to everything. But these 'Lone Rangers' don't deserve to be pilloried and imprisoned and their lives destroyed, just because they aren't satisfied with the official story. As long as someone does not threaten murder, he can say pretty much what he likes. 'Sticks and stones ...' The trials against these deniers, particularly Doug Collins, were/are travesties of justice, threatening basic freedoms of the Canadian Charter of Rights and Freedoms. The most infamous of these figures, David Irving, who played a starring role in the Zundel trials, was finally convinced of the evidence for the gas chambers and recanted his earlier denials, though he was never forgiven.

The serious questioners—laymen and intellectuals, non-Jews and Jews—refer to themselves as **"revisionists"**, although this courtesy is not extended to them in mainstream media, where "antisemite" and "Holocaust denier" are slapped on one and all. Even Wikipedia notoriously labels people "Holocaust deniers", whether or not they have ever mentioned "the Holocaust", which can backfire spectacularly.[49] Jewish dissidents are called "self-hating" Jews or are ignored. Non-Jews are threatened with the antisemitic label. Many Israeli historians now are called "revisionist"[50] and are likewise vilified by the Zionist establishment for their criticism of the official line on Israeli history, including the depiction and interpretation of the *shoah*.

The Canada-Israel Nexus is the story of Canada's contribution to this tale. Most of it takes place in Palestine, but much here in the "New Jerusalem",[51] where Canada plays a special role as "Israel's best friend". It is in North America that the world's Jews found their real Promised Land, where they came in the millions from eastern Europe and Russia in the 19th and early 20th centuries,[52] and quickly became the shapers of western popular culture and the wheelers and dealers at the heart of the US empire as financiers, lawyers, pundits, viziers to the monarch (now it's advisers to presidents and prime ministers). Israel as the Promised Land came as more of an afterthought, though it too had been foreseen by British imperial planners two centuries ago. Israel is in fact an anachronism, a holdover from the British world empire, which ironically came to fruition as that motherland died after WWII.

The enduring Diaspora movement of mostly European Jews, the leverage of Jews within western states, and the founding of a specifically Jewish state, positioning Jews at the heart of world politics, has been met by resistance, and spawned various conspiracy theories. Jews have always been more than just *Like Everyone Else*. Conspiracy theories are hard to prove by definition, but often have a grain of truth. Hitler saw the phenomenal success of German Jews as frightening, ominous. Only an isolated handful are followers of Hitler today, but whatever the conspiracy at the heart of today's global world is, Jews are certain to be or be seen as at the center of it.

For whatever reason, Canada became a kind of magnet for 'Holocaust deniers', conspiracy theorists, in the 1980s. Though none of the Canadian Lone Rangers considered in Chapter 7 ever personally attacked or advocated attacking Jews, they all have faced legal and personal attacks and *bona fide* "incitement to hatred" by the Zionists, merely for their attempts to open the debate on the role of Jews in contemporary society, and to clarify certain important 'footnotes' to world history which the Zionists have put off limits. More restrained anti-Zionists distance themselves from these mainstream media pariahs (a handful of whom are indeed neo-Nazis), afraid of the Zionists' silver bullet—the accusation of antisemitism—marshaled to label manifestations of actual anti-Jewishness, but more often used as a slur against critics.

This book is a search for a sober, less tendentious view of the Canada-Israel nexus, and how to make it better serve both countries.[53]

Endnotes

1. Rima Khalaf, the head of ESCWA resigned from the UN after Secretary-General Antonio Guterres and Nikki Haley, the US ambassador to the UN, demanded that the report be withdrawn. Israel denounced it as akin to Nazi propaganda. The UN report argues that Israel is a 'racial regime' because its institutions are premised on maintaining a Jewish nation by techniques of suppression and expulsion. Even Palestinians who have Israeli citizenship (*ezrahut*) do not have the right to nationality insofar as the Israeli Supreme Court decision prevents their being regarded as "Israelis" and they cannot be regarded as Jews. This racialized regime has meant that they can only access inferior social services, face restrictive zoning laws, and find themselves unable freely to buy land. Palestinians in East Jerusalem are reduced to the status of permanent residents, who have to constantly prove that they live in the city and that they do not have any political ambitions. Palestinians in the West Bank live "in ways consistent with apartheid", and those who are exiled to the refugee camps in Lebanon, Syria and Jordan have absolutely no rights to their homeland. Article 7(a) of the Basic Law prohibits any political party from considering a challenge to the State's Jewish character. Since this description of the Israeli state renders Palestinians as second-class citizens, their voting rights are reduced to merely an affirmation of their subordination. The report has been removed from the ESCWA website, but it is available here: <https://www.scribd.com/document/342220531/UN-ESCWA-report-on-Israeli-apartheid#from_embed>
2. In 1994 together with Yitzhak Rabin and Yasser Arafat for the peace talks that produced the ill-fated Oslo Accords.
3. In 1996, as a pre-election gambit, "Grapes of Wrath", in the race for PM, killing 106 in a Palestinian refugee camp in Lebanon. He didn't even win the election. He was unrepentant, telling international critics they were antisemitic.
4. Held in Basel, Switzerland.
5. Basic syntax puts adjectives before the noun in English to modify the noun. The noun is the main signifier, the adjective a lesser signifier. In Israeli Jew, the noun Jew is the chief signifier, the adjective Israeli the lesser one. In Jewish Israeli, Israeli is used here as a noun, Jewish being the lesser signifier.
6. A linguistics term referring to the sign/ symbol that one identifies with psychologically.
7. Recently from 20 to 100 Arabs, mostly Christian or Bedouin, have volunteered to serve each year. It is a subtle way to help inch towards equal rights for Arabs. Says Yussef Salutta, "I need to be part of the country, to be like everybody else." The reservist ID card is an identity certificate of Israeli-ness, which can help integration," said Colonel Wajdi Sarhan, head of the IDF Minorities Unit. (Rinat Harash, "An increasing number of Israeli Arabs are choosing to fight for the Jewish state", *Reuters*, December 6, 2016.)

    At the 2011 Jerusalem Film Festival, the documentary *Ameer Got His Gun* showed the experience of Ameer, who faced daily racism, but was told, "If you are Arab or Ethiopian or Russian — they will always make fun of you." His uncle served and was ignored by his Jewish 'friends' and ostracized by his community when he returned. It is mandatory for the Druze to join, but they are starting to refuse, complaining that when they do, they are still considered a "dirty Arab". In 2004, a bomb at an IDF post near Gaza killed five Arab soldiers. The next day, a member of parliament ranted about how the Arabs are

8 all worms. (Jordan Hoffman, "His deep, dark secret: He's Arab, Muslim and serves in the IDF", *Times of Israel*, November 10, 2012.)

8 One of the laws ratified in 1949 was the "Law of Lands of Israel" which gives all lands acquired to be leased in perpetuity on the condition that these would never be alienated to non-Jews, which effectives denies 95% of Israel's land to 200,000 Arab Israelis. Only Arabs have their property confiscated, and legal appeals are almost always dismissed. (Joel Kovel, *Overcoming Zionism: Creating a Single Democratic State in Israel/Palestine*, 2007, 97.)

9 Yedidia Z. Stern and Jay Ruderman, "Op-Ed: Why 'Israeli' is not a nationality", *JTA*, March 3, 2014.

10 Jonathan Cook, "Jewish Israelis at Home and Abroad: Israeli Nationality Rejected", *Washington Report on Middle East Affairs*, December 2013.

11 "Arab League refuses recognizing Israel as 'Jewish state'", RT, March 10, 2014.

12 The only remedy Zionists propose is for all the world to insist to the world, Arabs especially, that "Israel has a right to exist as a Jewish state," to ignore international norms, to make an exception for Jews. To make it illegal to question this. But a state's legitimacy, its right to exist is based on a covenant (royal, suzerainty, or secular) with the citizenry, implying civil rights as part of that contract with the state. If there are no civil rights for some, then the state is illegitimate and the persecuted have a right to overthrow it. <https://en.wikipedia.org/wiki/Right_of_revolution>

13 To get backing from the US and others at the UN to overturn the 1975 UN 'Zionism is racism' resolution, which succeeded in 1991.

14 <http://www.pewforum.org/2016/03/08/israels-religiously-divided-society/>

15 A separate question about Hispanic origin has been asked of all households since 1980, and the census form specifically instructs respondents that Hispanic origins are not racial.

16 Afghanistan, Pakistan, Gambia and Mauritania also call themselves Islamic Republics.

17 In the past, Arabs have been marked in the US Census as White. This began in the early 20th century when Arabs coming to the US were marked as White in order to avoid entry quotas and have a greater chance of achieving success and avoiding discrimination.

18 Debra Nussbaum Cohen, "U.S. Census May Add Controversial 'Israeli' Category", *Haaretz*, June 19, 2015.

19 Ibid.

20 Currently Colonel Adam Sussman.

21 Kovel. op.cit., 18.

22 The unhyphenated spelling dispels the notion that there is an entity 'Semitism' which 'anti-Semitism' opposes. Semitic refers to a linguistic group (Arabic, Ethiopian, Assyrian, Hebrew). There is no such thing as "Semitism" just as there is no such thing as Arabism or Englishism, though there is philo-Semitism/philosemitism, or Judeophilia, a term also coined in the late 19th century, referring to an interest in the Jewish people, their historical significance, and the positive impacts of Judaism on the world. Semite was only ever used as a euphemism among the upper class for Jew.

"Anti-Semite", then, underlines the essentially racial attitude of contemporary Jews in describing themselves, emphasizing inherent and unchangeable inborn qualities (vs anti-Jewish, emphasizing the Jew as a socio-religious construct, a reaction to the dominant society). The use of the term Semite finesses a reasoned, rational objection to Jewish ideas and actions, and sticks to the mantra "It is because of what we are, not of what we do." And no fault can be found with that.

The German word *antisemitisch* was first used in 1860 by the Austrian Jewish scholar Moritz Steinschneider (1816-1907) in the phrase *antisemitische Vorurteile* (antisemitic prejudices) to characterize the French philosopher Ernest Renan's false ideas about how "Semitic races" were inferior to "Aryan races". (Avner Falk, *Anti-Semitism: a History and Psychoanalysis of Contemporary Hatred,* Westport, 2008, 21.) Prussian nationalistic historian Heinrich von Treitschke used the word to refer specifically to Jews, who were mostly not Semitic speakers, except for the use of Hebrew in religious matters.

The philosemite most revered among Israelis is Major-General Orde Charles Wingate (1903–1944), a Christian fundamentalist, who followed Pilgrim Brethen Judeophile doctrines. He was an eccentric, known for his brutal collective punishment in the late 1930s of Arab villagers suspected of harboring Muslim militants. He trained Jewish militants and advocated formation of a Jewish unit in WWII. Wingate is commemorated in Israeli sports facilities and a youth village.

23   Anti-Muslim is the equivalent for Muslims. Judeophobia would be congruent with Islamophobia but both terms are cumbersome.

24   This includes descendants of Babylonian Jews and Mountain Jews from modern Iraq, Syria, Bahrain, Kuwait, Dagestan, Azerbaijan, Iran, Uzbekistan, Caucasus, Kurdistan, Afghanistan, India and Pakistan. Yemeni Jews are sometimes also included as Mizrahis though their history is separate from Babylonian Jewry.

25   Reuben Slonim, *Both Sides Now: A 25-year encounter with Arabs and Israelis,* 1972, 6.

26   Franz Boa (a German Jew) made this clear, as have subsequent genetic studies. "We have just as little right to say there is a Jewish race as that there is a French race or a German race or a Spanish race. It is scientifically incorrect to refer to races as still existing. Attempts to characterize a genetic trait which may exist among a group of people as a racial trait simply indicates ignorance, because 85% of human genetic variation exists within any group. Genetic differences between individuals overwhelm all other attempts to differentiate mankind, while genetic differences between groups have no predictive value for any single individual. E Fuller Torrey, *Freudian Fraud: The malignant effect of Freud's Theory on American thought and culture,* 1992, 235. The term "race" was used loosely in the West and in the Canadian census to denote national or ethnic groups, including Jews, Poles, Italians, English, French, etc., until 1951, when it was replaced by "ethnic origin".

27   Deuteronomy 24;16.

28   John Brown, "Next head of 'Civil Administration' said Palestinians are sub-human", +972 Blog, May 8, 2015.

29   The name "Jerusalem" meanings "founded by the Canaanite god of dusk Shalem," based on the same root S-L-M from which the Hebrew word for "peace" is derived, making it the City of Peace. In Islam, it is simply referred to as al-Quds (the holy place), with no anachronistic pagan connotation.

30   All such claims to use the Bible as an archelogical map are bogus, according to Israeli historians such as Shlomo Sand. See Chapter 9.

31   The monarch referred to as the Crown.

32   Genesis 12:3.

33 Amassed, it is claimed, 2,000 to 4,000 years ago as a compilation of legends, the Old Testament is used today as a map justifying colonization.
34 At the conclusion of the Yom Kippur service and the Passover Seder outside of Jerusalem the words "Next Year in Jerusalem" are recited. In Jerusalem itself, the Passover Seder might conclude, "Next Year in Jerusalem, the rebuilt," referring likely to the Temple that was destroyed over two millennia ago.
35 By 2014, according to the Yesha Council, 382,031 Jewish settlers live in the 121 officially recognized settlements in the West Bank, over 300,000 Israelis live in settlements in East Jerusalem and over 20,000 live in settlements in the Golan Heights.
36 See British civil servant and historian Albert Montefiore Hyamson's *Palestine: A Policy* (1942).
37 Hannah Arendt, *Eichmann on Trial*, introduction by Amos Elon, and "Zionism Reconsidered", *Menorah Journal*, vol. 23, no. 2 (October–December, 1945), 172.
38 Kovel. op.cit., 221. Edward Said sets out the anti-Zionist platform in *The End of the Peace Process: Oslo and After* (2000).
39 "As for the Turkish atrocities ... helpless Armenians, men, women, and children together, whole districts blotted out in one administrative holocaust—these were beyond human redress." Winston Churchill, *The World in Crisis, volume 4: The Aftermath*, New York, 1923, 158.
40 Peter Novick, *The Holocaust in American Life*, Boston: Houghton Mifflin, 1999.
41 Nora Levin's 1968 book *The Holocaust: The Destruction of European Jewry, 1933-1945*, is the first to use the capital "H", which then entered popular usage in the 1970s, thanks to Yad Vashem's now authoritative publications on "the Holocaust".
42 Per the Simon Wiesenthal Center's web site "the recognized figure [of non-Jewish civilians murdered during World War II] is approximately five million."
43 Some in the Orthodox community—especially Haredim, including Hasidim—remember the victims on days of mourning declared by the rabbis before the *shoah*, such as the 9th of Av in the summer, and the 10th of Tevet, in the winter, because in the Jewish tradition the month of Nisan is considered a joyous month associated with Passover and messianic redemption.
44 Other days are marked as well: Austria, Bulgaria, Czech Republic, France, Netherlands, Poland, Romania, Serbia and the US, with specific historical events commemorated. Alberta, Manitoba and Nova Scotia all mark 27 Nisan along with Israel. The US has a whole week, Days of Remembrance of the Victims of the Holocaust, starting on 27 Nisan each year.
45 Peter Myers, "Fighting with Words: the word 'Holocaust'", *mailstar.net*, January 5, 2014. <http://www.mailstar.net/holocaus.html>
46 Richard Evans, *In Hitler's Shadow*, 1989, 142.
47 Ibid., 142.
48 "The Torah forbids us to end the exile and establish a state and army until the Holy One, blessed He, in His Glory and Essence will redeem us. This is forbidden even if the state is conducted according to the law of the Torah because arising from the exile itself is forbidden, and we are required to remain under the rule of the nations of the world, as is explained in the book VAYOEL MOSHE. If we transgress this injunction, He will bring upon us (may we be spared) terrible punishment." <http://www.nkusa.org/AboutUs/Zionism/opposition.cfm>

49	See the Wikipedia entry on Gerard Menuhin, who became a 9/11 truther in 2001, and was labelled a Holocaust denier in Wikipedia and elsewhere, though he had not made any public statement about the gas chambers and numbers of Jews killed in WWII. His request to Wikipedia to remove this insult was ignored, he started to look at WWII again and was convinced by the now-discredited Heuchter Report. His flamboyant artistic personality got the better of him and, incensed by what he now saw as the Zionist stranglehold on thought, he defiantly embraced the slur of 'Holocaust denier' and wrote his own version of WWII and the Jews, *Tell the Truth and Shame the Devil: As told to the author by a little old man* (Barnes Review, 2015), along the lines of Harwood. Wikipedia effectively created a new, proud 'Holocaust denier', and Menuhin's entry continues to begin, proudly, with that blast. (See Chapter 7)
50	For example, Israel Shahak, Benny Morris, Ilan Pappe, Israel Shamir.
51	The New Jerusalem was an important theme in the Puritan colonization of New England in the 17th century. The Puritans were inspired by the passages in Revelation about the New Jerusalem, which they interpreted as being a symbol for the New World. The Puritans saw themselves as the builders of the New Jerusalem on earth. This idea was foundational to American nationalism.
52	From 1880–1900, 2,800,000 Jewish Europeans immigrated to the United States, with 94% of them coming from Eastern Europe, and over 100,000 to Canada.
53	My focus is on Canada rather than the US, so I will leave the material on US Israeli/Jewish lobbies to my earlier *Postmodern Imperialism* Chapter 3, focusing only on the Canadian lobbies in Part Two. However, Canadian culture adopts much that is American, so that requires including the US in dealing with our common imperial heritage, and is the focus of Part One here.

PART I
BIRTH OF TWO NATIONS

| Chapter One |

CREATING CANADA

Geopolitics: Great Game I (to 1945)

Since the 19th century, when the imperial powers seized most of the inhabitable world, we have all been living under the laws of capitalism and its military extension, imperialism. Capitalism and imperialism are really just fancy words for exploitation of things and people to reap profits. Britain was the winner in the 19th century sweepstakes, with Spain, Holland, France, later Japan and Germany, the losers.

Both Canada and Israel are heirs to British colonial regimes in North America and the Middle East. Other former British colonies that were conceived as white settler regimes include the US, South Africa, Australia, New Zealand which provide insights into the settler states of Canada and Israel, with their large native populations. Britain's colonies themselves became mini-imperialists, exploiting the natives and when push came to shove, shoving them. Indeed, decimating them.

Canada was Britain's favorite child, as it was the model colony, staying loyal to the motherland in the face of the rebellious southerners, taking the 'empire loyalists' as refugees, gratefully accepting the British version of independence, the British North American Act and Confederation in 1867, sending troops and money to support British wars in South Africa and Europe. Canadians were open to the British-sponsored idea of a binational state in Palestine to include Jews, as it was one itself (English and French), not a US-style melting pot.[1] Both the New England colonies and the Jews in the Palestine Mandate were the black sheep of the British colonial project, waging war against their colonial sponsor, launching their own mini-imperialisms against their native populations, leaving sorry legacies today which grate at least Canadian sensibilities. But the family connection remains, binding all three together.

Although *The Canada-Israel Nexus* is primarily concerned with Canada's relationship with Israel, North America was one borderless land of hundreds of tribes before the Europeans came, so Canada and the US share a common colonial history and a common Jewish immigrant history (with notable differences). Today, American Indians comprise about 1.5% of the population,[2] about half the number of Jewish immigrants. Natives in Canada constitute 4.3% of the national population (1.4 million),[3] about three times the number of Jews.[4]

Native Americans see the borders separating Canada and the United States as artificial, and traditionally did not recognize private property. Canadian and American natives still move across borders on ancestral lands (today, bringing to the settler populations' minds cigarette smuggling and not much else). Similarly, Palestinians, who, apart from the Bedouin, were settled farmers, nonetheless moved, like the North American natives, through lands where boundaries meant little, and Ottoman traditions ruled.

European Settler Colonies in North America

In 1763, the 13 American colonies were established as crown or proprietary colonies (Virginia was called a dominion), mostly called provinces.[5] The British imperial dream was to absorb the American colonies into a new imperial powerhouse. The 13 American colonies rudely disrupted the British strategy by declaring themselves a republic. Slavery was the engine of growth, and the then '14 colonies'[6] had achieved lift-off into the imperial space by the late 18th century.

Despite solemn declarations of 'the rights of man', the newly minted United States of America looked askance at the zealous British abolitionists across the Atlantic, calling to end slavery. The settlers were champing at the bit to expand westward, and faced British imperial opposition to dispossessing the natives *en masse*. The New England merchants were angry with the East India Company, which declared that all tea and other imports had to come from British India. The merchants had a point, but were really more worried about the prospect of Britain outlawing slavery, the backbone of the southern states, where the labor of tens of millions of slaves produced huge profits. And the remaining lands of the native nations beckoned. Like Israel, they were initially able to square democracy with ethnic cleansing and institutionalized racism, until it finally caught up with the colonies, precipitating a civil war between components of the settler population.

That left Canada, Australia, and New Zealand as Britain's hope for creating European-populated satellites to assist in keeping the resource-poor island of the motherland rich and lording over its less fortunate 'brown' colonies in Africa and Asia, which were not so suitable for colonization, and used mostly for resource extraction. Canada was given limited self-government—enough to prevent those European settlers who became Canadians from deciding to join those who became Americans. British imperial strategists classified Canada as a "dominion" in 1867, which meant in practice, a colony where Britain shed its (mostly poor, white) excess population, whom it encouraged to permanently emigrate as farmers and merchants. Australia and New Zealand followed a similar evolution towards dominion colonies within the empire.

This strategy—leading to a transplanted, more or less educated nascent proletariat in Canada, overseen by committed professional rulers and educators from elite British schools—was a stunning success, a profitable investment by the 'center'. The Anglo-Saxon dominions were fast-tracked, given preferential loans to build industrial infrastructure and lots of opportunities to come to the motherland for education, to find wives, to cement less exploitative economic ties among the settlers than in the brown colonies, and quickly achieved responsible government (for landowners and officials).

Canada catapulted into social parity with the rich motherland, even surpassing it eventually in standard of living, without the messy, violent revolt that created the 'New Jerusalem'[7] to the south. As settler colonies, these dominions were allowed to join the ranks of the imperial rich, unlike India and all the other British colonies, including Egypt and eventually Palestine. (Lawrence 'of Arabia' lobbied Churchill to create a united Arab British mandate centered in Palestine as the first 'brown dominion', with no success.)

This strategy was less successful in southern Africa and Kenya, where settler colonies were set up in the most hospitable, richest areas in Africa. From the start, this was more problematic, with far more (and far less yielding) natives to displace, and the legacy of slavery hanging over British designs like a pall. The growing domestic anti-slavery movement in 18th century Britain, culminated in the outlawing of slavery. Attempts to dominate Africans were less successful than those exploiting the captured African population in North America.[8]

Canada does not have the legacy of slavery, not having the climate where slave labor could work on a mass scale, or so much good farmland for European settlers. So the dispossession of Canada's natives was not so brutal as slavery and the elimination of natives in the US. Nor was the British policy towards native peoples as brutal as in the independent American colonies, which cemented their ethnic cleansing and slave economy with what came to be called their "Manifest Destiny".[9] Natives across the new border in Canada looked on with horror at the fate of natives to the south, who were decimated by the land-hungry waves of European settlers.

The American Dispossession of Native Nations

The colonial policy in the Americas was **assimilationist** from the start. Expansion of the European-American populations to the west after the American Revolution resulted in increasing pressure on Native American lands, warfare between the groups, and rising tensions. The settlers had a common enemy—the Indian—and needed to bury the old ethnic animosities of their European heritage.

Natives in what is now the US suffered the most. Only 10% remained after the initial ravages of small pox and other European diseases.[10] They put up resistance in the northwest during the period 1811–12 known as Tecumseh's War. During the War of 1812, Tecumseh's forces allied themselves with the British. After Tecumseh's death, the British ceased to aid the Native Americans south and west of Upper Canada and American expansion proceeded with little resistance.

In 1830, President Andrew Jackson had Congress pass the Indian Removal Act, authorizing the government to relocate native Americans from their homelands within established states to lands west of the Mississippi River, accommodating European-American expansion. This resulted in the ethnic cleansing of many tribes, with the brutal, forced marches along what came to be known as the Trail of Tears.

The Indian Appropriations Act of 1851 set the precedent for modern-day Native American reservations through allocating funds to move western tribes onto specified territories (reservations), since there were no more lands available for relocation. Native American nations on the plains in the west continued armed conflicts with the US throughout the 19th century, through what were generally called Indian Wars. The Lakota put up one of the great acts of resistance in 1890, now called the Wounded Knee Massacre, where 300 mostly old men, women and children were killed.

In a sign of changing times, in 1990, both houses of the US Congress passed a resolution formally expressing "deep regret" for the massacre. In 2009, an "apology to Native Peoples of the United States" was included in the defense appropriations act. It states that the US "apologizes on behalf of the people of the United States to all Native Peoples for the many instances of violence, maltreatment, and neglect inflicted on Native Peoples by citizens of the United States."

In 1975, the US government passed the Indian Self-Determination and Education Assistance Act. It resulted from American Indian activism, the Civil Rights Movement, and community development aspects of President Lyndon Johnson's social programs of the 1960s. Natives in North America never abandoned tribal self-determination though some tribes in the US have been manipulated and defrauded by such 'businessmen' as Jack Abramoff.[11] Contemporary Native Americans have a unique relationship with the US because they may be members of nations, tribes, or bands with sovereignty and treaty rights, 'nations within a nation', much like Jews have traditionally claimed in the Diaspora, though Jews are supposedly only one 'nation'. Cultural activism since the late 1960s has increased political participation and led to an expansion of efforts to teach and preserve indigenous language for younger generations and to establish a greater cultural infrastructure.

Indigenous Dispossession, Canada-Style

Aboriginal Canadians, (also known as Indigenous[12] peoples in Canada and Indigenous Canadians) include the First Nations, Inuit and Metis. Indian is a term still commonly used in legal documents. There are several differences between natives in Canada (here referred to simply as natives) and Native Americans. First, the prominence of Metis, who constitute a third of natives (almost half million), view themselves as a people, and are gaining institutional recognition as such in contemporary Canada. The less genocidal nature of Canadian history meant that while only 1% of Americans claim tribal status, 4.3% of Canadians do. First Nations, Inuit and Metis peoples of all backgrounds have become prominent figures and have served as role models in the Aboriginal community and help to shape the Canadian cultural identity.[13]

But the ravage of European disease, and policies of land theft and forced assimilation were similar to those pursued in the US. The

British and the Americans were able to play tribes off against each other, providing guns for natives to kill natives, and whiskey to kill natives by their own hand. In Upper Canada, the Iroquois, the most warlike tribe, now armed with rifles, decimated the Huron, gaining control of the St Lawrence region, and prompting France to declare war against them in 1661. There were only 3,200 colonists by then, mostly French.

The Seven Years' War (1756–1763) pitted the colonies of British America against those of New France, mobilizing native allies on both the British and French sides. At the start of the war, the French North American colonies had a population of roughly 60,000 European settlers, compared with 2 million in the British North American colonies. The outnumbered French particularly depended on the Indians. The war, dubbed by Americans the "French and Indian War", refers to the two main enemies of the British colonists: the royal French forces and the various indigenous forces allied with them. For many native populations, the elimination of French power in North America meant the disappearance of a strong ally and counterweight to British expansion, leading to their ultimate dispossession.

The Native Americans were not enthusiastic supporters of the American revolution of 1776, and grudgingly supported the British from Canada. This war was among the colonists and did not promise anything but trouble for the native peoples. The conclusion of the American war of independence with Britain in 1783 meant no more British support for the natives south of the new border, allowing a rapid acceleration in the genocide being committed in the US, and a harsher policy—but still far less ruthless towards them—in the rump British North American colony, Canada. 1783 can be compared to 1947, when the British stopped providing any support to the native Palestinians faced with the Jewish invasion.

Tecumseh

Tecumseh (1768–1813), the great chief of the Shawnees, is the heroic Indian figure of this war. He saw that the British were the lesser of the two evils and steadfastly adhered to the policy of an alliance with Great

Britain, when many of his own and his confederate people were opposed to his diplomacy. He commanded forces that captured Detroit and kept the Americans from seizing what is now the heartland of Canada, southwestern Ontario. Ironically, Tecumseh is officially honored in both Canada and the US as a hero and military commander, with a park and other tributes in his honor in Canada.[14] Many native groups fled to Canada, as had the United Empire Loyalists following the 1776 revolution (when natives also fled north), and put themselves at the mercy of the British/Canadians.

Canadian historian Duncan Campbell Scott outlined the Canadian policy in 1915: "To keep the Indians at bay by friendship, to distrust them profoundly while cementing treaties with them, to heal each treachery with the salve of presents, to be ready with ample rewards for negative services—these were to be the actuating principles until the increase of population should abate the terror of the savage, and the pressure of civilization should turn him into a peaceful subject."[15]

Canada saw no equivalent to the Indian Wars and Wounded Knee Massacre. Native warriors were valued, playing an important role in defending Canada in the War of 1812. But they gained nothing from it, nor did native Americans fighting for the US side. Both the non-native Americans and Canadians insist 'we won the War of 1812'. But who lost? The answer: the natives. An addendum: the Canadian natives lost a bit less than their American cousins.

But the dispossession of Canadian natives proceeded apace, albeit in a more British, genteel way, reaching a climax in the late 19th and early 20th centuries, with a series of initiatives that aimed at complete assimilation-integration, starting with the Gradual Civilization Act and the Indian Act (1857), "for the protection of the Indians in Upper Canada from imposition and the property occupied or enjoyed by them, from trespass and injury."

The attempt at **Christianization** of the aboriginal peoples was much more vigorous than in the US, and had been ongoing since the first missionaries arrived in the 1600s. It became more systematic with the Indian Act in 1876, which would apply new sanctions upon those who did not convert to Christianity. For example, the new laws prevented non-Christian aboriginal people from testifying or having their cases heard in court, and banned alcohol consumption. When the Indian Act was amended in 1884, traditional religious and social practices, such as the Potlatch, were banned, and further amendments in 1920 prevented "status Indians" from wearing traditional dress or performing traditional dances in an attempt to stop all non-Christian practices. This interference with native culture was not part of Israel's plan, which emphasized Arab separation from the Jewish colonists.

Another focus of the Canadian government was to make the Aboriginal groups within Canada sedentary, in the thought that this would make them easier to assimilate. In the 19th century, the government began to support the creation of model farming villages. When most of these model farming villages failed, the government turned instead to the creation of Indian reserves with the Indian Act of 1876, in line with the US Indian Removal Act.

Through the Gradual Civilization Act in 1857, the government would encourage Indians to "enfranchise"—to "remove all legal distinctions between themselves and 'Her Majesty's other Canadian Subjects'".[16] If Aboriginals chose to enfranchise, it would strip them and their family of Aboriginal title; the plan was that they would then not only become more integrated into Canadian society but their lands would be available for purchase. However, they were often still regarded as non-citizens by Europeans, and those few who did enfranchise were often met with indifference, and never accepted by a race-conscious settler population.

The final government strategy of assimilation was the **residential school system,** which paralleled the US policy, though more aggressively, given the larger population of natives proportional to the settler population. Of all the initiatives that were undertaken in the first century of Confederation, none was more ambitious or central to the civilizing strategy of the Department of Indian Affairs, to its goal of assimilation, than the residential school system. It was the residential school experience that would lift children out of their "savage" communities into "higher civilization" and "full citizenship". Beginning in 1847 and lasting until 1996, the Canadian government, in partnership with the Catholic Church and later the Anglican and other Protestant churches, ran 130 residential boarding schools across Canada for native children, who were forcibly taken from their homes. This contrasts sharply with settler procedure in Israel, except for under-funding of Palestinian education and restrictions on their higher learning.

US natives benefited from the 1930s 'New Deal', which meant their government schools were less brutal from then on. The Canadian residential schools were underfunded, plagued by disease and abuse. Then Canada was made to face its possible violation of the United

Nations Genocide Convention that Canada signed in 1949 and passed in Parliament in 1952. Academics joined forces with newly empowered native leaders to take the government to court. A legal case resulted in settlement of $2 billion in 2006 and the establishment of a Truth and Reconciliation Commission[17] which confirmed the injurious effect on children of the residential schools system, and the turmoil created between native Canadians and Canadian society. In 2008 Prime Minister Harper issued an apology on behalf of the Canadian government and its citizens for the residential school system (even as he continued to underfund native education and promote the assimilationist policies).

A cynical question (relevant to the dilemma of the Palestinians) posed by some Canadians today: Is Canada's cultural genocide not better than the physical genocide of natives like in the US? The Liberal answer: Canada's bungled cultural genocide. At least a solid corps of natives are still alive to revive their cultures—if that is indeed possible, given the extent to which the residential schools severed succeeding generations from the languages and traditions of their forefathers. Fortunately for American natives, Roosevelt's socialism came to the rescue in the 1930s, and the physical genocide ended, with some aspects of Canada's cultural genocide finally ending by the 1960s. In some respects, the US natives have now 'caught up' to their culturally mutilated northern cousins.

Three thousand natives volunteered to fight with Canadian forces in WWII, about their proportion in the population, despite there being no conscription in Canada. Discrimination against them in the services was significant, unlike in the US forces, where natives were now admired for their courage and their exotic languages, used to generate encryption codes that couldn't be cracked. During wartime action, Canada's government confiscated native reserve land as a useable resource to assist the war effort. Native communities suffered displacement and extreme poverty both during and after the war as a result of the War Measures Act and the Veterans' Land Act, which effectively disregarded the efforts of native soldiers in the war.[18]

There have been three notable late 20th-century events in Canada comparable to the Wounded Knee incident on the Pine Ridge Indian Reservation in 1975, both also related to infringements of native lands. Again, comparing the situation of natives in Canada to that of the indigenous Arabs in Palestine, think: *intifadas*.[19]

The **Oka Crisis** was a land dispute between a group of Mohawk people and the town of Oka, Quebec, which began on July 11, 1990, and lasted 6 weeks. Sûreté du Québec (SQ) Corporal Marcel Lemay was killed by a bullet whose source has never been officially determined. Rumors circulated that the reason no source had been determined was that it had been a police bullet and that Lemay had been conducting an internal investigation which was connecting the death of two Mohawk men to SQ guns. The dispute was the first well-publicized violent conflict between First Nations and the Canadian government in the late 20th century.

The crisis developed from a local dispute between the town of Oka and the Mohawk community of Kanesatake over plans by Oka mayor Jean Ouellette to expand a golf course and residential development onto land which had traditionally been used by the Mohawk. It included pineland and a burial ground, marked by standing tombstones of their ancestors. The Mohawks had filed a land claim for the sacred grove and burial ground near Kanehsatake, but their claim had been rejected in 1986 on technical grounds.

The golf course expansion which had originally triggered the crisis was canceled by the mayor of Oka. The Oka Crisis galvanized, throughout Canada, a subsequent process of developing a First Nations Policing Policy to try to prevent future such events, but that policy led to further complications.

Throughout the 1990s, Kanehsatake became the focus of attention for alleged lawlessness, drug crimes (mostly involving cannabis), and connections to organized crime. The SQ were unwilling to patrol Kanehsatake, resulting in the surge in criminal activity. Since the 1990 crisis, Kanehsatake has been ruled by a pro-assimilation band council with its own police force established in 1997. In 1999, these police shot and paralyzed Joe David, a warrior active during the crisis. The band council has also pursued self-government agreements with Canada and Quebec, further undermining Mohawk sovereignty.

In January 2004, Kanehsatake was again headline news when local residents, fed up with their traitorous council, barricaded 60 police officers in the Kanehsatake Mohawk police station. In addition, police chief James Gabriel's house and vehicles were set on fire, after he had fled to Montreal. The Aboriginal officers had been brought in from across the province to reinforce local police. The pretext used was that of criminal activities and drug trafficking, the result of the SQ refusal to undertake that task. Previously, in 1991, Ouellette had been re-elected mayor of Oka by acclamation.

The **Ipperwash Crisis** took place at Ipperwash Provincial

Park, Ontario in 1995. Several members of the Stoney Point Ojibway band occupied the park in order to assert their claim to nearby land which had been expropriated from them during WWII. During a violent confrontation, the Ontario Provincial Police (OPP) killed unarmed protester Dudley George, purportedly believing the flashlight he held in his hand was a weapon. The shooting of Dudley George came a day after newly elected Conservative Premier of Ontario Mike Harris ordered OPP to "get the fucking Indians out of Ipperwash Park". The ensuing controversy was a major event in Canadian politics.

In 2003 a provincial inquiry was started after the Liberals were elected. In 2007, the Ontario government announced its intention to return the 56-hectare Ipperwash Provincial Park to its original owners, the Chippewas of the Kettle and Stony Point First Nation. The settlement was finalized in 2016, along with a $95 million payment, by Minister of National Defence Harjit Sajjan and Minister of Indigenous and Northern Affairs Carolyn Bennett. Chief Thomas Bressette signed the agreement on behalf of the band. Happier ending.

BC has its own blackmark—the incident at **Gustafsen Lake** in BC in August 1995, when several tribal groups, led by the Ts'peten Defenders, tried to conduct a sundance and the BC and federal governments tried to stop it after the owner of the land, Lyle James, tried unsuccessfully to evict the natives. They had erected a fence to keep defecating cattle from the ceremonial area. James believed the occupiers were staking their territory and ranch hands impaled the eviction notice on a sacred spear. The occupiers believed their religion was under attack and the Sun Dance leader, Splitting the Sky, called for an armed defensive stance. The involvement of the local elected Shuswap leadership further aggravated occupiers, who saw their elected leadership as serving the Canadian state.

The police wanted the dispute to be settled through negotiations. But the BC NDP government wanted to look tough on natives as an election ploy, and senior RCMP officers saw it as an opportunity to carry out a major paramilitary operation to intimidate natives. All through the spring there had been roadblocks at one location or another in the province. The RCMP got their 'war games'; the operation was the largest paramilitary operation in British Columbia history and cost $5.5 million. The standoff ended peacefully on September 17 when the few remaining occupiers left the site under the guidance of medicine man John Stevens.

James Pitawanakwat, sentenced to three years in jail

for endangering life, fled to the US when released on parole, and successfully fought extradition to Canada to complete his sentence, becoming the only Native ever granted political asylum in the United States. According to Janice Stewart, the magistrate justice of the US District Court in Oregon, "The Gustafsen Lake incident involved an organized group of native people rising up in their homeland against an occupation by the government of Canada of their sacred and unceded tribal land." She also asserted that "the Canadian government engaged in a smear and disinformation campaign to prevent the media from learning and publicizing the true extent and political nature of these events".[20] Respect and tolerance for the natives could have avoided these crises, revealing how thin the veneer of accommodation is when land is at stake.

Assimilations, Treaties

Here we can see some parallels between the US, Canadian and Israeli settler colonies and their treatment of the natives—the unsuccessful but enduring native resistance, the poor education provided by the state, the willful violation of international norms, though in some respects the North American natives have a stronger basis for resistance than the Palestinians.

Assimilation has been official government policy in both the US and Canada since the 18th century. This is in sharp contrast with Palestine, both under British and Israeli occupation. In Canada, *inter alia* due to the extent of overt racism and lack of English skills, there was no hope of successful native assimilation until after WWII, which had served to push natives into the mainstream as soldiers, where they achieved at last some respect for bravery and fighting skills. But this respect and a new access to education worked more to politicize natives, than to make them cede their rights more quickly to an encroaching system.

From the start of Confederation, the issues of native peoples in Canada were downplayed. The nation-to-nation negotiations between the British Crown and Indigenous nations reflected in the 1763 Royal Proclamation were not recognized in the 1867 Constitution. In the last 150 years, recognition of Aboriginal and Indigenous rights has fared better in the courts than in the political and economic arenas addressing their actual realization. Advances have been disappointing, and tragic living circumstances for Native Peoples ongoing and all too prevalent.

In Canada, there are stronger native claims, both in theory

and practice, than in the US, based on efforts to secure the honoring of **treaties** made with the British crown. This has meant native issues play a much more prominent role in both national and regional politics. Numbered treaties, the Indian Act, the Constitution Act of 1982 and case laws form the basis of treaty regulation. British Columbia is the weak link, as most of the native nations residing in British Columbia have no treaty with Canada, and still retain their original claim and rights to their lands. Canadian efforts to negotiate treaties have been largely unsuccessful. Aboriginal peoples construe these agreements as being between them and the Crown of Canada through the district Indian Agents, and not the Cabinet of Canada. The contrast with Palestine is stark, as neither the British nor Israelis have made treaties with the native Palestinians, though the Palestinians have a UN-based right to a state, subsequently recognized by most of the world. The Oslo Accords can be seen as a form of treaty, though it was never honored.

A series of eleven treaties were signed between First Nations in Canada and the reigning Monarch of Canada from 1871 to 1921.[21] The government of Canada created the policy, appointed the Treaty Commissioners, and ratified the agreements. These treaties are agreements with the government of Canada, administered by Canadian Aboriginal law and overseen by the Minister of Indian Affairs and Northern Development. According to the First Nations–Federal Crown Political Accord, "cooperation will be a cornerstone for partnership between Canada and First Nations, wherein Canada is the short-form reference to Her Majesty the Queen in Right of Canada." In a victory for the natives, the Supreme Court argued that treaties "served to reconcile pre-existing Aboriginal sovereignty with assumed Crown sovereignty, and to define Aboriginal rights". First Nations peoples were confirmed in interpreting agreements covered in treaty 8-to last "as long as the sun shines, grass grows and rivers flow."[22]

The fight over treaty rights employs a veritable army of lawyers. The push to dispossess natives of their remaining rights, to eliminate special status in legislation and assimilate them into the mainstream capitalist system picked up with the 1969 White Paper on Indian Policy, which was quickly shelved when natives read it. The Conservatives tried again with what came to be called "Buffalo Jump of the 1980s"—a secret federal Cabinet report leaked to the media by a Department of Indian Affairs and Northern Development (DIAND) employee, which proposed to eventually end all federal responsibility for native issues, devolving management to the provinces and cutting DIAND funding. It would have meant cultural suicide and again only made natives more hostile to anything coming from Ottawa.

In 1992, Aboriginal organizations and the federal government agreed, as part of the 1992 Charlottetown Accord, on amendments to the Constitution Act of 1982 that would have included recognition of the inherent right of self-government for Aboriginal people. For the first time, Aboriginal organizations had been full participants in the talks. However, the Accord was rejected in a national referendum.

There was some hope for a new government approach under the ill-fated Paul Martin Liberal government in 2005, but that government lasted only a year, and the new Conservative government dusted off the past failures and once again proposed ending the natives' special status. In 2012, the Harper government proposed the First Nations Property Ownership Act (FNPOA) to implement private property regimes on First Nations reserves in Canada, using fee simple property title on reserves, cast as "restoring pre-colonial property rights regimes."[23] Land claims and self-government final agreements proposed converting First Nations into municipalities, their reserves into fee simple lands and extinguishing their inherent aboriginal and treaty rights. To do this the Harper government announced a "results-based" approach to negotiating modern treaties and self-government agreements, terminating federal funding to those First Nations political organizations that refuse to 'negotiate'.[24]

But despite these fancy words, natives saw what was up. They had become more politically active since the 1960s, in both Canada and the US, and assimilation policies, which hadn't worked before, still did not work, despite the acquiescence of some tribes like the Kanehsatake.

Justin Trudeau made ambitious promises to Canada's Aboriginal peoples during his election campaign in 2015. He told the Assembly of First Nations General Assembly in July:

> The constitutionally guaranteed rights of Aboriginal Peoples in Canada are not an inconvenience but rather a sacred obligation. Our futures are inextricably intertwined. When I say that we must complete the unfinished work of Confederation, I mean that Canada needs a renewed, nation-to-nation relationship with Aboriginal communities.

This in the first place should have meant replacing the Indian Act and negotiating self-government. But upon election he moved instead to use his majority government to break or manipulate his promises, aided and abetted by his (token native) Justice Minister Jody Wilson-Raybould and his Indigenous Affairs Minister Carolyn Bennett.

Trudeau's biggest betrayal so far is his backsliding on his promise to adopt the United Nations Declaration on the Rights of Indigenous Peoples (UNDRIP). The Justin Trudeau government is attempting to take the international minimum standards of Human Rights of Indigenous Peoples' contained in the Articles of UNDRIP and interpret them through a Canadian constitutional framework, which continues to be used to dispossess, impoverish and oppress Indigenous peoples. All policies have traditionally been worded to terminate Indigenous rights and assimilate Indigenous People's into becoming, as Justin Trudeau calls them, "Indigenous Canadians". This is postmodern multiculturalism, which is fine for colonists, but ignores the fundamental right of the Indigenous Peoples to special legal status in addition to equality with the colonial settlers before the law.

The contrast between this projected place of native nations in the postmodern multicultural Canadian state and the situation of Palestinians in Israel is startling. The indigenous Palestinians have yet to be offered a place in a postmodern multicultural (one-state) Palestine/Israel despite many of their cultural practices being similar to those of most Israeli Jews. To the contrary: they remain locked in a separate legal regimen (apartheid, as so termed recently even by former Secretary of State, John Kerry) on a serially-reduced portion of the land which was originally theirs, and face the threat of ongoing ethnic cleansing removing them even from that. Despite Palestinians having UN approval of their right to a State, Observer Status at the UN and recognition by the world's states, Israel maintains what is internationally recognized as an illegal occupation of all of their territories. They must struggle for the right to mere existence.

However the Canadian multicultural projection is far from accomplished as it concerns native peoples. The Supreme Court of Canada supported the government by setting out a constitutional analytical framework of legal tests that continue to rely on the Doctrine of Christian Discovery[25] while placing the burden of proof on Indigenous groups to prove they have "existing" Aboriginal or treaty rights. These legal tests cost millions of dollars to meet and the collection of evidence in order to sustain a constitutional challenge in the courts is immense. They are unaffordable for most Indigenous Peoples, which is why most Chiefs and Councils across Canada are at what Diabo calls "federal Termination Tables", negotiating away their peoples' rights.[26]

In July 2016, Justice Minister Jody Wilson-Raybould told the Chiefs at a National Assembly of First Nations Assembly in Niagara Falls that, "adopting UNDRIP as being Canadian law is unworkable and, respectfully, a political distraction to undertaking the hard work required to actually implement it. Ultimately, UNDRIP will be articulated through the constitutional framework of section 35." Her statement contrasts with NDP MP Romeo Saganash's private members Bill 262, "An Act to ensure that the laws of Canada are in harmony with the United Nations Declaration on the Rights of Indigenous Peoples." Saganash's bill has been endorsed by many Indigenous and supporting groups, including The Coalition for the Human Rights of Indigenous Peoples.

Again, the contrast with Israel is instructive. Israel didn't even bother to show up when UNDRIP was voted on and says it does not apply in Israel, even though the UN ruled that at the very least, the Bedouin are covered.

But, by interpreting UNDRIP through the lens of Canadian constitutional law (as interpreted by the federal government and the Supreme Court of Canada), the Trudeau government is replacing the high international standard in UNDRIP of free, prior, informed *consent* (and thereby, veto power for dissent) with the lower domestic legal standard of the Crown's *duty to consult* with Indigenous groups. All the government has to do is justify infringement of Indigenous rights as being for the public good, and, like the IDF in Israel, expropriate the desired land 'in the national interest'. In Canada's most recent case, that means approving the Site C dam project in Peace Valley, the Liquified Natural Gas project on Lelu Island, and the Kinder-Morgan pipeline. As long as 50% of Canadians approve, that's all that matters. No need to resort to 'rights of indigenous peoples'.

The other British colony that warrants its own study as an 'Israel nexus' is **apartheid South Africa**, which was merely Nazi Germany without the 'Final Solution'. Both were expansionist, racist colonial regimes. There were various powerful South African fascist groups in the 1930s and debate about which side to support in WWII. Prime Minister Smuts sensibly joined the Allies, despite knowing that post-war pressures against the racist regime would be a problem. As in

Israel, the Old Testament justification for colonizing lesser peoples was the bible for Apartheid, but it proved thin material a half century later in the 1990s. In 1948 both declared independence. In 1961 PM Henrik Verwoerd: "Israel, like South Africa is an apartheid state."[27]

In 1973 PM John Vorster made a state visit to Israel. In 1976, he was toasted by Yitzhak Rabin for "the ideals shared by Israel and South Africa; the hopes for justice and peaceful coexistence." Israel cooperated with South Africa on nuclear arms development, joining in supporting the pro-imperialist faction in the Angolan war, providing anti-riot vehicles to manage the "townships". South Africa provided crucial, quiet support for Israel though officially Israel was anti-apartheid. South Africa was abandoned by the West as

- there was no South African lobby in the US,
- it was not so strategic geopolitically,
- US blacks and the civil rights movement created a popular world movement with the US now onside to boycott, disinvest and sanction,
- the segregation was more overt (black and white) in South Africa, while Israel is more mixed in its multicultural Jewish population, close to the Arabs.

In South Africa's favor, the state provided health and some welfare to blacks (they needed their labor) vs Israel. There, the EU/US/UN have to fund the Arabs.[28]

Ireland also provides some hint of the future for Israel-Palestine. The conquest from the 12th century culminating in the union treaty in the 19th century saw conquerors intermarry and become the Anglo gentry in the south, first the Normans and then the English, and waves of poor Scots create a troubled north that still maintains its colonial status. The 19th century potato famine provided the 'natural' cause that decimated the population, recapitulating the earlier decimation of natives in North America, forcing millions to emigrate to this newly freed land, much like Palestinians are doing on a smaller scale today, faced with the 'Anglo' invasion. But it didn't wipe out Irish culture. Israel mimics British Northern Ireland, tied to the US 'motherland' for safety from the native population.

The stand-off in Ireland is enduring and sparked terrorism for a century, both in the 'colony' and the 'motherland', though it has lost steam. Independence of the Catholic south was the result of a long and vicious guerrilla war that left Ireland crippled and isolated. Paralleling Canada, Ireland now is an enthusiastic member of the multicultural EU, with many immigrants and a shift from religiosity to secularism. Following Ireland, just as largely secular Israel faces a similar process of absorption into the local Arab culture, Palestinians face the prospect of a loss of Islamic devotion under the colonial pressures such as Ireland experienced in the past two centuries. Peace could mean acceptance of the invaders throughout Palestine as a similar conqueror gentry (the one-state solution). The main difference could be the greater resilience of Islam than Christianity, and the greater tribalism of Judaism, preventing intermarriage and assimilation—a mix of the criollo[29] and the Irish 'models'.

Canada was largely populated in the 19th century by destitute English and destitute Irish, both Catholics from the south and Protestants from the north, escaping the common enemy, famine. My own maternal grandparents are Irish and English Protestants, their descendants now assimilated and celebrating their Irish/ Englishness through the echoes of religious and cultural heritage—multiculturalism.

Endnotes

1   Canada celebrates two national holidays: the Queen's birthday (in Quebec, Patriots' Day) in late May and Canada Day, referring to the signing of the Confederation document uniting the four original Canadian provinces Nova Scotia, New Brunswick, Upper and Lower Canada on July 1. According to Binette referring to "Confederation (which was a confederation in name only), on July 1. Neither has any relation to its independence. Canada does not celebrate the date of its accession to independence, which legally occurred on December 11, 1931 through the adoption of a British law called the Statute of Westminster. Canadian citizenship did not appear until 1947."
1867 was supposed to be the final solution to the 1837-8 rebellion of the Patriotes of Lower Canada and a parallel revolt in Upper Canada, but it concerned only the distribution of powers among Anglophones, namely the British governor and the local élite. The Act of Union in 1840, which merged Upper and Lower Canada, had been designed to dilute the power of the Francophone majority of Lower Canada at a time when responsible government was becoming inevitable. However, the Act of Union was a failure since the political and national realities were obvious: in effect, there were two co-premiers and two attorneys general in United Canada; two parliamentary majorities were required if laws were to be adopted. The stand-off continues. Bi-nationalism is not an easy path. André Binette *L'Aut'journal*. 2017. <https://socialistproject.ca/bullet/1411.php#continue>

2	2.9 million people self-identified as Native American, Native Hawaiian, and Alaska Native alone, and 5.2 million people identified as US Native Americans, either alone or in combination with one or more ethnicity or other races. 1.8 million are recognized as enrolled tribal members.
3	See:https://www12.statcan.gc.ca/nhs-enm/2011/as-sa/99-011-x/99-011-x2011001-eng.cfm
4	As of 2011, Statistics Canada listed 329,500 adherents to the Jewish religion in Canada.
5	<https://en.wikipedia.org/wiki/Thirteen_Colonies>
6	Nova Scotia/New Brunswick was the 14th British colony in North America at the time of the American revolution. Nova Scotia was ceded to Britain by France in 1713 (Treaty of Utrecht), but a formal colony was established only in 1749 on what was still French territory (really Micmac, with French farmer settlers). It and Quebec were just barely British colonies in 1763 and the Americans initially invited them to attend official sessions of the new republic, the United States of America, but they demurred, remaining as British colonies, welcoming dissident 'Americans' as "Empire Loyalists". <http://www.myhartt.com/families/fourteen_colonies.htm> This is probably the source of Trump's claim during the 2016 election campaign that the US "should never have allowed" Canada to gain independence, that the United States owned Canada "at some point", and giving it back was a "major mistake". The former reality TV star was responding to a question about Puerto Rico possibly becoming the 51st of the United States, when he made the statement. "It used to be 51 you know, when we had Canada."
7	Puritan settlers called their first settlement at Plymouth in the 17th century "our New Jerusalem".
8	The exception was the Belgian Congo, where King Leopold instigated a genocide that still ranks as one of the worst in history, with estimates of 3-10m killed.
9	The term coined in 1845 and understood as belonging to the "Anglo-Saxon race".
10	Up to 90% of the American natives (18 million) died from European diseases, especially small pox, measles, scarlet fever, typhoid, typhus, influenza, whooping cough, tuberculosis, cholera, diphtheria, chickenpox, the common cold, and sexually transmitted diseases. While mostly this transfer was inadvertent, there are proven cases of intentionally infecting natives with contaminated blankets and other materials, a case of germ warfare.
11	In 2006, Abramoff pleaded guilty to three felony counts—conspiracy, fraud, and tax evasion—involving charges stemming principally from his lobbying activities in Washington on behalf of Native American tribes. In addition, Abramoff and other defendants must make restitution of at least $25 million that was defrauded from his Native clients. In 2006, he was sentenced to 6 years in federal prison, released in 2010, and wrote *Capital Punishment: The Hard Truth About Corruption From America's Most Notorious Lobbyist* in 2011.
12	"Indigenous" is most in line with UN laws and best emphasizes the issue of treaty obligations of the colonial power.
13	Including Metis leader Louis Riel and author George R. D. Goulet, actors Chief Dan George of the Tsleil-Waututh (Coast Salish) Nation and Graham Greene from the Oneida tribe.
14	Many towns and schools in Canada and the US are named in his honor. Union

	Civil War general William Tecumseh Sherman was given the name Tecumseh because "my father...had caught a fancy for the great chief of the Shawnees." The *USS Tecumseh* is a submarine commissioned in 1993. In contrast, no Israeli parent would call their son Arafat.
15	Duncan Scott, "Indian Affairs, 1763-1841", in Adam Shortt and Arthur Doughty, eds., *Canada and Its Provinces*, Vol. IV, Toronto, Glasgow, Brook and Company, 1914. <http://faculty.marianopolis.edu/c.belanger/QuebecHistory/encyclopedia/HistoryofCanadianIndians-1763-1840.htm>
16	<http://caid.ca/GraCivAct1857.pdf>
17	<http://ir.lib.uwo.ca/cgi/viewcontent.cgi?article=1034&context=iipj>
18	<https://ubcatlas.files.wordpress.com/2012/04/2008-carson.pdf>
19	Arabic for uprising, resistance, rebellion.
20	<https://en.wikipedia.org/wiki/Gustafsen_Lake_standoff>
21	Victoria, Edward VII, George V.
22	Assembly of First Nations; Elizabeth II (2004). "The Indian Act of Canada – Origins: Legislation Concerning Canada's First Peoples".
23	Michael Fabris, "Beyond the New Dawes Act: A Critique of the First Nations Property Ownership Act", MA thesis, University of British Columbia, 2014.
24	The 2006 Conservative Platform promised a "modern legislative framework" to replace the Indian Act (and related legislation) with a modern legislative framework which provides for the devolution of full legal and democratic responsibility to aboriginal Canadians for their own affairs within the Constitution, including the Charter of Rights and Freedoms. Russell Diabo "Harper Launches Major First Nations Termination Plan: As Negotiating Tables Legitimize Canada's Colonialism", *Intercontinental Cry*, November 9, 2012.
25	For the native perspective, see Steve Newcomb, "Five Hundred Years of Injustice: The Legacy of Fifteenth Century Religious Prejudice," < http://ili.nativeweb.org/sdrm_art.html>
26	Russell Diabo, "Justin Trudeau continuing proud Liberal tradition of betraying Indigenous peoples", *rabble.ca*, October 28, 2016, originally published in *Iori:wase*, Volume 4, Issue 28 on October 27, 2016.
27	Kovel, op.cit., 212.
28	Israel lets infrastructure be built for the Palestinians, but siphons funds before distributing them to the Palestinians, and then cynically destroys the infrastructure in bombing raids, knowing the EU et al will cough up. <https://www.democracynow.org/2006/7/28/headlines/israel_bombs_infrastructure_relief_trucks_ambulance>
29	'Creole' refers to a white person, not only whose *ancestros* are from Spain, but any Euro-descendant that lives in Spanish America. The prevailing racial reality is the "mestizo" (a person who is product of mixing white and amerindian) or mulatto (white and black), the Creole white people in Latin-America are a dominant minority.

| Chapter Two |

CREATING ISRAEL

Great Game II (1945–1991)

Imperialism has gone through three distinct stages since the term "Great Game" was coined in the nineteenth century to describe the rivalry between imperialist powers, primarily Russia and Britain. Imperial strategy was simpler then, but the basic elements were in place. Already by the nineteenth century there was no such thing as neutral territory. The entire world was now a gigantic playing field for the major industrial powers, and the Middle East was the center of this playing field.

The notion of a separate homeland for the Jews had long been an intimate, even essential part of the imperialist dream, or rather conspiracy, to capture Eurasia, and indeed, the world. The motif "a people without a land for a land without a people" was coined by Lord Shaftesbuet in 1839 in relation to a home for the British Jews.[1] Geopolitical theorist Halford Mackinder, one of the conspirators at the imperial Round Table in London, proposed a less formal empire to be called the British Commonwealth of Nations, with supporters including liberals such as H.G. Wells. Canada's Prime Minister Mackenzie King was an early convert, as was Goldwin Smith.[2]

In the global empire foreseen by Mackinder, a "Jewish-dominated Palestine, beholden to England for its tenuous survival, surrounded by a balkanized group of squabbling Arab states"[3] was a key linchpin: "If Arabia, as the passage-land from Europe to the Indies and from the Northern to the Southern Heartland,[4] be central to the World-Island, then the hill citadel of Jerusalem has a strategical position."[5] Mackinder's aspiration was not Zionist but imperial, and by putting Jews in a Palestinian homeland, he was assembling the pieces of today's imperial order, but for a different "World-Island" and with a very different "hill citadel" at the heart of that world-island empire.

Mackinder was a realist in foreseeing that the new Crusade to capture the Holy Land would be a political and economic quest rather than the supposedly spiritual (but actually military) quest that the original Crusades were. Mackinder realized that this one last formal colony was necessary to complete the empire geopolitically.

The Ottoman Caliphate was tottering by the late 19th century, and Britain wanted Iraq for its oil and Palestine for a Jewish state, "the hill citadel of Jerusalem" according to Mackinder, the last link in the chain of British Empire.

Though Zionism already had its following in the British political elite,[6] the plan for an 'Israel' was actually a subtle appeal to anti-Jewish prejudice in Britain, a selling point for those who wanted to rid Britain of Jews, foreshadowing Hitler's unofficial alliance with Zionists from 1933 on, and even for the post-WWII West, not anxious to absorb more Jewish refugees than necessary. It "always appealed to white European racists, from Hitler to Churchill to Lord Balfour. ... a fine way to impel Jews to leave Britain, Germany, wherever, [now] cleansed of a 'foreign element' perceived by them to be troublesome, subversive or simply distasteful. Many Jews opposed Zionism for the same reason."[7]

A European Settler Colony in Palestine

At the **Paris Peace Conference in 1919**, the World Zionist Organization (WZO), represented by its president Chaim Weizmann, along with the Zionist Organization of America, was able to pressure 'emir' Faisal, son of Hussein, nominally emir of the holy cities (but totally dependent on the British, soon to be overthrown by the Saudi Bedouin, Ibn Saud). "The Zionist Organization will use its best efforts to assist the Arab State in providing the means for developing the natural resources and economic possibilities thereof." At the same time, Weizmann stated at the conference that "the Zionist objective was gradually to make Palestine as Jewish as England was English."

Weizmann lobbied his British friends, arguing that western Jews would bring technology and investment to Palestine, helping the locals, not ethnically cleansing them, as the Ottomans did to the Armenians, as the newly liberated Balkan states were doing to Turks and Muslims who had long lived there as part of the Ottoman Caliphate.

He signed the agreement on behalf of the powerful WZO, while Faisal signed on behalf of the short-lived and powerless Arab Kingdom of Hedjaz. Neither represented an official government, but the WZO and ZOA represented the British and American Jewish elite, embodied in the Rothschilds, for whom the Balfour Declaration was written in 1917, though it was prepared long earlier, as revealed in the Campbell-Bannerman Report (1907).[8] Faisal was merely put there by the British as the token Arab. He was tricked into coming to an agreement with the Zionists based on the 1917 Declaration, which allowed mass immigration of European Jews to Palestine, so the British could blame any future problems on the Arabs themselves. It appeared to work, but, like Faisal and Hussein's kingdom, had no substance.

It is this Zionist promise of peace and prosperity for the Palestinians that Obama had in mind as he dropped his pressing concerns of state to rush to Peres's funeral in October 2016, and piously state, "My friend Shimon Peres showed us that justice and hope are at the heart of the Zionist idea." At 92, Peres could surely have recalled Weizmann's lobbying Churchill and other British leaders in the 1930s with this promise of a bright future, the legacy of the British Empire, brought 'free of charge' to the Arabs by British Jews and their relatives in Europe. The same promise British colonists brought to Canada two centuries earlier. Till the end, Peres seemed to believe this was still the real intention of Zionism. His last act was to promote a 'Marshall Plan', with Israel leading a transformation of the entire Middle East.[9]

There was a longstanding community of a few thousand religious Jews living peacefully in Israel before the influx. The number of Jews migrating to Palestine rose between the 13th and 19th centuries, mainly due to religious persecution by Christians. The expulsion of Jews from England (1290), France (1391), Austria (1421), and Spain (1492) contributed greatly to the messianic spirit of the time.

The Protestant Reformation's biblical literalism spurred Zionism. In 1649 two English Puritans in Amsterdam suggested to London, "that this nation of England, with the inhabitants of the Netherlands, shall be the first and the readiest to transport Israel's sons and daughters on their ships to the land promised to their forefathers, Abraham, Isaac and Jacob for an everlasting inheritance."[10]

Canada played a historic role in fostering the Christian Zionist dream. Henry Wentworth Monk (1827–1896) was a Canadian Christian Zionist, mystic, Messianist, and millenarian, who interpreted *Revelation* to imply Jerusalem as the center of a world government, complete with an international tribunal. Monk established the Palestine Restoration Fund in 1875 and tried to set up a farm settlement, which didn't succeed. He was inspired by the Earl of Shaftesbury who got Britain's foreign secretary to appoint the first British consul to Jerusalem in 1839, and he in turn inspired Herzl, who held the first Zionist Congress in 1897.

Canadian minister Albert Thompson returned from travels to Palestine in the 1910s to lecture widely on "the Jewish colonies" in the holy land "turning the wilderness into a very garden of the Lord."[11] In 1897 Zionist organizations were established in Toronto, Kingston, Winnipeg, Hamilton, Ottawa, Quebec and Montreal, attended by Christians, receiving greetings from Cabinet ministers, mayors, lieutenant governors.[12] This was in keeping with Canada's model role as a loyal, very British colony, now embracing with enthusiasm the completion of the imperial project, the British imperial 'conspiracy'.[13]

Settlement in Palestine by European Jews began in the 19th century and accelerated by the early 20th century. The sudden surge of immigration in the late 19th century parallels the surge of east European Jews emigrating to America, though the 2.8 million who went to North America puts the 40,000 who made aliyah to Palestine in the shade. They saw the 'promised land' as America. The following table indicates the leaps in growth of the Jewish population going to Palestine.[14]

Migration	Jews	Christians	Muslims	Total
1890	43,000	57,000	432,000	532,000
1914	94,000	70,000	525,000	689,000
1922	84,000	71,000	589,000	752,000
1931	175,000	89,000	760,000	1,033,000
1947	630,000	143,000	1,181,000	1,970,000

The period of the British mandate, from 1918–1947, marked the endgame of Great Game I, with Britain long past its imperial zenith, and incapable of carrying out a Canada-style colonization of Palestine. The British were dismissive of the Arabs, who had been duped by the empire's 'Lawrence of Arabia' into scuttling the Ottoman Caliphate on the promise of independence. Instead, the British began establishing the makings of a Jewish state, infuriating the locals, who saw their hoped-for independence betrayed. Balfour wrote: "We do not propose to go through the form of consulting the wishes of the present inhabitants. The four great powers are committed to Zionism... rooted in age-long tradition, in present needs, in future hopes, of far profounder import than the desire and prejudices of the 700,000 Arabs who now inhabit that ancient land."[15] Thus, the undeclared, endless war began, even as the 'war to end all wars' was signed off at Versailles.

The British (and Canadian) imperial dreamers Mackinder, Monk et al didn't live to see their dream realized, but the Zionist dream was now picked up by the British Jewish elite, with their own interpretation of *Revelation*: a Jewish state in Palestine but without Monk's international tribunal to govern world affairs. Again Canada played a key role in nurturing this new version. Federation of Zionist Societies of Canada President Clarence de Sola mobilized Jews to join Allenby's Jewish Legion (1917–1921) against the Ottomans.[16] Montrealer Dov Joseph made aliyah (immigrated) to Palestine in 1918 with the Canadian Jewish Legion. After the end of World War I, Joseph, now Yosef, worked as an attorney for the Jewish Agency.[17] Already in 1913, Young Judea clubs sprouted in Canada, preparing Jews for the dream of a homeland in Palestine. 1917 was a signal year for Jews—the Russian revolution and the Balfour letter both held promise for Jewish emancipation.[18]

Canadian Jews were more in line with Britain's imperial mission than Americans, and were able to balance their dual loyalties to the British scheme and their own. The Jewish elite supported WWI despite the alliance with the hated Russia, seeing an Israel as a future British colony, and Zionism consistent with British Canadian nationalism. Devout Christian Canadians were themselves colonists who had come to Canada to seize 'backward' peoples' lands, so in their eyes it was no crime for Jews to do this to Arabs in Palestine. Dual loyalty, yes; as long as Canada and Israel were bosom buddies, this was not a problem.

The Dispossession of the Palestinians

Formerly peaceful relations between Arabs and Jews were replaced by suspicion and animosity. Arabs, good merchants, but unprepared for the march of capitalism, protested as Jewish immigration accelerated. Zionists raised millions of pounds to buy up absentee landlords' lands and eject the peasants who farmed them. The idea was to buy enough property, expel the Arabs legally—*et voila!*—a Jewish state.

It would not be quite so simple. This conspiracy culminated in riots in 1929. It was time for hard power. Jewish guerrilla forces, especially the Haganah, smuggled arms into the country after the riots. The discovery of a shipment disguised as barrels of cement at the docks in Jaffa in 1935 (the "Cement Incident") proved that the Jews of Palestine were arming on a large scale, sparking the 1936–39 Arab revolt and seven-month general strike of 1936.[19]

The British occupiers were siding with the Jewish settlers, now European and even North American. The British had neither the will nor strength to make treaties with the natives, as they had done in Canada, providing some grounds for the natives to defend their rights upon independence. Major-General Orde Charles Wingate was the most (in)famous officer, training Jewish security forces, noted for his relish in torturing and killing suspected Arab resistance fighters.[20] Although the British administration did not officially recognize the Haganah, the British security forces cooperated with it by forming the Jewish Settlement Police, Jewish Supernumerary Police, and Special Night Squads. The British authorities maintained, financed and armed the Jewish police from this point onward until the end of the Mandate, and by the end of September 1939 around 20,000 Jewish policeman, supernumeraries and settlement guards had been authorized to carry arms by the government.

The Zionists were saved by the outbreak of WWII. They were able to hide behind their British overlords, whom they now saw as their enemies even as the British were fighting to save European Jews from Hitler. The Palestinians, logically, were either indifferent to the British-German spat, or rooting for a German victory to prevent European Jews from taking over Palestine, as the British had seemingly promised. Effectively war by the British and Jews against the local Arabs had erupted, and as the nations descended into world war, the Jewish immigrants used the preoccupation of the British with Germany to conduct a war of terror against both the Arabs and Palestine's British masters. Jews pushed for their own brigades to fight the Nazis, which the British at first declined. So Jews joined the British army and eventually got their Jewish Brigade Group in 1945, stationed in Tarvisio, near the border triangle of Italy, Yugoslavia, and Austria, where it played a key role in efforts to help Jews escape Europe to Palestine, a role many of its members would continue to perform after the brigade was disbanded. Later, veterans of the Jewish Brigade became key participants of the new state's Israel Defense Forces (IDF).

Jewish terrorist groups multiplied, now attacking British

occupiers and civilians alike, attempting to accelerate their departure. In 1944, Lehi assassinated a British minister, Lord Moyne in Cairo. The most destructive terrorist attack was the bombing of the King David Hotel in 1946 by Irgun, killing 91.

Like the settlers of the US and Canada, with their substantial Jewish contingent, the European Jews became the British Mandate's settlers, displacing the native Palestinians, a replay of British and US colonial policy in North America (and Australia, New Zealand, etc.), albeit more than a century later. Just as the Americans were more ruthless than the British, the Jewish terrorists were worse than British colonial administrators and their local police. The Special Night Squads engaged in activities, described by colonial administrator Sir Hugh Foot, as "extreme and cruel" involving the torture, whipping, abuse and execution of Arabs.

The Arab-Israeli war that followed the declaration of a Jewish state in Palestine meant the fractured, inexperienced UN had to immediately deal with the problem it had created in endorsing a two-state solution. (Notably, Britain abstained on the vote to recognize Israel.) Swedish Count Folke Bernadotte of Wisborg was agreed as mediator, but was promptly assassinated by the Zionist Stern Gang. After more than a year of painstaking negotiations, his assistant, African-American Ralph Bunche, managed to secure separate armistice agreements between Israel and Egypt, Lebanon, Transjordan and Syria, which left Israel with all the territory it had gone on to conquer, hundreds of thousands of Palestinian refugees in neighboring Jordan and Syrian, and no state of Palestine—a template for all future Israeli 'compromises', for which Bunche was awarded the Nobel Peace Prize in 1950.

From this Great Game II[21] to the present, there have been three UN peacekeeping missions protecting Israel at UN expense, despite the fact that Israel has killed dozens of UN peacekeepers over the years with impunity. The first fully fledged UN peacekeeping effort was covering the withdrawal of British, French and Israeli forces from Egypt in 1956, following their invasion in the wake of the nationalization of the Suez Canal. UN troops were stationed in Sinai afterwards as part of a deal to get Israel to withdraw, and when Egypt finally ordered them to leave in 1967 to reassert its sovereignty, Israel invaded and re-occupied Sinai and all of Palestine.

Israel was created in 1948, as the original Great Game I reached its end with the destruction of all the imperial rivals to the US: Germany,

Japan (the 'enemy' ones), and France, Britain, Holland (the 'allies'). Spain was long out of the imperial league, by then a hermit kingdom, or rather a fascist dictatorship. Israel was the new kid on the block, and soon joined all these retired imperialists, supposedly as just another innocuous postmodern nation in the new Great Game II of imperialists united against communism.

Intense Zionist lobbying of the US and the Soviet Union, and constant outright terrorism, forced a beleaguered Britain to cede control of Palestine, paralleling the horror of the partition of India happening at the same time. A united Palestine would have required resolute support by the West for the indigenous Arabs in the face of international Zionist hostility, not something Britain, the US or the Soviet Union had any interest in or the ability to enforce.

The **partition of Palestine** was an even worse disaster for the native Palestinians than partition was for the Indians, but like the division of India, eventually proved to be a geostrategic coup for the US in its geopolitical divide-and-rule strategy for the Middle East, providing the US with Mackinder's "hill citadel", a western outpost promising imperial control over the Middle East and a stepping stone to control over Eurasia. A much greater prize than the Raj-equivalent Pakistan, which became a mostly obedient postmodern state, one which later came to play an outsize role in imperial plans.

Originally the Zionists were courted by both the US and the Soviet Union, each hoping, based on very different reasoning, that the creation of a Jewish state in Palestine would afford an opportunity to gain influence in the Middle East after Britain pulled out.

How was the Soviet Union so easily duped by the Zionists' real plan?

Prior to WWII, the religious convictions of Muslim society gave the atheist communists little hope for allies among the emerging Arab nations, whereas Jews were the very backbone of communism and revolution in Europe and America. The Soviets saw in Israel a potential pro-communist junior partner, and provided weapons at the time of independence, ensuring its survival in the face of Arab hostility, counting on their gratitude.

However, American and European Zionist lobbyists, representing powerful financial and business interests, had assured British and US political leaders in the 1970s–80s that the Jewish state would remain onside. They had used the same ploy in WWI, assuring the British they could bring the US into the war on the allies' side as long as they were promised a homeland after the war. Unlike Muslims, Jewish elites have through the centuries been prominent in imperial politics as advisers to kings, and in imperial finance and banking, and the Zionists used this ace masterfully in 1948.

In the new Great Game II, the sole remaining imperial power, the US, faced off against the only apparent rival, the Soviet Union, capitalism's would-be nemesis, threatening to spread communist revolution around the world, with the Jewish state onside.

There was supposed to be less hard power guns and more soft power butter in this new Great Game. However, hard power falling short of outright world war has still relied on a world network of military bases, arms production and sales, nuclear weapons, proxies, and soon, missile defense and now cyber warfare.

Soft power meant promoting 'aid' and 'education', using NGOs, color revolutions, co-opting regimes, anti-piracy, drugs, and resorting to domestic repression when the imperialists' own natives got restless. To say nothing of political subversion, financial pressures through institutions such as the UN, IMF, and NATO, destabilization when necessary, and mass culture courtesy of Hollywood.

Jews and Empires

The real history of Jews and empire is not considered polite to talk about, just as it is not kosher to remind the Zionists that their romantic dream was actually put into action as a very unromantic un-Zionist, even anti-Jewish plan—part of the conspiracy by British imperialists in the mid-19th century. Napoleon also had his 'Jewish conspiracy' plans to which his European wars brought a swift end.[22]

Canada took in British Jews from the 18th century on. The US was even more attractive to European Jews, and Canada was, by the mid-19th century, just a short train ride to the nascent world financial capital, New York, a magnet for the European Jewish banking elite. Canada would do very nicely as a 'promised land' of freedom for the Jews.

It is vital to understand the relationship between Canada and Israel in this context. Hannah Arendt states in *The Origins of Totalitarianism* that the key to understanding "the rise and fall of the Jews" is "the relationship between Jews and the state". Historically, in response to the hostile attitudes and actions of their neighbors, Jews frequently sought the protection of the state. As Ginsberg argues in *The Fatal Embrace: Jews and the State*, for their own purposes, rulers often were happy to accommodate the Jews in exchange for their services, resulting in "the rise to great power by Jewish elites, but creating conditions for their subsequent fall."[23]

They made alliances "responsible for the construction of some of the most powerful states of the Mediterranean and European worlds, including the Hapsburg, Hohenzollern, and Ottoman empires ... [though] in Wilhelmian Germany and Hapsburg Austria-Hungary, the regimes provided access to a small number of very wealthy Jews while subjecting the remainder to various forms of exclusion."[24] This led to the paradoxical situation where some Jews were ministers or viziers while the majority of them were oppressed and rebels, a foretaste of the twentieth century Great Games.

Jewish history shows considerable periods of peace and prosperity, mostly under the Caliphates, with spasms of persecution, massacre and exile, when Jews were forced into exile, especially in Christian Europe. Their embrace of money lending (forbidden to Christians and Muslims) eventually became the foundation of modern capitalism and led to a period of unprecedented prosperity culminating in the disastrous WWII.

While Jews prospered in 19th century Britain, there was always a latent resentment. Prime Minister Disraeli's influence on Lionel Rothschild and Henry Oppenheim, to ensure financial and local Egyptian support for taking control of the Suez Canal in 1878, led Hobson to allude to "men of a single and peculiar race, who have behind them centuries of financial experience" and who formed "the central ganglion of international capitalism".[25]

The TV series *Downton Abbey* (2010–15) is a metaphor for what happened to Britain during the past century and a half—a fading empire, whose rulers are craven and decadent, where the enterprising British Jews, though only 0.5% of the population, are prominent in political life, presiding over a politically correct culture where the Downton Abbey bigots (the anti-Jewish fourth Earl and the homophobes) are vanquished.[26]

Apartness gave Jews an edge, but it cut both ways, making Jews a source of distrust, embodying the Other, the fears and self-doubt of mainstream society, society's 'shadow' in Jungian terms. Just as for Jews, mainstream society represented the 'shadow', the unknowable

Other. English Professor Michael Keefer analyzes the anti-Jewish meme in literature where Jews are the "ineradicable other", known by Gentiles "through the mediations of fiction" which are projected onto Jews around them.[27]

This cultural distinction has always been celebrated by Jews, and indeed is essential to prevent their feared assimilation into the larger Christian/Muslim societies they lived in. It implies rejection of the Jewish messiah, Jesus, making them for Christians the Jungian shadow threat to their beliefs, their essence. This, like the importance of Jews to empire, must be addressed if there is to be any real understanding of the nexus between any nation, here Canada, and its Jews, and an unresolvable cause of conflict. The religious basis of conflict is less now, as religion is not of much importance anymore, either for Jews or Christians. In a 2013 Pew Forum study, only 60% of US Jews said that belief in Jesus as the Messiah was not "compatible with being Jewish", while 34% found it compatible and 4% didn't know. Vatican II put paid to the idea that all Jews are responsible for the crucifixion.

When religion was the core of one's being, resentment against the self-proclaimed murderers of Jesus, seen by his devoted followers as part of the Godhead through the Trinity, is of course going to lead to hostility.[28] Constant pressure to convert, both external and as an individual choice, has not led to total Jewish assimilation. The fact that a third of American Jews accept Jesus as a legitimate prophet and even the 'messiah' and still consider themselves Jews shows that Jewishness is not just about theology. For religious Jews who rejected Jesus, there was/is no middle ground. 'Better dead than Christian.' The age-old antagonism was only a problem under Christian rule, with the Muslim caliphs simply seeing Jews as misguided 'people of the book', much like Jews see Christians and Muslims. True, Muslims considered Jews untrustworthy as allies, as Jews' behavior in early Medina made clear, prompting certain passages comparing Jews unfavorably to Christians in the Quran.[29] But a well-governed Islamic state could keep harmony, allowing the Jews to prosper, and even maintain their own religion, as is the case in Iran.

Other 'Others'

There is a strong parallel with the fate of another despised minority in European and Middle Eastern society—gay men, who were/are also a small minority (3-5%) of men, a social 'shadow' which threatens the sacredness of marriage and the character of manliness,[30] just as Jews threaten Christian spirituality. They suffered side-by-side with Jews and witches under Christendom (much less so under Islamic rule) right up until the Nazis, who decided they were just as bad, in their own way, as Jews, and both should be wiped out. Their fate today—legality, tolerance, outsize prosperity and apartness—parallels that of Jews.

Because they have no homeland to colonize, homosexuals are no political threat. The rise of gaylib in the era of identity politics has brought about the rise of a weak gay tribal identity, but these sexual inverts have always striven for the most part to assimilate and be invisible, rather than to stand out and demand special treatment. However, their psychological threat as Other remains, again by definition. Interestingly, their cause has been enthusiastically embraced by Zionists, though not without problems, as the difficulties of life in supposedly gay-friendly Israel makes abundantly clear.[31] They are an important part of the "yerida" (emigration from Israel) and are also an untrustworthy ally in the Diaspora, many embracing not the Zionist, but the Palestinian cause, despite homosexuality being frowned upon in the Muslim world.

Those Jews who have not assimilated stubbornly remain aloof, with their apartness being a choice (unlike homosexuals), taking pride in their persecution as God's 'chosen people', above Gentile society. Otto Weininger, a 19th century German Jewish philosopher, described Judaism as a state of mind. For some, the focus is on the rituals; for some, the tribal solidarity; for others, the supposed superiority. But while you may be born a Jew, there's nothing to stop you from not being a Jew whenever you like, as many (most?) have done in the past, including hundreds of thousands of immigrants to America over the past 200 years. It's easy to move, change your name, join a church (or not), and blend in. But insofar as these assimilationists are no longer Jews, their former identity becomes untraceable.

The 1967 war with Egypt and the resulting sense of empowerment of Israel parallels the rise of gaylib since the 1969 Stonewall riots.[32] Jews are now much more up front about their Jewishness, and gays about their gayness. In the US, it is now 'cool' to be 'Jewcy', as some young Jews flaunt on their t-shirts. It is now 'cool' to be gay, too. Just as many Jews make their identification with Israel their primary signifier, there are many people who identify themselves first and foremost as gays, rather than as, say, Canadians or socialists. This is the age of personal "identity politics". And Canada leads the way, with Prime Minister Trudeau and NDP leader Tom Mulcair marching together at Toronto's gay pride parade.

This Jewish-homosexual parallel recapitulates a 19th century one: the Dreyfus trial in 1894 and the Oscar Wilde trial in 1895. Dreyfus, an obscure Jewish officer convicted of treason, became the cause célèbre of Victor Hugo and other prominent figures and was rehabilitated, while Wilde, the greatest 19th century playwright, died broken and abandoned. Ironically, these historic trials were a kind of swan song for civilization's overt repression of Jews *and* gays. Now books about the Holocaust are part of children's curricula, just as story books where 'Susie has two daddies' (at least in the most 'progressive' schools).

Of course, the barbarian holocausts of Hitler against Jews *and* gays were yet to come, but again, look at the difference. Only 9% of Jews reject Israel as a Jewish state (though most secular Jews put it in fifth place in their priorities 'as a Jew'),[33] and the Zionist organizations have used this tragedy to reap billions of dollars in reparations for Israel, themselves and individual survivors, while, by creating what is a racist state, inflicting an equally tragic fate on the Palestinians. No gays (or relatives) received reparations for their suffering, let alone Hitler's other Others—Roma (gypsies) and communists. Gays and Roma have not used their new freedom to inflict suffering on others claiming that it is justified because of Hitler's holocaust. Their threat to society is only psychological, which Zionists have tried to exploit, making Tel Aviv the "gay capital in the Middle East",[34] but with little success.

Conundrum of Jewish Nationalism and Democracy

So Jews are a much more imposing Other than gays, Roma, or any other minority. Tribalism is still a powerful political force with an equally powerful historical legacy, which is why some of the 'chosen people' refuse to abandon it, whether or not they abide by Judaism the religion. Given their new prominence in the 19th century British Empire, in keeping with their age-old tradition of uniqueness, chosenness, the Jewish people fashioned a secular, *imperial ideology of their own*, Zionism, which appealed to the growing secular Jewish community. In the US one-third of Jews describe themselves as having no religion, and identify as Jewish on the basis of ancestry, ethnicity or culture. In

Israel, it is *half*. The Jewish state is *de jure* religious but *de facto* secular. In the tradition of Great Game I, the new proto-state set out to carve a nation on Palestinian lands, employing the traditional policy of war and occupation of others' lands, appealing primarily to a secular nationalism rather than religion. This contrasts with Canada, which was founded on Christian morality, where Christianity was assumed to be the dominant cultural force. In direct contradiction to Israel, Canada was never *de jure* a religious state (no modern states were religious in the 19th century), but it was one *de facto* (at least until recently).

It follows from this that when Jews achieved their own state, those who approved of this state in the Diaspora would use their embedded influence in their host countries to promote their own (national) state, and as a corollary even undermine or abandon a host if it interferes with the goals of the Jewish state. The genuine specter of dual loyalty now raises its head, something that, say, dual Canadian German citizenship doesn't pose, as your true nationality is where you live, pay your taxes and vote. You are a German Canadian. Israel calls for the firm commitment of world Jewry in all countries to the cause of the Jewish state, something that Germany doesn't require of German emigres newly settled in other countries.

In Great Games I&II, Jews and Zionists played a strong supportive role to the empire—in Great Game I as loyal ally (and financier) to the various imperial teams; in Great Game II, both as US or Canadian citizens and later, as embodied in Israel, as a "strategic ally" of the US, as prophesied by Mackinder. Up to this point, Israel was really just a new pawn in the British-American imperialist Great Game. If Israel 'played by the rules' it would simply be another postmodern nation, part of the US fold.

But in anticipation of what we call here Great Game III, an independent, even leading role by Jews on the world stage, with specific strategies and goals, was already being charted formally for the first time at the First Zionist Congress in 1897, with Lionel Walter Rothschild the chief funder and inspiration for the creation of a Jewish state in Palestine. The British mandate for Palestine (1918–47) was the embryo of a new state, much like Canada from 1763 to 1932, whether or not Britain or the US liked it.[35]

The Israel factor has been implicit in all of the Great Games. The *professed* goal of Zionism during Great Game I was to create a modest Jewish state in the Middle East based on a negotiated accommodation with the Palestinian Arabs. The *underlying* goal from the start was to create a Greater Israel incorporating all the so-called Biblical lands, including Sinai, by displacing the natives, as indicated in Zionist discourse from Theodor Herzl and Zeev Jabotinsky[36] on—the Jewish version of Manifest Destiny.[37]

This was mostly fine from mainstream Canada's point of view. Most Canadians are Christian, and have been (at least until recently)[38] easily convinced that it's OK that the 'holy lands' are in Jewish hands. 'They suffered so in WWII, let the Arabs move somewhere else,' is a refrain heard all too often from secular or religious Canadians, echoing Herzl and Jabotinsky.

Jews have never had it better at any other time in history or in any other country—at the top of Canada's elite in the economy, media and in political influence. Even in the 1920–30s, when anti-Jewish sentiment was growing in Europe and the potential flood of penurious east European Jews, demanding special consideration, was frightening a still-WASP population, they did everything possible to come to Canada. This, despite a tighter entry requirement in 1910 allowing refusal to immigrants "belonging to any race deemed unsuited to the climate or requirements of Canada, or of immigrants of any specified class, occupation or character". But from 1945 on, Canada has, indeed, as prime minister Stephen Harper boasted been "Israel's best friend". By that, he also means, of course, "Jews' best friend".

Endnotes

1   Cited at Yves Engler, *Canada and Israel: Building Apartheid*, Vancouver: Fernwood Publishing, 2010, 12.

2   See Chapter 5.

3   Cited at William Engdahl, *A Century of War: Anglo-American Oil Politics and the New World Order*, revised ed., London: Pluto, [1992] 2004, 47.)

4   Heartland (Germany, Eurasia) contrasts geopolitically with Rimlands (Britain, US, Japan).

5   Halford Mackinder, *Democratic Ideals and Reality: a study in the politics of reconstruction*, New York: W.W. Norton, [1919] 1969., 89.

6   What came to be known as "Christian Zionism" emerged in England in the early 1800s. In 1839 the evangelical Anthony Ashley-Cooper called on parliament to support creation of a Jewish state in Palestine, prompting Lord Palmerston to appoint the first British Consul to Jerusalem, supporting the idea of a "Jewish entity" allied to the Ottoman Empire as a counterweight to Egypt "to blend the biblical interest in Jews and their ancient homeland with the cold realities of [British imperial] foreign policy". Yves Engler, *Canada and Israel: Building Apartheid*, Vancouver: Fernwood Publishing, 2010, 12.

7   Ed Janzen, in Walsh, Bill, Cy Gonick, *A Very Red Life*, 2008, 355.
8   "There are people [the Arabs] who control spacious territories teeming with manifest and hidden resources. They dominate the intersections of world routes. Their lands were the cradles of human civilizations and religions. These people have one faith, one language, one history and the same aspirations. No natural barriers can isolate these people from one another ... if, per chance, this nation were to be unified into one state, it would then take the fate of the world into its hands and would separate Europe from the rest of the world. Taking these considerations seriously, a foreign body should be planted in the heart of this nation to prevent the convergence of its wings in such a way that it could exhaust its powers in never-ending wars. It could also serve as a springboard for the West to gain its coveted objects." From the Campbell-Bannerman Report, 1907. <http://palestine2014.weebly.com/bannerman-report.html>
9   "The solution must come from the universities, using the model that already exists in Israel. There must be greenhouses for students, high tech and entrepreneurship. There are now 13,000 startup companies in Israel that were founded by students. Some of these students are already millionaires. They go to school, become entrepreneurs, receive money from investors and return the loans once they succeed. This model should be copied by the Arab world. Israel is a high-tech nation, but high tech has no flags. It is universal. The Middle East should be blanketed with high tech. I have been busy recruiting eight gigantic corporations for this project. High tech now has $24 trillion in reserve, $6 trillion of it in the United States. The investment funds are enormous. ... We need to recruit the Israeli Arab community for this, as well as high-tech leaders around the world. ... We don't need governments. They're just a big headache with very little money. We need to recruit international corporations. I'm in talks with Cisco, Facebook, Google, everyone.
    We have to present an enormous Marshall Plan for information, not money. We have to transform the universities into centers of entrepreneurship and technology. The leaders in the Middle East are making huge mistakes. Sisi is wasting billions of dollars on the Suez Canal. That is a mistake. I would not be surprised if I woke up tomorrow morning and read that Egypt or Saudi Arabia has collapsed. We have to propose this plan as quickly as possible. Anyone who wants can join." Ben Caspit, "Peres' secret Marshall Plan for the Middle East", *Middle East Monitor*, October 3, 2016.
10 Regina Sherif, *Non-Jewish Zionism: its roots in Western history*, Zed, 1983, 24.
11 Ruth Klein and Frank Diomant, *From Immigration to Integration: the Canadian Jewish experience*, 2001, 124.
12 Irving Abella, *A Coat of Many Colours: Two Centuries of Jewish Life in Canada*, 1990,149.
13 See Chapter 7.
14 <https://en.wikipedia.org/wiki/First_Aliyah>, <https://en.wikipedia.org/wiki/Zionism>
15 Edward Said, *The End of the Peace Process: Oslo and after*, 2001, 216.
16 Jonathan Plautm, *Jews of Windsor*, Dundurn Press, 2008, 75.
17 Joseph was military governor of Jerusalem in the 1948 war and cabinet minister is several govts. Yves Engler, *Canada and Israel: Building Apartheid*, 2010, 19.
18 Tulchinsky, *Taking Roots: The Origins of the Canadian Jewish Community*, Lester, 1992.
19 5,000 Palestinians, 300 Jews and 262 British troops died.

20	See Introduction endnote 24.
21	Great Game I being classical imperialism, Great Game II the united imperialists against communism.
22	"Bonaparte has published a proclamation in which he invites all the Jews of Asia and Africa to gather under his flag in order to re-establish the ancient Jerusalem. He has already given arms to a great number, and their battalions threaten Aleppo." Ben Weider (1997). *Napoléon et les Juifs* (in French) (PDF). Also, "Bonaparte, Commandant en chef des Armées de la République Française en Afrique et en Asie, aux héritiers légitimes de la Palestine" <wodka.overblog.com/article-2977379.html>
23	Benjamin Ginsberg, *The Fatal Embrace: Jews and the State*, 1993, ix. Benjamin Ginsberg is a libertarian political scientist and professor at John Hopkins University since 1992, best known for his critique of corporate control of American politics.
24	Ibid., 9–10.
25	J.A. Hobson, *Imperialism: A Study*, 3d ed., London: Allen and Unwin, [1902] 1938, 56-7.
26	One key plot device is the delicate treatment of the crucial role that Jewish banking money played in the elite's fortunes. Lady Grantham (Cora Crawley) is revealed in passing as an American Jewess, whose money saved the Abbey from bankruptcy, but whose origins are (sort of) a family secret. The outcast, though still privileged, role of Jews in British society is implicitly highlighted by the will of the fourth Earl, the father of the Downton Abbey's Lord Grantham, Robert Crawley. He had put an "entail" on the estate, stipulating that unless Cora produced a male heir (which she didn't), the estate would pass over to the closest male relative in the family, a third cousin. He wanted no truck with the 'Jewish conspiracy' of automatically inheriting Jewishness through the mother, undermining the 'Britishness' of the aristocratic lineage. The actual historical basis for the TV series has a similar Cora Crawley heroine, the daughter of Alfred de Rothschild's mistress, Amina (making her technically not a Jew at all), but still inheritor of a Rothschild fortune.
27	Michael Keefer, *Antisemitism Real and Imagined*, 2010, 154.
28	See Introduction endnote 29 for Talmudic acknowledgment of responsibility for the execution of Jesus. A simple apology and a kind of compromise is what Christian Jews (Messianic Jews), a Jewish sect which originated at the time of the Apostle Paul, offers. They accepted Jesus as the messiah but maintain their primary identity as Jews. There are 350,000 worldwide (10,000-20,000 in Israel), though they are not formally recognized there, performing aliyah according to their maternal Jewish ancestry and considered merely Jews, along with the secular and atheist Jews (half of all Israeli Jews). There is also Jews for Jesus, founded in 1973 in San Francisco. Their membership is not clear; they are not a 'church' but a missionary group. Presumably converts just join a Christian church. They are not a small operation. Their income in 2010 was $20,728,530. Their missionary activity involves handing out literature on the street, one-on-one Bible studies, full-page ads in leading newspapers and magazines, ISSUES (an eight-page evangelistic publication for "Jewish seekers") and internet evangelism.
29	E.g., Quran 5:82.
30	Lesbians are not such a threat, generally unacknowledged in legal codes, the Bible or popular culture.

31	See for instance, Jason Koutsoukis, "Homophobia in Israel still high but declining slowly, says survey", *http://www.smh.com.au/world/*, August 7, 2009.
32	A series of spontaneous, violent demonstrations by members of the gay (LGBT) community against a police raid that took place in the early morning hours of June 28, 1969, at the Stonewall Inn, located in the Greenwich Village neighborhood of Manhattan, New York City. They are widely considered to constitute the single most important event leading to the gay liberation movement and the modern fight for LGBT rights in the United States. <https://en.wikipedia.org/wiki/Stonewall_riots>
33	30% of American Jews answered "very attached" when asked the level of their "emotional attachment to Israel." 40% said "somewhat attached" and 22% said "not very attached," with only 9% citing no attachment.

Pew came up with nine different traits commonly associated with Jewish identity and asked Jewish respondents to answer whether each is "essential to being Jewish." Among those nine traits, "caring about Israel" was the fifth most likely to be selected. 43% called "caring about Israel" essential. "Only 15% of Jews said that Israel was a key voting issue." Eric M. Uslaner, "Two Front War: Jews, Identity, Liberalism, and Voting", Israeli Democracy Institute, 2007.

Traits more likely to be considered "essential to being Jewish" than caring about Israel: 1/ being intellectually curious, 2/ working for justice/equality, 3/ leading an ethical and moral life, 4/ remembering the Holocaust.

Among religious Jews, only half called caring about Israel an essential Jewish trait. It still ranks fifth for this group.

Among secular Jews, only 23% called caring about Israel an essential Jewish trait. It ranks sixth, behind "having a good sense of humor."

Only Orthodox Jews and Evangelical Christians strongly believe God gave Palestine to the Jews (84%, 82%). Overall, 40% of American Jews believe the land that is now Israel was given to the Jewish people by God vs 55% of American Christians. Max Fisher, "8 fascinating trends in how American Jews think about Israel", *Washington Post*, October 3, 2013. |
34	<https://www.touristisrael.com/gay-tel-aviv-for-beginners/5686/>
35	See Chapter 5.
36	Theodor Herzl (1860–1904) is the founder of political Zionism. Zeev Jabontinsky (1880–1940) is the most renowned Zionist revolutionary and inspiration of the Jewish Defense League.
37	The idea of population transfer accompanied the Zionist movement from its very beginnings, first appearing in Theodore Herzl's diary. There was little dispute among Zionists about the desirability or morality of forced transfer. In the late 1930s, Ben-Gurion wrote: "What is inconceivable in normal times is possible in revolutionary times; and if at this time the opportunity is missed and what is possible in such great hours is not carried out—a whole world is lost." The 'revolutionary times' would come with the first Arab-Israeli war in 1948, when the Zionists were able to expel 750,000 Palestinians (more than 80% of the indigenous population), and thus achieve an overwhelmingly Jewish state, though not including all the land the Zionist leaders wanted. According to Ilan Pappe, the mindset of Israelis has always been "Palestine is by sacred and irrefutable right the political, cultural and religious possession of the Jewish people represented by the Zionist movement and later the state of Israel." Any concession made to Palestinians is at best temporary or "an act of ultimate and unprecedented international generosity". "Any Palestinian, or for that matter

international, dissatisfaction with every deal offered by Israel since 1948, has therefore been seen as insulting ingratitude in the face of an accommodating and enlightened policy," explaining the "righteous fury" that Israelis show. See Ilan Pappe, "What drives Israel?", *HeraldScotland.com*, 6 June 2010.

38 A similar poll would reflect much the same statistics among Christians. More church-going Christians support the biblical legends than most Jews. Another poll in 2014 found only 17% of Canadians support Israeli policies, and among those with strong opinions, the split between supporters of Israel and Palestinians was 50:50. Support for Israel actually fell under Harper, reflecting public disapproval of Harper's Evangelical position. "Canadians split on support for Israel and Palestinians, poll finds", *JTA*, June 17, 2014.

| Chapter Three |

THE SEEDS OF A NEW EMPIRE

Hard Power

US hard and soft support were essential to the creation and survival of Israel. Britain was both a reluctant ally and increasingly the 'enemy' of the Zionists, as their program gathered steam and Britain tried without much commitment to carry out its obligations as the colonial administrator of Palestine after WWI. **Jewish terrorists** in the British Mandate for Palestine targeted British occupiers and even assassinated top British officials. Zionist terrorist groups killed at least a thousand Arabs and British soldiers and officers in the 1930–40s, including:

- July 25, 1938. The Irgun threw a bomb into the melon market in Haifa resulting in 49 deaths.
- November 6, 1944. Lehi (the Stern Gang) assassinated British minister Lord Moyne in Cairo, Egypt. The action was condemned by the Yishuv at the time, but the bodies of the assassins were brought home from Egypt in 1975 to a state funeral and burial on Mount Herzl.
- July 26, 1946. The bombing of British administrative headquarters at the King David Hotel killed 91 people (28 British, 41 Arab, 17 Jewish, and 5 others). Some 45 people were injured. In the literature about the practice and history of terrorism, it has been called one of the most lethal terrorist attacks of the 20th century. Irgun was described as a terrorist

organization by the United Nations, British, and United States governments, and in media such as *The New York Times*, and by the Anglo-American Committee of Inquiry.

This upset the genteel Canadians. Canadian Prime Minister Mackenzie King was not happy about the recreation of another aggressive US-type nation in an already volatile region, and delayed recognizing Israel. But his protégé Lester Pearson, Canada's first UN ambassador, was a committed Zionist. Even the assassination of UN mediator Count Bernadotte in 1948 did not deter him, and as soon as Mackenzie King retired in 1948, Pearson was able to convince the new PM, Louis St. Laurent, to recognize Israel and set Canada's new pro-Israel policy. Pearson went on to help Israel get out of its dilemma in 1956, after its undeclared war against Egypt, which had shut down the Suez Canal.[1]

The ingathering of Jews to Palestine in the 1920–30s was very much the focus of Canadian Jews, who raised funds to build kibbutzim and send the early makers of aliyah, including a handful of Canadians. By the time Israel was recognized in 1948 and the war with the Arabs began, hundreds of Canadian ex-soldiers (Jewish, but some non-Jewish)[2] were there, fighting the war of liberation. Most came 'home' to Canada, another handful stayed to build the new self-proclaimed Jewish republic.

Israeli invasions have included wars with Egypt/ Syria (1948, 1956, 1967), later Lebanon (1980s, 2006) and then invasions of Gaza (2009, 2014, 2016). Israel didn't have the scope of the US in Great Games III for innovative color-revolution/regime-change hard power, only the use of pro-Israel local proxies (the Druze and Maronite Christians in Lebanon), who could be installed or just used as allies. Israel was/is still in its infancy, though growing up fast. Cultivating Arab proxies is still not feasible, but the number of Muslim countries that recognize Israel is growing.[3]

Israel was able to use **black-ops** to encourage immigration, first from Muslim countries. In the 1940–50s, Israeli secret services orchestrated bombings in Egypt, Iraq and Morocco, purportedly by Arabs against local Jews. Given the suspicions that fell on all Jews in the countries after the brutal war to establish Israel, where Jewish invaders killed tens of thousands of innocent locals, the traditional friendly relations in north African Muslim countries with the local Jews collapsed, and a few well-placed bombs in public places did the trick. Most fled to the open arms of Israel, eager to populate the now empty homes and villages of Palestinian refugees.

The 1950–51 Baghdad bombings, widely attributed to Israel, targeted Jews to encourage them to leave Iraq. The most infamous terrorist act to be exposed was the so-called Lavon affair in Egypt in 1954, when local *sayanim*,[4] were used by Israeli agents to plant bombs in the US and British information centers in Alexandria with other bombings planned, both intended to force Egyptian Jews to flee 'antisemitism' and to create a schism between Egypt and the US.

The creation of local Arab proxies was envisioned by the Oded Yinon Plan,[5] a geopolitical doctrine of the 1980s calling for the partition of large powerful Arab states, like Iraq, into weak, feuding governments in the tradition of divide-and-rule. This came to fruition after the US invasion of Iraq and proxy insurgencies in Syria.

Blackops continue in new variants. The wild fires in Israel of November 2016 immediately led to accusations of Palestinian arsonists. The trees had been planted to obliterate the remains of Palestinian villages using fast-growing European furs unsuitable to the hot, dry climate, in an attempt to create a 'little Switzerland'. They went up like match sticks, without much by way of arson necessary. Even if one or two fires had been started, it was the policy of the Zionists—obliterating villages with unsuitable trees—that is the source of the problem.[6] Netanyahu's **collective blame strategy**[7] punished many Israeli Arabs who had no conceivable connection to the wildfires and only aggravated tensions between Jews and Arabs. Education Minister Naftali Bennett dismissed as "an isolated incident" the arsons committed regularly by settlers against Palestinians and their crops.

Homes of Jews who burned Palestinian homes are left inviolate, while the families of suspected Palestinian 'terrorists' see their homes demolished by the Israeli authorities. Fires are set by Jews (West Bank settlers) in Palestinian fields, their olive trees chopped down, and lands stolen with impunity.[8]

The racism and violence of the Zionists today prompts many to compare their tactics to those of Hitler.[9] The same fascist psychology—ends justify means, terrorize your victims into submission or, better, herd them into concentration/refugee camps, hoping they will just leave, or kill them—is at work. It's just more calculating, less extreme, camouflaging itself as an 'eye for an eye'.

Arms production for export is an important indirect game strategy, purportedly to defend freedom, but implicitly to tie the acquiring countries to Israel economically and politically. Azerbaijan, a Muslim nation, is a major importer of Israeli military equipment in its confrontation with Armenia, and now has a direct oil pipeline to the Mediterranean and warm relations with Israel. Israel tried to sell US military planes to China but faced the rare US fist under Bush Jr, and backed off. Canada has an agreement with Israel on military hardware.

Israel has an extensive arms industry and is tied with France as fourth largest global arms exporter (after the US, Russia and Germany), its export sales accounting for 80% of defense industrial capacity, about $7.3 billion in 2010. Despite Israeli claims of Arab or Iranian desires to drive them into the sea, there is almost no defensive need for Israel's armed might, including its substantial, still unacknowledged **nuclear arsenal**, except to threaten its neighbors, the US and Europe.[10] As argued here, the Palestinians would welcome a reasonable compromise that gives them full civil rights, whether in a two- or one-state format. Israeli leaders who suggest a willingness to seek a legitimate compromise are pilloried or assassinated. When Ben-Gurion called for Israel to give up the gains of 1967 for a settlement in 1973 before he died, he was dismissed as a senile has-been. Yitzhak Rabin was assassinated in 1994 for a much less radical compromise. Its outsized military capacity is necessary to allow Israel to keep expanding, dispossessing with impunity.

Soft Power

The extent of Israel's subversive role in the context of Canadian society is debatable, the subject of the remaining chapters here. But there is no doubt that Israel employs both hard and soft power wherever necessary in pursuit of its agenda. There are Israeli spies/agents (*sayanim*),[11] just as there are spies from the US, Russia and a few other countries, but the *sayanim* are much more effective insofar as they are part of the tribe, inspired by ideology.

Israel hoped to achieve what Canada, Australia, New Zealand and the US had: the global acceptance of its existence as a state without tedious international law-based questions as to the justness of its domination of native peoples and seizure of their lands. But the pesky Arab natives were not so yielding, naive, or lacking in external support as were the indigenous peoples in Canada and elsewhere. Arabs are identical ethnically to north African Jews, even speaking the same language and having similar cultures, so Israel's plan was not so easy to carry out.

Rather than face the vicissitudes of British fair play or US inexperience, the Zionists took matters into their own hands in the 1930s. The Jewish Agency for Palestine **made deals with the Nazis** to transfer Jewish assets from Germany, and pay for (young, able-bodied) German and other Jews to be allowed to emigrate to Palestine before (and even after) the Nazi meat grinder was in complete control. Yf'aat Weiss explains in an essay for the Holocaust Memorial Center at Yad Vashem that the Haavara (transfer) Agreement between Germany and German Zionists allowed "German Jews emigrating to Palestine to retain some of the value of their property in Germany by purchasing German goods for the Yishuv [the Jewish settlement in Mandatory Palestine], which would redeem them in Palestine local currency". The Haavara agreement did not have in mind the foundation of a Jewish state in Palestine. By late 1937 an anti-Nazi German official involved in administering the agreement suggested that fear in Nazi circles that it might lead to a Jewish state, to which Hitler was implacably opposed, was leading to suggestions "it should be terminated."[12] Adolph Eichmann visited Haifa in 1938 to meet with Zionist officials connected with Aliyah Beth (the organization for illegal immigration to Palestine) to conduct secret negotiations before the British deported him. He then moved on to Cairo to meet a Haganah representative.

There was even an attempt to negotiation a mass transfer of Jews to Palestine with the Nazis. In a letter in 1941 to high Nazi officials, Avraham Stern, known as Yair, a leading early Zionist fighter and member in the 1930s of Irgun, and later, Lehi, proposed to collaborate with "Herr Hitler" on "solving the Jewish question" by achieving a "Jewish free Europe". The solution can be achieved, Stern continued, only through the "settlement of these masses in the home of the Jewish people, Palestine". To that end, he suggested a collaboration with the Germans' "war efforts", and establishing a Jewish state on a "national and totalitarian basis", which will be "bound by treaty with the German Reich."[13]

The Transfer of Goods Agreement between the Zionists and the Nazis enabled German Jews to transfer some of their frozen assets to Palestine at a highly punitive exchange rate, flooding Palestine with German goods at the same time that world Jewry was boycotting German goods. Zionists justified this as a "dialectical necessity".[14] Foreign Jewish organizations transferred money to let local German Jews buy exit permits, providing Germany with a flourishing income stream right up until 1945.[15]

In 1944 Himmler offered to exchange a million Jews for ten thousand trucks and negotiated in Budapest for the emigration of

Jews in exchange for cash. This consorting with the Nazis ended very badly, as "daily contacts between the Jewish organizations and the Nazi bureaucracy made it easier for the Jewish functionaries (*judenrate*) to cross the abyss between helping Jews to escape and helping the Nazis to deport them."[16]

This willingness to consort with the enemy occurred again during Irangate.[17] It finds its equivalent today in Israel's secret cooperation with Saudi Arabia, supposedly Israel's most implacable enemy, about 'security matters'. Saudi Arabia does nothing to stop Israeli atrocities against Palestinians, and targets Iran, Israel's sworn enemy and the only state unequivocally supporting the Palestinians. Clearly 'security matters' means quelling genuine Palestinian resistance (Hamas) and anti-Iranian scheming. This willingness surfaced once again in the 2015 invitation to Israel extended to Heinz-Christian Strache, leader of Austria's far-right Freedom Party, founded by ex-Nazis. Strache was embraced by top members of Benjamin Netanyahu's coalition based on their mutual antipathy to Arabs. Similarly, Israel pays court to France's *Front National* and the English Defence League.

The mutual embrace of Jewish **financial elites** and western states from the Middle Ages on is an important form of **parapolitics**, the pursuit of politics by covert means. Jewish prominence in finance (both legal and criminal)[18] in all the Games has meant that throughout, while only a tiny percentage of a host nation's population is Jewish, an outsize percentage belongs to the super-rich. In Britain on the eve of WWI Jews constituted 1% of the population and 23% of its millionaires, and in Great Games III in the US, 2% of the population and 50% of its billionaires.[19] In Canada, Jews are 1.6% of the population and 25% of the billionaires.[20]

However, the charge that the Rothschilds and a few other elite Jewish families exercise complete control over the world overly simplifies geopolitics and the increasingly vast and complex world of global finance, attributing superhuman powers to humans, a fetishism that Marx would be the first to criticize. Karl Marx (1818–1883), grandson of the rabbi of Trier,[21] famously criticized nineteenth century Jews in the context of the triumph of capitalism as follows:

> What is the secular basis of Judaism? Practical need, self-interest. What is the worldly religion of the Jew? Huckstering. What is his worldly God? Money. The Jew has emancipated himself in the

Jewish fashion not only by acquiring money power but through money's having become (with him or without him) the world power and the Jewish spirit's having become the practical spirit of the Christian peoples.[22]

With the decline of Christianity, for proponents of what is now western Judeo-Christian civilization, "we are all Jews". Or, as Vice President Joe Biden put it, "You don't have to be Jewish to be a Zionist." Despite the fact that it violates current international law which represents the positive evolution of four centuries, the secular Zionist project is now largely embraced by western ruling elites, and it came about largely because of the financial power of the Rothschilds, the principal promoters of a Jewish state in Palestine from the nineteenth century onward.

The parasitical nature of finance capital, claiming magically to produce value through the manipulation of money, was recognized and condemned by all the montheisms, though the Hebrew Bible allows interest[23] to be charged to strangers but not "to thy brother".[24] This exception became the foundation in the Middle Ages for Jewish lending to non-Jews, and with the rise of banking, Jewish dominance in the role of state financier. Christianity also outlawed it; hence, Jews became the usurers of the Middle Ages. With the rise of capitalism, it was accepted by Christianity too,[25] and is the sense behind the statement of founder and spiritual leader of the Shas Party (a key member of the current Likud coalition government) and former Sephardi Chief Rabbi of Israel, Ovadia Yosef, in a Sabbath sermon: "Goyim were born only to serve us. Without that, they have no place in the world; only to serve the People of Israel."[26] Islam is the only monotheism that still forbids usury and interest.

The most famous Jewish financier in history was Mayer Rothschild (1744–1812), who famously quipped, "Give me control of a nation's money and I care not who makes the laws." He founded the dynasty that still acts as *eminence grise* in the shadowy world of banking today. His most famous son, Nathan Rothschild, and Nathan's son, Lionel Walter, were committed Zionists, the latter responsible for the Balfour Declaration, which was a letter addressed to him by the British foreign minister, Alfred Balfour.[27] The letter and financial blackmail, convincing Britain that the 'Jewish lobby' could bring the US into the war on Britain's side, was a masterful use of parapolitics (a term coined by Peter Dale Scott as one aspect of "deep politics", emphasizing the clandestine nature of primarily soft power). Deploying the *perception* of unrivaled power based on financial prominence.[8] was a decisive replay of the age-old win-win for Jews in European wars of the past,[29] now used in the promotion of their own state.

The Germans ended up paying the Zionists all and more of the capital they had stolen from Jews from 1933 to 1945 after the war. The 1952 Reparations Agreement between Israel and West Germany initially paid Israel 3 billion marks over the next fourteen years and the World Jewish Congress—450 million marks. The payments played a vital role in Israel's survival—87.5% of the state income in 1956. Later, Swiss banks and German banks, such companies as Deutsche Bank, Siemens, BMW, Volkswagen and Opel, and the ex-socialist Hungarian government were also required to pay additional reparations to the state of Israel on behalf of Jews who suffered under Nazism. Arendt criticized Ben-Gurion's cynicism in staging the Eichmann trial at least partly to "force more reparations money out of the German government."[30] In 2009, Israeli Finance Minister Yuval Steinitz demanded a further 1 billion euros from Germany as well as a discount on the purchase of two German-built warships.

A significant new development in this cultural war for 'hearts and minds' is the phenomenal growth of the ultra-Orthodox **Chabad-Lubavitch** community. The most famous leader of Chabad was Rabbi Menachem Mendel Schneerson (1902–94), the "Lubavitcher Rebbe" who is worshiped as the messiah by his most devoted followers. The movement began an outreach program in the US in the 1950s in reaction to the assimilation of American Jews, founding a collective of Jewish religious cultural centers across the US. Today it has blossomed into a movement with 4,000 full-time emissary families directing 3,300 institutions and a workforce that numbers in the tens of thousands dedicated to the welfare of the Jewish people worldwide.

They are particularly important in the former Soviet Union through the Federation of Jewish Communities, promoting emigration to Israel and possibly acting as a cover for Israeli intelligence gathering and subversive activity. The Lubavitchers actively lobby all levels of the US government and were able to get Congress and President Carter to declare 18 April 1978 Education and Sharing Day (ESD) in honor of Schneerson, for his efforts for "education and sharing" for Jews and non-Jews alike. Since then each year in April, the US president proclaims ESD on a day close to Schneerson's birthday (11 Nisan).

**President George W. Bush signs a
proclamation declaring ESD April 16, 2008**

In the 1991 bill declaring ESD, the Noahide laws—a version of Judaism for non-Jews—were described as the "ethical values and principles" that are "the basis of civilized society and upon which our great Nation was founded".[31] In a further move, in 2006 Bush II announced that May would henceforth be celebrated as Jewish American Heritage Month (JAHM), In 2009 Obama inaugurated April 5, 2009 as a yearly Education and Sharing Day and said: "Few have better understood or more successfully promoted these ideas than Rabbi Menachem Mendel Schneerson, the Lubavitcher Rebbe, who emphasized the importance of education and good character. ... On this day, we raise his call anew." In 2010 Obama held the first JAHM White House reception "to highlight and celebrate the range and depth of Jewish American heritage and contributions to American culture."

Hundreds of Chabad Houses now span the world. There are 50 Chabad Houses in Canada. They managed to have their movement praised in Hansard by the Liberals, Conservatives and NDP in a kind of 'all party' tribute in 2003,[32] though they have yet to enshrine the Noahide Laws in a parliamentary endorsement as has the US.

The Chabad movement is an Orthodox sect, but now recognizes Israel—unlike some Satmar and Neturei Karta—as a Jewish state in the tradition of the ancient Israelite kingdoms. *Sayanim* can use Chabad Houses as safe houses, where there would be no record of a person's stay. Senior Israeli government and military officials visit and stay there alongside Israeli backpackers. The Chabad House in Mumbai was at the center of a still unsolved terrorist event in 2009 where up to 200 people were killed, including Chabad emissary Rabbi Gavriel and five other Chabad visitors.

Though Muslims played no role whatsoever in the persecution of Jews in Europe under the Nazis, what Norman Finkelstein calls the "Holocaust industry" is a central part of the **campaign to vilify Islam**. David Horowitz has organized "Islamofascism Awareness Week" (IFAW) on close to 100 college campuses since 2007, identifying Islam with Nazism. At the same time, Michigan State University Young Americans for Freedom invited a *bona fide* fascist—Nick Griffin, the head of the British National Party—to speak on how Europe is becoming "Eurabia". IFAW is now an annual event, with seminars on jihad and Islamic totalitarianism. Canadian Jews are more discrete in their lobbying in multicultural Canada, which is less tolerant of ethnic targeting, not promoting anti-Muslim sentiment so openly, and restricting lobbying to Parliament Hill, and editorial offices. None of these ventures represent any mass movement, but given the Zionist power in the media and politically, hate crimes against Muslims have increased alarmingly since 9/11, as has Jewish Defense League-type targeting of Muslims and those defending Palestine. Despite (or because of?) the Jewish presence there, the creative world of Hollywood has done very little to promote or resist this, given its (albeit selective) tradition of political correctness and sympathy for the persecuted.

Many 9/11 skeptics claim Israel orchestrated that tragedy, intent on creating a "new Pearl Harbor", as called for in 1996 by the Project for a New American Century (PNAC) to facilitate American intervention in the Middle East. It is impossible to prove such allegations, but then the official explanation for the sudden, precision collapse of the World Trade Center has many weak points, and there are hints that some players had foreknowledge.[33] Such tragedies are quickly made use of to promote the Zionist agenda, as might be expected. Expressing his delight immediately following 9/11, Benjamin Netanyahu exclaimed, "It's very good." Such statements, while tasteless, do not prove anything other than *schadenfreud* and the eagerness and ability to move forward with Israel's agenda.

Yiddishkeit as US-Canadian-Israeli Culture

Jewish dominance of **Hollywood** is well known. Prominent Hollywood Jews such as Ben Stein even boast "Do Jews run Hollywood?

You bet they do... & what of it?" Jewish humorists Bryan Fogel and Sam Wolfson confirm Jewish dominance in Hollywood, noting that of the ten major studios, nine were created by Jews (Walt Disney was a Gentile), and as of 2006 all ten studios were run by Jews.[34] "Yes, we do control the movie studios," they write. "All Jews please report to the World Conspiracy Headquarters immediately (don't forget to bring your pass code)."[35]

In a more serious vein, playwright David Mamet noted that Jewish control of Hollywood extends beyond studio ownership. "For those who have not been paying attention, this group [Ashkenazi Jews] constitutes, and has constituted since its earliest days, the bulk of America's movie directors and studio heads." As for American TV network control, Fogel and Wolfson claim the figure is 75%; for print media, they found that seven of ten major publications are run by Jews. "Conclusion: Jews have lots of opinions that they love to write about and charge you money to read! Cool."[36]

Unsurprisingly, among Jews prominent in the finance and economic elite in the US and Canada there are no publicly proclaimed anti-Zionists, resulting in an implicit bias towards Israel in US media. Reinforcing this bias, the (tax exempt) Israel Project was set up in 2002 as a propaganda arm of Israel with 18 members of Congress on its board of directors, buying commercial time to air pro-Israeli advertising on CNN, MSNBC, Fox News and other cable networks. It also provides "media fellowships" for US students, and conducts focus-group public opinion research. A member of one such group said she was "called in for what seemed an unusual assignment: to help test-market language that could be used to sell military action against Iran to the American public."[37]

Canada has a similar history. Canadians watch US TV[38] and Hollywood movies, and are, for all intents and purposes, very similar to Americans culturally—no matter how much they pride themselves on their difference. A popular (Canadian) joke goes: what is the difference between an American and a Canadian? Well, that Canadians are NOT Americans.

At a conference in 2009, Zionist media magnate Haim Saban described his pro-Israeli formula, outlining "three ways to be influential in American politics ... make donations to political parties, establish think tanks, and control media outlets."[39] The extensive activities by Zionists to promote Israel in the US media by the early 1960s was confirmed by the release in 2010 of declassified files from the 1962–63 Senate investigation revealing Israel's clandestine programs for "cultivation of editors," the "stimulation and placement of suitable articles in the major consumer magazines" as well as for controlling US reporting about sensitive subjects such as the Dimona nuclear weapons facility.[40] While the national Zionist organizations procured the journalists and academic writers and editors, it was the local affiliates who carried the message and implemented the line. Though there has been no Senate investigation of this influence in Canada, the same process has taken place in Canada. The Canadian variant of this is discussed in Part Two: Canada: Israel's "best friend". As Ginsberg explains, Jews have played the same paradoxical cultural role of vizier to the monarch as part of their home nation's elite, guiding public policy, and at the same time, as shapers of popular culture (storytellers), advocates of the oppressed and rebels. In the era of popular journalism, they also play the dual role of controllers of media and the content, which is paradoxically sometimes advocating for the oppressed, and sometimes for the vizier (who is advocating for Israel). As documented in Part 2, this remarkable situation, repeated throughout Jewish history in the diaspora, has been identical in Canada. Jews play the same roles, in Canada's case, making them direct shapers of both government policy and popular culture.

This focus by Jewish elites on media is nothing new. Reuters news agency was established by a German Jew, Paul Reuter, in 1851 and came to specialize in swashbuckling, sensational British imperial news, enthusiastically supporting empire, in line with the interests of Jewish financial capital at the time. Jewish interests controlled much of German media until the rise of Hitler. By the 1870s, while 1% of Germany's population, Jews controlled 13 out of 21 daily newspapers and had strong presence in four others.[41]

Management vs Popular Culture Creation

The 20th century were halcyon days for Jews in North America, where they quickly integrated into US and (less so) Canadian society, especially the budding mass media, both films, radio and newspapers. Ex-vice president Joe Biden boasted of this to a gathering of Jewish leaders in Washington, DC, stating that the "immense" and "outsized" Jewish role in the US mass media and cultural life has been the single most important factor in shaping American attitudes over the past century, and in driving major cultural-political changes. "Jewish heritage has shaped who we are—all of us—as much or more than any other factor in the last 223 years. And that's a fact."[42]

Biden said elsewhere, "You don't have to be Jewish to be a Zionist. I'm a Zionist, too."[43] By sheer presence and wealth, the Jewish/Zionist lobby overwhelms North American media culture, and enforces strict censorship on Israel and things Jewish. Reflecting on the purchase of *The New York Times* in 1904, historian Goldwin Smith lamented, "Is there such a thing as a paper or periodical which is not controlled by Jews or afraid to print the truth ... about them."[44]

The focus of Jewish elites on the media and manipulating it to serve their ends is a corollary of the 'fatal embrace' of Jews and the state, an outgrowth of Jewish culture, an instinctual attempt to protect group interests in the face of the host country's population whose interests are not the same, and at times can be hostile. This need to control public opinion became a science in the early twentieth century—public relations—founded by Edward Bernays,[45] nephew of Sigmund Freud, whose influence he promoted, and friend of presidents Roosevelt and Kennedy. This technique of social mind control was quickly seized by commerce, used to create advertising, the largest 'service' industry in world. Another two-edged sword, invented by a Jew and used soon against Jews to devastating effect by the Nazis.

Culture has always been a vital tool of the ruling elite managed to secure the economic and political system as a whole. With the creation of Israel in Great Game II, it took on a special meaning. Imperial state support was no longer required just for a small Jewish financial elite within the empire, but for an aggressive Jewish state fighting wars, and increasingly determining US policy in the strategic Middle East.

Soft power became more important under advanced capitalism. The east European Jews in America helped produce a new voice for capitalism which, combined with technology and advertising, swamped the other Jewish-inspired voice of Marxism and revolution against it. The new elite created a truly mass society, but a commercial one, not a socialist one, where family and traditions are replaced by mass media manipulation with a view to promoting product consumption. The Soviet Union managed to escape this transformation but eventually succumbed. Whether or not this was a conscious 'conspiracy', looking back on it, it clearly produced a *de facto* situation of Jewish domination of media and economic power, inevitably benefiting Israel.

There can be no culture without an economic base. It is only because of enduring Jewish prominence in the world of finance and hence the economy as a whole, and then via a commanding presence in the media world, that Jews have been able to achieve a considerable degree of hegemony in the world of culture. This cultural hegemony was relatively benign, at least in the US, until the creation of Israel.

The Hollywood film industry was at the heart of American culture in the twentieth century, largely the creation of 'liberal'[46] media-savvy Jews. Before the creation of Israel, the Hollywood cultural message was generally one of social justice within the system, fighting for the rights of the underdog and minorities, themes deriving from Yiddish folk traditions.

Early Hollywood: Mad Supermen

"God bless America" was written as the Zionists were coming into their own in 1938 by lyricist Israel Baline and Irving Berlin, one of America's greatest popular composers. His many tuneful scores and definitive stamp on American culture remind us daily of our debt to the Pale.[47] The definitive stamp that Jews put on American culture via Hollywood cemented post-WWII America as the Promised Land of the Free World at the very moment that the Zionist dream was coming to fruition, the path of history now careening on a linear, apocalyptic trajectory, all the time inspired by the Zionist myth.

The first half of the 20th century witnessed a golden age of liberalism and even socialist tendencies among writers and actors in Hollywood, when Jews were more or less assimilated into American life and were for the most part progressive in outlook. US Jews assimilated more than did Canadians, both before and after the creation of Israel. The anti-Jewish pressures were stronger in the US, as was/is the sense of American patriotism, and the draw of US culture. But the pattern was the same in Canadian entertainment (Wayne and Shuster, S.C.T.V.). The intimate links are exemplified by the fact that Canadian Frank Shuster was the cousin of American Joe Shuster, co-creator of Superman. (See below.) Jews are at heart of Hollywood and culture in general, shaping it, prospering as secular pseudo-goys, for the most part invisible as Jews.

Progressive Jewish, really east European Yiddish, culture, was greeted with open arms by the masses. It spoke to the poor and the oppressed. The Jewish creators, like most Americans in the early

20th century were new penniless immigrants, with poor English, more interested in integrating than reproducing the narrow ghetto tribalism that they so readily left behind. The common people enjoyed the antics of Yiddish artists regardless of their ethnicity. Only the mysterious Hungarian Harry Houdini (Ehrich Weisz) was openly Jewish. It was only in the 1930s that assimilated Jews like Melvyn Douglas (Hesselberg) became stars in their own right. Until his early teens, Douglas did not even know his father was Jewish, knowing him only as an immigrant from Latvia. His parents were determined that their children would integrate fully into American society. But then neither did Madeleine Albright, who learned only in 1997 that her father was Jewish.

The new Hollywood studios were dominated by Jewish financiers, impresarios who determined what films Americans would watch, with an eye on profits over preaching old-fashioned Sunday school morality. This frightened, even incensed, the pseudo-genteel Gentile cultural and political elite in the US, and not entirely without reason. The decadence of Hollywood in the 1920–30s was and still is shocking in retrospect. *Anything goes*[48] captured the dissolution, lack of respect for traditional mores, government, everything 'boring', the triumph of promiscuity as the norm, the escape into fantasy, the Hollywood dream world over the harsh reality of the Depression. Happy endings, yes, but what happened on the way pushed sensibilities to the limit. Finally, the Hays Code to censor films was introduced in 1934. The cinema had taken the place of religion in American minds and it had not been a good role model.

Talented Jewish artists were at the heart of this, eager to jettison their stuffy religious-ghetto Russian/ Polish traditions. The adaptability of the 'wandering Jew' meant willingness to become just ordinary Americans who liked matzo balls and might celebrate a second News Years in September. Many (in Hollywood, *all*) changed their names, even forgot about these few shibboleths of their grandparents. The rise of film and recording allowed them to move to the top in the entertainment world.

Originally the new Jewish-American culture was unashamedly left wing—even worse to the old Gentile elites than just being Jewish—as captured by the 1920s poster depicting Marx as the new Moses – "Marx the Wonder Worker". By the 1930s, this radical politics had softened into commercial (but still working class) culture with its new heroes.

Der Groysser Kundes (1915)

The new mass culture, best represented by comics, found Jews at its heart, with such Jewish superstars as Superman, Batman and Spiderman. Louis B. Mayer (1884–1957), born in a Ukrainian shtetl, emigrated to New Brunswick, Canada, and went on to become the (benign, fatherly) Jewish kingpin in Hollywood. New York intellectuals flocked to Hollywood starting in the 1920s, continuing through to today, an outsize contingent being Jews, the majority left wing, many communists, though Mayer was at best a liberal and struggled to tone down the political subtexts of films.

This hothouse reproduced in microcosm Ginsberg's scenario of the two Jews–the vizier-banker and rebel. Mayer himself played both roles, the nice capitalist, in this scenario. The more typical case was that of penniless teens Jerry Siegel and Joey Shuster, who created Superman in 1933 and sold the rights in 1936 for $130 to promoter Max Gaines. Penniless Bob Kane (ne Kahn) and Bill Finger created Batman in 1939, commissioned by Jack Liebowitz as a rival to Superman at his now iconic DC Comics.[49] The creators were poor New York Jews, the publishers were richer (just barely) New York Jews, recapitulating the remarkable hegemony of Jews in popular culture, both as creators and hard-nosed financier-producers.

Superman and Batman were originally socialists, fighting for social justice, even for racial equality in subtle flashes (the comic censor was keeping an eye on anything too political). With the creation of Israel and the onset of the Cold War, Hollywood and US culture lost much of its anti-capitalist, occasionally socialist message, though the rights of minorities continue to be an important Hollywood theme, the remnant of social justice, which became today's "identity politics", nurtured by the Zionists.

Superman always remained Jewish because he "will always be of Krypton, subject to laws foreign to his countrymen." No matter how apparently assimilated he is as Clark Kent, he is "haunted by a past he relives over and over" as he fights for Truth, Justice and the American Way.[50] He renounces his Jewishness as his primary signifier, replacing it with the humble apple-pie Clark Kent, but he doesn't forget his roots. The bitter-sweetness of 'good assimilation'.

Batman was created in 1939 by Bob Kane (Kahn) in collaboration with writer Bill Finger. It already has a film noir feeling, with Gotham City a kind of violent, ominous dark place of murder and corruption. Spiderman was created by Stan Lee (Liber) in 1962. Superman, Batman and Spiderman have the same basic plot; Spiderman's alias, Peter Parker, is uncertain of himself and his identity—perennial Jewish themes, but universal in the modern world of insecurity, shiftless migration and now gender identity alienation.[51] They precipitated a slew of other Captain Marvel superheroes, who lost as often as they won, tragic heroes who hark back to Samson. Spiderman was insecure, always the outsider. He became the 20th century Everyman, Colin Wilson''s *Outsider*. The Jewish archetype of the supersmart, obsessively logical, with the Gentile 20th century techno-brawn thrown in.

Al Capp (Caplin)'s Li'l Abner (1934) was another highly popular cartoon strip, though as an adult strip, it did not have the cultural impact on teens that the superheroes did. The importance of Jewishness in the cartoon world is shown by the National Cartoonists Society's Reuben Award for Cartoonist of the Year (to Al Capp in 1947), and the Elzie Segar Award for "unique and outstanding contribution to the profession of cartooning" (to Al Capp posthumously in 1979). Why this prominence? Unmerited? No, Jews from the 1920s on were at the top of the cartoon pile. And they were/are at the top on the production side, consummate wheeler-dealers (schmoozer is Yiddish), making millions, and endowing awards (not to mention university chairs and whole departments on the Middle East).

"What me worry?" brings us to the greatest of all Jewish cartoon figures, Harvey Kurtzman's Alfred E Neuman, and *Mad* magazine (1952–55), which went viral within months, electrifying social dissidents and eventually just about everyone, with its "Fan-Addict" clubs and membership cards. Kurtzman explained that 'fan' meant 'fanatic', coining the term and satirizing the obsession with 'belonging to the communist party', spying (who cares?). Nothing was sacred to Neuman: in 1952, he introduced Superduperman, assistant copy boy at the *Daily Dirt* and sexy Lois Pain, who ends up selling reefers to schoolchildren. Superduperman must battle Captain Marbles, prompting Lois to crack, "Big deal. You're still a creep." The Shadow keeps himself hypnotized so as not to remember he lives in a dump and is homely. There is Starchie and Mickey Rodent. Originally it was in b/w to avoid the comics code censorship. This was a kind of last gasp of Yiddish progressive art. Kurtzman eventually ended up in advertising.[52]

Jews were the perfect Others—writing, acting, directing and in all manners seeking to present and represent the lives and feelings of non-Jews and their shadow selves. Gays were also prominent though incognito in Hollywood both as writers and actors, and today, as much as 'straights', find solace in this golden age of Hollywood, recapitulating the parallel between the two minorities in society. As commerical entertainers, as artists or both, Jews had/have no choice but to 'play to the crowd'. By shunning the narrow tribalism and as leftwingers, they reject a Jewishness dominated by a wealthy and rightwing Jewish establishment.[53] They reject a prescribed slot. They just want to be American (or rather, North American, as the border between the US and Canada was porous, and creative Canadians often migrated to the US).

The zenith of Yiddishkeit (Yiddishness, cultural Jewishness) was 1935–55. How could Jews not be drawn to left wing ideology of the times? The "New Deal" was jokingly referred to as the "Jew Deal".[54] And then, just as quickly, they discarded socialism as the wrath of McCarthy descended on them. The world proletariat was replaced with world Jewry as the organizing force for what was left of 'revolution', with the goal, not of world socialism, but of a national Jewish state. Zionist communists like Ben-Gurion and Begin[55] replaced Stalin's version of communism as 'socialism in one country' with 'Jews in one country'.

The horrors of WWII and the creation of Israel electrified Jews, and the anti-Jewish subtext of HUAAC[56] forced a radical retrenchment. McCarthyism was effectively a **postmodern pogrom**, from which progressive Hollywood never fully recovered. The cultural elite increasingly discarded any open advocacy of working class ideals, and Hollywood came to rely on more and more explicit sex and violence to mesmerize audiences, as if to lull them into an ideological stupor, as the reality of US imperialism and Zionist expansion became more and more violent in the real world.

Jewish culture was radically altered. A new pact was made with the sovereign after this latest crisis between the state and its Jews. Hollywood producers fired and then rehabilitated the least 'guilty' of their blacklisted, chastened pariahs by the early 1960s. The creation of Israel and the anticommunist witch-hunting in the US following the collapse of the 1941–48 alliance with communist Russia abruptly changed the flavor of popular culture in the West. The aftershock of WWII Jewish suffering put paid to residual anti-Jewish bigotry. All criticism henceforth would be limited to 'the system'—greedy corporations or corruption, but within bounds. No more hints of revolution.

But the question nags: So who needs Israel, the troublemaker new kid on the block? Jewishness itself was transformed with Israel, arresting the Jewish assimilation of the pre-Israel period, recreating the rift between Jews and non-Jews which Yiddish American culture had overcome by cultural blending, reviving the mistrust of Jews as an unfriendly alien Other, and raising again the specter of dual loyalty.

The Yiddishkeit that inspired Hollywood is the benign Jewish shadow presence that Zionists love to hate. It led (and continued to lead) to Jewish assimilation, weakened the tribal nature of Jewish life, made it secondary. Yiddish was outlawed in Israel as a language of public discourse. Even the rich theatrical heritage of Yiddish theatre and literature was forbidden–except if performed in Hebrew. This happened in the 1950s, even as McCarthy was destroying progressive Yiddish Hollywood.

But Yiddish culture was stronger than its foes. It is the bread and butter of American Jewish life, and even as the Hebrew language replaced (obliterated) Yiddish as the official Jewish *lingua franca* in Israel, its legacy is alive and well across the Atlantic. The Zionists know this, and secretly revel in the success of Woody Allen and *Seinfeld, Saturday Night Live, Jon Stewart, Colbert, S.C.T.V.*—any one of the dozens of sitcoms that blossomed from the 1950s on TV, and studiously avoid any mention of Israel or Zionism, which is not a selling point for anyone. America (that includes Canada) would be a dull place without Yiddishkeit. Its broader cultural meaning, including the language, literature and music, is even being revived today in North America and Israel. The 'happy ending' without Israel would have been assimilation, Jewishness as just a quaint ethnic heritage from east Europe, now embedded in world culture via Hollywood.

Israel benefits from the solid Yiddishkeit roots of North American (really world) culture. Without the support nurtured through this soft power, supplemented by lots of grim reminders of the *shoah*, Israel would be seen immediately for what it was and is. Who wants to root for a ruthless Goliath? The Zionist project needed/needs this universalized Yiddish culture, despite its underlying logic of Jewish assimilation in North America, as it has broad popular support, and even if not enthusiastically Zionist, helps buttress the US special relationship with this thorny ally.

The Hollywood Jewish apotheosis was Otto Preminger's *Exodus* (1960) with a syrupy Oscar-winning theme song, a love poem to the new Israel, airbrushed of massacres and ethnic cleansing of

Arabs, complete with Paul Newman marrying an American *shiksa*, symbolizing the secular Israeli Jew wooing America. Surveys showed the film powerfully affected American Jews, reasserting their (secular) Jewishness, but it is a sleeper, rarely seen today,[57] unlike the safe, swashbuckler *Ten Commandments* (1956), which people love precisely because they know it is only legend.

Schindler's List (1993) is the most notable of the **Holocaust films**. *Life Is Beautiful* (1997), an Italian comedy-drama, the only upbeat one.[58] Both won multiple Academy Awards. They are the best of the new Hollywood genre— "Holocaust" movies, which started in the 1970s and became a major focus of Hollywood, becoming part of what Norman Finkelstein, as a son of Holocaust survivors, dubbed the "Holocaust industry", promoting an indirect justification of Israel to assure unconditional US support. Israel has few real fans anywhere except for a minority of Jews (and of course evangelical Christians), so the Holocaust is the best way for Zionist financiers to promote Israel. There have been over 40 US and Canadian feature films about the Holocaust produced in the past two decades, none about the war of 1948 and from 1967 to the present from the Palestinian perspective, supposedly justified by "the Holocaust".

"The Holocaust may yet turn out to be the greatest robbery in the history of mankind," says Norman Finkelstein. "The Holocaust industry has clearly gone berserk." It has replaced Christianity as a quasi-religious moral foundation in the West, seeking to keep Jews together, reduce assimilation, and keep goys subservient, according to Israel Shamir. "Christ suffered for us and came back to life. The Holocaust believers believe that the Jewish people suffered and came back by creating the Jewish state."[59] That is the not-so-subtle message of the Holocaust films.

But Israel lacks the powerful draw that both British imperial culture and US mass culture have as elements of soft power. There are three fronts on this 'battle for hearts and minds' for the Zionists: Jews in Israel, Jews outside of Israel, and general public opinion. The Brits had it easy on the cultural front, relying on the prestige of its old culture and the pomp of empire, benign or otherwise. The Americans have their incredible wealth, the 'American Dream', technology, IT and mass culture.

Just as Zionists piggy-backed on British imperial power until 1948, they continue to piggy-back on US imperial hard power, using soft power as much as possible. The Jewish soft power at the top levels of western society translates into unwavering support of Israel in politics. English is the *lingua franca* of Israel. More than a thousand Americans and Canadians serve in the IDF on short stints every year.

The trouble is Yiddishkeit, which the Zionists don't control. While media is owned by Zionists, the creators of Hollywood culture are not for the most part Zionist, and even if they are, they are still critical of Israel, as Spielberg demonstrated in *Munich*.[60] Sympathy for the Palestinians, as the disenfranchised, oppressed underdog, is a natural for popular culture, like the beleaguered Jews in the 1930s, not the ruthless jack-booted Israeli occupier of today.

The progressive element behind Yiddish culture trumps the vainglory of Zionism. No one loves to be hated, and anti-Jewish prejudice is inevitable now that people finally see on TV the Jewish Goliath killing stone-throwing Palestinian Davids. Spielberg is spurned by official Israel, with no honorary doctorates, etc., but he isn't fazed. Spurning—or being spurned by—Israel is increasingly a badge of honor for artists and intellectuals.

The Zionists are far from hegemonic in Hollywood, despite the surge of Holocaust movies since the 1980s, when they launched their legal battles with anti-Zionists and WWII bad guys.[61] "Holocaust fatigue" has set in in Hollywood.[62]

The Israel/Jewish/Zionist/whatever Lobby are the heavy guns, but they blast indiscriminately, and are feared more than respected. They are neither funny nor sexy. They touch only the surface: Mao's 'paper tiger', but still dangerous to foes. The Zionists are right to be suspicious of Yiddishkeit, as Yiddish culture never liked Israel. Its universalism is the nontribal version of Judaism, evolved in 19th–20th centuries in Europe and then the US, and undermines the tribal essence of Zionism. US/Canada are the Yiddishers' 'promised land'. Irving Berlin, Leonard Bernstein, Aaron Copland, Saul Bellow, Philip Roth, Woody Allen, Tony Kushner, Mordechai Richler, Leonard Cohen ... The list is long and still growing.

Yiddishkeit Resurrected

By the 1980s, the Yiddish cultural transformation came to living rooms through television **sitcoms**. It no longer mattered who was of Jewish heritage. We all are schmucks, schmoozers, shnors, shysters ... So the slew of sitcoms written, produced and often starring Jewish

Americans were fun but generally shallow, reflecting the shallowness of life in the Promised Land. Nobody's fault, really.

There's *Phil Silvers, Car 54, Barney Miller, Dick van Dyke, Mary Tyler Moore, Rhoda, Lou Grant, Tracy Ullman, Maude, Carol Burnett, All in the Family*, leading the way for the first black sitcom *Sanford and Son* and the only anti-imperialist sitcom *M.A.S.H.* (It made so much money, it was tolerated.) Not to mention *The Simpsons* and *Seinfeld.* Truly breathtaking. Canada's contribution via *Saturday Night Live* was *S.C.T.V.*, and its Jewish/non-Jewish cast John Candy, Joe Flaherty, Eugene Levy, Andrea Martin, Rick Moranis, Catherine O'Hara, Harold Ramis, Martin Short, Dave Thomas, all of whom went on to have Hollywood careers. We have all—Americans, Canadians—been nurtured on Yiddish culture. The promised land came about in our own backyard despite Israel.

But the decline of US culture set in at the same time, not due to anything Jewish, but due to the imperial, commercial mindset of the US. The social accommodation, which started with Roosevelt's New Deal, transformed the working class in the 1950s into a quietist 'middle class', focused solely on material pursuits, leaving politics (Cold War, Vietnam, the Middle East) to the big boys, where Jews were prominent as advisers to the monarch and media moguls, but not calling the shots—except in relation to Israel. Not the fault of Jewish influence, but rather of imperialism itself.

Cracks in the cement reveal fresh shoots of the old Yiddish Hollywood humanism.

- Palestine itself has produced Oscar-nominated films, including *Paradise Now* (2005), *Omar* (2013), and *Ave Maria (*2015).
- Palestinians and Israelis work together on films exploring their problems such as *Oriented* (2015).
- The US film *West Bank Story* (2005) by Ari Sandel won the 2006 Oscar for Best Live Action Short Film. It is straight-up Yiddishkeit, a parody of *West Side Story* (Bernstein and Sondheim), with Kosher King and Hummus Hut competitors in Israel mimicking American multicultural life.
- In *You Don't Mess with the Zohan (*2008), Superman (Adam Sandler) is an Israeli counter-terrorist army commando who fakes his own death in order to pursue his dream of becoming a hairstylist in New York City. Zohan tells Palestinian American

Dalia, "I come to States to stop the fighting. Here in America, we all same." Ferando Croce calls it "a beautiful vision, a clown's utopia where prejudice gets a pie in the puss."[64]

- Harvey Pekar (1939–2010), the legendary Yiddish cartoonist, in his final autobiographical graphic novel, finally took on Israel in *Not the Israel My Parents Promised Me* (2012). He is the classic Jewish American 'storyteller', working class, socialist, thumbing his nose at the Jewish 'viziers' advising on US politics and the economy. He got Zionism in both flavors —religious from his father and secular from his mother. At his funeral, he asked that the Kaddish prayer replace Cleveland for Israel as his home.
- Eli Valley, political cartoonist in the mold of Yiddish cartoons of the past, especially MAD, takes aim at the Jewish world's sacred cows, including American organizational leaders like Abe Foxman, tycoon Sheldon Adelson and Israeli Prime Minister Benjamin Netanyahu. His goal with *Diaspora Boy: Comics on Crisis in American and Israel* (2017) is to energize a "besieged Jewish left: We've been told we're self-haters and Jewishly ignorant, and my book says, enough of that shit. This is a moment of transformation in America and Israel. We're in a cataclysm. There's an enormous shift going on."[65]

There has been a remarkable resurgence of Yiddishkeit's Superman, Spiderman and Batman. They were the Canadian top box office hits of the 2000s, with multiple remakes of all three as trilogies, with spin-offs *Man of Steel* (2013), even confrontations between the various icons battling it out *(Batman vs Superman (*2016*)*, still with a hint of social justice for the underdog and environmentalism. It couldn't be otherwise, as Yiddishkeit was always subversive and good hearted. Ideology in the West has been reduced to consumerism and anomie, and Yiddishkeit is stepping in to fill the gap. Hollywood is less and less clearly Jewish, but very Yiddish. A 1998 survey of Jewish directors in Hollywood found most unwilling to designate any Jewish influence or Jewish element to their work. They think of themselves as artists who happen to be Jews. Marx said it first, with something else in mind, and Obama more recently,[66] but nothing has changed since Marx's observation in 1844 about "the Jewish spirit's having become the practical spirit of the Christian peoples."

Endnotes

1   The first fully fledged UN peacekeeping effort was covering the withdrawal of British, French and Israeli forces from Egypt in 1956, following their invasion in the wake of the nationalization of the Suez Canal. UN troops were stationed in Sinai afterwards as part of a deal to get Israel to withdraw, and when Egypt finally ordered them to leave in 1967 to reassert its sovereignty, Israel invaded and re-occupied Sinai and all of Palestine, murdering the UN troops, including Canadians stationed there, a sad denouement to. Pearson's Nobel Peace Prize for his efforts followed Bunche's equally questionable peace prize in 1950.

2   <https://en.wikipedia.org/wiki/Israeli_Air_Force>

3   Ten Muslim majority countries recognize Israel. Turkey (1949), Egypt (1979), Albania (1991), Azerbaijan (1992), Kazakhstan (1992), Kyrgyzistan (1992), Uzbekistan (1992), Tajikistan (1992), Turkmenistan (1992), Jordan (1994).

4   Egyptian Jews.

5   See <https://www.scribd.com/doc/155650153/A-Strategy-for-Israel-in-the-Nineteen-Eighties-Oded-Yinon>

6   According to Jewish National Fund statistics, 6 out of every 10 saplings planted do not survive. Those few trees that did survive formed nothing but a firetrap.

7   On the basis of flimsy evidentce (a broken bottle smelling of gasoline found near a fire), Netanyahu ordered suspected Palestinian homes or just any nearby homes to be burned and their inhabitants collectively punished, evicting them in the cold of winter, taking a page from Nazi strategy to cow civilians in occupied territories.

8   Akiva Eldar, "Will Netanyahu's collective blame sink Israel?" *Al-Monitor*, December 1, 2016.

9   Roger Tucker, "Zionism and Nazism: Is there a difference that makes a difference?", One Democratic State. <https://sites.google.com/site/onedemocraticstatesite/Home/today-s-headlines/zionism-and-nazism-is-there-a-difference-that-makes-a-difference-by-roger-tucker>

10   "We possess several hundred atomic warheads and rockets and can launch them at targets in all directions, perhaps even at Rome. Most European capitals are targets for our air force.... Our armed forces, however, are not the thirtieth strongest in the world, but rather the second or third. We have the capability to take the world down with us. And I can assure you that that will happen before Israel goes under." Martin Levi van Creveld, professor of military history at the Hebrew University in Jerusalem, *Guardian*, November 23, 2012.

11   *Sayanim* (sing. *Sayan*) refer to "diaspora Jews who provide assistance to the Mossad". This entry at the English language Wikipedia was deleted in 2010 but is still available at other Wikipedias, including the Dutch site <http://nl.wikipedia.org/wiki/Sayanim>.

12   <https://www.theguardian.com/politics/2016/apr/30/livingstone-muddies-history-to-support-hitler-and-zionism-claims>

13   Omri Boehm, "Liberal Zionism in the Age of Trump", *The New York Times*, December 20, 2016. Another plan, by Nazi leaders opposed to Hitler (Goerdeler) in the case of German victory, was to transport Jews from Europe after the war to Palestine, Madagascar or some "independent state in a colonial country" like Canada or South America. Hannah Arendt, *Eichmann in Jerusalem*, 47, 103.

14   Arendt, ibid., Introduction by Amos Elon, x.

15   Ibid., 25.

16 Ibid., 11.
17 The apparent conspiracy between the Republicans and the Iranian government during the 1980 presidential elections led to the subsequent Iran-Contra scandal. Senior administration officials secretly facilitated the sale of arms to Iran, which was the subject of an arms embargo. They hoped, thereby, to fund the Contras in Nicaragua while at the same time negotiating the release of several U.S. hostages. It was planned that Israel would ship weapons to Iran, and then the United States would resupply Israel and receive the Israeli payment. See <https://en.wikipedia.org/wiki/Iran%E2%80%93Contra_affair>
18 Marc Rich, living in exile and pardoned by Clinton in 2001, the most notorious in recent times. <http://www.rense.com/general63/oky.htm>
19 Ginsberg, op.cit., 22; Israel Shamir, *Pardes: An etude in Cabbala*.
20 The 2011 *Forbes'* list of billionaires listed 24 Canadian billionaires.
21 Marx's father converted to Lutheranism shortly before Karl's birth.
22 I.e., the practical money-oriented life of 19th century secular (Christian) society. Karl Marx, "On the Jewish Question", 1844. available at <http://www.marxists.org/archive/marx/works/1844/jewish-question/index.htm>.
23 Interest and usury have the same meaning. The term usury derives from medieval Latin *usuria* (interest) referring to the monetary charge imposed on loans. Usury is now understood as only excessive interest charges, but the underlying argument that money in itself is sterile is true whatever the rate of interest proposed.
24 Deuteronomy 23:19.
25 As late as the reign of Pope Leo XIII (1878—1903) usury and speculation were condemned by the Catholic Church as harmful forms of lending and investment.
26 Jonah Mandel, "Yosef: Gentiles exist only to serve Jews", *Jerusalem Post*, November 18, 2010.
27 The Rothschild stamp is everywhere in Israel. Between 1890 and 1924 Edmond Rothschild funded many settlements in Palestine through the Jewish National Fund. Later his son, James, established Yad Hanadiv, the family charity fund which sponsored the construction of the Knesset building and the Israeli Supreme Court. Jacob Rothschild is now head of Yad Hanadiv, an Honorary Fellow of Jerusalem and president of Institute for Jewish Policy Research. Daniel Rothschild is head of the Interdisciplinary Center Herzliya in Israel, which sponsors the Herzliya Conference, where Israeli foreign policy is formulated.
28 This strategy is admitted by the ADL's Abe Foxman who boasts how he bullies foreign governments to acquiesce to his demands, claiming influence in top US government circles, at the same time as he denies accusation of excessive Jewish power. See Yoav Shamir, "Defamation", 2009. <http://www.defamation-thefilm.com/html/about_yoav_shamir.html>
29 Such as the 30 Years War in the seventeenth century, where all states in "central Europe and Scandinavia make use of resources and talents of Jews to compete with their rivals." Ginsberg, op.cit., 17.
30 Arendt, op.cit, 13.
31 Bill Text 102nd Congress (1991—1992) <http://thomas.loc.gov/cgi-bin/query/z?c102:H.J.RES.104.ENR>.
32 Hansard, vol. 138, number 117, 2nd session, 37th Parliament, House of Commons, June 11, 2003. "Jewish sleeper law remains dormant in Canadian

House of Commons", Fitzpatrick Informer, September 8, 2012. <http://fitzinfo.wordpress.com/2012/09/08/jewish-sleeper-law-remains-dormant-in-canadian-house-of-commons/>

33 See David Griffin (*The Mysterious Collapse of World Trade Center* 7, 111-121; *9-11 Contradictions* 226-236). Israeli instant messaging company Odigo admitted that two of its employees received instant messages warning of an impending attack 2 hours prior to the first plane hitting. This warning was NOT passed on to the authorities. Odigo had a feature on its service that allowed the passing on of messages through a search feature based on nationality. Knowing these two particular Israelis were forewarned, it is possible that they passed the message on to other Israelis. Out of the 4,000 Israelis believed to have worked in and around the WTC and the Pentagon only five died. <https://wikispooks.com/wiki/9-11/Israel_did_it#Israeli_Citizens_Get_Tipped_Off> But a more mainstream, cautious view among 9/11 skeptics does not point to Israel as a culprit, speculating rather that authors and supporters of PNAC with positions of power in the US government were behind it. These 'neocons,' as is well-known, were bent on taking out regimes in the Middle East perceived to be hostile to Israel.

34 Jewish directors include Turner Broadcasting System chairman and CEO Philip Kent, TimeWarner CEO Jeffrey Bewkes, FOX NewsCorp CEO Peter Chernin, Chairman of the Board of the National Amusements theatre chain Sumner Redstone, Paramount CEO Brad Grey, Walt Disney/ABC? CEO Robert Iger, CBS CEO Leslie Moonves and NBC Universal CEO Jeff Zucker.

35 Bryan Fogel and Sam Wolfson, *Jewtopia: The Chosen Book for the Chosen People*. James Petras, Jeff Blankfort and Israel Shamir document Zionist media control in their writings.

36 Fogel, op.cit.

37 Focus Grouping War with Iran *Mother Jones*, 19 November 2007.

38 As with most media in Canada, the television industry and television programming are "strongly influenced by media in the United States, perhaps to an extent not seen in any other major industrialized nation outside the US." There are quotas for Canadian content, and new content is often aimed at a broader North American audience. <https://en.wikipedia.org/wiki/Television_in_Canada> In 2015, Canada's top ten "most-Watched entertainment TV events", including the Academy Awards, were American. The most-watched regularly scheduled TV programs were mostly American (including #1 a spin-off "The Amazing Race Canada" of the American original). <http://www.bellmedia.ca/pr/press/tv-top-10-canadians-watched-2015/>

39 Connie Bruck, The Influencer, *New Yorker*, 10 May 2010.

40 <http://www.irmep.org/11-121960AZC.pdf>.

41 Ginsberg, op.cit., 25.

42 Jennifer Epstein, "Biden: 'Jewish heritage is American heritage'," *Politico*, May 21, 2013.

43 <http://www.israelnationalnews.com/News/Flash.aspx/182160>

44 Davies, ed. 77.

45 Bernays' most successful work was titled *Propaganda*, a term which did not then carry the pejorative connotations of manipulation for ulterior purposes that it does today, hence its later replacement by the anodyne term, "public relations" [also known in official circles as "perception management"].

46 Hollywood has lost much of its old-fashioned liberalism since the 1950s.

"For the most part, this is not a very liberal Hollywood. With few exceptions, Hollywood is in tune with the heartland, where they sell a lot of popcorn and are very pro-America, anti-controversy and pro-war. It makes for big movies that make a lot of money. And movies that make a lot of money are good movies." Tony Sokol, "The Myth of the Hollywood Liberal", http://www.denofgeek.com/, March 21, 2013.

47 A western region of Imperial Russia with varying borders that existed from 1791 to 1917, in which permanent residency by Jews was allowed and beyond which Jewish permanent residency was generally prohibited. <https://en.wikipedia.org/wiki/Pale_of_Settlement>

48 1934 musical and the hit song by Cole Porter made famous by Ethel Merman, not Jewish, but unashamedly advocating promiscuity and decadence, and an honorary Jew among the Hollywood crowd.

49 Paul Buhle, *From the Lower East Side to Hollywood: Jews in American Popular Culture*, 105.

50 Scott Raab, "Is Superman Jewish?" in *Superman at Fifty: The persistence of a legend*, Colliers, 1988.167.

51 Buhle, op cit., 115.

52 Ibid., 193.

53 Ibid., 52-5.

54 Ginsberg, op.cit., 115.

55 Ben-Gurion published a eulogy to Lenin following his death in 1923, where he compared himself to Lenin. (Reprinted in *Midstream*, October 1996, in an article by Eli Tzur.) Menachem Begin was an NKVD agent, recruited as part of the Polish army which the Soviet secret police set up in Russia as a rival to the free Polish army operating from London. He served with the Soviet-created Polish army in Transjordan and then Palestine in 1942–43. See, for instance, www.mail-archive.com, 11 April 2006. <http://www.mail-archive.com/osint@yahoogroups.com/msg20338.html>.

56 House Un-American Activities Committee, created in 1938. From 1969 until it was abolished in 1975, renamed "House Committee on Internal Security".

57 Also in 1960, the more assimilationist Stanley Kubrick directed *Spartacus*, with the rebel, universal Jewish subtext still intact. Kubrick, like most of Hollywood, never dealt with Israel in his work.

58 Only 5% of Italian Jews died as a result of the pact with Hitler. Mussolini refused to comply with Hitler's demands as did Italians after the Germans occupied Italy in 1943. Denmark and Bulgaria also defied the Nazis. This side of WWII has yet to be explored in Hollywood.

59 Norman Finkelstein, *The Holocaust Industry: Reflections on the Exploitation of Jewish Suffering*, 2000.

60 *The Jewish Week*, preferring cardboard heroes, complained of his "equating the Israeli assassins with 'terrorists'". Eli Valley, "Steven Spielberg's unforgivable 'sin'" Jerusalem Post, March 1, 2006, and Stewar Ain, "'Munich' Refuels Debate Over Moral Equivalency", *The Jewish Week*, December 16, 2005.

61 See Chapter 7.

62 For example, a comedy skit on Ricky Gervais' *Extras* in 2005 featured Kate Winslet who plays a nun protecting Jews in a basement in a WWII movie. Gervais, the 'extra', asks Winslet, "Why are you making the film? To expose the Holocaust?"
Winslet: "No. We don't need another film about the Holocaust. We get it. It was

grim. Move on. I'm doing it because if you do a film about the Holocaust, you'll be guaranteed an Oscar. I've been nominated 4 times and never won. The whole world is going 'Why hasn't Kate won'? Schlinder's bloody List, The Pianist. Oscars coming out of their arse."

A happy ending: Winslet got her Oscar at last in 2008 in *The Reader*, a 'Holocaust film'.

Jon Stewart's "Israel" video in 2014 went viral with 1.2 million views before it was blocked. On the *Daily Show*, he merely mentioned the word Israel and ten correspondents popped up to scream at him. "Look, obviously there are many strong opinions on this," Stewart said when the shouting subsided. "But just merely mentioning Israel or questioning in any way the effectiveness or humanity of Israel's policies is not the same thing as being pro-Hamas." That of course led to a new round of shouts and insults, prompting Stewart to turn to a "lighter" topic: Ukraine.

In *Denial* (2016) about the David Irving trial, some of Deborah Lipstadt's legal team complain, after hundreds of hours of researching Irving's diaries, about the Jews being "obsessed with the Holocaust", asking when will they make peace and move on. Irving was a leading WWII historian until the 1980s, when he fell victim to the dubious Heuchter Report, leading to his famous trial and conviction in 1998, still the greatest court victory for "the Holocaust". (See Chapter 7.)

63 An Israeli soldier falls in love with a Palestinian, the Israelis build a wall and the soldier smashes it to be with his true love. Both stands burn down in a fight, but customers arrive and David and Fatima scrape together some of the remaining food, merging the two falafel stands. At the very end, Fatima asks what will happen if their families cannot stop fighting. David says he will "take you to a place called... Beverly Hills", alluding to the song "Somewhere" in *West Side Story*.

64 <http://www.cinepassion.org/Archives/FallZohanStrangers.html>
65 < http://www.haaretz.com/jewish/features/1.806807>
66 <https://www.washingtonpost.com/news/post-politics/wp/2016/01/28/obama-we-are-all-jews-in-face-of-rising-anti-semitism/>

| Chapter Four |

THE ENEMY OF MY FRIEND IS MY ENEMY

US-Canada-Israel vs Soviet Union

The enthusiasm of many American Jews for communism was a dilemma as the Cold War got under way. Remarkably, the later purging of left wing Jews, most famously the electrocution of the Rosenbergs, was orchestrated purely as an anticommunist move, with no public mention of Jews and Judaism *per se*, despite the anti-Jewish hatred dripping from the House Un-American Activities Committee. The days of blatant prejudice—'No Jews or dogs allowed'—were over. The powers that be were sure to make Jews the judge and prosecution in the Rosenberg trial to forestall any charge of antisemitism, turning the trial into an intra-tribal affair. Letting the Jews purge their ranks. The suffering of Jews in Nazi Germany gave Jews a clean bill of health in the US, despite their subversive (socialist) role culturally, which the witch hunts could not completely undo.

The few communists in Hollywood were decimated in a spectacular **postmodern pogrom**. No mention of the J word, but the point was made. A few Jewish scapegoats were sacrificed publicly along with their Gentile comrades, making sure the anti*communist* message was heard, but leaving the predominance of Jews in the media untouched. The subtle threat of blackmail over any past political activity hanging over everyone's head was a kind of a shadow boxing by the state with the Jewish community, one of Ginsberg's moments of crisis in the relationship between Jews and the state, which culminated in the harnessing of Jewish critical culture to the service of US imperialism.

Most far left Jews, such as Irving Kristol, Daniel Bell (ne Bolotsky) and Norman Podhoretz, once Trotskyists, quickly refashioned themselves as hard right anticommunists.

At precisely the same time, and just as remarkably, Israel was severing its intimate ties with the Soviet Union. Initially the Zionists had played both sides against the other in the budding Cold War. Soviet support was essential both for official recognition by the UN and for military support, given the US embargo on arms, intended to stop the exploding civil war in Palestine. Without Soviet arms, intended by Stalin to ensure Israel would be *its* strategic ally, Israel could have been overwhelmed by the local Arabs it was intent on displacing. Most of the Jews who came to Palestine in the 1920-40s were socialists or communists and lived on communes (kibbutzim). Menachem Begin was an NKVD agent, recruited as part of the Polish army which the Soviet secret police set up in Russia as a rival to the Free Polish Armed Forces operating from London. He served with the Soviet-created Polish army in Transjordan and then Palestine in 1942-43.[1]

Despite Arab Muslim suspicions of the atheist Soviet Union and Stalin's initial support for Israel, the Palestinians and the frontline states, Egypt and Syria, were forced to seek support from the only world power willing to provide it—the Soviet Union—making them reluctant allies of the new US enemy. In 1955, Moscow began providing military assistance to Syria and Egypt. This followed from Israel's new unconditional allegiance to the US, and confirmed Israel's role as a born-again 'bulwark against communism' in the Middle East. Ironically, "without Israel, there was little chance that any of the Arab regimes would turn away from their dependence on the West."[2] Already, the Jewish state was playing clever games with the superpowers.

As the 1950s progressed, the US moved ever closer to Israel, but its support would often be covert so as not to further antagonize the Arabs and maintain its position as neutral arbiter. The shift toward Israel was not as rapid as it might have been, because Eisenhower was popular as a wartime hero and could politically afford to buck the new, energetic domestic Israel lobby. Eisenhower's threat of UN Security Council sanctions in 1956 brought about Israel's withdrawal from Sinai.

For Israel, victory in the 1967 war was a vital turning point in its relationship with the US and the world. Its own regional Great Game II was now won, long before the US Great Game II against the Soviet Union was. 1967 gave it all of Palestine, destroyed the Arab dream of defeating Israel in the field, and eventually knocked Israel's main foe—Egypt—out of the game. By decisively defeating the forces of Arab nationalism, Israel proved its value to the United States, if indeed the Arab nationalists' defeat was in the US imperial interest. After all, whatever threat the Arab nationalists posed to western interests had been initially caused by Israel in the first place.

Israel's 1967 victory "imparted fresh momentum to forces, ascendant since the late 1950s, that were pushing for a stronger US commitment to Israel as a strategic asset."[3] The specifically Zionist logic was entrenched at this point at the heart of US strategic thinking. 1967 was time to move into Great Game III Israeli style, which came to fruition only in the 1980s, in conjunction with US domestic political developments and the sudden rapid decline of the Soviet Union.

With the advent of Gorbachev in 1985 and his version of "socialism with a human face",[4] relations between the Soviet Union and Israel improved dramatically. Gorbachev tried to undo the legacy of Soviet-era anti-Zionism by opening the doors to the emigration of Soviet Jews in 1988 and preparing to renew full diplomatic relations with Israel. At the same time Gorbachev promised Arafat during a state visit that year that the Soviet Union would recognize an independent Palestinian state if proclaimed, naively hoping that Israel would show gratitude for his generosity by negotiating a genuine peace with the Palestinians.

Arafat declared independence in November 1988 and got Soviet recognition the next year, while Israel was busy setting up consular offices in Moscow. Hundreds of thousands of Russian Jews got instant Israeli citizenship and emigrated, many of them settling illegally in the Occupied Territories, nominally part of what would be a Soviet-recognized Palestinian state. By the end of 1991 when full diplomatic relations with Israel were restored, over 325,000 Soviet Jews had emigrated.

Gorbachev's hopes to bring a quick peace to the Middle East were dashed as he was ousted from power, leaving the PLO abandoned and Israel stronger than ever. Just as the Zionists had hoodwinked Stalin into recognizing Israel, they once again hoodwinked another Soviet leader into re-recognizing it. Instead of increasing Soviet/Russian influence by this dual recognition, all influence was lost. The Palestinians were hurt by the Soviet betrayal, while the Israelis welcomed a million new Jewish immigrants. Gorbachev got the 1990 Nobel Peace Prize for all his efforts.

Israel had had a 24-year head start over the US in the region, so by 1991, when the US formally entered the new game, Israel, flush with a million new Jewish citizens, was in no mood to put the brakes on its colonial agenda of total, permanent occupation of Palestine. This conflicted with the US Great Game III, and forced Bush I to refuse to finance the illegal settlements in 1991–92. This turned the Israeli Lobby against him during the presidential elections, and ensuring his defeat in favor of the more zealously pro-Israel Bill Clinton. Canada was merely a cheering spectator to all this, only becoming head cheerleader in 2006 with the rise to power in Canada of Stephen Harper.

The traditional roles of Jews as both financiers of the imperial state and as mobilizers of political opinion are present in all three Great Games, with the "political mobilization" now focused more and more exclusively around ensuring support for America's new 'half' empire— Greater Israel—from Great Game II onward. The creation of Israel made it "virtually impossible for a secular Jew anywhere not to be Zionist",[5] trumping traditional leftist leanings, sapping the energies that once fueled Jewish support for liberal and communist causes.

The 1967 war reinforced this dynamic and led some radical leftist Jews and others with strong sympathy for Israel to shift sharply to the right, founding the neoconservative movement. The neocons encouraged the rapid colonization of the Occupied Territories, and an end to the UN plan, agreed to by both the US and Israel in 1948, of partition and "two states for two peoples", making it now a "'five states for two peoples' plan: one contiguous state, surrounded by settlement blocs, for Israel, and four isolated enclaves for the Palestinians."[6] (See map next page.)

Iran, Egypt

Despite having nationalized much of British industry, the British Labour government demanded Great Game I-style 'gunboat diplomacy' in **Iran,** when Prime Minister Mossadegh had nationalized the oil company owned by British interests in 1951. Prime Minister Attlee's minister of defense Lord Emanuel Shinwell[7] warned that if tough action was not taken, "Egypt and other Middle Eastern countries would be encouraged to think they could try things on; the next thing might be an attempt to nationalize the Suez Canal."[8] The result was, when Churchill came to power in October that year, he was able to urge the US to 'send in the marines' and overthrow the democratically elected Iranian prime minister.

The Enemy of My Friend is My Enemy | 109

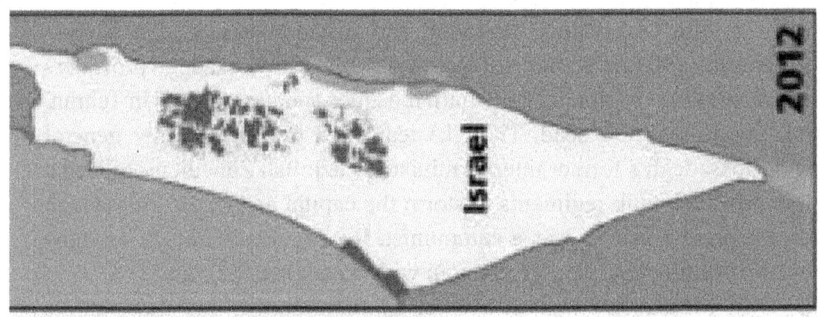

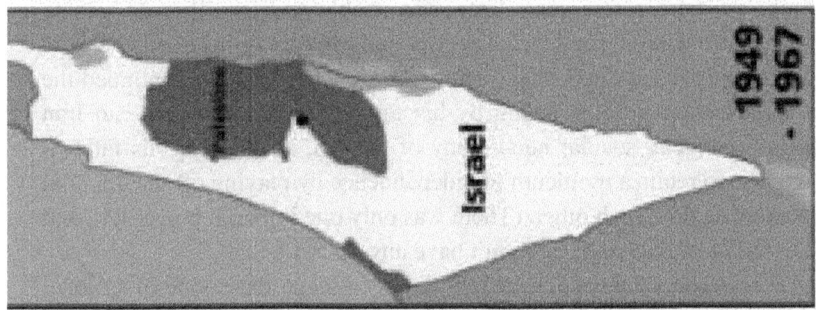

PALESTINE 1948 TO 2012

The CIA vetoed the plan, and instead, organized a coup—supposedly soft power, but still messy, paying anti-Mossadegh protesters and street thugs to riot, loot and burn mosques and newspapers in Tehran, leaving almost 300 dead. The CIA team, led by retired army general and Mossadegh's former interior minister, Fazlollah Zahedi, mobilized a few pro-Shah tank regiments to storm the capital and arrest Mossadegh on the pretext that he was a communist. It was a classic black-op, now openly admitted by the CIA, though with no apology to Iran.

Mossadegh was an avowed *anti*communist, and thus, unlike Cuba's Castro a few years later, was unable and unwilling to turn to the Soviet Union for help. The US and Britain re-installed the now thoroughly discredited Shah junior in Iran, who dutifully continued the secularization process begun by his father. He proceeded to run Iran as an obedient, secular neo-colony of the US, abandoning his father's attempt to retain a modicum of independence by playing off the imperial powers against each other. (There was only one imperial power left, and he was no socialist, so he didn't have any option.)

The weakness of Britain did not escape the notice of Colonel Abdel-Nasser, who forced most westerners out of Egypt in 1954 and nationalized the Suez Canal in 1956, in a rare win for a periphery player in Great Game II. Encouraged by their 'success' in Iran, British Prime Minister Anthony Eden believed that a British-French-Israeli attack on **Egypt** would not only remove Nasser, getting back the canal, but would also strengthen the British position vis-à-vis the United States.

As early as 1954, Eden had complained that the Americans "want to replace us in Egypt," indeed, "they want to run the world." The British and French conspired behind the US back and concocted a ruse—Israel sending in military forces presumably on its own with Britain and France coming in to mediate. But it fooled nobody. The Eisenhower administration forced a humiliating unilateral withdrawal on all parties, including—for the first and last time—Israel. Britain once again had to bow to US dictate, watching its empire continue to slip away.

Canada had sold US fighter planes (at US behest) to Israel just prior to the attack, thus playing a crucial role in the drama as the fall guy, allowing Eisenhower to play the hero, boosting the US image in the Arab world. Pearson then stepped in as the supposedly neutral mediator and reaped a Nobel Peace Prize for his efforts in 1957. Egypt was supposedly the victor, but not for long. The 1967 war gave Israel Palestine and Sinai, and as a result Egypt was soon battered into joining the US imperial project as a willing postmodern state alongside Canada.

When Egypt was knocked out of the race after 1967, Iran, Turkey and Pakistan were left as the only important Muslim countries in the imperial fold. The imperial project itself was rocky after 1967, with a cocky Israel flexing its own imperial, very 'modern' muscles.[9] Turkey was in NATO but it was not as pliable as Iran under the Shah. The 1953 coup in Iran remained the centerpiece for the new imperialism. It was only natural that the US embassy in Tehran became a "nest of spies", as it has been dubbed since then, 'mission control center' for all US (and, by definition, Israeli) espionage activity in the Muslim world. Iran was the most reliable US ally in the Muslim world, along with Turkey, the only other Muslim country (neither Arab) that recognized Israel. But the 1953 wound continued to fester.

The US completed the Egyptian transition to postmodern state in 1979 with the peace treaty with Israel. But 1979 also witnessed the overthrow of the Shah of Iran. Even as the US launched a war against the Soviet enemy through the Afghan Islamic jihad next door, **Iran had its own Islamic revolution**. Carter refused the Shah asylum, and actually facilitated the return of Ayatollah Khomeini to Iran in 1979, in keeping with the strategy that when a rupture is imminent, it is best to try to control the outcome. Soft power. No one was more 'soft' than Carter, trying to create a grateful (and, hopefully, loyal) new proxy in the Great Game II war against communism which was, after all, Islamic. It didn't work. Instead, angry Iranian students occupied the US embassy and held the staff (which of course included CIA agents) hostage for over a year. (See Chapter 6.)

The Soviet Union collapsed, and Bush Sr's "New World Order" speech in 1991 would be parodied by Bush Jr in Iraq as Saddam Hussein's regime was destroyed in 2003. But from 1979 on, Iran would continue to gain strength and respect as the new centerpiece, this time for anti-imperialism. For three decades, it had looked like a win-win for the US and Israel. But 1979 proved a day of reckoning for both. Islamic Iran now had both the US and Israel in its sites, both for the 1953 coup and for the treatment of Palestinians. Iran would go on to become both the US and Israel's *bête noire,* and the new Great Game III role of Israel as an imperialist in its own right would make Iran a *bête noire* of Israel's 'best friend' Canada, too.

Palestinian Resistance

The Palestinians were not quite as helpless as the North American natives, being citizens of the once powerful Ottoman caliphate, and familiar with western imperialism in its medieval form, since the 11th–13th century Crusades. They were not overwhelmed by European diseases, like the North American natives, which had conveniently freed much land for the American settlers, obviating blatant genocide.

Like the American colonists, the European Jews who began to colonize the land did so primarily by buying lands, the Americans did it through trickery, as the natives did not understand what private property meant. The Jews bought land from absentee landlords, rich Arabs living in Egypt, Lebanon and elsewhere, who were indifferent to the plight of the peasants farming them. When Palestine became a British colony ("mandate") in 1919, this process accelerated, though official British colonial policy was to restrict Jewish immigration in the interests of maintaining peace. No treaties with the natives. It was dog-eat-dog capitalism.

The policy of the British occupation of Palestine, vs Israeli occupation, is similar to that of British North America vs the US. Britain was still trying to appear sporting, genteel, though it was now bankrupt, and could not control the angry Arabs and the determined, increasingly desperate Jews. After the 1948 war, Israel re-enacted the US practice in its unashamed, ruthless dispossession of the natives—Roman style murder and plunder of Palestine, recalling the destruction of Jerusalem in 70 AD, this time by the Jews. While Britain had taken 300 years to colonize Canada, and solemnly made treaties (many, but not all, 'honored in the breach'), Britain had only 30 years as occupier of Palestine, and was immediately overwhelmed and cast out by its colonial settlers, fanatical Zionists, from the start bent on expelling and/or killing all the native Palestinians. Animosity grew daily through the 1920–30s, with the Jews determined on independence and eventual total control, requiring a policy of elimination and herding natives into ever-shrinking 'reserves'.

Palestine is a *thousand* times smaller than North America (27,000 km² vs 25 million km²), and in 1948 had more than a half million Jewish colonists but still twice as many native Arabs. Even the brief nightmare period of British occupation of Palestine looks much better in retrospect than the Israeli reality, just as British occupation of New England/ Canada was not as cruel as the post-British reality for North American natives. True, Jews were facing the specter of annihilation in Europe by the mid-1930s, with the British Mandate 'motherland' in denial. They were on their own, accounting for their fanaticism.

The Jews had many advantages over the natives, including their tribal unity in the build-up to 1948—the great banking families (especially the Rothschilds), contact with if not serving in high office in Europe (French Prime Minister Leon Blum). The Palestinians were/are more or less united as Muslims (90% Muslim, 10% Christian) and were in solidarity in the face of the Jewish invasion, but nationalism is a European concept, alien to the Muslim world. The Arab world has never been united except under the various Muslim Caliphates, which, except for the first century, were not Arab. The Campbell-Bannerman Report in 1907 intended to create a Jewish state "to prevent the convergence of [the Arab world] in such a way that it could exhaust its powers in never-ending wars."[10] Add in the prospect of fighting an all-out modern, high-tech war, and the Arab failures in the past century were inevitable.

The importance of unity was put poignantly by Tecumseh in a letter to US General William Henry Harrison in 1810: "The only way to stop this evil [white settlement of the Indians' land], is for all the red men to unite in claiming a common and equal right in the land as it was at first, and should be now—for it never was divided, but belongs to all… Sell a country! Why not sell the air, the clouds and the great sea, as well as the earth? Did not the Great Spirit make them all for the use of his children?"[11] Nasser tried to unify the Arab world in defense of Palestine, but he wasn't even Arab himself,[12] and was poorly educated.

The 1936–39 Arab revolt and general strike, demanding Arab independence and the end of Jewish immigration, as the League of Nations had authorized in 1922,[13] brought the creeping imperialism under the British Mandate to a head. Roughly 5,000 Arabs and a similar number of British died during that war of occupation of Palestine.

From the 1920s on, massacres of Palestinians accelerated reaching peaks in 1948 (20,000 Arabs-Palestinians), 1967 (23,000 mostly Egyptians), the Intifadas (1987–91, 2000–05) (5,300 Palestinians), the invasions of Gaza (2008, 2014) (3,700 Palestinians). According to official Israeli security data, between 750,000 and 800,000 Palestinians have been arrested and imprisoned by Israel since 1967. A high-placed Palestinian told *Al-Monitor*, "Around a third of our people are familiar with the inside of your prisons. Almost a million human beings have rubbed shoulders with Israeli prison guards over the last 50 years. There is hardly a Palestinian household without a shahid [suicide attacker] or prisoner."[14] The actual killings to date are more than 50,000, dispossessing millions, and creating a Palestinian diaspora rivaling the Jewish one, the largest refugee population in the world. This is the equivalent of 170 Wounded Knees. Then there are the invasions of Lebanon in 1982 and 2006, where Israel was accused of war crimes, in particular, held indirectly responsible by its own Kahan Commission for failing to control its Christian Lebanese proxies managing the Sabra/Shatila Palestinian refugee camp.

It was 'easier' in North America, where most natives were wiped out by disease, and the few who were left had no western-style sense of ownership of the land, no modern transport or organized, professional armies, and almost no modern weapons, and no foreign powers helping them. No mass media to relay the news of massacres to the world, and no indignation. It became' 'harder' for Israel, requiring constant wartime mobilization, and the constant activity of hasbarah, explaining its atrocities as somehow justified, juggling to avoid the fate of South Africa—a world united to bring it to account.

The Palestinians were left out in the cold in Great Game II, unprepared to confront the highly organized, determined Zionists, who were able, unlike the Palestinians, to count on powerful allies around the world in addition to seasoned troops trained primarily by the British and armed by the West and the Soviets during and after WWII. The British made no effort to prepare the Palestinians to form a government after the occupier's hurried departure. The Arab Liberation Army was hastily put together in 1948 by the fledgling Arab states, but untrained and without proper weapons, it was routed by the Zionists, and most of the Palestinians forced into exile in refugee camps.

The Palestinians remained without a unifying secular political organization until **Fatah** was founded in the late 1950s, and the **Palestinian Liberation Organization** was sponsored by Egypt in 1964. PLO head Yasser Arafat was recognized as the *de facto* leader of Palestine, and the PLO gained Observer status at the UN in 1974. The PLO declared Palestinian independence in 1988 in Algiers. These moves were important to legitimizing the Palestinian cause in the West.

From the start, for Arab regimes in the region, intent on maintaining their neocolonial power, and intimidated by the fierce commitment and powerful western backing of Israel, support for the PLO was more about finding a way "to co-opt and restrain the Palestinian resistance movement" to prevent them from drawing Arab states inadvertently into war.

But the Palestinians have had foreign power backing them—the Soviet Union, Saudi Arabia, Iraq (briefly), and, after 1979, Iran. Only the Soviet Union—after Stalin recognized his fatal error in recognizing Israel in 1948—was a firm supporter of the Palestinian cause throughout Great Game II. But it was ineffectual, concerned in the first place with its own survival in the face of the overwhelming economic and military might of the US empire.[15] Then it collapsed, leaving Palestinians with only the support of the Saudis, who are allied with the US (and by implication Israel), the erratic Saddam Hussein, and the Iranians who are far away, Shia, and threatened with invasion themselves.

So the Palestinians are in much the same position as South African blacks, who were without any support, powerless against their white masters, until the US was shamed into supporting a world movement to overthrow Apartheid. Once that happened in the 1980s, it took only a few years to bring the supposedly intransigent white racists to heel. The key difference is the power of Israel, not only in the Congress of the United States,[16] but in high offices throughout Europe.[17]

In the meantime, wounds similar to those of native nations in the US and Canada fester, keeping resistance alive.

Israel's complicated citizenship laws discriminate not only against Palestinians living in the "Occupied Palestinian Territory",[18] making it virtually impossible for them to travel abroad, but also against Arab Israelis, who live in a citizenship purgatory. These are able to vote, attend most universities (in Hebrew only) and receive health care, but again, are often prohibited from travel, subject to arbitrary arrest, censorship, and are prevented from owning land. Natives living on reserves in Canada can have a normal (Canadian) passport, and have land reserves totaling three million hectares.[19] Off-reserve natives lose their status but can buy and sell land like non-natives.

Israel has pressured Bedouin natives in the eastern occupied territories to settle into villages, much like natives in Canada were forced to do in the 19th century. Both programs had proved a disaster, and the Bedouin are no more eager to do the Israeli bidding than were the natives in Canada.[20] Any Bedouin tribes that have agreed have been destroyed through poverty, inertia and the tedium of settled lives. Some have simply returned to their pastoral lives, each time with less and less access to grazing lands. When Israelis demolish their settlements, they return to try to rebuild, only to have them destroyed again.

Unlike Canada which has a multi-ethnic settler population and officially practices multiculturalism and multinationalism (as it relates to the French and English speaking populations), Israel has never encouraged assimilation, being founded as a Jewish state, 'Jewish' being mostly a religious-racial category hence excluding Arab Muslims, who neither are Jews by religion, nor by 'race', a word without real substance. In fact, the notion of Jews as a race has recently come under fierce attack.[21] Jews from north Africa and Iraq (along with all Arabs) are the true 'Semites', where the term means 'speaker of a Semitic language'. They are called pejoratively mizrahi (oriental), considered second class citizens by the 'white' secular European Jews in Israel, identified with Arabs. Now they are the dominant political force, yet still in thrall to Zionism.

The one big difference that has made the Palestinian struggle much harder than that of the natives in North America is their lack of any treaties from Britain and then Israel. Canada signed 11 "numbered treaties" made between 1701 and 1923 on native land claims. They are considered sacred by the natives, with holidays celebrating them, and are the basis of the complex issue of unresolved land claims, land use and native relations with both the government and the people of Canada. There are no such treaties signed between the Palestinians and the Israel government. The closest to an agreement is still the ceasefire after the 1948 war, and after that, Egypt's peace accord in 1979, where the vague promise was made to agree to create a Palestinian state, but never acted on.[22] That said, there is UN recognition to the extent that it decreed a two-state solution for the territory that was originally Palestinian, a decision which is officially adhered to by the UN and all world governments, including Canada.[23]

Perpetual War

It's Israel's agenda of expansion, despite its self-promoted "existentially" perilous state, surrounded by enemies (including the supposedly friendly Egypt), that pushes it to further antagonize the local Arabs, rather than make concessions to obtain peace. Without hostile neighbors, the US would have no need of Israel as reliable Middle East gendarme keeping unreliable, anti-American Arab states in line.

This is a most unusual and risky strategy for a weak, heartland country surrounded by enemies. Heartland Nazi Germany dominated its neighbors by sheer might. Israel also has such a potential, deriving from its unacknowledged nuclear weapons able to strike all major cities—of Europe and the Middle East.[24]

Nonetheless, for Israel, this strategy of constant war has worked because of the widespread perception of the international power of world Jewry, promoted by the Jewish elite in the US, who were able to convince the US leaders of their own domestic power despite their small numbers, and the importance of Israel as a dependable Middle East ally. (And failing convincing US leaders, filling the Congressional and presidential electoral coffers to the extent that that issue remains moot.) As a result, the powerful Jewish/Zionist lobby has been able to get a yearly virtual blank check for arms and even (illegal) settlement building.

This need for hostile neighbors has been reiterated time and again throughout Israel's history; for example, future Israeli prime minister and would-be peacemaker Yitzhak Rabin as a general in 1991 bemoaned that "Israel was doomed to live forever in war, or under the threat of war with the entire Arab world."[25] That Israelis implicitly accept this as the normal state of affairs was confirmed by a 2010 poll by *Time*: "Asked to name the 'most urgent problem' facing Israel, just 8% of Israeli Jews cited the conflict with Palestinians ... Israeli Arabs placed peace first, but among Jews here, the issue that President Obama calls 'critical for the world' just doesn't seem critical."[26]

Hostility and war are more than just a strategy for Israel, they are its *raison d'etre*, along with *Lebensraum*, which is the underlying goal of the Zionists in Great Games II and III. While Jewish elites traditionally benefited from wars between states, they never had any interest in being involved directly in perpetual war, being able to prosper during peacetime as well, and appreciating the stability of their host nations, whether it be Britain, Germany, the US or whatever. This state of perpetual war is a new strategy made necessary by the enduring colonial nature of Israel itself.[27]

So, in a move that is startlingly counter-intuitive to that agenda, Israel at first promoted *Muslim* organizations among the Palestinians, counting on a supposedly quietist Islam (the Saudi variant) dampening nationalist sentiment of the then predominant, officially secular-socialist PLO. This contrasts with the brutal treatment of native nations by Canada, which in an effort to assimilate them, forcibly seized their children and banned their languages and culture in favor of English and Christianity. This made a good contrast for the Zionist hasbarah folks, and they indeed have been highlighting to North American natives this difference between

Israel and the racist British/Canadian/American colonial masters.[28]) But it has backfired. Not only with the rise of Hamas, but with cooperation between religious and secular liberation movements both among Palestinians and around the world. Despite Islamophobia following 9/11, westerners are converting to Islam, especially women. Arab/Muslim is the new chic, quite possibly because of empathy for the Palestinians, and an interest in Islam and its traditions.[29] Paradoxically, Donald Trump's Muslim ban has fueled Americans' sympathy for Muslims.

And Israel is at least indirectly responsible not only for Hamas, but for the spawning of new types of resistance—the Taliban, Hizbullah, al-Qaeda, ISIS and others—that were not present in Great Games I and II. During those games, resistance to imperialism was primarily by communists and nationalists, both within the imperial center and/or institutionalized in the Soviet Union, forces which responded to traditional state strategies, and were eventually defanged with the collapse of the Soviet Union. The new forms of resistance don't respond to traditional US/Israeli imperial force, though both the US and Israel have tried to use them, and even supported and infiltrated them initially to try to make sure they served imperial aims.

These resistance groups are committed to overthrow the colonial constructs imposed on the Middle East by the imperial powers in Great Games I and II, and the walled ghettoes built in Great Game III by Israel. They continue to resist and gather strength, biding their time. Though Hizbullah participates in the political rituals of the Lebanese state, it grew out of local needs, like the Taliban, and both are genuine movements, not dependent on state institutions or infrastructure for their existence. They are parallel organizations to the state, militias that cannot be intimidated or bullied by the state or outside forces. Neither the US invasion of Afghanistan nor Israel's invasion of Lebanon in 2006 were able to destroy them, though the result was to destroy those countries' infrastructure and cause unimaginable grief.[30]

Al-Qaeda and the Taliban are more a problem for the US than for Israel. Israel is more concerned about Hizbullah, and the resilience of Hamas and the Palestinians, who live in concentration camp conditions, refusing to give up their last bits of land. They also face the now sizable Palestinian Diaspora, which rivals that of the Jews themselves, and continue to demand the right to return. The lightning expansion of ISIS (Islamic State in Iraq and Syria) since 2014 has put al-Qaeda on Israel's doorstep now, with an attack in 2016 in Jerusalem attributed to ISIS.[31]

At some point, the best simulation models break down. Sharon and Yinon's plans to win Great Game III with the US in tow, which were even translated into mathematical game theory strategies for the IDF by Israeli Nobel laureate Robert Aumann,[32] no longer make sense when the real enemy—the offspring of Israeli terrorism[33]—exists at the sub-state level in both 'host' countries (the US, France, Britain and Israel) and those of the 'enemies' (Iraq, Syria, Afghanistan), in defiance of the entire system of nation states operating according to the principle of balance of power and market capitalism.

Violations of International Norms

Israel is notorious for the dozens of UN motions sanctioning its violation of human rights, which it ignores with little if any sanction.[34] It picks and chooses which UN treaties to sign, and then argues they don't apply when brought to account:

- Though Israel has signed the UN Declaration of Human Rights, even the US criticizes Israel on a human rights violation (its policy of marriage discrimination), but in fact Israel violates all the clauses.[35]
- Israel signed the UN Convention on the Elimination of Racial Discrimination (1969), and is regularly condemned for widespread racism, but does not consider itself bound by any criticism.[36] Israel denied in 2005 that the International Covenant on Civil and Political Rights (1976) and the International Covenant on Economic, Social and Cultural Rights (1976), both of which it has signed, are applicable to the occupied Palestinian territory.
- Israel refused to sign the United Nations Declaration on the Rights of Indigenous Peoples, and denied the UN ruling that it applies at the very least to the Bedouin in Israel.

The definition of Israel as a "Jewish and democratic state" was adopted in 1985 as the basis of a future constitution, to include in the Basic Law: Human Dignity and Liberty. But the contradiction between nationality and citizenship was there right from 1948 and remains unsolvable, leaving Israel without a constitution, or constitutionally-defined borders, its passport a confidence trick.

Endnotes

1   See Chapter 3, endnote 43. Also www.mail-archive.com, 11 April 2006. <http://www.mail-archive.com/osint@yahoogroups.com/msg20338.html>.
2   M Shahid Alam, *Israeli Exceptionalism: The Destabilizing Logic of Zionism*, 2009, 206.
3   Ibid., 206.
4   The political program announced by Alexander Dubcek in Czechoslovakia on April 1968.
5   Yakov Rabkin, *A Threat from Within: A History of Jewish Opposition to Zionism*, 2006, 48.
6   Ariel Sharon's description of the current reality, as reported in *Haaretz*, June 18, 2007.
7   "The poor Jewish boy from London's East End", Shinwell was responsible for Attlee's nationalization of industry in 1947, and then became a fervent Zionist. "Lord Shinwell Dead at 101", *jta.org*, May 9, 1986.
8   William Roger Louis, *The British Empire in the Middle East*, Oxford: Oxford University Press, 1984, 673.
9   'Modern' in the political sense of having genuine independence as a sovereign nation.
10 See Chapter 2, endnote 8.
11 <http://indiancountrytodaymedianetwork.com/2012/06/18/war-1812-could-have-been-war-indian-independence-118851>
12 His father was a Saidi from Upper Egypt.
13 The Churchill White Paper that was the basis of the Mandate emphasized that the establishment of a Jewish National Home would not impose a Jewish nationality on the Arab inhabitants of Palestine, and "the status of all citizens of Palestine in the eyes of the law shall be Palestinian." To reduce tensions between the Arabs and Jews in Palestine the paper called for a limitation of Jewish immigration to "the economic capacity of the country to absorb new arrivals."
14 Ben Caspit, "The real story behind Trump's meetings with Abbas and Netanyahu" www.al-monitor.com, May 31, 2017. http://www.al-monitor.com/pulse/originals/2017/05/israel-palestinians-benjamin-netanyahu-donald-trump-abbas.html#ixzz4iqWPnX6d
15 In 1948, communism had no following among the Arab masses, while the creation of a Jewish state was a leftwing and liberal *cause célébre* in the West. *The New York Times* reported in 1948 a 10,000 strong demonstration in support of Progressive Party presidential candidate Henry Wallace composed of communists and Leftist labor leaders that marched under the banner of the United Committee to Save the Jewish State and the United Nations. The combination of new Israeli communists, Arab conservatism, and the rising Cold War prompted Stalin to recognize Israel as a means of ensuring imperial instability in the Middle East having his own strategic ally there. The failure of this strategy led to a reversion to Soviet anticolonial policy and support for the Palestinians and Israel's other neighbors. The Soviet Union continued to support the Arab states, even when it got little in return. It was the first country to recognize Saudi Arabia in 1932 but the Saudis broke relations in 1938. Its influence was never strong and by 1972, not only were the Soviets unceremoniously expelled from Egypt, but soon all the Arab countries would

be at least implicitly backing the *mujahideen* to wage war on the Soviet Union, financed by the US and egged on by Israel.

16 See, inter alia: http://www.foreignpolicyjournal.com/2016/03/22/the-best-congress-aipac-can-buy/; https://www.nytimes.com/2015/04/05/us/politics/gops-israel-support-deepens-as-political-contributions-shift.html?_r=1

17 See David Cronin, Sarah Manusek and David Miller, *The Israel lobby and the European Union,* Europal Forum Public Interest Investigations, (downloadable at http://powerbase.info/index.php/File:PII_IsraelLobbyEUreport2016_Cronin_Mursak_Miller.pdf) http://www.spinwatch.org/index.php/issues/lobbying/item/5864-press-release-new-report-details-extent-of-israel-lobby-in-brussels-connections-to-us-islamophobia-industry-and-illegal-settlements and also https://www.middleeastmonitor.com/20160513-new-report-breaks-down-the-israel-lobby-in-the-european-union/

18 This is the official designation used by the UN Office of the High Commissioner for Human Rights, see http://www.ohchr.org/EN/Countries/MENARegion/Pages/PSIndex.aspx

19 Tom Flanagan, "First nations property rights: Going beyond the Indian Act", Globe and Mail, March 22, 2010.

20 For example, "Israel to demolish Bedouin village for national-religious Jewish town", *rt.com,* November 11, 2013.

21 See Rita Rubin, "'Jews a Race' Genetic Theory Comes Under Fierce Attack by DNA Expert", http://forward.com/news/israel/175912/jews-a-race-genetic-theory-comes-under-fierce-atta/

22 The 1979 treaty called for "Transitional arrangements for the West Bank and Gaza for a period not exceeding five years in order to provide full autonomy to the inhabitants." <https://en.wikipedia.org/wiki/Camp_David_Accords#Key_points_of_the_West_Bank_and_Gaza_section>

23 For key Canadian policies in relation to Israel, see http://www.international.gc.ca/name-anmo/peace_process-processus_paix/canadian_policy-politique_canadienne.aspx?lang=eng

24 See also Nadim Ladki, "Israel Professor: 'We Could Destroy All European Capitals", http://www.rense.com/general34/esde.htm

25 Israel Shahak, *Open Secrets: Israel Nuclear and Foreign Policies,* 1993, 46.

26 Karl Vick, "Why Israel Doesn't Care About Peace", *Time,* 2 September 2010.

27 Perpetual war was posited by Orwell in *1984* as the Great Game II endgame, where the West has adopted the worst features of the Soviet Union, which Orwell dismissed as just another empire, and the world is held in thrall by a state of permanent war between competing *faux* communist empires. It was written before the creation of Israel, which he opposed. See John Rodden, *George Orwell: the politics of literary reputation,* 2002, 318.

28 See Chapter 8.

29 See Chapter 8 and my *From Postmodernism to Postsecularism: Re-emerging Islamic Civilization* (2013).

30 US actions in Syria since 2012 have aided ISIS. There are critics who insist the US still assists the Taliban even as it fights them in Afghanistan. While this may be in Israel's interests, it is unlikely that the US is still pursuing this policy. While it helped create al-Qaeda and initially supported the Taliban, it is now trying to put the genie back in the bottle. Sibel Edmonds, "The Three-Decade US-Mujahideen Partnership Still Going Strong", *informationclearinghouse. info,* 14 October 2010.

31	"Jerusalem truck attack: Suspect may have supported ISIS, Netanyahu says", *CNN*, January 9, 2017.
32	Robert J. Aumann, "War and peace", Proceedings of the National Academy of Sciences of the United States of America, vol. 103 no. 46.
33	Two top al-Qaeda spokesmen, taking the place of Osama bin Laden, were revealed on Youtube as American-born Jews, but the videos were removed immediately and the news removed from the press. 'Crotch bomber' Abdul Mohammad's computer showed a trail of emails to Israel and he passed through airports without a passport or visa in Ghana, Nigeria and the Netherlands where airport security personnel are largely either Israeli or employees of Israeli companies. Are they part of a new ultra-Zionist movement anxious to promote *faux* terrorist attacks or genuine rebels against Zionism? Gordon Duff, "Dazed and confused: Why Jews are joining al-Qaeda", *veteranstoday.com*, June 29, 2010.
34	Marriages in Israel can be performed only under the auspices of the religious community to which couples belong, and no religious intermarriages can be performed legally in Israel. Israel's other violations can be viewed at <https://en.wikipedia.org/wiki/List_of_the_UN_resolutions_concerning_Israel_and_Palestine>
35	<https://sites.google.com/site/palestinegenocideessays/universal-declaration-of-human-rights-palestinians>
36	The 2012 CERD report indicates that racial prejudice can be found in almost every facet of Israeli life ("Concluding observations of the Committee on the Elimination of Racial Discrimination," 9 March 2012.)

PART II

CANADA: ISRAEL'S "BEST FRIEND"

| Chapter Five |

JEWS IN CANADIAN HISTORY

Introduction

My writings about Canada and Israel began in 2008 at *Al-Ahram Weekly* in Cairo with an account of the sixth (and last) international **Cairo Conference against Imperialism and Zionism**.[1] Egypt was in the dying days of dictator Hosni Mubarak's regime, caught between the anti-imperialism and socialism of Gamal Abdul Nasser and his pro-American successor Anwar Sadat. Sadat, to his credit, was trying to move forward when he made peace with the enemy in 1979. But his embrace of Israel and US neoliberalism won him no supporters, and his assassination in 1981 resulted in no outpouring of grief, unlike the death of his beloved predecessor in 1970.[2] His successor, Hosni Mubarak continued Sadat's policies, resulting in Egypt regaining membership in the Arab League in 1987, and maintaining a pseudo-democracy, where real opposition (the Muslim Brotherhood) was repressed.

The fellah in the sugar cane fields had a more sophisticated analysis of world events than most Canadian Middle East experts. He knew all about his violent, unpredictable next-door neighbor. So while the political atmosphere in Egypt was oppressive, it was still less oppressive than in Canada, where holding an anti-Zionist conference would have been impossible (then and now). Only Iran dares do that, which is a major part of why Iran is so victimized by the West. The Canadian Security Intelligence Service (CSIS), assisted by Israeli intelligence and B'nai Brith, has a blacklist of prominent anti-Zionists and pro-Palestinian activists, who are denied entry to Canada if they are foreigners. The plucky students who organize the annual Israeli Apartheid Weeks across Canada are demonized, and have now been subject to a (thankfully still toothless) motion condemning all organizations which support the "boycott of Israel". The only other anti-Zionist conferences, held three times in Tehran,[3] raised shouts of "antisemitism" against all westerners (including religious Jews) who attended them. The rule of Harper's Conservatives, during which they were held, was surely the low point in Canadian political history, though it really didn't differ in substance from earlier regimes or the post-Harper one.

The conference featured children of jailed Muslim Brothers, pleading for public awareness about their fathers being tortured and robbed. Since Egyptians are uniformly hostile to Israel,[4] the cause of unending tragedy, not only for Palestinians, but for Egyptians, holding the conference was good politics for the unpopular dictator Hosni Mubarak, despite its strong anti-US tone, the presence of major Egyptian opposition representatives, and the absence of any Mubarak supporters.

Fourteen members of the Canadian Peace Alliance (CPA) and others from student organizations represented Canada. Delegates to this and the previous Cairo conference were attacked in the *National Post* and *Ottawa Citizen* for consorting with "terrorists", and "shouldn't be surprised if they come under scrutiny of the Canadian security services", simply for their willingness to dialogue with Muslims fighting the various wars now being inflicted on them. My article "Zionism in Canada: Political poison" and a later article "Canada's First Nations: Expect resistance" prompted a reference to me in the *National Post* as a "terrorist", and derided my comparison of the struggle of Canada's natives and Palestinians, fine examples of how pro-Zionist reporting masquerades as news. My reply to the *Post*[5] was not printed, nor did I get an acknowledgment.

As the conference was taking place, 2,500 Canadian troops in the dangerous southern Kandahar region of Afghanistan had their mission extended to 2011 in what was billed as a fateful parliamentary vote, as the pro-war Conservatives had only a minority government and the war was unpopular among Canadians. Only 15% of Canadians favored extending the troop presence to 2011, with 60% in favor of bringing the troops home. Nonetheless, the vote was a walk-over, with the Liberals voting alongside the minority Conservative government, and only the small social democratic New Democratic Party (NDP) and the Bloc Quebecois voting 'no'.[6]

Pseudo democracy reigned in both Egypt and Canada. A crude dictatorship in the former, but with more freedom of thought and speech, more understanding of the reality of Middle East politics, than in the latter, with all its sophistication and democracy. Debate on the Middle East had shut down completely in Canada by that time. Canada had become a haven for refugees, both Arab and Jewish, from Israel and Palestine, a source of passports for Israel's illegal activities, a laughing stock, a plaything of Zionist hardliners. How did Canada become such a disappointment when it came to the Middle East? The road was long and troubling.

17th–19th Centuries: Golden Age for Jews in Canada

'Discovered' mostly by French explorers, Canada was created as a settler colony of the French empire, *Nouvelle France*, which forbade Jewish colons in the 17th–18th centuries. After the French defeat in 1763, the British encouraged Jewish settlers to Canada. They came primarily to Montreal, as it was the financial hub of Canada in the 18-19th centuries, and close to the US financial hub, New York City. They lived discretely apart in French Canadian society, seen by the Quebecois as just some more *anglais* merchants, or worse, Americans, crowding out the French and threatening French culture.

France and England had expelled the Jews in the 12-14th centuries (Spain also from 15th century), so there were almost no Jews (none officially) in 17th century France or Britain.[7] European nations like France and England referred to themselves as Christian in opposition to heathen (Muslim) countries. By the 17th century, they tolerated Jews but gave them no political rights. Jews and Christians alike accepted the Jewish claim to be a different and separate 'nation', which meant they had no inherent political rights in the predominantly Christian countries[8] in which they actually lived.

Amsterdam and eventually London and Paris admitted Jews as "new Christians", so they finally had full rights—to a degree. Britain allowed Jews to be naturalized in colonies by 1740, as they were the preeminent traders and bankers of the empire. This led to a steady flow of cultured Jewish settlers (bankers, merchants, businessmen) to North America, descendants of the Sephardic branch of Judaism. British Jews were eager to emigrate. Life was freer in America. No need to simulate being "new Christians", though the tribal snag remained implicit. The French Canadian Catholics were more visibly anti-Jewish than anti-Anglo, as anti-Jewish resentment was more politically correct then than open resentment of *les anglais*. The few Jews were English speaking, originally from Britain and then east Europe, adopting English as their *lingua franca*. Some assimilated and intermarried, leaving little trace of their Jewishness, but many cherished their apartness. Jews were not included in official records, like Presbyterians, Methodists and Quakers. Only Anglicans were full-fledged citizens in the 18th century.

The battle for Quebec in 1759 saw Jewish suppliers on both sides. Abraham Gradis, nominally a Catholic convert, was called "my right-hand man" by General Montcalm, and helped negotiate prisoner exchanges. On the British side, Alexander Schomberg converted to join the navy and rose to command the frigate Diana, helping Wolfe conquer Quebec.

Wolfe's key supplier was Aaron Hart, who had come up from New York to help the British in the war with France, and decided to stay, locating in Trois-Rivières, halfway between Montreal and Quebec City. As a wealthy merchant, he lent money to poor farmers, and when they couldn't repay, he was able to take their lands. At the same time, he made donations to the local nunnery. He went to London to find a Jewish wife, and sired 11 children.

His eldest son, Moses, opened a bank and issued his own currency, ran three times unsuccessfully for a seat in parliament, and was finally appointed high constable. His son, Ezekiel, won a seat in 1807 but refused to sign on the Sabbath, then signed, crossing out "the year of our Lord", but was then not allowed to take his seat. This established an

Hart dollars

open, politely defiant presence. The Hart family's challenges led to the 1832 Emancipation Act giving full legal citizenship to Jews, including the right to hold elected office. The Harts lived a prosperous, public life despite the snag of being separate culturally.

Samuel Hart (no relation) settled in Nova Scotia and in 1793 became the first Jewish legislator, wisely taking his oath as required. His wife and children were Anglican. Samuel Jacob, another prominent merchant also assimilated, marrying a French Canadian. As did Nathan Levy, a German working for the British, who converted to Lutheranism. Jews were not formally allowed to own land until 1803, even though there were established Jewish communities by then. Jews fought for the British in the war of 1812. In 1831, Papineau, speaker of the Lower Canada assembly, sponsored a bill providing full political rights to Jews (this happened in Britain only in 1855 when London elected a Jewish mayor David Salomon).

The first Jew in Toronto arrived in 1835. Arthur Hart, grandson of Aaron Hart of Trois-Rivières, scion of one of the oldest Jewish families in British North America, established a branch of his father's Montreal wholesale mercantile house in York (population 9,000). He didn't stay long, but Judah and Henry Joseph, also merchants, came a few years later. The latter converted to Christianity and married out of the faith, assimilating, as did Samuel Nordheimer who came from Bavaria via New York, and Jacob Hirschfelder, a former tutor in Hebrew at King's College. The willingness to convert was taken as a desire to integrate in society, even if, like many conversions, it was *pro forma*, indicating more a secular outlook, at a time when secularism was on the rise in mainstream society. "These Jews were readily accepted as Englishmen."[9] Though most Jewish merchants opened for business on Saturday, Judah Joseph was strictly Orthodox and closed his shop—losing much business—but was respected and patronized.

British Jews came as part of servicing the empire, as they did throughout the colonies. They were well educated, competent administrators and part of a world merchant and banking network. British Jews constituted a "significant proportion (10%) of Quebec's small English mercantile community in the 18th century, accepted reasonably well within that community simply because they were needed."[10] French resentment grew when the Jews were seen as pushing the French commercial class out with "superior political and trade connections",[11] but the strong, cultured Jewish presence by the mid-19th century made it a "the golden age for Jews in Canada."[12] They were essential to the success of empire, and were respected as such, despite their aloofness and unfamiliar traditions.

That, plus the huge wave of immigration from the 1870s–1920s, helps account for the eventual strong presence and influence of Jews in America, including Canada. In emigration, old prejudices (on both sides) died, providing a new life for Jews. "Rather than 'anti-Jew sentiment', all doors were open to Jews."[13]

Prime Minister John A. Macdonald welcomed Jews: "A sprinkling of Jews in the North-West would be good. They would at once go in for peddling and politicking, and be of as much use to the new country as cheap jacks and chapmen [peddlers]."[14] Macdonald was eager for financial backing for the Canadian Pacific Railway, and was well aware of the stronghold that the Rothschild dynasty had on the British Empire, headed at the time by the Jewish British prime minister, Benjamin Disraeli. This political acceptance, and a lax immigration regime which classified Jews simply as east European whites, led to a mass immigration of destitute east European peasants, primarily Yiddish-speaking Jews, until the 1920s.

Early 20th Century: Mass Immigration and Assimilation

Relatively few Jewish immigrants came to Canada before 1896. In fact, Canada was far more a land of *emigration* than immigration, as thousands of Canadians, including Jews, left for the US where industry was in need of cheap labor. Until WWII, the US border was very open, which was especially advantageous to Jewish immigrants to both countries, with extended families on both sides. The official policy was to give priority to white immigrants. The model was white, Anglo-Saxon, Protestant (WASP), which meant Britain and northern Europe. The thinking was: the closer you were to the model, the more likely you were to be accepted by the government and the previous immigrants. The more you diverted from the model, the more "foreign" you were, the more difficult for you to enter and the more likely you will face discrimination by ordinary (WASP) Canadians once here. So this notion that an ethnically homogenized population was required for nation-building and required assimilationist policies impacted more groups than just the colonized native nations. Section 38 of the Canadian Immigration Act of 1910 gave the Canadian Government the power to prohibit the entry "of immigrants belonging to any race deemed unsuited to the climate or requirements of Canada". People from "warm countries" were deemed unsuited for immigration to Canada.[15]

This policy of assimilation had worked well in the 18th–19th centuries. But, faced with a US always looking to expand, Canada needed immigrants, especially for farming (immigration was the responsibility of the Ministry of Agriculture). Nonetheless, Jews from eastern Europe were accepted, though they were not Christian and not noted as farmers. Once the word got out, there was a flood of poor Jewish immigrants. Canadian Jews sent their savings to relatives and friends in the east European and Russian ghettoes to buy steamship third class tickets.

From the start, Jews were the largest non-Christian minority (only surpassed by Muslims in 1991). Because the Jewish immigrants were mostly from east Europe and Russia, and weren't cut out for farming, they gravitated to slums in the cities and worked as peddlers and merchants, not really what the Canadian government had in mind, needing skilled, hardy farmers. In 1921, only 4% of Canadian Jews lived in rural Canada.

The Jewish population exploded, increasing 15 times from 1871 to 1901 to 16,401, as happened in the US. As 'white' Europeans (the genuine Semitic speakers, Arab Jews and Muslims, from 'warm countries', were mostly barred), the doors were open to them, even for those with no farming skills. By the outbreak of WWI, their numbers had increased another 6 times to reach 100,000, of whom three-quarters lived in either Montreal or Toronto. Many of the children of the European refugees started out as peddlers, eventually working their way up to owning established businesses, as retailers and wholesalers. Jewish Canadians played an essential role in the development of the Canadian clothing and textile industry. Most worked as laborers in sweatshops, with a select few as the sweatshop owners.

The archetype was of the old, poor Jew as rag picker. This form of employment was partly unavoidable, since older, unlettered immigrants without skills could do little else. So it was done by the devout, who wanted a flexible schedule in order to be able to observe prayer times and the Sabbath, and were not concerned with riches. More prosperous east Europeans became rag-*processors* who (in Toronto) sold to the Frankel brothers, the largest waste-processing establishment in the city. Others were purveyors of peddlers' supplies, some itinerant repairmen, knife sharpeners, but all these jobs were exhausting, and involved abuse.

In 1916, Toronto had 600 rag pickers, mostly Jews. Jewish immigration fell sharply when the 1923 ruling put Jews into the "special permit" group

Jewish Ragpicker

of immigrants from "non-preferred" countries, requiring their cabinet approval. The Toronto *Telegram* op-ed in September 1924 reflected the mainstream anger at the tribal success of Jewish immigrants, who were sending earnings to kinsmen in eastern Europe to allow penniless ghetto dwellers to come to settle in urban slums. It called for a "poll tax so high that friends in Montreal and Toronto and Winnipeg would have their resources strained to the utmost to lend their tribesmen through foreign post more than enough to bring a baker's dozen per annum."[16]

Unsurprisingly the immigration rules tightened. The lowest in the category of "not preferred" among whites were the Jews. By the 1930s, Canada's Jews were almost exclusively living in the larger cities in Jewish communities, and they were primarily poor Yiddish Europeans, mostly merchants, peddlers, bootleggers. From the 1920s on, under tighter rules, the few Jews permitted entry were businessmen and cultured Jews—German scientists/academics/musicians—the so-called Ashkenazis. The already more-or-less assimilated Jews were Ashkenazi and resented their Yiddish ghetto co-religionists, and even joined the call to limit the new immigrants from the Pale.[17]

Resentment against Jews festered. In a 1933 survey, 70% of Toronto businessmen said they would not deal with Jewish firms. Jewish scholars today point to this period as a shameful, racist one in Canadian history,[18] overlooking how Jews themselves benefited from the 'white' racism which prioritized their immigration to Canada in the first place, and how benign it was/is compared to the genuine horrors of the other British colonies, and the racism of the US and Nazi Germany at the time.

Despite the prejudice, Jews prospered in business, setting up their own when shunned by the Gentiles, becoming the only immigrant minority who made it into the Anglo-French economic elite. "They were separate yet interlocked in a peripheral way with the Canadian Anglo-dominated elite."[19]

There was little overt violence against Jews. The legendary 1933 Christie Pits riot is still remembered by Toronto Jews as a brave stand against Nazism. The baseball team that sparked the riot was Harbord Playground, consisting of the local Jews and Italians, who battled the Swastika Club members in the gathering, ripping down their swastika, sparking a riot of 10,000. No one was killed, and there were no further riots. Jews represented the largest minority in Toronto in 1933, followed by the Italians, lumped together in the WASP imagination as second-class citizens. The incident is a metaphor for how anti-Jewish prejudice evaporates when Jews join their non-Jewish neighbors in normal life. Within a few years all these boys would be fighting the Nazis side by side in common cause. The event had some parallels to the 1875 Jubilee riots, an outbreak of Protestant-Catholic sectarian violence in Toronto, and anti-Greek riots in 1918.

There were quotas on Jews at universities and in the professions, which came with the wave of immigrants from the 1870s on. Placements were still much higher for Jews (10% or more vs their 1.6% as a percentage of the population), but based on grades alone, Jews would have had much higher enrolments at the medical and law schools and universities, with the inevitable resentment. Prior to WWII, Jews found it difficult to become practicing doctors in large cities, and were denied internships at the major hospitals. So they set up their own hospitals. This was also the pattern for law firms and businesses.

The fact is that Jews, for tribal or other reason, excel other groups in higher learning. Even with the handicaps they faced at the time, they still came out on top as a group. Without the quotas, as is seen in present day Canadian society, Jews would have quickly become the largest group at universities and in the professions. The restrictions were a kind of 'affirmative action' for less accomplished immigrants and WASPs in a society with many growing pains.

The implication was that Jews should assimilate. Assimilation has always been the bane of zealous Jews, who fear the tribe will disappear. But many Jewish immigrants were more interested in integrating into Canadian society, and leaving behind the source of anti-Jewish prejudice. They officially changed their names to Green, Stein, Smith, etc. from the more obviously Jewish Mandelbaum, Liebowitz, Finkelstein, etc. Landlords had the implicit right to discriminate by race and religion, and while an assimilated Joe Green, a "new Christian", could pass for a Gentile, get a good job, go to university, join elite clubs, Yehuda Finkelstein couldn't, and faced constant petty discrimination. It was just as much a problem for the grandparents of, say, Toronto aldermen Anthony Perruzza or Joe Mihevc. Jews had no monopoly as victims of prejudice at the time.

Even the teaching and medical professions were not off-bounds if Jews were willing to live in small towns. This is standard policy for immigrants, the government looking more favorably on immigrants who intend to live in smaller centers or as farmers, a policy which continues today. This is a kind of benign quota system, a pragmatic policy intended to benefit all Canadians. After a few years in a town, helping those Canadians not 'fortunate' enough to live in the big cities, many Jews found it possible to get a job back in Toronto or Montreal, now with experience and good (Gentile) recommendations. Many decided to stay in, say, Guelph, where my Jewish dentist was a respected Guelphite, sired a large, happy family, and was a regular synagogue goer. From 1921–41, the number of Jewish doctors and lawyers increased more than 5 times, the number of Jewish dentists more than tripled, and Jewish nurses quadrupled.[20]

The debate about assimilation raged in the aftermath of WWI, when Zionism was in its youth, given a boost with the Balfour 'Declaration' (really just a letter to Nathan Rothschild), and became a new factor in anti-Jewish prejudice. The most famous assimilationist of the period was the German foreign minister, Walther Rathenau. His views on internationalism and human rights were similar to those of Albert Einstein, though they disagreed on the Jewish question, with Einstein initially an enthusiast Zionist, only later ruing his support for a Jewish state.[21] Rathenau wrote: "I am a German of Jewish origin. My people are the German people, my home is German land, my belief is German belief, which stands above all denominations."[22]

The most successful campaign for assimilation of Jews was in the young Soviet Union, where the religious aspect of Jewishness was suppressed, and the cultural aspect celebrated, allowing Jews to integrate almost seamlessly and, like in the West, rise to the top of economic and cultural life (though not political life). Churchill vilified this communist experiment, marshalling both his anticommunism and his anti-Jewish prejudice: "The international Jews, the adherents of this sinister confederacy [Bolshevism] ... have become practically the undisputed masters of that enormous [Soviet] empire."[23] There was a brief experiment in allotting Jews a 'promised land' in Siberia (Birobaidjan) in 1928 (an attempt to scuttle the British plan for Jews to colonize Palestine), but Soviet Jews were not interested, preferring the comforts of big city life.

There were never any limitations on election to public office after 1832. Toronto's first alderman was Newman Steiner, born in Bohemia, arriving in Toronto in 1852, appointed justice of the peace in 1870, and elected alderman in St James's Ward in 1880 as a Liberal, converting to Lutheranism in 1890. Few of the Jewish elite were interested in politics, and the new arrivals from the 1890s also were not interested initially, partly because they had no concept of a 'state' or civil rights. Even Zionism was a messianic rather than a political idea. They saw politics as a Gentile preserve, and, lacking fluent English, avoided non-Jews in principle. By 1911, this was changing, and there were Jews in both the Conservative and Liberal parties, and their candidacies were sought in heavily Jewish ridings. Jacob Cohen used his sociability and English fluency to become a translator for Colonel George Taylor, the police magistrate, who appointed him justice of the peace and a bail magistrate, and to sit on the Bench and succeed him in 1918.

Jews have been prominent in mainstream politics ever since, including not only the Liberals and Conservatives, but the CCF/NDP (David and Stephen Lewis, Dave Barrett, Cy Gonick and Gerald Caplan) and the Communists. There were Jewish Liberal and Conservative MPs by the 1930s. Peter Bercovitch was a Liberal MPP and MP in Montreal from 1916–42. David Croll was elected as a Liberal MPP in Ontario in 1934 and became the first Jewish federal cabinet minister and first Jewish senator. Larry Grossman was Ontario Conservative Party leader 1985–87. There have been three Jewish mayors of Toronto—Nathan Phillips, Phil Givens and Mel Lastman. Jews have been close advisers to Mulroney, Chretien and Harper.[24]

Confirming Ginsberg's thesis about the dual aspect of Jews in history—as viziers and rabble-rousers—Jews formed an important part of Canada's fledgling communist movement from the 1920s onward. The 1930s saw the success of labor union organizers, who were primarily communists and Jewish. The Communist Party was the only one in the 1930s that promoted racial equality and welcomed Jews, though not Zionists. Legends of this period include Bill Walsh who organized the United Electrical Workers, Joe Salzberg (Toronto alderman from 1938, MPP for St Andrews from 1943), and Fred Rose (MP from Cartier 1943, beating the NDP's David Lewis).[25]

Education was a thorn, as Canada was founded on two nations, with Protestant and Catholic schools enshrined in the BNA act. There was no room for a third wheel, and Jews either went to Protestant schools or organized and paid for their own. The issue of taxation, representation on school boards and the demand for full student rights caused frictions.

Jewish integrationists/assimilationists were uncomfortable with the east European Jews, who stood out by "their appearance, way of life, poverty, religious practices and inability to speak English. They were an embarrassment to a community struggling to integrate and be accepted."[26] They now outnumbered by far the few thousand Jewish immigrants from colonial days, like Peter Bercovitch, Quebec MPP from 1916–38 and MP 1938–42, who was in favor of integrated education, arguing that schools should be a melting pot where children will get their education and the ideals for their province.

It was agreed that Jews should attend Protestant schools. In most provinces, this was not a problem, as school board trustees were elected and Jews could be elected as trustees and have some say in the school program. But the school boards were appointed in Quebec until well after WWII. There was no effort to include Jews on the school boards (trustees in Ontario, commissioners in Quebec). The lack of Jewish input into the Protestant school curricula was not seen as discriminatory. Protestants were footing almost all the bill, as the Jewish immigrants in the 1900–20s were too poor to pay property taxes. In 1913, the Montreal

Protestant school board relented, hiring Jewish teachers where the classes were predominantly Jewish.

But many of the new immigrants wanted Jewish education, resisting assimilation, and where a large plurality of students in the Montreal Jewish areas was Jewish, they wanted to make sure that the educational program fit their needs. Because they were poor, they called for a state subsidy to Jewish schools, which was denied, given the limitation of publicly funded education under Confederation to Protestant and Catholic schools.

The court case of Montreal high school student Jacob Pinsler, denied a scholarship in 1901 on the grounds that his parents did not pay taxes to the Protestant School Board, became a landmark. It resulted in a 1903 ruling in his favor, but Jews were still mostly excluded from the teaching profession. The daily Lord's Prayer and Christmas carols were also sticking points. Bullying of Jews at schools was a problem in a few Montreal schools because of the high concentration of the poor east European Yiddish Jews with their strange ways, "Christ-killers" in the eyes of children brought up in devoutly Christian homes.[27] Concerned Jewish mothers sensibly told their children not to stand out or attraction attention, though Jewish children held no monopoly on being bullied. What overt anti-Jewish prejudice there was ended with WWII.

The Jewish demands were seen as an "attack on the constitutional rights of Protestants."[28] The dispute became so heated that the school officials threatened to ban Jews from all schools, which Quebec premier Taschereau prevented, calling for a committee and some kind of legislative solution, a 'solution' which dragged on indefinitely until it disappeared altogether with WWII.

After WWII, Jewish schools became popular in Toronto and Montreal, as Zionism instilled a new Jewish pride, and fears of too much assimilation took hold. Education is seen as essential to preserve Jewishness and prevent intermarriage. "Today's Jewish leaders worry as much about the rate of assimilation as of antisemitism".[29] As if to make up for its past sins, the Quebec government began multiculturalism early, subsidizing Jewish and Greek schools catering to those communities, but Ontario, the other province with a large number of Jews, did not follow suit, forcing Jews there to rely on school fees and philanthropy. Jewish organizations sued the Ontario government, demanding subsidies, but lost,[30] the court effectively blocking all denominational claims for financial support other than Catholic.

Ontario is the only province with 100% funding for Catholic schools and zero funding for all other religious schools. Quebec and Newfoundland eliminated their constitutionally-protected denominational schools in the late 1990s through constitutional amendments. The law for education in Quebec now focuses on language rather than religion, with students of any religious background now choosing English or French schools.[31] Despite eliminating denominational schools, Quebec also allowed for subsidies to special religious groups, allowing Jewish schools to flourish now with state subsidy.

This effectively undermined the whole purpose of the elimination of the Catholic-Protestant denominational debate, but was a boon to Jewish schools. The lack of state funding in Ontario has led most Jews to attend public high schools, and to a decline in private Jewish schools, where poor salaries mean poor teaching. Quebec now has more Jewish schools than Ontario despite a smaller population. In 1998, $20 million in government grants went to Jewish schooling in Quebec, perhaps a nod to the past conflicts and the shadow of Adrien Arcand, a kind of reparations for past sins.[32] It accounts for the more conservative nature of the Jewish community in Quebec today. Ontario Premier Mike Harris introduced a private school tax-credit for parents, but it was unpopular and the Liberals repealed it in 2003. The number of Jewish schools is much lower in US, where parents are not so worried about the dangers of assimilation, and where government grants are absent.

The restrictions on Jewish life were irksome, but not really so bad. Jews who wished to embrace received English values were welcomed, and reaped the rewards; other Jews, who wished to stand apart, were permitted to do so, but paid a small price in social exclusion. Julius Greenberg might not get a job as a clerk, but John Green would. Many Jews, as did many other immigrants, changed their names. Communist Moishe Wolofsky became Bill Walsh.

As a communist, Walsh was interned from 1939–42 before fighting in the army till 1945. He suffered as a communist, but felt no anti-Jewish discrimination from his comrades or the broader public. The communists were anti-Zionist, rejecting Zionism as a form of fascism like Hitler's Aryanism. Sam Carr attacked Zionists as "inspired by fascists". He and fellow communist Fred Rose carried out their anti-Nazi campaigning through the nonsectarian Canadian League against War and Fascism in the 1930s.

Canada was never an apartheid state, like South Africa or *ante bellum* US, so overt anti-Jewish prejudice was never a serious problem, as Jewish immigrants (or potential immigrants) were just getting the same treatment as other non-WASP immigrants whose customs and demands for special treatment disrupted the dominant social fabric. No Jew was killed as a Jew in Canada, and only one Jew was ever lynched in the US.[33]

The minor problems of prohibition from clubs and resorts to people with Jewish-sounding names or people who looked 'Jewish' or were poor and not dressed according to some implicit dress code, and the problem of employment and housing discrimination, or education restrictions, never seriously stood in the way of Jews prospering, getting education and normal health care, or setting up private businesses. There were minor inconveniences which arose from the specific Jewish tradition of tribalism and being a 'nation within a nation', which other minorities did not have, being ready to integrate and intermarry with other ethnicities.

Countries like Canada and Australia, where natives were pushed aside, and British and later other ethnicities immigrated to displace them, required these settlers to integrate in order to replace the original native cultures with something new and binding, much like Israel is still struggling to do. Jews immigrating to Canada partook of this process from the colonizer's point of view, but brought their own tribal identity *within* the settler community, the 'nation with a nation' being built on the territories of the original native inhabitants.

More than any other ethnic group, east European Jews were "used to minority status, tended to accept their inferior position more readily than did other immigrant groups," avoiding areas where they suspected discrimination might be encountered. They rebuilt their ghetto life, looking for security by moving *en masse*. For instance, in Toronto, they didn't go north and east. "The Ward" (Queen-Gerard, Yonge-Avenue Rd) was their home, until it moved west as the Jewish elite left when the new immigrants came, moving to Rosedale (despite supposed land restrictions) and north of Bloor (Huron and St George-Beverley). "As early as the turn of the century the *Jewish Times*, which reflected the opinion of the acculturated community both in Montreal and in Toronto, had found it necessary to publish a formula to minimize discrimination at summer resorts. Its readers were instructed to 'avoid loudness and assertiveness. To appear well-bred, people shun all display in dress, extravagance in expense and attempts to outshine others. '"[34]

There was an enduring conflict in neighborhoods with an

Orthodox community, demanding silence on Saturdays. At the same time, they were very sensitive to criticism by the dominant group, and obeyed when told to be quiet on Sundays. By 1914, "the image of the Jew as Englishman and solid citizen, which for many years had been projected by Holy Blossom, had been supplanted ... by that of the exotic, boisterous and poverty-stricken east European Jew of the Ward and by the stereotype of the Jewish peddler."[35] Most Gentiles saw only the Ward ghetto from a trolley on Dundas St or the rag peddler.

The Jewish experience in Canada, from the start through the rocky immigrant wave and the world wars, allowed them to blossom. What Jews were *not* able to do was to play a full, participatory role in Canadian society on their own terms.[36] Jews as a minority group stood apart as being more insular, requiring "self-imposed exclusion" in even a secular society, seeing the latter as actually a "liability" in that it implies that all religions are a private concern, that no religion has priority.[37] Ironically, a state where "church and state" are fused (as was feudal Christian or Muslim practice) lets Judaism define itself more concretely, and maintain its sense of identity within society, though at a high cost. If all religions are to be treated the same, as they are in secular society where church and state are separate, then this identity is denied.

The most notable case of the pre-WWII insensitivity to Jews trying to escape the Nazis was the plight of the *MS. St Louis*, a German ocean liner whose captain, Gustav Schröder, set sail against orders on the "voyage of the damned", on May 3, 1939 for Cuba, trying to find homes for 936 Jewish refugees from Germany. After those without valid visas were denied entry to Cuba, the United States had a gunboat following it up the coast so it couldn't land until it reached Halifax, before heading home. The 902 remaining refugees were finally accepted in various European countries (Britain, France, Belgium, Netherlands).

This is considered a shameful act now,[38] but it's not fair to condemn prime minister Mackenzie King for turning the *St. Louis* away. He was following what Washington did and/or told him to do, and was committed to maintaining Canadian unity. Letting them in would have been a sensation, an act of defiance to the US, something that the wily King would or could not do, and which would have caused riots in, at least, Quebec.

The fear was, with the German persecution from 1933 on under Hitler, that any large influx of Jews at this point would be the thin edge of a wedge of a huge wave of desperate, penniless immigrants swamping and drowning the fledgling Gentile British colony, already faced with its own assimilation woes with the US to the south, turning 'Canada' into something unknown and undesirable. There was lingering resentment that Canadian Jews had not fought in proportion to their presence in WWI. Jews were hostile to the war, where Germany, with which most Jews identified, was the enemy, and few indeed enlisted to fight. Many were communists and revolutionary.

There was little sense that the large wave of Jewish immigrants from before WWI had really embraced Canada as their homeland, especially with the new Jewish colony then being built in Palestine. Many Jews moved on to the US, using Canada as a stepping stone. Canada needed committed new Canadians, especially farmers. Jews had proved to be a demanding group, much less open than others to assimilation, as frictions especially in Montreal over education showed. Jewish immigrants who professed to be farmers had almost all headed to Montreal, Toronto and Winnipeg to join the Jewish immigrant ghettos and do city things to survive. There was no chance of King throwing aside the government policy against all immigration, and no reason to think better of Jewish immigrants than past experience had shown.

Petitions in Quebec in the late 1930s against the admission of Jewish refugees were signed by hundreds of thousands, notably the St Jean Baptiste Society's 128,000 signatures calling for no immigration whatsoever. Jewish historiography particularly damns French Canadians, like Esther Delisle's *The Traitor and the Jew* (1993) and Mordechai Richler's *Oh Canada! Oh Quebec! Requiem for a Divided Country* (1992), as if there is only one valid side to the story of the times. Immigration was unpopular, especially in Quebec, where a complete loss of French language and culture was feared. King could not ignore both political reality and the will of the majority. He told a delegation from the Canadian National Committee on Refugees that only a huge public outcry could bring about a liberalization of Canada's immigration policy, and he urged the committee to educate the general public about immigration.

It is not surprising that the government was reluctant to accept a massive increase of Jewish immigrants as WWII approached, given the pervasive unemployment experienced during the Depression. Nor is it surprising that a few years later, after the war, they were welcomed with (more or less) open arms, given their suffering under the Nazis. These policies reflected the thinking of the time. Canada (i.e., King) was just doing what his big brothers the UK/US were doing. There was nothing inherently racist or bigoted about this. All our political leaders failed us in the 1930s for complex reasons, King least of all.

Overall immigration had slowed to a trickle in the 1930s, from 166,783 in 1928 to 14,382 in 1933, under the Conservative R.B. Bennett, and continued to decrease. Tighter regulations meant that, by 1932, only Americans, British subjects and agriculturalists with enough capital to start farming in Canada could be admitted without problem. Immigration was at its most unpopular level since Confederation. Still, 5,000 Jews immigrated in the 1930s, the same percentage in the overall number of immigrants as from 1896 to 1929, when the big wave of Jewish immigrants came.

The persecution of Jews under Hitler led Australia to allow in 20,000, Britain 70,000 and the US 100,000. But their cases were very different. Australia was far away from Europe and North America, and could be sure that the Jews would work hard to become Australians. Britain and the US had an obligation as the ones responsible for allowing Hitler to get away with his victimization and war preparations.

Canadians were being swept up into their own nightmare as the world descended into war two months later. This confirms the operative principle governing Canada's relations with Jews and Israel: do what the US does or tells you to do. Washington too was worried about the blowback from a surge of Jewish refugees, which the *St. Louis* epitomized, and certainly did not need Canada showing it up. Canada was already a postmodern nation, where Canadians have no independent foreign policy. But then neither do Americans have any say in their foreign policy, given the nature of 'postmodern democracy'.

No one asks about the fate of the ghost ship *St. Louis*. Mercifully, only a quarter of those interned died in death camps during World War II. Three-quarters survived. Schroder survived the war in Germany and went on to be feted as one of Israel's "Righteous Among the Nations". The famous voyage was a success after all, bringing the plight of the Jews dramatically to the world's attention and saving many of the refugees' lives.

One of the lucky Jews to make it into Canada was Thomas Bata (1914–2008), who fled Czechoslovakia to England after the Germans invaded in March 1938. Bata chose to continue on to Canada in 1939 because he believed that it incorporated the best of two worlds, or as he phrased it, "a blend of British traditions with the progressiveness and dynamism of the United States." Only 24, he gained admission with the help of the Canadian National Committee on Refugees, which popularized his plight and the took advantage of the immigration loophole for admitting entrepreneurs. Bata and 82 of his key Czech workers settled just outside of Frankford, Ontario, where they laid the groundwork for a business that would employ over 700 workers by the fall of 1940 and become an international success story in the post-war years.

Of the 1,200 Canadians and Americans in the Mackenzie-Papineau Battalion during the Spanish civil war, there were 38 Jewish Canadians (3.2%) and 13 Americans, a respectable showing, after WWI.

When WWII began, clearly putting the Jewish plight as a top priority on the war agenda, there was again, as in WWI, a reluctance by Jews to join. This was embarrassing, given the clear threat to Jews that Canada's declared enemy posed. It frustrated the budding Zionist movement as well, which was eager to have battled-trained Jews ready for the planned creation of Israel, and they worked with the now pro-Zionist Canadian Jewish Congress, headed by Samuel Bronfman in 1939, to promote conscription.

Mackenzie King

Jews enlisted at a slightly lower rate than average, many opting for the "zombies", those who refused to sign up for overseas service (the highest rate of refusal among religious groups). That, and the fact that Jews had a higher education level, meant many were assigned to desk jobs and rear-echelon duties, and that their casualty rate was the lowest (2.6% vs average 4.1%) among soldiers. One reason was the possibility of being captured by Nazis. This was groundless, as Tulchinsky found out when interviewing some Jewish veterans who were captured and treated well by the Germans. In one case, the German police captain asked the prisoner, "Jude?" to which he remained silent, and he wasn't bothered further. In one camp, the German commandant allowed Jewish prisoners to hold Yom Kippur services.[39] Tulchinsky also found no systematic prejudice among Canadian soldiers. A British officer in the RAF singled out Sam Finkelstein and asked if he was Jewish. Why? "Well, Jews are smart, and I want a smart navigator."

Britain's Chamberlain government had appeased Hitler since 1933, leaving Poland open to invasion and the subsequent slaughter of Europe's Jews. The coming disaster was clear to at least Churchill and the communists. FDR called a conference in Evian, France, in 1938 to address the mounting Jewish refugee problem. No one had a proposal. Diplomats at Evian worried that accepting a blank check of Jewish refugees from Hitler would "serve to justify his policy against Jewry." King stated indignantly, "No country should be allowed to throw upon other countries the responsibility of solving its own internal difficulties."[40] The lack of determination at Evian led one Nazi newspaper to gloat, "The Evian Conference serves to justify Germany's policy against Jewry," i.e., the Jews were on their own.

In September 1939, the Nazis offered the Intergovernmental Committee on Refugees all of Poland's Jews, suggesting they be sent to Madagascar, an idea that had been tossed around since 1933. Zionists were quite willing to take up this offer.[41] With the Zionists in league with the Allies (and in touch with the Nazis),[42] it was not completely insane. In 1940, Britain would mobilized hundreds of boats and saved 380,000 troops from the Nazis at "the Miracle of Dunkirk".

British foreign secretary Anthony Eden washed his hands of the bizarre scheme, warning FDR his government "could no longer help solve the refugee problem" because "no country at war with Germany could assist in any way the exodus of enemy nationals from territories under enemy control" or agree to talk about stateless citizens after the collapse of Poland."[43] All too true, but it was Britain's cowardice in the 1930s that had let Hitler get that far.

As the war progressed, nothing much changed. The Bermuda conference in 1943 came to the same conclusion. No miracle for Jews in the works, only the possibility of setting up some camps in North Africa to receive refugees from Portugal, the convocation of yet another conference, and a joint declaration that refugees were a problem for the United Nations. The invasion of Normandy would come in a few months and the fate of the remaining Nazi prisoners, Jews and non-Jews, would have to await the collapse of the Reich. Canada stayed in the sidelines as this tragedy played itself out, wondering about what to do with 250,000 Displaced Persons looking for new homes after the war, 30% of them Jewish.

Israel as an Escape Clause for Unwanted Refugees

Adolph Eichmann complained during his trial in 1961 in Jerusalem that no countries wanted the Jews in the 1930s. During the war, Franco issued passports to 600 Jews of Spanish descent though they never had been in Spain. "If only one could be sure they wouldn't be liquidated," opined Franco as he let them in.[44] Ironically, the mass murderer Eichmann actually saved thousands of select Jews for emigration in 1944. He admired the Zionists as idealists like himself, who thought in "national terms".[45]

Chaim Weizmann, President of the Zionist Organization and later Israel's first president, was busy lobbying the Allies, pointing out not just the slaughter of Jews, but the advantage to the Allies of supporting the creation of Israel. He baldly told Vincent Massey, Canada's High Commissioner to London, in 1945: "Canadians are unlikely to welcome Jewish mass immigration and from the Jewish point of view it is far more desirable to resettle immigration on a solid national basis in a Jewish state rather than to send them where they are bound to create new problems."[46] Canada's immigration chief, Frederick Blair, vilified now as an antisemite, would have smiled, as Weizmann was admitting what Blair had been saying all along.

There was no popular position in Canada on the creation of a Jewish state, other than among the Zionist minority among Canada's Jews. It was seen as a dangerous anomaly, a racial state at a time when the Aryan racial state was the scourge of the world. CCF head J.S. Woodsworth, a former Methodist minister, saw through the pro-Zionist hypocrisy: "It was easy for Canadians, Americans and the British to agree to a Jewish colony, as long as it was somewhere else. Why 'pick on the Arabs' other than for 'strategic' and 'imperialistic' considerations?" The 1942 CCF convention read, "The Jewish problem can be solved only in a socialist and democratic society, which recognized no racial or class differences."[47]

To prod Canada into action on refugees, both Jewish and non-Jewish, the US and Britain proposed Canada as an executive member of the Intergovernmental Committee on Refugees as decided at the Bermuda conference. This was good PR for King, as it showed Canada in the important inner circle of postwar international planning, and provided a weapon against those protesting Canada was not doing enough for refugees.

Already in May 1945, External Affairs was shopping for

good refugees, visiting camps and sizing up the applicants. Massey particularly liked the Balts, especially the Latvians. "Clean, hard working, conscientious and resourceful, they are very anxious to be employed in some way, and more than others they put this desire into practice." Jews were everywhere at bottom of the ranking, below Poles and Ukrainians. Major Bordet complained that "after two years doing absolutely nothing, their apathy is amazing. They are unwilling to face the hardships of life in a war-ravaged country. These people might be the most worthy of our sympathy but are the most undesirable people as immigrants."[48] Colonel Scott, of the Canadian Military Mission also liked the Balts and was not impressed by the Jews. "They are not popular, but how far this is anti-Semitism and how far based upon practical experience is hard to say. No administrator talks like an anti-Semite, though some of them are strong against Zionists. It is universally stated that the Jews are physically lazy, and (though not so universally) they will not even do their own camp work. They are great black marketeers, but whether worse, or only more patient than the Poles, is hard to say."[49]

Only UNRRA's Charity Grant argued in a convoluted way in their favor: "The very resourcefulness necessary to survive gave rise to much of the anti-Semitism even then flourishing in Europe, yet it was this very resourcefulness, if transplanted to a friendly environment, that would make these Jews strong, independent and successful settlers. Where can they go and what can they do? No one wants them."[50]

Originally, the plan was *repatriation* of everyone wherever possible. This was the Soviet position, and their DPs returned home and adapted, though that was no picnic for those who had worked for the Germans. But no refugees wanted to return to war-devastated lands, and Jews were able to convince the Allies that "while presumably safe from physical violence, Jews who had been victims of German persecution in concentration camps could no longer expect to be spiritually at home in Germany or live normal lives here."[51] Of course, everyone wanted to go to Canada or the US. So the massive transfer of DPs become the central concern of Canadian officials well into the 1950s. Given the Blairite suspicion of the value of Jewish immigrants, they were initially excluded (though not officially) from bulk-labor programs in forestry, mining and carpentry, where it was assumed they would probably not finish the 2-year required work assignment and instead slip away to the big city. Jews were noted as tailors, and finally were accepted in the needle trade and the quota was pushed up to 60%.

"Folk wisdom understood Jews as clannish, aggressive, cosmopolitan. Jews, many concluded, 'did not fit in', their political sensitivities were suspect, their loyalties forever in doubt, their religion based on the continued rejection of Christ, their sole preoccupation, making and hoarding money."[52] Jewish Canadian historian Irving Abella, author of *None is Too Many: Canada and the Jews of Europe 1933-1948* (1983), the source for the above citations, doesn't dispute this "folk wisdom" and his praise of Canada is faint. King had been faced with the economic crisis, "the vocal anti-Jewish sentiment of Quebec politicians, the government's fear of Canada being made the dumping ground of any British or American scheme to resettle Jews," and the worry that any "momentary sympathy ... would quickly be washed away", leaving King and Canada high and dry.[53] "Canadian Jewry sought to tap the wellspring of human kindness, only to find it dry. Prepared to eulogize the Jews, [Canada] was not prepared to offer them a new home."[54]

Abella refers to King and the time's "virulent anti-Semitism"[55] yet recounts how King personally expedited the case of Carl Goldenberg, a Montreal lawyer whose family faced death if they were not granted a visa within the next 48 hours. He wrote King in desperation after his appeals to the immigration official stalled. King acted immediately and saved Goldenberg's family. No doubt Abella took offense at King's reference in his personal diary to Goldwin Smith's characterization of Jews as "a poison in the veins of a community".[56] After decades of problems with Jewish immigration, the Jews' tragic fate in WWII, and their involvement in the Soviet spy ring exposed by Soviet embassy worker Igor Gouzenko in 1946, implicating several prominent Jews, including MP Fred Rose, it is hardly surprising that King would reflect on Smith's eerie prediction of trouble as he witnessed the mass immigration of Jews in the 1890s. (See below re Smith and Rose.)

Abella's charges are hardly fair. He quotes "folk wisdom" without admitting the grain of truth behind it. Jews were a problematic immigrant group from the start, energetic, smart, but demanding, tribal, refusing to assimilate, to become Jewish Canadians or merely Canadians. And despite Canadian officials' reservations, Canada's contribution to settling Jewish refugees 1946–50 was outdone only by Israel and the US.[57] Canada's refugee quota by 1948 was 180,000 immigrants, including 8,000 Jewish DPs. By 1948, with Israel having won its war of independence and having seized much of Palestine, the road to immigration to Israel was open. 13,500–20,000 refugees arrived in Israel every month from 1948 to 1950, when most of Europe's Jewish refugees were finally settled. In 1948 a new immigration act erased any official reservations about the desirability of Jewish immigrants, and they came without any restrictions.

Post-WWII: Resurgent Identity

After WWII, "Antisemitism does not present an immediate menace to the Jewish community today," wrote Saul Hayes, the best known public spokesman in the Jewish community, in May 1949.[58] At the same time, Canadians seemed to prefer almost any type of immigrant—including their erstwhile enemies, the Germans—to Jews. A Canadian Gallup poll in 1946 found half of Canadians held negative views of Jews. Only the Japanese scored higher (60%). Jews "continued to live in a profoundly Jewish solitude, both by choice as well as for reasons of exclusion."[59] In what many Jews considered an affront, German scientists (Nazi members by definition) were settled in Canada at the request of the US and Britain to keep them out of Soviet hands. Even a few war criminals slipped in.[60]

At the same time, 64% of Canadians approved of legislation to combat discrimination in employment, which came to pass for all Canadians in the 1950s. The 1944 Ontario Racial Discrimination Act declared illegal "restrictive covenants barring Jews and other minority groups from acquiring and owning certain properties, or the use of language referring to 'Jews or other persons of objectionable nationality.'"[61] In 1955 Nathan Phillips became mayor of Toronto, and the last restrictions on land sales and club membership were annulled. In 1945 only a handful of Jews were on university faculties; by 1961, there were 132; by 1971, there were 1,280, a tenfold increase.

The creation of Israel should have reduced the need for Jewish immigration to Canada. But as most Jews looking for a new home were still not Zionist, wanting, like all other poor Europeans, to come to the generic 'promised land' of Canada/ US, Jewish immigration increased after WWII. In the post-WWII flood of immigrants, Jews were now welcomed – 46,000 from 1946 to 1960, mostly refugees from Europe and north Africa,[62] a far higher proportion of post-war immigration than the 160,000 to the US. By 1990, Holocaust survivors accounted for 30% of Jews in Canada vs 8% in the US. Half came to Toronto and a third to Montreal. In the 1960s–70s, there was a new wave, including South African Jews. About 30,000 Jews immigrated to Canada from 1981 to 1991, mainly from the former Soviet Union, Israel, South Africa and the US.[63]

World Jewish population is estimated at 20 million (0.2% of the population), with 6.4 million in Israel, 6.8 million in the US (2.6% of the US population)) and 392,000 in Canada (1.2%). Canada is now home to the fifth largest Jewish community in the world, following the US, Israel, the former USSR and France.[64] Jewish immigration continues, mostly from France, Israel and South Africa.

For Jewish historians, formerly "blighted with an oppressive anti-Semitism in which Jews were the pariahs of Canadian society, demeaned, despised, and discriminated against," Canada was now "far different—generous, open, decent, human."[65] Jewish scholars and leaders in both the US and Canada recognize that Jews in Canada are more 'Jewish', less assimilated than in the US. Canada was taking in proportionately more Jews than the US now. In 1990, only 10% of US Jews were immigrants, compared to 30% in Canada, where they were providing a constant stream to reinforce tribal solidarity. Canada's policy of multiculturalism encouraged ethnic identity unlike the US 'melting pot'. Canada is 10% the size of the population of the US, and though Jews are a smaller percentage in Canada than in the US (1.1% vs 3%), their outsize presence in the economy and culture, alongside the larger, more assimilated Jewish population in the US, reinforces their sense of identity.

As Jewishness penetrates mainstream culture through the Hollywood melting pot, all North Americans in a sense were assimilating Jewish (Yiddish) culture. Assimilation works both ways as multiculturalists argue, the Gentiles absorbing the 'creative spark' of Jews, the Jews enjoying the advantages of freedom in the broader society, no longer so isolated and limited by the restrictions of a narrow tribal outlook. Potentially win-win without the complication that the sudden dual loyalty introduced with the creation of Israel.

Jews finally achieved all the perks of Canada, especially in education:

- 10% of Jews earn more than $75,000 vs 2.6% on average.
- 40% of Toronto's doctors and dentists were Jewish in 1991. At the same time only 13% are in manual trades vs 41% on average.
- 50% of Jews age fifteen and over were either enrolled in

university or had completed a BA in 1991 vs 20% on average.
- 16% of Jews had an MA, MD, or PhD in 1991 vs 4% on average.[66]

Israel as the 'Promised Land'

The creation of the State of Israel in 1948 marked the crowning success of the Zionist movement and initiated a period of gradually closer ties between the new "Israeli" nationality and Canadian Jews. By default, after 1948, Canadian Jews were henceforth *de facto* dual citizens of Canada and Israel in the eyes of Israeli leaders, whether or not they opted for an Israeli passport. Nazi racism had been defeated, but, in the state it had spawned, it looked like a Jewish version was in the works, as Palestinians were dispossessed and pushed into refugee camps while their land and property was seized by Jews and Israeli Arabs were denied full citizenship.

Overnight, on May 14, 1948, virtually all Jews everywhere became Zionists. Zionism became the Jews' "civil religion", more so in Canada than in the US.[67] With the exception of the Jewish communists, all Jewish organizations, be they secular, reform or Orthodox, became Zionist, and cultivated close relations with Israel. The Canada-Israel Committee was set up as a Jewish mouthpiece to inform Canadians about Israel. Specialized organizations connected Canadian Jews with particular parts of Israeli society—universities, hospitals, social welfare projects. Visits to Israel became more and more frequent, often in the form of sponsored tours, cultivating bonding between Canadian Jews and their second 'homeland'. Most adult Canadian Jews have visited Israel; many have visited more than once; many have relatives there.[68]

Among non-Jews, there was little enthusiasm in Canada when Israel declared itself a state in 1948. The United Church was vocal in its opposition to the creation of Israel. "Much of the sympathy for the Jews which was so general and genuine has been lost by their actions since the close of the war."[69] "Zionist insistence on the implementation of the Balfour Declaration according to their wishes will lead to a new focal centre of antisemitism, not alone in the Near East, but in the whole world. Let's not have to say that 'the Jews seem to have a positive genius for making enemies".[70]

Mackenzie King feared Canada would be drawn into an increasingly violent conflict between the British, Jews and Arabs. Ottawa withheld *de facto* recognition of Israel until December 1948, after King retired. Israel failed in its first attempt to gain admission to the UN because Canada abstained when the issue came to a vote in the Security Council. Canada granted *de jure* recognition only in May 1949, once the Jewish state had been admitted to the UN.[71]

But the enthusiasm for Israel meant that Jews were more visibly seen as prey to dual loyalty, perceived as outsiders. Many were apprehensive about being seen as advocating too aggressively on behalf of a foreign country. Thus the need for a new relationship with the state, the "time honored tradition of entrusting a handful of prominent *shtadlans* to make Israel's case in the corridors of power."[72] This special relationship with the state was what worried King, but he would only admit it in his private diaries. Only the United Church had courage enough to raise the danger of Israel as a Jewish state publicly. (See below.)

Almost two-thirds of Canadians have been indifferent or non-committal from the start, and sympathy for Israel vs the Palestinians has always been evenly split. Among those Canadians who consider themselves most familiar with the Israeli-Palestinian dispute, 32% express sympathy towards the Palestinians while only 26% are sympathetic towards Israel.[73] This has been a sore point with Zionists, unable to drum up enthusiasm despite their flag waving. Legally Jews had never had it so good anywhere in now "multicultural" Canada, but Canadians are just not interested in Jewish matters, whether in Canada or in the Jewish homeland. Underlying resentments remained, but it was increasingly difficult to express them publicly.

In the 1930s, it was not clear if Israel would be a national home for all Jews or only a refuge for the persecuted. With the creation of Israel, the Zionists insisted it was the national home of every Jew in the entire world. In 1938, the Zionist Organization of Canada stated, "Zionism strives to establish a Home for the Jewish people and not a refuge. The task of the Zionist movement involves more than the settlement of refugees."[74] An intense propaganda campaign still continues today urging Canadian Jews to perform aliyah[75] with mixed success.

Canada is still the preferred home for Jews. Toronto has become the 'safe haven' within the Canadian 'save haven', the 'Mecca' for ex-Soviet and Israeli Jews. Toronto has the largest Jewish community, about half in all Canada (188,000). The two decades since the collapse of the Soviet Union saw twice as many Jews coming to Toronto as in the previous two decades (1990–2011: 33,000), the largest arrival from a single country or region to Toronto since the pre-1921 immigration wave.

Many educated and skilled Israeli youth emigrate to Canada. "Canada, especially, had become their 'golden realm'. The land of promise in Israel, the promised land. Israelis are immigrating to maple-leaf territory in rapidly increasing numbers, reversing the process that created a Jewish state after 2,000 yrs of exile," wrote Reuben Slonim in the *Telegram* in 1965. "A symbol of a new start for the disappointed and the disillusioned." There were 1,500 Israeli immigrants to Canada in 1967 alone, even as Israel was taking over all of Palestine and Sinai. Slonim recounts a popular joke about Canada in Israel in the 1960s. Moses was noted as a stammerer. The Lord asks him, 'Where do you wanted the children of Israel to settle?' Moses stutters, "Can ... Can ... Can ..."[76]

Of the estimated 1,000,000 Israelis who have emigrated *from* Israel up to 2003, two-thirds have migrated to the US and an additional one-sixth have settled in Canada. That means 750,000 in the US, about 12.5% of the Jewish population of Israel. For Canada, that means 167,000, a third of Canadian Jews. Other estimates are as high as 1.2 million emigres in Canada.[77]

Yerida (emigration) skyrocketed in the mid-1980s, due to a combination of the effects of the 1982 Lebanon War, exposure of Israeli tourists to other cultures and new opportunities in other western countries. In 1984 and 1985, more Jews emigrated from Israel than immigrated to it. The American *Moment* magazine editor Leonard Fein said that "the disturbing data on emigration from Israel" were only one part of "an internal Jewish malady. . . [a]ssimilation in this community, apathy and ignorance, fatigue and demoralization." Former Knesset Speaker Avraham Burg caused a stir in 2004 by telling an interviewer that he had a French passport and that "whoever can" should likewise seek a second citizenship.[78] Stephen Walt, professor of international relations at Harvard University suggests that "the Zionist ideal is losing hold within Israel itself" because the Israeli government "endlessly delays the [peace] process."[79]

The rate of immigration of young Israelis to Canada has tripled since 1970 (pre-1970 1,385, 2000–2011 3,900), half indirectly from the ex-Soviet Union (7,965, 47% of Jewish immigrants to Canada). This surge in immigration suggests that Soviet and Israeli Jews prefer Canada to Israel, which suggests that the hostility and tensions in the Middle East far outweigh any perceived racism in Canada, and that Canada is the preferred 'promised land'. Israeli migration to Canada continues, with Canadian Israelis, "reported to be 'completely alienated' from the organized Jewish communities",⁸⁰ i.e., these Israelis are assimilating as Canadians, Jewish Canadians, making Jewishness a secondary signifier in their lives.

Second generation Canadian Sephardi youth feel more affinity with Italians and Portuguese than with Israeli or Canadian Jewish organizations. Quebec is the preferred destination for Sephardi immigrants from north Africa and France, half marrying non-Jews. They want to integrate with Quebec French culture, and don't identify with Anglo-Jews. 20% expressed outright dislike of the Ashkenazi, seeing Canadian Jews as less observant and cold.⁸¹ The Ashkenazi dismiss them as Arabs, primitive, but they are proud of their Arab heritage and culture. They have no identification with Israel, don't consider making aliyah, as opposed to Ashkenazi Canadians, about 350 of whom made aliyah in 2016.⁸²

Given the existence of Israel, the logic should have been (should be?) for Jews to emigrate there from Europe, rather than to Canada. In the past decade, there has been a sharp increase in emigration from France to both Canada and Israel. The extreme actions of Zionists in France, exemplified in the *Charlie Hebdo* scandal,⁸³ which turned into a tragedy in 2014, show how aliyah can be 'encouraged'. For years, Israel has been trying to coax European Jews to immigrate, and now has succeeded, with French emigration to Israel increasing while it falls from all other countries. France has a complex history of friction with ex-colonies, especially Algeria. 12% of the French population are Muslim, and the educated French have an enduring love of Arab culture. They are just dismissed by the Zionists as inherently bigoted, which only makes anti-Jewish sentiment worse, but encourages aliyah.

Canada has a cleaner slate, and remains the preferred destination for Jews. In 1995, a Canadian Federal Court decision stated that Jews from any country could *not* claim refugee status in Canada because they have automatic citizenship in Israel, underlining the anomaly of the Jewish state—but immigration to Canada by Israelis and Jews proceeds normally. Some estimates claim that more than 100,000 Israelis live in Toronto alone, though exact numbers are not possible to determine, as many Israelis come and go frequently, with a broad network of friends and relatives in the more peaceful Canada, a welcome 'haven' from the Israeli 'haven'.

This growing assimilation is happening among non-Israeli Jewish Canadians too. The current intermarriage rate is 20%, an increase of almost 70% since 1991. In cases where both spouses are less than 30 years of age, the level of intermarriage is 28.3%. A third of intermarried children are identified by their parents as Jews; half are assigned no religious affiliation.[84] This is still lower than in the US, where the intermarriage rate is 50%.

As Jews become more secular, Jewish culture loses its tribalism, emphasizing "its universal values – love and reverence for life, human worth and dignity, humility, learning and joy – as essential elements of identity in the modern world."[85] This process recalls the vision of the communists in the 1920s–30s and the Soviet policy of assimilation, with Jews embracing Yiddish language and culture, while still seeking integration into the countries where they lived.

A New York spokesman for the Jewish left, Irving Howe, echoed Hannah Arendt, when he forecast the end of secular Jewish culture at a lecture at the University of Toronto in 1979. The Holocaust and dispersal of the ghetto tradition "destroyed the cultural well that had fostered this tradition, and North American Jews had fallen victim to the 'enticements of liberal democracy'."

Many Jews observe religious externalities but do not actively engage in religious life. Others champion Israel but "this translated into only weak support for substantive Jewish continuity."[86] The end of the Canada-Israel Committee in 2011 symbolized that the days of Zionism are numbered. Zionism is "largely a spectator sport ... for diaspora Jews, cheering—and occasionally heckling from the sidelines."[87] Israeli Zionists lecture their American cousins: "Your duty is to live in the land of Israel, but since you prefer the fleshpots of North America, pay for the privilege."[88]

Quebec's 'Jewish Problem'

Quebec's resistance to special treatment of Jews is seen by Jews as bigotry, whereas the French see themselves as the first Canadians—after the First Nations—needing special treatment in the Anglo-dominated world, and resent the attention given to this small, late-comer minority with its own special demands. Canada was founded as a binational country of English and French, later acknowledging the natives as the real 'first nations', and the assumption is that other immigrants will be grateful for their welcome and will assimilate into either the French or English communities, as part of "multicultural" Canada. Jews were demanding to be put on the same level as French Canadians in the French province, and were bound to face resistance. Canada's compromise since WWII is a 'good' multiculturalism. Everyone enjoys equal civil rights for all, Jews included (but not above).

The heyday of anti-Jewish sentiment in Quebec, like elsewhere, was in the 1920–30s, which exacerbated the problems of education, and the French concern about the largely Anglo immigration of the past two centuries—now here were these new special Anglos concentrating in Montreal, with their special demands. Adrien Arcand (1899–1967), a self-proclaimed fascist, was the chief rabble-rouser, who published and edited several anti-Jewish newspapers during this period, most notably *Le Goglu, Le Miroir, Le Chameau, Le Patriote, Le Fasciste Canadien* and *Le Combat National*. He was a brilliant journalist and charismatic speaker, but his bark was worse than his bite, and his star faded with the outbreak of WWII. He was interned during WWII as a fascist, but was never prosecuted for his anti-Jewish speeches.

The negative legacy of Quebec-Jewish relations from the school controversy of the 1920–30s and the Arcand period no doubt accounts for the subsequent generosity of the Quebec government from the 1960s, providing government support for Jewish schools, Canada's only province where Jewish schools are flourishing.

Now, it is the Jews' current nemesis, Muslims, who through sheer numbers are eclipsing the Jewish minority in Canada, especially in Quebec, where cultural clashes feed the 'antisemitic' accusation, despite the real discrimination being against Muslims, rather than Jews. The Quebec City murder of 6 Muslims at their mosque in January 2017 shows that Quebec still has a problem, but now a Muslim one. In 2011, there were one million Muslims (3.2% of the population) making them the second largest religion after Christianity. In Greater Montreal, 6% of the population is Muslim, in the Greater Toronto Area, 7.7%.

Arab Muslim and Sephardi Jewish immigrants in Quebec have more in common with each other than Sephardi and Ashkenazi Jews, and both embrace French Canadian culture, adding an Arab flavor. Many Muslims come to Quebec from French-speaking African countries, especially Algeria, Morocco, Rwanda and Burundi. The Anglo and east European Jews have always had a problem in French Canada. They are still the Other to the French. Now they are eclipsed in French Canada by Muslims, Hindus, Sikhs, with only Israel as the source of resentment of Jews by Quebecois.

A exodus of 30,000–40,000 Jews from Quebec took place in

the 1990s over fears of Quebec independence (most moved to Toronto). Parti Quebecois Premier Jacques Parizeau hinted that the Jews ("money and the ethnic vote") were responsible for the narrow 'no' vote. Indeed, Montreal Jews were against Quebec independence. Sympathy for the Palestinians was always strong in Quebec, which worried the conservative Jewish elite in case of independence. After 1967, members of the separatist Quebec movement sided with the Arabs in the conflict, and began to see Canada and Quebec as a kind of replay of Israel and Palestine. Some Front de libération du Québec militants went to the PLO for guerrilla training. Canada's kowtowing to Israeli colonialism fed separatists' anger, and it was only logical for Canada (even more so a Quebec nation) to distance itself from the world's pariah.

Once again, Jews left because they couldn't fit in. In Montreal, "the Jewish community remains largely isolated from and mysterious to the surrounding francophone milieu."[89] This of course is the Anglo-Jewish perspective, as the French-speaking Jewish Quebeckers integrate and assimilate.

The Formation of Jewish/ Zionist Organizations

Prior to the creation of Israel, Zionist 'soft power' relied mainly on calling people "anti-Semite", a kind of silver bullet. 'The slur is mightier than the sword.' This soft power became more systemized after WWII, channeled into various political lobbies, institutions, museums and other public displays.

Given the success that Jews have had in Canada, especially since WWII, it is puzzling that "antisemitism" studies and literature dissecting this canard continue to multiply. The campaign to fight what had become "a marginal phenomenon ... unacceptable in mainstream society,"[90] reached the highest political levels in 2009 with the creation of the Inter-parliamentary Coalition for Combating Antisemitism (ICCA), a coalition of parliamentarians from around the world. Its first annual conference was held in London, its second in Ottawa in 2010, hosted by the **Canadian All-Party Parliamentary Inquiry into Antisemitism.**

The London Declaration on Combating Antisemitism was signed by former British Prime Minister Gordon Brown and by several prime ministers across the globe and more than 600 parliamentarians worldwide. The Canadian 'All-Party' Parliamentary Inquiry was boycotted by the Bloc Quebecois, which complained it was one-sided, and quit. Its 2011 report stated "Canada is turning into a hotbed of antisemitic activity, especially on university campuses."[91] It quoted 2011 Statistics Canada's finding that there was a 42% increase in hate crimes and a 71% increase in religiously motivated crimes targeting Jews. So is "antisemitism" "marginalized, unacceptable" or growing in leaps and bounds? And if the latter, why?

The many recent institutions devoted solely to "antisemitism" have their legacy in Jewish organizations founded in the 19th century. The oldest transnational Jewish defense organization is B'nai Brith International (from Hebrew "Children of the Covenant", 1843). It is predominantly North American and has become the most powerful Jewish organization within the American Israel Public Affairs Committee (AIPAC, 1951), the most important pro-Israel lobbying group. In the first two decades of the 20th century B'nai Brith launched the Anti-Defamation League (ADL, 1913) and Hillel (1923). A Canadian branch was set up in 1875, and it remains the most aggressive organization pursuing "antisemitism", keeping track of any incidents which smack of anti-Jewish prejudice.

The Canadian Jewish Congress was founded in 1915 and is the main umbrella Canadian Jewish organization (renamed, significantly, Centre for Israeli and Jewish Affairs [(CIJA) in 2011)]. Zionist activities now are conducted through CJC/CIJA. The pro-communist United Jewish Peoples' Order (UJPO) was founded in 1926, the only anti-Zionist organization. It was expelled by CJC president Samuel Bronfman in 1951, readmitted in 1995, and expelled again in 2011 for its outspoken criticism of Israel.

These and other[92] groups, a confusing, overlapping array, are the main Zionist organizations. As the pro-Soviet Jewish movement and UJPO faded, its critical mantle was picked up by Independent Jewish Voices (IJV, 2008) (see Chapter 9.).

There are unashamedly terrorist ones too, heirs to the notorious Lehi (1940–48, aka Stern Gang), Haganah (1921–48), Mossad (1949) and other Israeli formations. Among openly functioning Jewish terrorist organizations in the West, the Jewish Defense League is the best known, operating in Europe, North America and South Africa. Founded at the height of Great Game II by Rabbi Meir Kahane[93] in New York City in 1968, the JDL's purpose is purportedly to protect Jews from local manifestations of antisemitism, but instead it became a loud proponent of anticommunism and Islamophobia, bombing Soviet and Arab properties in the US, and targeting for assassination alleged "enemies of the Jewish people", ranging from Arab-American political activists to neo-Nazis. In "Terrorism 2000/2001", the FBI referred to the JDL as a "violent extremist Jewish organization", though it still operates openly in the US and Canada. This marks a new strategy for Israel, a hands-off openly terrorist international Israeli-first organization, a luxury the US itself can't afford in pursuit of its own imperial goals. The JDL operates sort-of openly in Canada, its presence seen, but its activities not necessarily acknowledged, clearly operating in Israel's interests.

The plethora of Zionist organizations locally and internationally is impressive, but hide the hollowness of Zionism, flush with the money and media access of the diaspora Jewish elite, comfortable in their own 'promised lands' outside Israel (but enthusiastically supporting it), puffing itself up to look powerful, but mostly on paper, as it excites passion only among a fraction of one percent of Canadians.

The above organizations, with the exception of the UJPO and IJV, are the activist arm of the Zionists. They have been joined by new museums, institutes and foundations, providing vehicles for outreach. Holocaust museums and monuments have sprouted in the West, mostly from the 1990s. There are at least 6 in Canada:

- Holocaust Memorial sculpture (Edmonton),
- Montreal Holocaust Memorial Centre (1979),
- National Holocaust Monument (planned) (Ottawa),
- Sarah and Chaim Neuberger Holocaust Education Centre (Toronto, 1994),
- Vancouver Holocaust Education Centre (1994),
- Canadian Museum for Human Rights (Winnipeg, 2014).[94]

The Canadian War Museum in Ottawa planned to include a holocaust section in 1977, but veterans protested and the idea was abandoned.

There are 60 Holocaust museums in the US, 54 in France, 11 in Israel (including the only one commemorating homosexuals killed), 7 in Germany. In comparison, there is no museum devoted to the onslaught suffered by indigenous nations in Canada or the US.[95]

Foundations to study "antisemitism" have been established, funded by Jewish philanthropists and the Canadian government. The Canadian Institute for Jewish Research, Canadian Friends of the Simon

Wiesenthal Center, Honest Reporting Canada, the Canadian Institute for the Study of Antisemitism (CISA) and others award scholarships and facilitate public education on the subject of "antisemitism in its classic and contemporary forms" and instruct students on the Holocaust. CISA sponsors the leading academic journal on the subject, *Antisemitism Studies*, which is published by Indiana University Press and is edited by the Institute's director, Catherine Chatterley, who teaches history at the University of Manitoba. In *The Antisemitic Imagination*,[96] Chatterley argues that "the Jew" is "a libelous fictitious abstraction first generated and then propagated by Christian Europe, and must be uprooted from our imagination in the interests of truth, morality, and justice."[97]

The Holocaust had been avoided by Jews after 1948 as a shameful legacy, more a critique of Jewish failure than part of the greater tragedy of WWII. The Eichmann trial in 1961 was used to justify Israel's massive land grab in 1948, but interest in WWII as hasbarah began only after the 1967 war, as Israeli leaders worried that they had risen too high and risked a fall, as Ginsberg argues. In 1972, the CJC establish standing committees on the Holocaust, erecting the first Holocaust memorial in 1977 (in Montreal).

Holocaust studies are included in all schools now. Holocaust Education Week has been held each November in Toronto since 1979 on the anniversary of Kristallnacht. Israeli and Jewish Studies courses are found at 40 universities, funded in part by Jewish philanthropists, in the first place, Samuel Bronfman and Peter Munk.[98] The first Jewish studies program was launched at McGill in 1969, which has the only full Department of Jewish Studies. The Israeli nationalist tilt of McGill's Jewish studies is actually inscribed in a major funding agreement. In 2012 the estate of Simon and Ethel Flegg contributed $1 million to McGill's Jewish Studies department partly for an "education initiative in conjunction with McGill Hillel."

The University of Toronto has a Jewish Studies program, and York and Concordia operate a joint Centre for Canadian Jewish Studies.[99] Inaugurating the Andrea and Charles Bronfman Chair in Israeli Studies at the University of Toronto in 1997, Bronfman enthused, "The miracle of modern Israel is of broad interest. Andy and I are happy that students at the U of T will have the opportunity to delve into the social, political and economic revolutions that have taken place within this remarkable society." Bronfman added yet another center, the Anne Tanenbaum Centre for Jewish Studies in 2008, helped by more millions from Larry and Ken Tanenbaum.

University of Manitoba sends 40 students to Ben-Gurion

University each year. The University of Manitoba's Asper Centre for Entrepreneurship has an exchange with Tel-Aviv University. CIJA hosted a week-long tour of Israel in 2008 for presidents of Ryerson, University of Waterloo, University of Toronto/Montreal/Saskatchewan/Ottawa/Kings' College/McGill. University of Toronto's president Naylor returned and pushed to scuttle (unsuccessfully) Israeli Apartheid Week on campus.[100] The most prominent 'junket hasbarah' organization is financed by Bronfman, who founded Birthright Israel in 2000, offering 10-day free education tours every summer for all Canadian Jews interested. Half of Canadian Jewish youth go to Israel gratis on group trips, 80% whose "main motive is to have fun," 46% "to see the homeland of the Jewish people".

There are also educational tours to Holocaust sites.[101] Some worry about the effect on young children of "heavy-handed shock treatment. It socializes Jewish children into a fearsome commitment to survival," reducing the "complex rich Jewish heritage into a vale of tears." They complain that the Holocaust is "now a trendy, low-cost way for some largely secular Jewish intellectuals to identify publicly as Jews. ... This 'Holocaust chic' is the ultimate in political correctness for Jews who do not want to be too Jewish."[102]

The agenda is militantly pro-Zionist, condemning Canadian social history and exonerating Jews and Israel of any contribution to what Chatterley sees as an eternally present and growing problem of anti-Jewish prejudice. Part of this offensive is to paint Canada as a nation of bigots – until tragedy struck and Jewish influence became strong and fought off the bigotry. The goal of the educational offensive is to capture both Jewish and Gentile minds in the school years, teaching them the truth about Jews as understood by Zionists. Effectively: Zionist 'soft power' for Canadians, colonizing their minds, vs the 'hard power' deployed against Palestinians, colonizing their lands.

This soft power is devastating for many Canadians. When Pierre Lacert complained about the lack of courtesy of his Hassidic neighbors, they accused him of antisemitism and sued him. Though he was exonerated by the Quebec Court of Appeals, he was vilified in the *National Post*,[103] and the taint remains. "Not many things as damaging to one's reputation as being called anti-Semitic ... not even pedophilia."[104]

But Zionists take no prisoners. And they actively harness Gentiles to prepare Gentiles to engage in future battles against anyone critical of Israel (i.e., antisemites). Elizabeth and Tony Comper started Fighting Anti-Semitism Together (FAST), a coalition of supposedly non-Jewish business leaders and prominent individuals. FAST sponsored a lesson plan for Grades 6 to 8 called "Choose Your Voice: Antisemitism in Canada". Over 2.4 million students in 19,000 schools have been through the FAST program. A year ago FAST added "Voices into Action", an anti-racism lesson for Canadian high schools that devotes a third of its plan to the Nazi Holocaust in Europe. The Toronto couple also sponsored the Elizabeth and Tony Comper Interdisciplinary Center for the Study of Antisemitism and Racism at the University of Haifa in Israel. The Center operates an online Ambassadors Program, which "gives students intellectual material and technical skills to combat online the global boycott, divestment and sanctions anti-Israel movement."[105]

Tony and Elizabeth Comper were/are Anglicans. Elizabeth taught at the Beth Rivkah Academy for Jewish girls in Montreal. Tony earned his millions as CEO of the BMO Financial Group in 1999–2004, where he was criticized for his high salary and bonus. His policy of "service shrinkage", or decreasing the number of services offered for the same banking fee, attracted criticism from customers. In 2006, on his watch, BMO was forced to refund overcharges on mortgage payments of approximately $250 per customer.

Launched in 1982 at the time of the Keegstra and Zundel trials (see Chapter 7), B'nai Brith's League for Human Rights annual *Audit of Antisemitic Incidents* purports to document all antisemitic incidents in Canada. It shows a peak 331 incidents in 1995. Examples of antisemitic incidents include:

- A Jewish student assaulted in the laundry room of his residence at the University of Toronto.[106]
- An attempt to boycott an Israeli brand of hummus at the University of Ottawa cafeteria. It monitors teachers for any anti-Israeli activities.
- A teacher was hounded in 2013 simply for posting a link to an Iranian website, and to an article by Richard Falk.
- After unidentified "activists" replaced the flag of Israel with an Algerian one during a multicultural festival at the University of Ontario Institute of Technology (UOIT) in 2017, B'nai Brith worked closely with the administration in an effort to hold those responsible to account.

It succeeded in having Nadia Shoufani suspended in Mississauga in 2016 for telling demonstrators at an al-Quds Day rally that Palestinians have a right to resist the occupation. B'nai Brith Canada accused her of "glorifying terrorists". Its 2014 ad about antisemitism in the *Jewish Tribune* was titled "Almost 4 Million Canadians Are Afflicted by This Disease".[107]

A few brave Jews have protested against this hounding. French Jewish academics Esther Benbassa and Jean-Christophe Attias stated, "Relentlessly condemning every speech that is not entirely standard, in relentlessly tracking down the smallest indices of hatred, rejection, or mere indifference, one undoubtedly creates a community of fantasied suffering."[108]

National Post's Jonathan Kay says "many essentially trifling antisemitic incidents are being blown out of proportion." He accused B'nai Brith of cynically using its exaggerated figures and claims to terrify older Jews so that "donations come rolling in."[109]

Elah Feder poses the dilemma of all these attempts to eradicate antisemitism: "The more we talk about anti-Semitism, the more appealing it becomes."[110] Needlessly crying "wolf!" is not only cynical but is another example of foot-shooting, undermining the credibility of the accusation while tarring all Jews in the process.

And what do Canadians think about Israel after all the hard work of B'nai Brith? Virtually all Canadians say it is not 'antisemitic' to criticize Israel, even Conservatives (80%). Forty-six percent of Canadians have a negative view of Israel and only 28% have a positive view. Omitting the Conservatives, it was 61% negative, 55% among Liberal supporters (only 22% positive), and 74% saw Canada's policy as biased in favor of Israel.[111] Only the politicians on Parliament Hill or Queen's Park, etc.—under the B'nai Brith axe—support Israel. Soft power is only so effective where there is a shred of free thinking left among the people.

Tagging the Early "Antisemites"

Goldwin Smith (1823–1910), appointed Oxford University professor of modern history at the age of 36, was very much the Victorian liberal. His predecessor as modern history professor at Oxford, Matthew Arnold, wrote Smith always "remained true to his insight, unshakeable, unseduced, unterrified." His successor, E.A. Smith called him "a prophet of righteousness, who never feared the face of man wherever there was truth to be asserted or wrong to be denounced."¹¹²

He was a brilliant essayist and journalist, tutor and friend of the future Edward VII, a leading figure in Toronto literary life, co-founder of the *Toronto Evening Telegram* (since 1971, the *Toronto Sun*), *Canadian Monthly* and others including the *National Review*, where in 1872 he adopted the nom de plume that would become his own literary journal, *A Bystander*.

Goldwin Smith

His only real biography, Elisabeth Wallace's *Goldwin Smith: Victorian Liberal* (1957), completely censors his most intriguing and important intellectual passion: a critique both theological and sociological of Judaism and Jewishness. Ramsay Cook's scholarly *The Regenerators, Social Criticism in Late Victorian English Canada* (1986), focuses on Smith's writings about the decline of Christian belief and the moral problems of technology, and like Wallace's biography, completely ignores this central element, which Cook describes as a "severe case of 'cultural despair'."¹¹³ Tulchinsky slams Smith's work as a projection of "visceral feeling rather than of cool reason about the Jewish 'danger'," saying Smith intended it as "a clarion call to awareness and action."¹¹⁴ Erased from Toronto history, dismissed by contemporary Jewish writers like Tulchinsky as a "Jew-hater",¹¹⁵ only a few of Smith's writings are available at the Toronto Reference Library, and only on request.

In his vilification of Smith, Tulchinsky never addresses any of Smith's criticisms, though he provides quotes.¹¹⁶ For instance,

- "There was a Judaism of the Prophets, and a Judaism of the Law, ... the first broadened into Christianity, while the second was narrowed into Pharisaism and the Talmud."¹¹⁷
- "Those who refuse to mingle with humanity must take the consequences of their refusal. They cannot expect to enjoy at once the pride of exclusiveness, and the sympathies of brotherhood."¹¹⁸

Tulchinsky, the only academic to address Smith's critique of Jewishness, concludes that Smith "challenged the legitimacy of Judaism and the right of the Jewish people to survive as a distinct cultural group in the modern world. This was antisemitism of the most fundamental and dangerous kind."[119] In contrast, Catholics and Muslims on the whole easily integrated in the Protestant-dominated American colonies without losing their heritage, and Jews were integrating to some extent in Europe in the 19th century, including German Jews. However, the elite Jews still worked in the economy tribally (with the exception of isolated figures such as Rathenau), making them an easy target in the post-WWI period.

His criticisms in theology were in line with the current scientific dismissal of much of both the Old and New Testaments as of dubious origin, full of inconsistencies, but including divine truths, moral and ethical principles. He saw Christianity as the completion of the Judaic messianic religion, and Judaism as a denial of the universality of Christianity, a tribal throwback that made Jews a danger to the unity of the human race. "As a manifestation of the Divine, the Hebrew books teaching righteousness and purity, may keep their place in our love and admiration forever; while of their tribalism, their intolerance, their religious cruelty, we forever take our leave."[120] He felt Jews should accept the human race as their only 'tribe', and assimilate within their respective nation states rather than existing as a "nation within nations". His goal was a society based on "social justice and free religious convictions".[121] His ethics were based on a "rational Christianity".[122] Though he moved closer to agnosticism in his life, he insisted that morality depended on religious belief, "the only lasting spring of the unselfish affections and actions which bind men into a community and save that community from dissolution."[123]

His vision of world unity and peace, and his disdain for the idle, incompetent aristocracy still governing Britain, made him an early critic of imperialism. Though describing himself as "anti-Imperialistic to the core" ironically he believed in the greatness of the British race. For him, 'race' was a cultural term, and Jews could easily fit in by rejecting the tribal aspects of Judaism and embracing Christian universalism, without the need for an acceptance of the specifics of Christian dogma, most of which he himself rejected. Indeed, for many secular English Jews, this appears to be the case.

He wrote histories of the US, Canada, and Britain, strongly advocating commercial union with the US and the eventual reunion of the US, Britain and Canada as part of a commonwealth of former British colonies. The subsequent US invasion of the Philippines destroyed his illusion of a non-imperialist America and he eventually reversed his belief that Canada should join the growing imperialist next door.

He was one of the only public figures who dared oppose the Boer War in a jingoistic British Empire, and criticized as "most extraordinary this English opposition to Russia," when British media was denouncing Russia for the rioting and pogroms at the time. He argued that the animosity towards Jews in the Pale was because of their self-imposed isolation from Russian life, their disdain for Russian spirituality, combined with the practice of usury, which always led to misery and resentment. In correspondence in 1907, he writes that the "rising in Roumania [is due to] the sense of Jewish intrusion and oppression."[124] "Only because they will not fuse with the peoples among whom they live does [the Gentile] so gird at the Jews."

Smith had regular correspondence with Jewish writers, contributed to the Holy Blossom Temple, and attended its inauguration in 1897. In a letter to a Jewish friend Jonas Rosenfield, he writes, "The Jewish race has done much for which the world must be grateful; but socially the sense of estrangement almost inevitably prevails ... The wanderer comes rather to live upon them rather than with them ... the main source of all that we have had to deplore."[125] "Jews have one code of ethics for themselves, another for Gentiles,"[126] which historically was the case as it related to the practice of usury. Smith took pains to deny any racism on his part, saying he was merely rejecting the tribal aspect of Judaism, calling for assimilation.

Jewish media control was already evident in the US at the time (less so in Canada), but already a concern to Smith. Adolph Simon Ochs, the son of German Jewish immigrants, bought *The New York Times* in 1904.[127] "A paper or periodical which is not controlled by the Jews or afraid to print the truth temperately expressed, about them? Meanwhile, the semitic influence grows and not entirely for the good."[128] Smith's view that Jews "seem to be behind the press everywhere, or at least be able to muzzle it" predates Israel Asper and Canwest Media (now Postmedia), which came to dominate Canadian media ownership a century later, including Smith's *Telegram*, now the Toronto *Sun*, Canada's leading pro-Zionist newspaper.

His most detailed analysis of things Jewish is found in "The

Jewish Question", in *Essays on the Questions of the Day Political and Social* (1893), written at the time that the Jewish population was exploding on his very doorstep, the Grange, but still only 16,401 in 1901.

> Judaism is not, like Unitarianism or Methodism, merely a religious belief in no way affecting the secular relations of the citizen; it is a distinction of race, the religion being identified with the race, as is the case in the whole group of primaeval and tribal religions, of which Judaism is a survival. A Jew is not an Englishman or Frenchman holding particular tenets: He is a Jew with a special deity for his own race. [It is] from hatred of their financial practices, not on account of their religion, that the people of Europe, and especially the peasantry, began rising against them.

In the 1890s, when "philosemitism" was the rage among his Oxford peers, he proudly took the monicker "antisemite", accepting the (mistaken) implication that all Jews (wherever they came from and whatever language they spoke) and Arabs were of the same race, rather than most Jews being European. "The term 'anti-Semite' is applicable to me if it means simply fear of political, social and financial influence without the slightest shadow of religious apathy."[129]

He was pessimistic about reforming Judaism, seeing assimilation as the only long-term solution: "Jewish monotheism is so bound up with other elements of Semitism or Judaism, that it would be impossible to disentangle it, and make it the foundation of a united Church." Instead, he felt we must rely on "spontaneous and informal approximation which will lead gradually to a unity of action."[130]

The most famous Jew of 19th century England was prime minister Benjamin Disraeli, who satirized Smith in *Lothair* (1870) as a "social sycophant", and with whom Smith corresponded and opposed politically, though he didn't stoop to publicly humiliating Disraeli, as the latter had done to him. A Sephardi, Disraeli indeed could be fairly called Semitic, at least distantly having north African roots.[131] Disraeli was an enthusiastic imperialist, happy to use his power to expand the empire around the world, unlike the anti-imperialist Smith. Jews were at the financial and political heart of British imperialism, as both were well aware.

Paradoxically, Smith had a strong influence on both Mackenzie King and French Canadian nationalist, Henri Bourassa. King called for the British Empire to be transformed into a Commonwealth in the 1920s, taking his inspiration from Smith. Smith saw a future "where Jew and Gentile will merge." His credo was "Above All Nations is Humanity," further averring that "Jews who did not want to assimilate should go to Palestine, or at least not come to Canada."[132] He is much like the great 17th century philosopher, Baruch Spinoza, and the great 19th century philosopher, Karl Marx, both Jews by birth, who rejected tribal Jewishness and were excommunicated, though eventually honored as great universalists.

This open nonracist criticism of Jewishness comes from both right (Smith) and left. Karl Marx (1818–1883) had made a more telling critique of Judaism from the socialist end not long before Smith took up his professorship at Oxford.[133]

The United Church

As the flood of east European Jewish settlers started arriving in the 1880s, the Protestant churches provided charity facilities, with an eye to proselytizing in 'the Ward' in Toronto. The interdenominational Toronto Jewish Mission opened there in 1894, hiring Henry Singer, a Polish Jewish convert to Christianity from Boston. The Presbyterian mission (the United Church was formed in 1925) opened in 1898 and became a priority in 1907 with Rev J. McPherson Scott heading the Jewish Mission Committee on Elizabeth and Elm Streets, later called The Christian Synagogue.

"The very intellectual superiority of the Jew is not in favor of missions for his conversion," wrote an editorial in the *Telegram*.[134] Such public efforts were bound to fail; any Jew wanting to convert would want to do so privately. Public conversion is humiliating to the individual and considered an insult to the disavowed community; the proselytizing probably did more harm to the churches' image than good. B'nai Zion began an intimidation campaign at the Christian missions, with toughs standing outside threatening Jews who entered, playing loud music at public gatherings to drive them away. One incident caused a riot in 1911 and 8 Jewish protesters were arrested. An Anti-Missionary League was set up in 1914, uniting elite and ghetto Jews. After WWI, the need for church charity among the poor Jews fell as Jewish charitable organizations grew.

Morris Zeidman (1894–1964), a Polish immigrant, arrested in youth as a Jewish socialist in Poland, converted to Presbyterianism in Toronto in 1908, attracted by the "Christian Synagogue", and became superintendent of the Scott Institute, both to fight anti-Jewish bigotry and as a missionary to convert Jews. He also founded the historic Scott Mission. He did not make many conversions, but provided help to immigrant Jews who were ignored by Toronto's establishment Jews, and fought anti-Jewish prejudice. His family stayed behind in Poland and were killed in WWII.

United Church minister Claris Silcox (1888–1961) started his interfaith dialogues at Columbia University in 1929, and in 1934, set up the first Canadian seminar on Jewish-Gentile relations in Toronto. He was general secretary of the Christian Social Service Council of Canada, the predecessor of the Canadian Council of Churches, and in 1940 director of the Canadian National Conference of Christians and Jews, founded by E.M. Howse. Criticism of fascist anti-Jewish propaganda was conducted by the Committee on Jewish-Gentile Relations in Toronto, headed by Silcox and Rabbi Maurice Eisendrath of Holy Blossom Temple.

Silcox was not a fan of Zionism nor the creation of Israel, and Jewish critics still dismiss him as having the "odour of Christian sanctimoniousness", and not "free from certain dubious and cliche-ridden assumptions about Jews and Judaism", holding "opinions on the Middle East, which came to fruition in the post-war years", and even "a possible antisemite himself", having "residual antisemitism". He showed "ignorance of the nature and history of the Zionist idea", believing rather in the "Jewish passion for social justice ... the supreme contribution of the Jews ... in the field of religion."[135] This was at a time when social justice was being replaced with Zionism in Jewish ideology.

The Zionist media has a particular grudge against the United Church, the only Christian denomination that spoke out strongly against Zionism. Particularly irritating for Zionists were editorials in 1946–47, 1956, and in 1967–73 in the *Observer*, when Israeli aggression and expansionism were at their height.

Silcox's 1956 article in the United Church *Observer* criticizing Israel's invasion of Egypt stood out as his worst sin, undoing for the Zionists all his brave efforts fighting anti-Jewish prejudice and fascism in the 1930s. The *Observer* rarely mentioned Zionism and Israel after that, the new editor, A. E. Forrest explaining, following the 1967 war, "Christians hesitate to voice any criticism of Israel for fear of being charged with prejudice. We cannot expect Jews to be objective about Israel, so it is the right and duty of Christians to see at least two sides of this many-sided problem."[136] Christian anger boiled over when the June 1967 victory was busily being consolidated, with thousands of new Palestinian refugees permanently settled in refugee camps, even as the Zionists were publicly exhorting the world's Jews to immigrate and settle on their stolen land. "Israel has no more intention of complying with the wishes of the World Council of Churches than with the UN." The op-ed bemoaned the imbalance between slick Israeli PR, and Arabs shooting themselves in the foot by denying all western Jews visas and refusing to engage the Zionists in world media.

The op-ed concluded by denouncing the "intolerable racist policies followed by Israel."[137] Now it was necessary to face down the Zionists in Canada, who were celebrating Israel's theft with many making aliyah or going to Israel to join the army to fight the Palestinians, both Muslim and Christian. Forrest condemned Israeli policies strongly after 1967, comparing Israel to apartheid South Africa, and even Nazi Germany. M.J. Nurenberger, editor of the *Canadian Jewish News*, called Forrest "the most dangerous enemy of Israel because he is subtle and articulate."

Forrest published a travel book, *The Unholy Land,* in 1968 after a ten-month tour of the Middle East. He was shocked at the condition of the refugees, who had been promised a return to their homes and were betrayed. Like Smith and all later critics of Zionism he was opposed to the tribalism of Judaism, quoting approvingly from the Jewish socialist Bund literature that: "Jews, although they are of different and distinct national origin, are – or should be – equal citizens of their countries, and that they should unite with all other citizens, in the common struggle for the victory of labour, democracy and Socialism."[138]

Zionism was "secular messianism", which for a religious person of any faith smacks of apostasy. Forrest quotes Uri Avnery, whom he befriended in his travels in Israel. Avnery had been a Zionist, but began to revise his views after the 1956 Suez Crisis, and called for a de-zionification of Israel to make it "in a sense just another state."[139] Already in 1968, Avnery said, young Israelis weren't eager for more Jews to immigrate. The 'right of return' for Jews should be abolished, as it feeds the fear of Israel's neighbors that its intention is constant expansion and seizing of territory. Israel should be reformed as a secular, multinational state.[140]

"The US's next Vietnam will be in the Holy Land," Forrest warned.[141] Just as France had argued in the *Observer* in 1946, Forrest warned that the growing tide of Soviet Jews emigrating to Israel after 1967 to claim stolen land was provocation to Arabs and increased the likelihood of further war. Zionists writing today about Forrest charge that he was 'antisemitic' and prey to the belief that there was "a sinister Zionist plot to expel the Palestinians."[142]

At the time, Ernest Howse, a former United Church moderator, added his voice, criticizing Israel for taking the phrase 'next year in Jerusalem' literally. CJN editor Nurenberger called him an "apostle of neo-antisemitism" and a disseminator "of distrust and mutual suspicion among Jews and Christians." These ministers cried out in anguish, but were pilloried and ignored.

The last open confrontation with Zionism in Canadian mainstream media was in 1972, when *Observer* editor A.E. Forrest commissioned an article by a Canadian minister in Florida, John Booth. "How Zionists Manipulate Your News", appearing in the March 1972 *Observer*, infuriated Zionist critics, especially the now powerful B'nai Brith which had already set up its surveillance network across North America through the Anit-Defamation League (ADL).[143]

The ADL is tax exempt as a charity, despite openly advocating for a foreign government, and being heavily involved in political advocacy.[144] This special government favor could only be explained by the now powerful Israel lobby, explained Booth, able to twist laws to its needs. No other such organization openly lobbying on behalf of a foreign state was given this privilege. The ADL boasted that it subsidized journalists, with junkets for fluff pieces, launched boycotts, defamation suits, employed undercover agents, used entrapment and impersonation to create 'incidents'. Booth quotes Rabbi Elmer Berger, an American Jewish critic, charging that the ADL was "reprehensible, arrogant, suppressive".

The Zionists used character assassination to humiliate Toynbee, Bertrand Russell and FDR—all called antisemites for questioning the wisdom of Zionist statehood. *The New York Times* publisher Arthur Sulzberger wrote that he "objected to attempts of character assassination." When Booth tried to speak anywhere, he was monitored, and faced with angry demonstrations, forcing hosts to cancel his talks. There was even a bomb threat to New York Community Church where he was to speak. He called on B'nai Brith to engage him in an open debate, which they refused.[145]

There was nothing untrue in "How Zionists manipulate your news," just embarrassing facts stated boldly in a mainstream publication, showing how media control had advanced through ownership and effective lobbying by the powerful Jewish lobbies. The inability of the Zionists to control the United Church was frustrating and called for war. B'nai Brith demanded a formal retraction be published in the *Observer* for the "errors and distortions," and for the church to end criticism of Israel.

Forrest at first refused and launched a law suit for defamation, to which B'nai Brith responded with their own lawsuit. This open scandal had to be resolved and United Church officials crafted an apology for any errors, explaining that the article was not addressing Canada but the US. Forrest refused to sign the apology, asking first that any errors be pointed out, but his letter was not answered. As was the case when Booth was harassed and denounced in the US, no refutation of his statements was forthcoming, only angry calls of 'antisemitism'. On the contrary, B'nai Brith was unhappy with the mild retraction, calling it "not only inadequate but totally unacceptable, that in fact, its wording aggravates the offense,"[146] and demanded a formal apology on their terms.

The new moderator, Bruce McLeod, was also pro-Palestinian but had a church to run, and was determined to soothe Jewish egos. Few people outside the Jewish community really cared much about the Middle East, and the church had to deal with the strong Jewish lobby and constant, shrill calls in the mainstream press of 'antisemitism'. He gave in and agreed—at B'nai Brith headquarters—to a new, groveling apology about "inaccuracies" and "the church's sorry role in fostering hostility between Christians and Jews."[147] Forrest felt betrayed, blacklisted, as no mainstream paper would publish his "statement for the press" explaining his side.

Forrest still had the *Observer* to edit, and called on his friend Rabbi Reuben Slonim to write an article for the *Observer* to clear the air of anti-Jewish feelings in the July 1974 issue. "The Real Middle East Crisis is Still to Come" did little to mollify B'nai Brith, as Slonim basically agreed with Booth and Forrest, but as he later wrote in *Family Quarrel: The United Church and the Jews* (1977), he was more concerned that the tone of the piece was angry, a personal attack after Booth had been hounded by B'nai Brith. Holy Blossom Rabbi Gunter Plaut told B'nai Brith to put an end to the scandal and leave the United Church alone, as it was clear Forrest represented overwhelming church opinion, and pressure on officials would merely create more anti-Jewish sentiment. The lawsuits were withdrawn.

Despite pressure from some of his colleagues and even friends, who just stopped short of calling him 'antisemitic', the church had stood by Forrest, a popular editor since 1955. The 25th General Council of the United Church even had the chutzpah in August 1972 to urge the government to cancel a $100 million loan to Israel to pressure Israel to change its policies of colonizing Palestinian lands and leaving refugees in limbo. At the meeting Forrest had been given a standing ovation and shouts of "We love you, Al."[148]

Forrest was principled on his rejection of the Jewish state (as opposed to the Israeli state) till the end, stating "How can I uphold a racist state?" Forrest retired in 1978, too controversial to be nominated moderator, and died shortly afterwards, worn out by his struggles, having been labeled a Red, a crypto-Fascist, and an antisemite.

The Jewish press in Toronto had labeled three former moderators—E.M. Howse, Robert McClure and Bruce McLeod, among others—as antisemitic. Relations remained testy with the United Church, Jews claiming 'antisemitism' with every criticism of Israel, and their Christian protagonists fighting to defend what they saw as the truth and the cause of social justice. Moderator Bill Phipps (1997–2001) issued the 1997 report "Bearing Faithful Witness: United Church-Jewish Relations", calling for a radical reinterpretation of theology, including ending any attempts to convert Jews (other religions are still fair game) and the belief that "Christianity does not supersede Judaism". In line with the Vatican II *Nostra Aetate*, the report downplays the 'fact' that Jewish high priests conspired to kill Jesus. "Blame is shifted to the Jewish crowd, the Jewish people. They shout, 'His blood be on us and on our children!' (27:25) This horrible saying, undoubtedly a creation of the writer."[149]

Phipps goes quite a bit further, questioning the resurrection of Jesus as a scientific fact, and said, "I don't believe Jesus was God."[150] The report and Phipps's other musing effectively end all differences with Judaism – except that Judaism denies Jesus is the Christ, thereby denying an existential creed of official Christianity. A hard 'bargain'. United Church members are still active in fighting Israeli crimes, and the church supports BDS, but the passion and honesty of Forrest and the *Observer* is muted.

The latest demand from the Jewish establishment is to insist that the Protestant Church apologize for Martin Luther's views of the Jews. The *Jewish Algemeiner* writes that "the 500th anniversary of the Reformation would be the 'perfect time' for Protestant leaders to recognize and apologize for the 'horrific antisemitism' of their movement's founder, Martin Luther."[151]

Paradoxically, Luther was actually reforming the Catholic Church along Judaic lines, getting rid of statues of saints and Jesus, considering them, as did Jews, idol worship. Originally, he hoped that Jews would convert to his new, more Jewish Christianity. In 1523, Luther accused Catholics of being unfair to Jews and treating them "as if they were dogs", thus making it difficult for Jews to convert. "I would request and advise that one deal gently with them [the Jews]," he wrote. "If we really want to help them, we must be guided in our dealings with them not by papal law but by the law of Christian love. We must receive them cordially, and permit them to trade and work with us, hear our Christian teaching."[152] But they refused, which is when his tirades against them began.

It was the Catholic Church that condoned prosecuting Jews throughout the Middle Ages, Catholic monarchs expelling them from Spain, France, Britain and elsewhere. Despite Luther's angry words when his offer to Jewish leaders was spurned, Protestants welcomed them in Holland and Germany, where they prospered. In Canada, Jews studied in Protestant schools, originally not paying taxes, and the Presbyterians and Anglicans provided charity in the early 20th century to penniless Jews struggling to get their feet on the ground.

The claim that Jesus is the Messiah will always remain in dispute. Judaism has had dozens of claimants to messiah-hood since, most famously Sabbatai Zevi (1626–1676), an Ottoman Jew who claimed to be the Messiah, but then converted to Islam and still has followers today (Donmeh). The most enduring is Menachem Schneerson (1902–1994), son of Yosef Yitzchak Schneersohn (1880–1950), who founded the Chabad-Lubovich organization in 1923, the largest Jewish organization in the world. During the 1990s, many people believed that the son would be revealed as the Messiah. Even after his death in 1994, people still believed that he will be the Messiah.

Reuben Slonim (1915–2000) was born in Winnipeg, and spent his early years at the Jewish orphanage where his mother worked as a cook. He took the only road to advancement, a Bronfman memorial scholarship to study at the Hebrew Theological College in Chicago. He became the first Canadian-born rabbi in Canada, at the

McCaul Street synagogue from the 1930s, and then Beth Habonim, the synagogue built specifically for Holocaust survivors, appropriately when he discovered in 1945 that his father's home town, Slonim, in Belarus, which was mostly Jewish, had been destroyed and its inhabitants, including many of his relatives, murdered.

A follower of Reform and Conservative Judaism, Slonim was a journalist, and became associate editor of John Roberston and Goldwin Smith's *Evening Telegram*, which under its new editor John Bassett, became the most pro-Zionist mainstream paper. He traveled to Israel reporting on the development of Israel from 1948 on, and went from enthusiast to increasingly critical Zionist till he became a post-Zionist, which made him a pariah in the Canadian community after WWII. Later, he reflected that three quarters of Toronto Jews actually preferred the more neutral *Toronto Star*, appreciating neither the gung-ho pro-Israel flavor to the news nor Slonim's critical op-eds.

After the Six Day War of 1967, part of which he spent in a bomb shelter in Israel with his daughter, Slonim returned to his synagogue and said that Israel might win the war, but it would lose the peace if it did not show magnanimity towards the Arabs. He maintained that the deepest ethical values of Judaism were being jeopardized and betrayed by Israel's blatant ghettoization and suffering of another Semitic people, the Palestinians. His journalistic memoirs, *Both Sides Now: A 25-year encounter with Arabs and Israelis* (1972), shows the transition that took place in many Jews upset with Israel's refusal to stop its colonial march, making any peace agreement increasingly remote.

After 1967, he argued that the days of Zionism were over, that Israel had its state now and had to make peace and become a regular nation, entering an era of post-Zionism, that "politically, ideologically and culturally, Israel must follow the Middle East rather than the needs of Jews abroad,"[153] agreeing with Uri Avnery that once Zionism did have a meaningful purpose. In the 1910–30s period, the national-home idea was a necessary rallying point. Israel was "not a Jewish state but a free state established by Jews. There should be no special rights for Jews. All citizens should have full equality." Israeli Arabs are a vital link with the Arab world, he felt. You can't sit back and wait for peace. Israel must take the initiative, solve the refugee problem unilaterally to promote a full settlement.[154]

Forrest had commissioned Slonim's article to heal the rift with B'nai Brith in 1973, but Slonim was hardly the man to mollify the Zionists. Slonim had been pushed out of his McCaul St congregation and called an "Arab lover" and an "enemy of the Jews" for criticizing the occupation and mistreatment of Palestinians, never flagging in his defense of Jewish universalist values. He was the only one to actually address the errors of the Booth article, pointing out that Jean-Paul Sartre wasn't a Jew as claimed by Booth.

In 2000, his daughter wrote in his obituary, "In the past year my father was too sick to know about the negotiations between Israel and Syria, but he felt vindicated by the peace accords signed in Oslo. He never at any time expressed anger at the Jewish community where his views were unpopular."[155] Yet his post-Zionism was qualified. He was not confident that Jewish traditions would survive unless the state was assured a majority of Jews. He was caught in a conundrum as a devout Jew, because any settlement of the refugee problem could well deny that. In which case, 'Israeli' would not necessarily mean a specifically Jewish identity (Hebrew, customs, holidays) for Israel, and Slonim, like most supporters of Israel, were/are not confident that such an Israeli identity would be good enough. He was not willing to accept assimilation into a democratic nation, as Goldwin Smith, his 'antisemitic' predecessor at the *Telegram* advocated. Addressing this contradiction, Slonim quotes I. F. Stone, "to be a Jew is not quite to belong. Every society has its Jews. Israel's Jews are its Arabs.[156]

Endnotes

1   Eric Walberg, "Zionism in Canada: Political poison", *al-Ahram Weekly*, April 3, 2012. at <http://ericwalberg.com/index.php?option=com_content&view=article&id=119:political-poison&catid=39:europe-canada-and-us-&Itemid=92>
2   His funeral in Cairo drew five million mourners, the largest in history, and an outpouring of grief across the Arab world.
3   The International Conference to Review the Global Vision of the Holocaust in 2006 and two "New Horizon: The International Conference of Independent Thinkers" in 2012, 2014.
4   97% see Israel as the biggest threat to Egypt. <https://www.brookings.edu/research/what-do-egyptians-want-key-findings-from-the-egyptian-public-opinion-poll/>
5   Excerpt from my letter to the *National Post*: Hi Tristin, I read your deconstruction of my article "Respect Existence or Expect Resistance" with interest. <http://news.nationalpost.com/2013/01/08/idle-no-more-is-a-righteous-struggle-against-land-hungry-colons-iranian-state-tv/> I appreciate for someone who no doubt approves of the neoliberal nightmare that Canada now endures, my analysis comparing Canadian natives, Iranians, Palestinians and Egyptians is hard to fathom (you call it bizarre). I'm surprised you seem to doubt what

is as clear as day – that natives in Canada are the victims of British/French imperialism, just as Iranians are victims of British/French/US imperialism. The parallels are all too clear–and sadly unknown to 'colon' Canadian readers, though easily understood by Canadian natives, Iranians, Palestinians and Egyptians.

As a fellow journalist, you can appreciate that I 'follow the news'. In my case, with the virtual war being waged by the US and more recently Canada against Iran, recapping the criminal war against Iraq, I have focused my writing on trying to expose this infamy. The subtext of your article seems to hint at a conspiracy by Iran, using Canadians like myself and brave natives like Terrance Nelson. The underhanded treatment of natives in Canada is recognized by the UN as a blotch against Canada. Iran media is merely 'following the news'. The worse our natives fare, the more attention their plight gets in Iran. Don't look for conspiracies where there are none. Presstv and my criticisms of the Canadian government are open and above board. The conspiracy is perpetrated by Harper in league with mining and oil companies to further steal native resources, the profits going to the rich corporations, intent on leaving environmental and social devastation behind.

6   Bruce Campion-Smith, "MPs vote to extend Afghan mission to 2011", *Toronto Star*, March 13, 2008.
7   Louis XIV had seized Alsace-Lorraine in the 17th century, with a significant Jewish population; Cromwell and the Pilgrim Christians wanted to allow Jews to immigrate, but it didn't happen formally. They were just allowed to come without declaring themselves as Jews. Jews had same disabilities as all non-Anglicans who refused to take the official religious oath (required in order to hold municipal office, parliament, get university degree (till the mid-19th century). By mid-17th century, openly Jewish communities began to emerge. Germany and Holland consisted then of small principalities, better for Ginsberg's 'fatal embrace'. This changed when Germany unified in 1871, giving rise to a strident jingoism against the large, rich Jewish minority.
8   Laws were derived from Christianity, but no country was legally defined as "Christian" or according to "race".
9   Stephen Speilman, *The Jews of Toronto: A History to 1937*, 1979, 15-6.
10 Ira Robinson, *A History of Antisemitism in Canada*, 2015, 26.
11 Ibid., 26.
12 Irving Abella, *A Coat of Many Colours: Two Centuries of Jewish Life in Canada*, 1990, 32.
13 Denis Vaugeois, *The First Jews in North American*, 2012, 278.
14 Robinson, op.cit., 32.
15 "Canadian Immigration History", Marianopolis College.
16 Speilman, op.cit., 321.
17 The British *Jewish Chronicle* in 1909 criticized the "influx of foreign Jews who formed ghettos and fostered prejudice among French Canadians", advised restricting immigration, and public schools to promote assimilation. Tulchinsky, *Taking Roots: The Origins of the Canadian Jewish Community*, 1992, 247.
18 Irving Abella, *None Is Too Many*, 1982.
19 "The Canadian Corporate Elite: Ethnicity and Inequality of Access", in Rita Bienvenue and Jay Goldstein, *Ethnicity and Ethnic Relations in Canada*, Toronto Butterworths, 1985, 148--149.
20 Robinson, op.cit., 73.

21	Einstein's love affair with Zionism was short-lived, and he returned to assimilationism by the late 1930s when he saw what he described as the rise of fascism within Zionism. "Apart from practical consideration, my awareness of the essential nature of Judaism resists the idea of a Jewish state with borders, an army, and a measure of temporal power no matter how modest. I am afraid of the inner damage Judaism will sustain – especially from the development of a narrow nationalism within our own ranks, against which we have already had to fight strongly, even without a Jewish state." Albert Einstein, on April 17, 1938, in a speech at the Commodore Hotel in New York City. After the war, he spoke out strongly against Israeli atrocities, and became a fierce critic of the Zionists. (Alfred M. Lilienthal, in *What Price Israel?*, recounts that on April 1, 1952, in a message to the Children of Palestine, Inc., Einstein "spoke of the necessity to curb 'a kind of nationalism' which has arisen in Israel 'if only to permit a friendly and fruitful co-existence with the Arabs.'" Lilienthal also relates a personal conversation with Einstein: "Dr Einstein told me that, strangely enough, he had never been a Zionist and had never favored the creation of the State of Israel. Also, he told me of a significant conversation with [Chaim] Weizmann [leader of the World Zionist Organization.] Einstein had asked him: 'What about the Arabs if Palestine were given to the Jews?' And Weizman said: 'What Arabs? They are hardly of any consequence.'" [131]. <http://www.newdemocracyworld.org/old/Einstein.htm>
22	Walther Rathenau, *An Deutschlands Jugend*, 1918, p.9. Rathenau was assassinated in 1922 by a German nationalist, not so much as a Jew but as a member of the hated Weimar political regime, subservient to the crippling Versailles Treaty.
23	Winston Churchill, "Zionism vs Bolshevism: the struggle for the soul of the Jewish people", *Illustrated Sunday Herald*, 8 February 1920, and Jeffrey Wallin and Juan Williams, "Churchill's Greatness", *Fox News*, September 2001. <http://web.archive.org/web/20031216033237/http://www.winstonchurchill.org/i4a/pages/index.cfm?pageid=282, *Fox News*, September 2001.>
24	Morton Weinfeld, *Like Everyone Else ... But Different: The Paradoxical Success of Canadian Jews*, 265.
25	The rise and decline of the communist movement parallels the rise and decline now of Zionism as an ideology. The heroic days for the communists were the 1930s, but with the rise of the welfare state, the communist message was blurred. The heroic days for the Zionists were the 1930–40s, with the struggle to create Israel.
26	Abella, *Coat*, 83.
27	Up to 70% of students were Jewish in some schools in Montreal in the pre-WWI period.
28	Montreal Protestant School Board official Irving Rexford in 1924.The argument, made in 1935, was that "by becoming Canadian citizens, Jews had accepted to live in a Christian country. This fact implied a limit to the Jews' freedom in Canada. Jewish demands, however legitimate they may be, 'must never interfere with the character of our [Christian] institutions and our laws.'" M. Ceslas Forest "La question juive au Canada" in Robinson, op.cit. 60-2.
29	Abella, *Coat*, 235.
30	In 1994, the Ontario Court of Appeal ruled unanimously against a coalition of Jewish and Christian schools requesting provincial funding. The judgment held that, because public funding of Ontario's Roman Catholic school system (as of

Quebec's Protestant school system) was agreed to at the time of Confederation and was part of the Constitution Act, 1867, non-funding of other denominational schools does not constitute discrimination against them. <http://www.edu.gov.on.ca/eng/general/abcs/rcom/full/volume4/chapter16.html>

31 <http://secularalliance.ca/about/policies/public-financing-of-religious-schools/>
32 See below. Weinfeld, op.cit., 229, 231.
33 Leo Max Frank (1884–1915) was an American factory superintendent who was convicted in 1913 of the murder of a 13-year-old employee, Mary Phagan, in Atlanta, Georgia. Although antisemitism was not locally common, there were growing concerns regarding child labor at factories owned by members of the Jewish community. One of these children was Mary Phagan, who worked at the National Pencil Company where Frank was director. The girl was strangled and notes on the body implicated the night watchman, Newt Lee. Over the course of their investigations, the police arrested several men, including Lee, Frank, and Jim Conley, a black janitor at the factory. The prosecution relied heavily on the testimony of Conley, who described himself as an accomplice to the murder, and who the defense at the trial argued was in fact the perpetrator of the murder. Conley was sentenced to a year. In contrast, 4,000 black men, women, and children were lynched in the twelve Southern states between 1877 and 1950.
34 *Jewish Times*, July 5, 1901, p249. In Speilman, op.cit., 120.
35 Ibid., 122.
36 Anthony Julius, *Trials of the Diaspora: A History of Anti-Semitism in England*, Oxford University Press, 2010, 431.
37 Alan Davies, ed., *Anti-Semitism in Canada: History and Interpretation*, 1992, 71.
38 In 2000, the son of the immigration official Frederick Blair then responsible apologized. In 2011, a memorial monument at the Halifax pier called the Wheel of Conscience, was produced by the Canadian Jewish Congress.
39 Gerald Tulchinsky, *Canada's Jews: A People's Journey, 2008,* 378.)
40 Irving Abella, *None Is Too Many*, 1982, 27.
41 The Madagascar plan dates from Zionist Organization founder Chaim Weizmann, and was mooted by Hitler in the 1930s up until the Germans occupied France in 1940, but was impossible then, due to the British refusal to consider it. There was also a plan from 1937 according to Hoettl to send all Germany's Jews to Palestine under an international agreement. The Nazis had openly urged Jews to leave after 1933, and 50% (300,000) had done so. A Central Bureau for Jewish Emigration was set up, and Eichmann was sent to Palestine by Heydrich in 1937 to investigate the feasibility. In 1940, there were negotiations with Vichy France, but the British dismissed the project out of hand. It was only after the invasion of the Soviet Union in June 1941 that Heydrich switched to "transport to the East", which looks in retrospect to have meant extermination. According to Hoettl, Eichmann was "one of the most overrated figures of the Third Reich." Wilheim Hoettl, *The Secret Front: Nazi Political Espionage 1938--1945*, Weidenfeld and Nicholson, [1953] revised edition with appendix on Eichmann 1997, enigma books, 2003.
42 Ibid.
43 Abella, *None Is Too Many*. 68-9.
44 Arendt, op.cit., 156-7.
45 Ibid., 60. No defense witnesses were allowed at his trial, so the defense couldn't force agents of Aliyah Beth (the organization for illegal immigration) to testify.

46   Ibid., 184.
47   Zakhariah Kay, *Canada and Palestine: The Politics of Non-Commitment*, (1978), 80. The new leader, M.J. Coldwell, embraced Zionism in 1945.
48   Abella, op.cit., 226.
49   Ibid., 225.
50   Ibid., 227.
51   Ibid., 213.
52   Ibid., 281.
53   Ibid., 282.
54   Ibid., 284.
55   Ibid., 318 notes.
56   Ibid., 228. King never intended that his diaries be made public. See below re Smith.
57   Ibid., 274.
58   Franklin Bialystok, *Delayed Impact: The Holocaust and the Canadian Jewish Community*, 2000, 70.
59   Robinson, op.cit., 107.
60   See below and Chapter 8.
61   Ibid.
62   Israel used terror bombings in Egypt and Iraq to force Arab Jews to flee to Israel. Moroccan Jews also met with hostility due to the new Jewish state. The preferred 'promised land' was almost always Canada. A well-established Jewish immigration network was able to facilitate the surge in immigration.
63   The Canadian Encyclopedia, <http://thecanadianencyclopedia.ca/en/article/jewish-canadians/>
64   <https://en.wikipedia.org/wiki/American_Jews>,"World Jewish Population 2013" <jewishdatabank.org>
65   Irving Abella, "Never Again May Be None Too Many," *Globe and Mail*, February 26, 2013.
66   <https://en.wikipedia.org/wiki/History_of_the_Jews_in_Canada>
67   Ruth Klien and Frank Dimant, *From Immigration to Integration: The Canadian Jewish Experience*, 2001, 136.
68   <http://thecanadianencyclopedia.ca/en/article/jewish-canadians/>
69   A.E. Prince op-ed and CE Silcox, *University of Toronto Quarterly, 1947.*
70   A.E. Prince, *United Church Observer*, March 15, 1947, 4).
71   David J. Bercuson, *Canada and the Birth of Israel* (Toronto: University of Toronto Press, 1985). cited at <http://www.jewishvirtuallibrary.org/jsource/myths/canada.html#1>
72   Klien, op.cit., 252.
73   A 2002 GPC International (Ottawa) survey at <https://www.jewishvirtuallibrary.org/myths-and-facts-canada-israel-relations-chapter-26#_edn6> Also see text at endnote 109.
74   Tulchinsky, op.cit., 350
75   "The act of going up"—that is, towards Jerusalem—"making aliyah" by emigrating to Israel.
76   Meaning, of course, Canaan. Reuben Slonim, *Both Sides Now: A 25-year encounter with Arabs and Israelis*, 1972, 105-7.
77   Kilgore, Andrew, "Facts on the Ground: A Jewish Exodus From Israel". *Washington Report on Middle East Affairs*, March 2004. According to the 2011 census, there are only 30,000 Israelis in Canada.

78	"Going Down from Heaven—or Israel", *momentmag.com*, July 2013.
79	Lawrence Davidson, "Israel's Jewish Exodus", *consortiumnews.com*, June 15, 2011.
80	Tulchinsky, op.cit., 481.
81	Tulchinsky, op.cit., 450.
82	<http://www.moia.gov.il/Hebrew/InformationAndAdvertising/Statistics/Documents/2016/OLIM1A.xls>
83	<http://ericwalberg.com/index.php?option=com_content&view=article&id=544:hebdo-vs-al-jazeera-a-tale-of-two-journalisms&catid=40:middle-east&Itemid=93>
84	<http://www.jewishdatabank.org/Studies/downloadFile.cfm?FileID=3189>
85	Tulchinsky, op.cit., 456.
86	Tulchinsky, op.cit., 456-7.
87	Abella, *Coat*, 235.
88	Slonim, *Both Sides Now: A 25-year encounter with Arabs and Israelis*, 1972, 97.
89	Morton Weinfeld, "Quebec anti-Semitism and anti-Semitism in Quebec", *jcpa.org*, 2008.
90	A 1994 survey quoted in Robinson, op.cit.,124.
91	Robinson, op.cit.,173.
92	The other main Jewish organizations include **World Zionist Organization** (1897), founded at the initiative of Theodor Herzl at the First World Zionist Congress, specifically to achieve a nation state for Jews, the **Zionist Organization of America** (ZOA, 1897, affiliated with WZO), and the **American Jewish Committee** (AJC, 1906), most having international affiliations. The **American Jewish Congress** (1918) was the umbrella organization of all US Jewish organizations, which was instrumental in establishing the **World Jewish Congress** (1936) to unite world Jewry in the face of Nazism.
93	Patron of Baruch Goldstein, who emigrated to Israel in 1983 and murdered 29 Palestinian Muslim worshippers, wounding another 125.
94	The Canadian Museum for Human Rights (CMHR) is a national museum in Winnipeg which was/is sharply criticized as a showpiece for 'the Holocaust', with almost no representation of the Holodomor (Ukrainian for hunger-death) and other 20th century genocides, though with a special exhibition devoted to the Native American history. Prior to 1923, several Aboriginal graves had been uncovered while digging for foundations, indicating that the CMHR is located on an Aboriginal burial grounds, but the construction had started and went ahead anyway. The museum was the idea of the Asper Foundation, which donated $20 million, with the final $300 million cost covered by the Winnipeg, Manitoba, and Canadian governments. It became an important symbol for Harper in his eagerness to please his Zionist followers, finally opening after much controversy in 2014. A disgruntled Ukrainian Canadian leader, Lubomyr Luciuk, who had fought the hasbarah, complaining that the tiny Holodomor exhibit was placed near the washrooms, said, "the building is more mausoleum than museum." ("Museum doesn't deliver equally", *Kingston Whig Standard*, December 17, 2014."
95	The Canadian Museum of Civilization across from the parliament buildings in Ottawa is Canada's national museum of human history, which includes the most extensive museum honoring the First Nations. It and the Royal Ontario Museum have agreed to return many of their sacred artifacts to the tribes to whom they belonged. There are numerous smaller centers of native art and

culture across Canada, which document local native history. The US opened the National Museum of the American Indian within the Smithsonian Institution, with sites in New York and Washington, DC, and there are 31 other major museums for different native tribes across the US, but none dedicated to the destruction of the natives in the past 400 years.

96 Catherine Chatterley, *The Antisemitic Imagination*, Indiana University Press, 2016.
97 <http://catherinechatterley.com/writing.html>
98 Munk's endowment was made on the understanding that the university would match it, and the Canadian government would double that total, with Munk controlling the agenda of the program.
99 Weinfeld, op.cit., 247.
100 Engler op.cit., 127.
101 Ibid., 212.
102 Ibid., 215, 217.
103 Graeme Hamilton, "Nasty neighbours: Prominent Hasidic leaders take Montreal blogger to court over libel claims", *National Post*, January 16, 2013.
104 Robinson, op.cit., 183.
105 The Haifa Center was partly sponsored by Larry and Judy Tanenbaum. Tanenbaum was one of a half-dozen donors who scrapped the hundred-year-old Canadian Jewish Congress in 2011 and replaced it with the Centre for Israel and Jewish Affairs. They also helped Bronfman at University of Toronto (see above), and set up the Tony and Elizabeth Comper MAOF Environmental Experience. MAOF (the Hebrew word for flight and vision) is geared toward young immigrants and youth in underprivileged and peripheral areas of Israel. The educational program will teach about ecology and Zionism. Yves Engler, "The Holocaust Industry in Canada", *dissidentvoice.org*, January 2nd, 2017.
106 January 1999, Weinfeld, 340
107 Robinson, op. cit., 178-9.
108 Robinson, op. cit., 179.
109 Jonathan Kay, "B'nai Brith report on anti-Semitism debunked," *National Post*, December 5, 2010.
110 Robinson, op. cit., 180.
111 Criticism of Israel is not racist for 91% to 100% of Liberal, Green and NDP supporters. EKOS survey 2017 at Dmitri Lascaris, "Poll: Canada's politicians drastically out of touch with public on Israel", *mondweiss.net*, February 2017.
112 Goldwin Smith, *A selection from Goldwin Smith's correspondence*, 9, 10.
113 Ramsay Cook, *The Regenerators, Social Criticism in Late Victorian English Canada*, 1986, 36.
114 Davies, op. cit., 85.
115 Tulchinsky, op. cit., 127.
116 Smith's works are only available in his hometown Toronto, by special request at the Reference branch of the Toronto Public Library, or at the University of Toronto research library.
117 Smith, *The Bystander*, 1882, quoted in Tulchinksy, "Goldwin Smith: Victorian Canadian Antisemite", in Davies, ed., 76.
118 Smith, *The Bystander*, March 1980.
119 Davies, op. cit., 75.
120 Smith, *Guesses at the Riddle of Existence*, Toronto, 1897, 52.
121 Arnald Haultain, *Goldwin Smith: His Life, 1910*, 54.

122	Elizabeth Wallace, *Goldwin Smith: Vicorial Liberal, 1975,* 215.
123	Goldwin Smith, *A Plea for the Abolition of Religious Tests,* Oxford, 1864, 28. in Ramsay Cook, 28.
124	Smith, *Correspondence,* 1913, 482.
125	Ibid., 505.
126	Ibid., 103, 126.
127	Ochs was engaged in crusading against antisemitism. He was active in the early years of the Anti-Defamation League (1913), serving as an executive board member, and used his influence as publisher of *The New York Times* to convince other newspapers nationwide to cease the unjustified caricaturing and lampooning of Jews in the American press. His only daughter, Iphigene Bertha Ochs, married Arthur Hays Sulzberger, who became publisher of the *Times* after Adolph died. Her son-in-law Orvil Dryfoos was publisher from 1961–63, followed by her son Arthur Ochs "Punch" Sulzberger. Her daughter, Ruth Holmberg, became publisher of the *Chattanooga Times.* Ruth Holmberg's son is Arthur Golden, author of *Memoirs of a Geisha.* Ochs' great-grandson Arthur Ochs Sulzberger, Jr. has been publisher of *The New York Times* since 1992. One of his nephews, Julius Ochs Adler, worked at *The New York Times* for more than 40 years, becoming general manager in 1935, after Ochs died. Another nephew, John Bertram Oakes, the son of his brother George Washington Ochs Oakes, in 1961 became editorial page editor of *The Times'* editorial page, which he edited until 1976.
128	Smith, *Correspondence,* 462.
129	Smith, *Correspondence,* 441. Cook et al agree, though they assume 'antisemitism' is the same as racism, which Smith denies. "Smith's extreme ethnocentricity in the case of the Jewish people, as Gerald Tulchinsky has shown, can only be described as anti-Semitism." Ramsay Cook, *Dictionary of Canadian Biography,* Volume XIII (1901-1910) Goldwin Smith.
130	Smith *Correspondence,* in 1905 to his (Jewish) friend George Freeman in New York.
131	Disraeli (1804–1881) was a convert to the established Church of England and ardent imperialist. He did not speak Hebrew (so not strictly speaking 'Semitic', but was unashamed of his Jewish heritage, telling the House of Commons, "Jews are an ancient people, a famous people, who in the end have generally obtained their ends. They have outlived the Pharaohs, Roman Caesars, and Arabian Caliphs." (Smith, *Correspondence,* 218.)
132	Robinson, op. cit., 43.
133	Karl Marx, "On the Jewish Question", 1844.
134	*Evening Telegram* June 12, 1914.
135	Alan Davies, *How Silent Were the Churches?,* 1997, 42-3.
136	*Observer,* 1/3/67.
137	*Observer* 1/10/67.
138	International Jewish Labour Bund, in A.C. Forrest, The unholy land, 1968, 72.
139	Forrest, op.cit., 73.
140	Avnery, Uri (1968): *Israel Without Zionists: A Plea for Peace in the Middle East,* MacMillan Co., New York, in Forrest, op. cit., 44.
141	Ibid., 164.
142	Tulchinsky, op. cit., 436.
143	By 1972 the ADL already had 28 regional offices in US, 2 in Canada.
144	The CRA registers foreign charities involved in disaster relief, humanitarian

aid or "activities in the national interest of Canada." (Tax Alert - Canada, Issue No. 29, April 27, 2015) Canadian charities such as KAIROS promoting humanitarian aid to Palestinians were disqualified under the Harper government, accused of supporting terrorism, but the Canadian branch of the ADL and the Jewish National Fund are accepted.

145 *Observer*, March 1972.

146 Haim Genizi, *The Holocaust, Israel, and Canadian Protestant Churches*, 2002, 155.

147 Ibid., 165.

148 Ibid., 160.

149 "In all probability, it was an attempt to make some sense out of the overwhelming devastation that had already befallen Jerusalem, the Temple, and the Jewish people in the Roman war; it was not intended to apply to future generations of Jews as an open-ended curse. It is hard to imagine that Jews, who hated the Romans and the cruel Roman punishment of crucifixion, would mock one of their own hanging in agony on a cross. We are told that the high priests and elders did this (27:41). Their antagonism is said to have continued even after the resurrection (28:11–15). Perhaps Matthew told the story in this way out of anger over leadership that he perceived as misguided; he hoped that more Jews would adopt his interpretation of events. He was deeply committed to his vision of a renewed Judaism through Jesus. He would be surprised and hurt by the anti-Judaic sentiment inspired by his gospel. He stresses the importance of forgiveness, of living by an honorable code, and of love even for the enemy (5:21–26; 18:10–35)." <http://www.united-church.ca/sites/default/files/resources/study_bearing-faithful-witness.pdf>

150 Robert Mansfield, *Everything I Learned About Theology I Did Not Get From Sunday School*, Xulon Press, 2003, 106.

151 Gilad Atzmon, "Protestants get ready to grovel", November 9, 2016. <http://www.intrepidreport.com/archives/19645>

152 <http://www.christianitytoday.com/history/issues/issue-39/was-luther-anti-semitic.html >

153 Reuben Slonim, *United Church Observer*, July 1974.

154 Slonim, *Both Sides Now: A 25-year encounter with Arabs and Israelis* (1972), 97.

155 http://www.billgladstone.ca/?p=7369

156 Slonim, *Family Quarrel: The United Church and the Jews*, Clark & Co, Irwin, 1977, 106.

| Chapter Six |

ENTRENCHING A CANADIAN PRO-ISRAEL FOREIGN POLICY

We can think of both Canada and Israel as children with growing pains by the end of WWII. Canada had been struggling to achieve independence from Britain—not very hard, but it was time to fly the coop, or at least make the pretense of flying.

The British Empire Economic Conference was held in Ottawa in 1932, with Conservative R.B. Bennett as prime minister agreeing to "Imperial preference" or "Empire Free-Trade", based on the principle of "home producers first, empire producers second, and foreign producers last" initially for a period of 5 years. But with Mackenzie King returning to office in 1935, this was a last gasp of British imperialism in Canada. At the earlier 1921 Imperial Conference, King had rejected the demand to renew the pre-WWI empire, endorsing Goldwin Smith's call for a "commonwealth" of former colonies, and a move towards world government, as epitomized in the new League of Nations. As World War II drew to a close, Imperial Conferences were replaced by Commonwealth Prime Ministers' Conferences, but were of little consequence, the new United Nations taking precedent.

King insisted on Canada's right to declare war against Germany in 1939 rather than accept a blanket British declaration for Canada as a colony, as had been the case in WWI. Precisely one week after Britain's, Canada's declaration of war was a first tentative step towards Canada asserting its adulthood among nations, and marked Canada's real 'declaration of independence'.[1] King also prided himself as a kind of intermediary between the US and Britain, especially in the phony pre-

WWII period when FDR couldn't bring the US into the fray, facing a strong isolationist movement.

Unlike WWI, WWII was a popular cause from the start among Jews in Canada, with the birth of Israel, in embryo since 1917, due at the close of the war. The Arab world, still more or less under colonial occupation, knew this and was not interested in making room for a Jewish sibling, so naturally it was less than enthusiastic about the WWII allied cause, despite Egypt and the Levant (Syria, Lebanon, Jordan, Palestine) being British and French 'mandates', and by definition on the side of the 'allies'.

Charges by Israel that Arabs and Muslims were therefore traitors, and even fascists, are distortions of the reality. Living in mandates, they had no state to betray, and had every right to be suspicious. From their point of view a defeat of the British and French would work in their favor. Mussolini's fantasy of a Roman empire in north Africa was nonsense, Germany's plans for the Middle East were not clear, but British/French plans were clear and for them portended only further disaster. But the allies won, and battle-hardened Jews—from both Palestine and Canada—now directed their arms at the Arabs. Israel made up for lost time in a hurry, growing literally in spurts and starts, gathering Jews from around the world, pushing aside anyone that resisted.

Canada had very little by way of relations with the Arab world up to this point. Arabs were not part of the British imperial elite nor part of the immigrant waves that brought Jews to Canada. Far from it, they viewed interest-bearing banking as 'haram' (sinful) and their relations with non-Muslim nations were virtually impossible, as the Arab world was occupied by imperialists Britain and France—with the exception of Saudi Arabia, seat of the two most holy cities in Islam, and conveniently for the Saudis, a desolate wasteland at the time, of no interest to potential occupiers.

But that was changing rapidly now, with Canadian Jews enthusiastically supporting the fledgling Jewish state there, where Canadians were told there were no local Palestinians, or if there were, they were barbaric terrorists. Canada was thrown into the Middle East cauldron through its one-sided support for Israel, and the next 70 years have merely confirmed the embarrassing fact that Canadians have no independent foreign policy, especially in the Middle East.[2]

From Pearson to Chretien

Mackenzie King was not enthusiastic about what he foresaw as a recipe for conflict, and withheld recognition of Israel. As a devout Presbyterian, but not a literalist, he knew enough biblical history to be aware of the validity and implications of a self-proclaimed Jewish state, and did not condone Pearson's eagerness to recognize Israel. He was familiar with the strong dissent on Israeli recognition in the United Church, which most Presbyterians had joined in 1925.

With his retirement, **Louis St. Laurent** (PM 1948–57) appointed **Lester Pearson** (PM 1963–68), as Canada's first UN ambassador and foreign minister, and Canada moved away from King's British nostalgia to support the US and Israel. St. Laurent was staunchly anticommunist, pro-US, pro-NATO. Pearson was, too. He had been at the founding conference of the UN in San Francisco in 1945, and was chairman of the UN Special Committee on Palestine in 1947. The Arabs wanted the UN (now in charge of Palestine) to grant Palestine immediate independence as one democratic country, the European refugee issue excluded, in line with practice for Syria, Lebanon, Jordan and Egypt. But Britain's refusal to carry out her Mandate, handing over authority in Palestine to the UN meant that effectively now *the US* was in charge. Truman agreed to fashion a Jewish state under intense pressure from the Jewish lobby, and the Arabs boycotted what was clearly a rigged process, though their solution of one state was the only logical one.

Pearson's "adherence to the pro-partition fold was an important turning point" (vs a binational state), "a fitting climax to [Canadian] Justice Rand's work," according to David Horowitz, first governor of Bank of Israel.[3] Canadians Pearson and Rand made sure that Jews, one third of population owning 7% of the land, would receive 55% of the land. The only Middle East expert at the Department of External Affairs, Elizabeth MacCallum, said Canada supported partition, "because we didn't give two hoots for democracy."[4] She warned Pearson that the Middle East was now in for 40 years of war.[5]

"By the summer of 1950, Israeli arms requests were being placed in Canada."[6] Egyptian president Nasser condemned this when he took power. Canada wasn't interested and sold 24 F86 jets to Israel on behalf of the US in early 1956, just as Israel was preparing to launch a war against Egypt. The US used Ottawa as cover, because Canada had no interests in the region (other than supporting Israel). Pearson as external affairs minister in 1952 defended Israel unconditionally. "Israel is beginning to emerge as the only stable element in the whole Middle East area."[7] Pearson went on to explain how "Israel may assume an important role in western defence as the southern pivot of current plans for the defence" of the eastern Mediterranean. Liberal MP Don Carrick echoed geopolitical theorist MacKinder in a 1956 speech: "Israel could be an outpost and source of security for the western world in the Middle East. The Egyptians have driven the British out of the Suez ... Israel could constitute an arsenal for the democracies of the free world in the Middle East."[8]

Pearson's Nobel Prize in 1957 was earned in the service of Israel, the clear villain in Egypt's President Nasser's Bay of Pigs, when Israel invaded Egypt at the behest of Britain and France to try to seize Egypt's Suez Canal. Israel was forced by the US to withdraw, but suffered no ill effects for its crimes, and was assured of the presence of 'United Nations' peacekeepers (whom Israel would kill ten years later, when it reinvaded Egypt). Pearson's bumbling cheery smile convinced the very angry Egyptians that he had negotiated the best deal possible, though no one was fooled about who got the best deal.

Israel was not totally happy, having to give up Sinai, but the peace-keeping force Pearson set up there meant Egypt was no longer a threat to Israel, and the Straits of Tiran, closed by Egypt since 1951, were re-opened to Israeli shipping. As no peace settlement was agreed, Israel also had had a dry run for its future war plans. The ceasefire with Egypt laid the groundwork for the Six Day War in 1967, a mere 10 years later. "Pearson backed the Israeli move to secure control over the Palestinian lands in the West Bank and Gaza Strip after the war in 1967. He actively opposed moves within the UN to adopt resolutions calling on Israel to withdraw from occupied Palestinian territory, cornering Canada into an extreme minority while the majority of nations condemned Israeli occupation."[9]

Pearson was teased during and after 1947 as "Lord Balfour of Canada" and "Rabbi Pearson". In 1960 he was awarded Israel's Medallion of Valor, and in 1968, the Theodore Herzl award from the ZOA for "commitment to Jewish freedom and Israel".

The key to Israel's success in shaping Canada's foreign policy is not 'hard power', i.e., threatening to invade or otherwise terrorize Canadians militarily. It is Israeli **'soft power'**, built on Canada's relatively large, prominent and Zionist Jewish community, and the Old Testament meme among Christian literalists (including Pearson, whose father was a minister), who quickly became supportive of the Jewish state. To the old charge of "antisemitism" was now added the charge of 'wanting to destroy Israel', leveled at any criticism of Israel or rejection of the concept of a racially-based state, no matter how justified by international law. The sudden dual national identity of all Jews (by definition) created a new problem for non-Jewish Canadians, as Israel could gain support, not just at a government-to-government level, but through families and individual Jews, who could now operate in the interests of Israel both as fundraisers and as *sayanim,* agents of Israel. Hundreds of Canadians 'make aliyah' each year, gaining automatic Israeli citizenship, taking their Canadian passports with them, and are free to stay visa-free in either country. It is impossible to know who among them or the non-aliyahs is keen enough to carry out activities which might include 'destroying Canada'. (See 'Dual Loyalties' below.)

Increasing control of the media reached the point where Canada's largest media magnate, Israel Asper, controlling 60% of Canadian news media, was able to tell his newspapers not to publish articles critical of Israel.[10] Objectivity on news concerning Israel in mainstream Canadian media is mostly absent; serious criticism only available in alternative media. On the surface, Canada officially became "Israel's best friend" under Harper (now, under Justin Trudeau, just "friend").

As a postmodern nation, Canada has almost no independent foreign policy, following US and now Israeli directives on all key issues. The 'plus' side for Canadians is that there should be little need for Israel to spy on Canada, as Canada is already doing what it should. *Sayanim* are more important in hostile countries, like Iraq, Iran, and quasi-neutral countries in Europe, and in the imperial ally-rival, the US. Israel relies on the Jewish elite in Canada to convince Canadians that Israel's actions are necessary for promoting security and prosperity in the Middle East, to act as a watchdog on incipient "antisemitism" both in the broad public and at universities, on "Holocaust denial", grassroots campaigning exposing Israeli atrocities, etc.

The 'down' side of Canada's being weak and out-of-the-loop is that Israel feels free to violate Canadian laws when it's useful, knowing it will not be censured.

The Israel lobby's main purpose is to *shape* the discourse, leading to 'democratic consensus' and appropriate government policies, controlling culture through ownership, monitoring and attacking offenders. Occasionally this fails, but less often after 1956. Israel has become a bully, and a powerful one, with Canada in its thrall. "Jewish Power is the capacity to silence the debate on Jewish Power," writes Gilad Atzmon.[11]

Attempts to protest by a few brave Canadian officials over the years were unsuccessful, and by the 21st century had ceased altogether, leaving the task to a handful of grassroots organizations. That didn't mean an end to actual anti-Jewish prejudice, though it is now less visible. Israel as the Jewish state is no poster child for peace, as daily atrocities force media attention, however one-sidedly they are reported. Resentment of Canada's Zionist-dominated policies remains, however, inevitably generating anti-Jewish anger—given that Jews are automatically identified with the 'Jewish state', and increasingly from the rest of Canada's multicultural mosaic.

Pearson was derided by his own Liberal Party and prime minister successor, **Pierre Trudeau**, (PM 1968–1979, 1980–1984) as the "defrocked Prince of Peace". Pearson was so pro-Zionist/imperialist that Noam Chomsky turned Peter Gzowski's innocent question about his flight on Morningside radio into a shocking moment of ugly truth:[12]

> NC: I landed at War Criminal Airport.
> PG: What do you mean?
> NC: The Lester B. Pearson Airport.

Chomsky was expected to safely diss the US—a favourite pastime of Canadian media gadflies—but decided instead to tell some painful truths about Canada's phony peacenik image and its iconic Nobel Peace Prize prime minister. Gzowski lost it, was furious, and let Chomsky know it. Surprisingly, thousands of listeners phoned in and supported Chomsky, chastizing Gzowski for his un-Canadian-like rudeness, forcing Gzowski to eat crow and interview Chomsky later from Boston, though on the condition that Chomsky would throw no further punches.

Trudeau was not impressed by Pearson's strongly pro-Israel bias, but he was in the end unable to change Canada's foreign policy. Trudeau was already faced with a strong Zionist lobby, and was MP in the predominantly Jewish riding of Mount Royal. He distanced himself from Pearson's blanket endorsement of Israel, instead, promising

Canadian Jewish Congress lobbyists in 1970, that he would strive to persuade the Soviet government to "allow Jews cultural freedom and permit some emigration to Israel." When Premier Alexei Kosygin paid a state visit to Canada in October 1971, there were demonstrations. Already the plot to get Soviet Jews to Israel was underway. In 1971, 11 Soviet Jews hijacked a Russian airliner, which Canadian Jews responded to with demonstrations of support across the country. Sixty rabbis prayed in front of the Soviet embassy and on Parliament Hill. It worked. In 1971, Jewish emigration levels jumped to three times the 1968-70 rate, and they doubled again in 1972 and continued throughout the 1970s.

Trudeau had sympathy for the Palestinians, but the Jews were a stronger political force. Following the 1973 war, Canadian embassies and trade missions were opened in a number of Arab and Muslim capitals. Although Canada imported no oil from the Middle East, there was an increasing tendency on Ottawa's part to reach out to Arab countries, including abstaining on UN resolutions critical of Israel that Canada had traditionally opposed. Trudeau refused to pass anti-boycott legislation against the Arab boycott of Israel or publish a list of Canadian companies that were observing the boycott when pressured in 1977.

Although Canada had always supported the according of individual rights to Palestinian refugees, Trudeau increasingly focused on the collective rights of the Palestinians as a people. Canada also increasingly viewed the PLO as the political representative of the Palestinians and invited it to participate in international conferences scheduled for Toronto and Vancouver. By the late 1970s and early 1980s, Trudeau permitted Canadian diplomats to initiate mid-level contacts with the PLO, and senior Canadian officials for the first time declared support for the concept of a Palestinian "homeland" within identifiable boundaries (the West Bank and Gaza Strip). Trudeau questioned the benefit to Canada of participating in UN peacekeeping forces established in the Sinai and the Golan Heights in 1974 and 1975, agreeing to the UN missions only under pressure from the US.

Ontario premier Bill Davis, facing a close election race in 1975, bowed to pressure from Jewish groups to insist that Trudeau cancel the 5th UN Congress on the Prevention of Crime and the Treatment of Offenders, scheduled to take place in Toronto in September 1975 because the PLO had been granted observer status. But Trudeau did not block the May 1976 UN Habitat Conference, attended by PLO representatives. External Affairs Minister Allan MacEachen wanted to make contact with

PLO moderates. He told Canada-Israel Committee officials "Canada was not prepared to prejudge the PLO issue."[13]

In 1982, Trudeau sent a letter to Israel's Prime Minister Menachem Begin counseling restraint in the face of escalating PLO attacks across the Lebanese border. Trudeau also cautioned that Israeli counter-terrorism policies had given "Israel's friends certain cause for concern, to say nothing of its enemies." On June 9, Trudeau sent a second letter to Begin, expressing "dismay" over Israel's incursion into southern Lebanon and informed Begin that he could not "accept the proposition that the present military activities are justified or that they would provide the long-term security that you seek for the Israeli people."[14]

In 1981, Pierre Trudeau stated, Jews "opened the way to growing antisemitism by making their views known on matters related to Israel and anti-boycott legislation," echoing an op-ed in the *Toronto Star* by a former moderator of the United Church stating, "Jews could cause antisemitism if they continued to attack those who spoke out against Israel."[15]

Looking back on this period, Trudeau appears to have done his best to overcome the sorry legacy of the 'defrocked Prince of Peace'. A stronger pro-Palestinian movement in Canada at that time would have given Trudeau more credibility in his attempts to steer Canadian foreign policy in a more balanced direction, but young people were more interested in protesting the Vietnam War and defending war resisters. Just as King told Jewish lobbyists in 1939 that he needed a mass Canadian protest to take the controversial decision to allow the St Louis to unload its 900 Jewish refugees, Trudeau need grassroots support to resist the powerful Jewish lobby in his parliamentary waiting room. But Trudeau never faced opposition in his predominantly Jewish home riding. Measured criticism of Israel is secretly welcomed by many Jews, themselves afraid to speak out.

Progressive Conservative Party leader **Joe Clark** (PM 1979–80) pledged during the 1979 federal election campaign to move Canada's embassy in Israel from Tel Aviv to Jerusalem. However, once in office, Clark quickly rescinded the embassy transfer, after Arab threats of economic sanctions reached the ears of Bell Canada, Royal Bank, ATCO and Bombardier. He had not been versed on the intricacies of the Israel, Palestine and US nexus, and learned his lesson. Clark's successors have shown no similar inclination to move the embassy, though US presidential candidates George Bush and Donald Trump also raised the prospects. Clark's bungling continued, as he lost a vote of confidence and became Canada's shortest lived prime minister.

Back in opposition, Clark had his fingers burnt by Zionists closer to home, when he joined Prime Minister Trudeau to protest the brutal invasion of Lebanon. The new face of Canadian Jews was demonstrated when Clark issued a public rebuke to the CJC at its annual policy convention for its stance of unconditionally supporting Israel in that war. During the speech, Clark was interrupted with heckles from the crowd and approximately 50 people left the room in protest. Near the end of his remarks, the audience began to sing Hatikvah, the Israeli national anthem. The Zionist movement had become the sole voice of Canadian Jews, an increasingly strident and assertive one.

Clark was not intimidated. In a replay in 1988, at a Canada-Israel Committee function, back in power as foreign affairs minister, Clark accused Israel of grave human rights violations and "illegal" maintenance of control by "force and fear". CIC chair Sidney Spivak threatened to unleash a Jewish campaign against him at the next election. Many again walked out. The *Toronto Star* picked up the baton, charging Zionists with "dual loyalty", and commending Clark's words as "a necessary reminder to members of the Jewish community in Canada that they are citizens of Canada not Israel." The Ontario Press Council tried to cool tempers by telling the *Star* the op-ed should have specified only those who walked out.[16]

Brian Mulroney (PM 1984–1993) earned Zionist approval in 1985 by setting up the Deschênes Commission to prosecute Nazi war criminals residing in Canada. Its final report recommended changes to the Criminal Code to allow for their prosecution in Canada. In 1987, the federal government announced that those alleged to have been involved in the commission of war crimes or crimes against humanity would be subject to criminal prosecution or revocation of citizenship and deportation.

Its pickings were slim. The commission found evidence against 20 individuals, and only pressed charges against four men on allegations of participation in Holocaust war crimes. One case ended in acquittal; two cases were dropped for lack of evidence; the fourth case was stayed due to the health of the defendant. Since 1998, courts have found that six men, all Ukrainian, misrepresented their wartime activities and could have their citizenship revoked (they weren't deported). Another seven people subject to deportation died.

The only case to go to court was against Imre Finta (1987–90), and he was acquitted.[17] The commission was not popular among non-Jewish east Europeans, who saw it as a campaign to slur Ukrainians, Hungarians and others. Don Blenkarn, Conservative MP Mississauga South, criticized the commission for sensationalizing poorly documented cases, with the result that the "government pays heavily politically and the Jewish community is going to suffer."[18]

Mulroney was faced with a dilemma in 1987, when relations between the Jewish Community and the Canadian government became strained after the first Intifada. Clearly, Mulroney wanted to criticize Israel, but instead, let Clark be the fall guy, resulting in the above-mentioned intervention by Clark. Mulroney was unhappy with the fracas and to try to bring some accommodation, that same year sponsored a seminar on the Middle East at Montebello, where 15 Jews and 15 Arabs met to discuss peace and war. But no Zionist organizations were there to vet the invitations, and loudly denounced it. It was the first and last such seminar.

The Jewish/ Israeli lobby has determined all Canadian foreign policy relating to Israel since it got going for real in the 1960s, and, by the 1980s was in high gear, with the noisy trials of Holocaust revisionist historians Keegstra and Zundel starting in 1984, the latter's lasting almost a decade. But the seeds for this surrender of Canadian sovereignty were long ago planted under Lester Pearson.

Jean Chretien (PM 1993–2003) returned to Trudeau's slightly more critical attitude to Israel and indeed, the US imperial project, most notably in his refusal to send troops to Iraq in 2003. Massive demonstrations did for Chretien what King had called on his Jewish lobbyists to do in 1939 if they wanted to influence policy. The Zionists don't have all that much clout electorally, despite dominating the mainstream media. Their ability to mobilize others is less than that of any other ethnic group, so mass demonstrations are not on B'nai Brith's agenda. Better the vizier and lobbyists, the "handful of prominent *shtadlans*" to make Israel's case in the halls of power.

Few Canadian Jews vote based on Ottawa's policy towards Israel. Historically, there is actually an inverse correlation between pro-Israel governments and Jewish support. Pierre Trudeau and Jean Chretien, for instance, garnered more support from the Jewish community than Brian Mulroney, yet Mulroney was more supportive of Israel.[19] Harper found this out to his dismay. Writes *Globe and Mail* columnist Margaret

Wente, "Some of my Jewish friends can't decide what's more offensive – Mr. Harper's lovey-dovey friendship with Bibi Netanyahu (not their favorite guy), or the casual assumption in some parts of the media that all Jews think alike, that all they care about is Israel, and that their votes can be bought so cheaply."[20]

Harper

As a postmodern nation, Canada is the perfect "best friend" of Israel, a nice, modest foil masking the underlying imperial links of Canada-Israel. Both were colonial projects, 'white dominions' of Britain, now continuing their lives under US hegemony. Israel keeps a check on the Arab countries surrounding it and Canada helps out, trying to maintain a look of innocence, a softer version of the US-Israel hard power fist.

Support for Israel reached a zenith under Conservative Prime Minister **Stephen Harper** (PM 2006–2015). While most Catholics and Protestants have been ignorant or indifferent to Zionism, backing is strong among evangelicals who believe Jews need to "return" to the Middle East to hasten the second coming of Jesus and the Apocalypse as foretold in *Revelation*. In 2010, at a Christian Zionist event in Toronto. Jeff Watson, Conservative MP for Essex, delivered greetings from Prime Minister Stephen Harper, saying, "The creation of the state of Israel fulfills God's promise in Deuteronomy to gather the Jewish people from all corners of the world."[21] About 10% of Canadians identify themselves as evangelicals, including a number of Harper's cabinet ministers. The president of the right wing Canadian Centre for Policy Studies, Joseph Ben-Ami, explains: "The Jewish community in Canada is 380,000 strong; the evangelical community is 3.5 million. The real support base for Israel is Christians."[22]

All this is in fact an eerie replay of John Mearsheimer and Stephen Walt's argument about the Israeli lobby in the US, whose "core" is "American Jews who make a significant effort in their daily lives to bend US policy so that it furthers Israel's interests."[23] Its Canadian counterpart, led by the CJC/CIJA and B'nai Brith, through extensive media control and privileged access to the highest levels of government, have kept all the major parties onboard since the 1950s, ensuring the continuation of Pearson's pro-Israel policy as Harper took it to an extreme.

At the very moment I was creating a tizzy at the *National Post* for writing about the Cairo anti-imperialist conference,[24] Harper was carrying out a revolution in Canadian foreign policy, signing a **public security cooperation "partnership" in 2008** with Israel to "protect their respective countries' population, assets and interests from common threats". Israel security agents now officially assist Canada's security services in profiling Canadians citizens and monitoring individuals and/or organizations in Canada involved in supporting the rights of Palestinians. This had been going on for years, but now it was official. (See "Dual Loyalties" below.) At the same time, he introduced a novel foreign adviser, an **Israeli military attaché**, to his circle (the US has one too). In January 2011, Canada and Israel signed an umbrella pact for defense and military cooperation and then a **"strategic partnership"** in 2014, in order to "deepen their relationship by enhancing their bilateral engagement and cooperation across the widest possible spectrum." Included in this agreement are sections providing for increased security consultations and cooperation, frequent intergovernmental meetings, cooperation in joint research and development projects, and strengthening of counter-terrorism collaboration.

These moves resulted in a string of shameful one-sided votes and actions by Harper:

- Calling Israel's 2006 invasion of Lebanon a "measured response". A Canadian UN peacekeeper was targeted and killed by Israeli in the invasion. Harper refused to protest, asking rhetorically in parliament what they were doing there in the first place.
- Refusal to condemn the invasion of Gaza in December 2008 or the siege of Gaza (the only dissent at the UN Human Rights Council).
- Refusal to condemn the Israeli murder of 9 members of the Gaza Freedom Flotilla in May 2009.
- Opposition to an attempted IAEA probe of Israel's nuclear facilities as part of an effort to create a nuclear-weapons-free Middle East.
- Cutting off Canada's contribution to UN humanitarian aid to Gaza because it was going through the (democratically elected) Hamas government.
- Cutting funding to KAIROS and other Canadian NGOs which

supported Palestinians in 2009, ending 35 years of government funding for KAIROS, supposedly for supporting BDS (which it denied).
- Banning British MP George Galloway from coming to Canada to speak at a pro-Palestinian rally in 2009, though George Galloway was entering from the US and had spoken at such a gathering there. Such bans on peace activists have only multiplied since then.
- Opposing the successful Palestinian bid in 2012 to upgrade its status at the UN from "non-member observer entity" to "non-member observer state".
- Breaking off diplomatic relations with Iran in September 2012 at the height of the Israeli mania to invade Iran.
- Founding the Canadian Parliamentary Coalition to Combat Antisemitism (CPCCA) in 2009 and hosting the 2011 Inter-parliamentary Coalition for Combating Antisemitism, which only confirmed the *lack of antisemitism*.[25]
- Flirting openly with the Jewish Defence League, by including JDL Canada's 'event co-ordinator' Julius Suraski on an official delegation to Israel in 2014.
- In 2015, finalizing a deal with Israel for the purchase of Iron Dome radar technology.

UN Embroglio

It was Canada's turn to join the UN Security Council in a rotating regional seat in 2010, but UN members snubbed Canada, acknowledging Harper's affront on the Kyoto treaty[26] and the pro-Israeli bias of the Conservatives. The humiliating withdrawal by Canada from the race with Germany and Portugal for a coveted place on the United Nations Security Council revealed what close observers have long known—that the current Conservative government in Ottawa has nothing but disdain for the world's tattered peacekeeper and would most likely just use its seat to serve US and Israel's agenda. Harper blamed the snub on "a rising tide of antisemitism", and attacked Liberal Party leader Michael Ignatieff for scuttling the UN bid with his criticisms of Canadian foreign policy. Israeli-American analyst Israel Matzav laments, "Canada's candidacy was voted down because of its close relations with Israel."

Canada has served on the Security Council many times in the

past, once each decade since the 1950s, and was never refused when it ran for a seat. It had carved out a highly respected role of good cop to its southern neighbor's bad cop: Lester Pearson's Nobel Peace Prize in 1957 for negotiating the withdrawal from Egypt's Sinai of Israeli troops, replaced by UN peacekeepers; Canada's refusal to break relations with Cuba after the 1959 revolution; refusal to send troops to Vietnam (unlike another 'white' colony Australia); recognition of China in 1970; and refusal to send troops to Iraq in 2003.

Canadian Conservatives from the days of Confederation in 1867 until relatively recently stood for an independent Canada. The only arguably great Conservative leader since Confederation, John Diefenbaker, refused to break relations with Cuba, and refused to station US nuclear weapons on Canadian soil, defying a furious US president Kennedy.

But the old Progressive Conservative Party was hijacked in 2003 by predominantly small-town right-wingers, boosted by the rising evangelical Christian movement, a repeat of what happened to the US Republican Party in the 1990s. The fiasco at the UN was "the world's response to a Canadian foreign policy designed to please the most reactionary, short-sighted sectors of the Conservative Party's base—evangelical Christian Zionists, extreme right-wing Jews, Islamophobes, the military-industrial-academic-complex, mining and oil executives and old Cold-Warriors."[27]

The UN criticized Harper on native issues.[28] It also took note of the Canadian **Afghan detainee abuse** scandal in 2009, when Canadian diplomat Richard Colvin, appalled by his own complicity in the torture of hundreds if not thousands of innocent Afghans, blew the whistle. He submitted documents to a House of Commons Committee proving both Harper and MacKay knew of the torture. Canadian Joint Task Force 2 commandos were regularly taking part in illegal night-time assassination raids. The government's answer was to declare the documents top secret and dismiss parliament, just as it did in 2008 when the opposition agreed to join forces and replace the minority Conservative government.

The $15 million for UNRWA-Gaza canceled by Harper ended up being not actually canceled; it was transferred to **Operation PROTEUS**, a plan to train a Palestinian security force "to ensure that the Palestinian Authority maintains control of the West Bank against Hamas," according to Canadian Ambassador to Israel Jon Allen. Boasts Minister of State for Foreign Affairs of the Americas Peter Kent, this is the country's "second largest deployment after Afghanistan".

JDL Canada disappeared under the radar after 9/11, but came alive again in 2006 with the arrival in Ottawa of ... Stephen Harper. Meir Weinstein, national director of the JDL in Canada, boasted that the JDL was responsible for banning George Galloway.[29]

Kicking Out Iran

The vilification of Iran since the Islamic revolution on January 16, 1979 has a very real logic to it, though one that is never spoken of. Iran is one of the skeletons in imperialism's closet and came back to haunt it in 1979 with a vengeance. The Islamic revolution is at least as important in history as the other momentous events of that year: the peace accord between Egypt and Israel signed in March, the advent of neoliberalism with Margaret Thatcher's election in May, and the Soviet invasion of Afghanistan in December.

Iran's remarkable, almost bloodless overthrow of the Shah startled the world, and put Canada and Israel into sharp focus, the former as a saviour of US hostages in Tehran, the latter now confronted with an implacable enemy. One of the first acts of the new Iranian head of state, Ayatollah Khomeini, was to sever ties with Israel, a close ally of the now discredited Shah. Several days after the revolution, PLO chief Yasser Arafat led a Palestinian delegation to Iran. The Palestinian delegates were publicly welcomed, and symbolically handed the keys to the former Israeli embassy in Tehran, which later became the Palestinian embassy. In August, Iran declared the final day of Friday prayers of Ramadan al-Quds Day, a celebration that has become an annual international event. The liberation of Palestine became Iran's number one international priority.

Canada's beef with Iran is not really a question of Iran's 'human rights', as Canada has diplomatic relations with countries with far worse records, in particular, Saudi Arabia and of course Israel. It is because of its commitment to Palestinian liberation and its genuinely Islamic character, which opposes the western secular order, seeing it as dissolute, lacking any clear morality, and dominated by money. Islamic Iran is a kind of religious version of the secular Soviet Union, the vanquished enemy of the West.

That translates into support for the Palestinians, opposition to Israel as a Jewish state, and opposition to imperialism in general, as imperialism (exploiting and invading other countries for material gain and outright aggression) violates Islam. True, in March 1979, months after the Iranian revolution, for a brief moment, the US was onside on Israel, when US President Carter managed to get Israel to withdraw from Sinai in exchange for peace with Egypt and a vague promise to move towards a state for the Palestinians, but that amounted to nothing, and Carter was soon history.

Despite its Shia Islam differing from the Palestinians' Sunni Islam, Iran took over the role of Palestinian ally from the Soviet Union and Iraq, as the former tottered and collapsed, and the latter became less and less reliable. Only Saudi Arabia, like Iran an Islamic state from its founding in 1932, is a reliable supporter of Palestine from the Sunni camp, but it is more an ally of imperialism, and Islamic in name only, under Wahhabi Islamic authority, providing funds and shelter to Palestinian refugees, but unable to bring Israel towards negotiating a meaningful resolution. It is caught between the US and its obligations as protector of the holy cities. Saudi Arabia is really just a tribal state, much like Israel, with morality only applying to tribal members.

Neither Saudi Arabia nor Israel are model states in western eyes (apart from Israel in a declining majority of western Jewish eyes), and they both submit to US control of the Middle East agenda and support US imperialism, thereby getting a free pass. Saudi Arabia also has the world's largest reserves of high quality oil, so its absolutist domestic regime and promotion of Muslim terrorists abroad to carry out its international agenda is tolerated, despite strong US popular domestic opposition.

But Iran remains a real ideological threat to the western order and its example and influence among others dissatisfied with imperialism is feared. Hence the unremitting policy of undermining its economy, isolating it internationally, using soft and hard power in all its manifestations (sanctions, cyberattacks, assassination of scientists, support for opposition groups such as the terrorist Mujahedin-e Khalq and separatist Jundallah) to destroy the revolution. This is a carbon copy of Great Game II against communism, and is a mainspring of Great Game III, which was supposed to complete US world hegemony (with sidekick Israel policing the Middle East), but has degenerated into a woolly 'war on terror'. Iran is the only force (along with Russia) genuinely committed to quelling the al-Qaeda remnants now funded by the Saudis and the US itself, if only inadvertently. To recognize this and cooperate with Iran would be a threat to Zionism and the entire imperialist agenda, so Iran remains the bugbear.

That is the background to Canada's surprise breaking of relations with Iran out of the blue, hours after the premiere of the Oscar favorite, *Argot*, at the Toronto International Film Festival in September 2012, a tendentious depiction of the US hostage crisis in Iran shortly after the 1979 revolution.

On September 7, as *Argot* was being screened, Foreign Affairs Minister John Baird announced that Canada was suspending all diplomatic relations with Iran, expelling all Iranian diplomats, closing its embassy in Tehran, and authorizing Turkey to act on Canada's behalf for consular services there. Baird cited Iran's enmity with Israel, its support of Syria and terrorism. "Canada views the government of Iran as the most significant threat to global peace and security in the world today," Baird had said at the Asia Pacific Economic Conference in Vladivostok, Russia, a few weeks earlier. Canada had not had a full ambassador in Iran since 2007. Relations between the two countries cooled after Iranian-Canadian free-lance photographer Zahra Kazemi died in Iran in 2003 under disputed circumstances,[30] and went from bad to worse under the Conservative government in power in Ottawa since 2006.

There was no protest in parliament over Harper's unprovoked violation of diplomatic norms. There had been lots of sabre-rattling as warning. Environment Minister Peter Kent told his confreres at the G8 in 2010 in Toronto concerning Iran, "It's a matter of timing and it's a matter of how long we can wait without taking more serious pre-emptive action. An attack on Israel would be considered an attack on Canada."

The official opposition, the NDP, should have been against it, but Mulcair himself is a Zionist. After meeting with Israeli President Shimon Peres during his official visit to Canada in May 2012, Mulcair told the press, "My in-laws are Holocaust survivors. Their history is part of my daily life. That's why I am an ardent supporter of Israel in all circumstances." Mulcair's wife, Catherine Pinhas, was born in France to a Sephardi Jewish family from Turkey. Canadians for Peace and Justice in the Middle East and Independent Jewish Voices have in the past criticized Mulcair for accepting financial support from pro-Israel lobbyists.

Not a peep from the rump Liberals, unwilling to do anything to jeopardize their already low popularity and disarray. Interim Liberal leader Bob Rae met with Netanyahu on his official visit to Canada in February 2012, and afterwards said the visit "gives all Canadians the chance to reflect on the deep friendship and strong ties between Israel and Canada. Iran's regime is a threat to the security of the region and the world. A nuclear-armed Iran would mean the threat of even greater proliferation and instability in the region, is a direct flouting of international law, and obviously raises the deepest concerns in Israel for its security."

In fact, rumor had it that this Canadian move was actually in preparation for an Israeli-US attack on Iran, though Baird demurred when asked about this as the motive for his otherwise implausible advice to all Canadians to leave Iran immediately. Baird's claim that Iran supports terrorism was one that Israeli agents have been making in Ottawa under the public security cooperation "partnership" signed in 2008 by Canada and Israel. Harper publicly stated he is convinced that Iran is trying "beyond any doubt" to develop nuclear weapons, with 'evidence' supplied by Israeli advisers. The claims were eerily like Bush's claims of proof that Saddam Hussein had WMDs as a pretext to invade Iraq in 2003,[31] and recalls Hitler's plan to invade Poland on the pretext of self-defense.

Ottawa was ready and willing to join Israel in any such attack. Harper said more than once, "An attack on Israel is an attack on Canada." There were US-conducted military 'exercises' involving Canadian ships off Iran's coast. Israel's frenzy to attack Iran was at its height in 2012, But in retrospect, it looks like it was all a hoax, perhaps an attempt to intimidate or cow Iran into stopping its support for the Palestinians.

While indeed Iran has been the nation most outspokenly critical of Israel, and is actively working to thwart the western-backed insurgency in Syria, there is no evidence of its support for "terrorism". It is in fact the victim of terrorism on the part of Israel and the US, which boast about assassinating Iranian nuclear scientists and destroying Iranian computers with viruses made-to-order, among other officially-sponsored acts of subversion.

Iranian Foreign Ministry spokesman Ramin Mehmanparast suggested another reason for Harper's latest targeting of Iran: Iran's successful hosting of the Non-Aligned Movement (NAM) summit in Tehran in August 2012. Leader of the Islamic Revolution Ayatollah Ali Khamenei says Tehran's hosting of the 16th NAM Summit was a "humiliating defeat" for the West. Humiliation was indeed the operative word for Canada in particular. The previous five years of Conservative rule in Canada brought nothing but disgrace to Canada internationally, and this move added further humiliation.

As if scripted, Israeli Prime Minister Benjamin Netanyahu immediately commended Canada's decision to break relations. With good cause, as it looks suspiciously like a response to a direct Israeli request.

The 1979 hostage taking was never forgiven by the US, despite the fact that no one died, except for eight Marines whose helicopter crashed in the Iranian desert in Carter's first bungled rescue attempt in April 1980. The hostages (taken by the angry young students unprompted by the government) were treated respectfully, allowed books, priests, exercise, provided with Christmas turkey. The black embassy workers and women were freed at the beginning in a gesture of solidarity with the oppressed. Reagan representatives secretly negotiated with the Iranians during the presidential election campaign, the "October surprise", which caused Carter to lose the election.[32] No money changed hands as a result of the siege, but the Iranian demand for an apology for the CIA coup in Iran in 1953 was never met, and the US has treated Iran much like Cuba ever since (only worse).

Terrorism from Harperism

In June 2014, the Islamic State in Iraq and Syria (ISIS) announced a worldwide caliphate, swiftly occupying large swathes of Iraq and Syria, and electrifying the Islamic world. The rebels called on Muslims to come and fight with them against imperialism and Israel. Understandably, some foolhardy young Muslims in the West and the Middle East, outraged and humiliated by US invasions of Afghanistan and Iraq, took them at their word, scraped together a few thousand dollars, snuck out of their homes and through the front lines to join their jihadis.

These included some Canadians, who had especially suffered under Israel's "best friend's" prime minister for 8 long years. But CSIS was on the alert, arresting them before they got too far. Though Canadians fight in the Israeli Defense Force (in the service of a foreign state that the UN accuses of war crimes, which amounts to state terrorism) all the time without any problem, if they decide to fight with Islamic rebels in the Middle East, they find themselves accused by a 2013 law that criminalizes "leaving or attempting to leave Canada" to commit terrorism. Somali Canadian Mohamed Hersi was nabbed in July 2014 at Toronto's Pearson airport and sentenced to 10 years in prison merely for attempting to join al-Shabab, even though Hersi was not found guilty of committing or plotting a specific act of violence. According to the presiding judge, he was "poised to become a terror tourist".

Hamiltonian and York University student, Mohamud Mohamed Mohamud, also a Somali Canadian, known to his friends and family as sociable and well-adjusted, wearing the latest fashions, listening to pop music and watching teen movies like all the rest of Canada's multicultural happy family, made it past border officials. In September, Mohamud was declared the first Canadian killed by US-backed Kurdish forces in Syria. An estimated 11,000 such fighters had already made the leap. Up to 130 Canadians are estimated to have joined them.

Mohamud Mohamed

As Canadian prime minister, Stephen Harper enthusiastically volunteered to send Canadian bombers and ground forces to Iraq (70 of the proposed 600-member contingent were already there); soon Canadian soldiers would be targeting Canadian jihadists like Mohamud, far from home. Having presided over Canada's Afghanistan mission, which killed 159 and left almost 2,000 Canadian soldiers traumatized and wounded, Harper was eager to repeat this disaster, even as frustrated Canadian youth reacted by joining what they believed was the latest jihad *against* western occupation of the Middle East.

Both Mohamud/Mohamed and Harper's commitment to multiculturalism were clearly skin deep. For Harper and prime ministers before and after, multiculturalism was just about the annual Toronto multiculturalism fair, Caribana, and matzo balls, but the real glue that binds Canadian policies is Canada's privileged economic place in the Anglo-American-dominated global social order. For the would-be jihadis, to partake in this pie meant humiliation and moral decay.

Jingoism generated by fighting a war far from home is also a great vote-getter, and in 2014, Harper was preparing for the 2015 election. Canada has no conscription, so only the committed join the Canadian army. As a result, there is no big outcry as soldiers die. On the contrary, youth such as Mohamud/ Mohamed are denounced as misguided and naive. But they are really just responding to what is actually the West's own cynical call to prop up the US-installed Iraq government and overthrow the Syrian government, a decades-old western policy and still the goal of the US government, despite President Bashir Assad being the main force resisting ISIS. But fighting for the other side is forbidden in both the US and Canada.

Under Harper, Canada seemed to be developing a thriving Muslim-based extremism, or so CSIS would have us believe. Shortly after the Somali Canadians were caught in the crossfire, there was a hit-and-run killing of a Canadian soldier in a Quebec town by Martin Couture-Rouleau, and a shooting death of the War Memorial guard on Parliament Hill in Ottawa by Michael Zehaf-Bibeau, the worst incidents of terrorism since 1989.[33] Both attackers were recent converts to Islam. Both were among 90 people being tracked by the Royal Canadian Mounted Police on suspicion of planning to join jihadists in Syria, Iraq and elsewhere. Both recently had their passports confiscated, forcing them to turn their frustrations against local military targets.

Were Couture-Rouleau and Zehaf-Bibeau crazies? Perhaps. Both showed signs of mental imbalance in the months leading up to the attack. But then many Canadians were furious with Harper's warmongering. Something was just waiting to happen. And Zehaf-Bibeau's actions on Parliament Hill apparently inspired New Yorker Zale Thompson to attack a group of police officers with a hatchet the next day. Thompson was also considered troubled, and a convert to Islam.

These deaths would not have occurred without the Conservative Party's loud pro-Israeli bias and aggressive war agenda targeting Muslim countries during the past eight years. Stephen Harper came to power in 2006 and rushed ahead with an aggressive military policy in Afghanistan and then in virtually any Muslim country the US was currently opposed to (Libya, Mali, Syria, Iraq). The Canadian military was turned into a tool of US imperial strategists, assisting in the occupation of Afghanistan and now training Kurdish militia in Iraq.

El-Farouk Khaki, head of the secularist Muslim Canadian Congress, warned shortly after Harper came to power, "Canadians need to wake up and realize the recipe offered by George Bush and Tony Blair, and now being adopted by Stephen Harper, has only led to an increase in terrorism fueled by the invasion of Iraq and Afghanistan." People who empathize with those killed by Canadian bombs and bullets inevitably will consider attacking the military responsible for that violence. To give them their due, Couture-Rouleau and Zehaf-Bibeau were not targeting civilians. Even the latter's 20 scattered shots in the parliament building were directed against the politicians responsible for sending the soldiers to Iraq.

Canada did not experience Muslim-inspired violence prior to 9/11. Prime Minister Jean Chretien refused to send troops to Iraq in 2003 (though he sent them to Afghanistan). In 2006, Canadian counter-terrorism forces arrested the "Toronto 18", a group of youths inspired by al-Qaeda, intending to explode a truck-bomb. The group had been infiltrated and monitored by police agents. Harper had just been elected, and despite the shoddy evidence, the misguided teens were sentenced and the spectacular trial set the stage for his rule. Harper sent ever more troops to a failing occupation of Afghanistan, and welcoming Canada's first Israeli military attaché.

With the election of the Liberals in 2015, all Canadian soldiers were brought home from Syria, leaving behind a few dozen to train Kurds. Since Trudeau came to power on a policy of disengagement, there have not been any more Canadian jihadis caught in crossfire, or attacks by crazed Canadians on Parliament Hill. But there was one terrorist incident, this by another Quebecois, Alexandre Bissonnette, against Muslims praying at the Islamic cultural center in Quebec City in January 2016. Six Muslims died; 17 children were left without a father.

Justin Trudeau: Harper-lite

"It's hard to find a country friendlier to Israel than Canada these days," chirped Israeli Foreign Minister Avigdor Lieberman on his official visit in 2010. Though the perpetrator of this friendship was out of power in 2015, his legacy lived on in Justin Trudeau. Within months of Trudeau's electoral victory, Craig Murray, a former British ambassador to Uzbekistan who had resigned due to British acquiescence to torture there, was denied a visa to visit Canada in September 2016 (subsequently overturned).[34] The Harper-Kenney foreign policy remained in place on things Israeli under what Canadians were hoping would be a new direction in foreign policy, 'returning' Canada to a more neutral role in the world. That neutral role was a mirage for the most part, certainly with respect to Israel, as a sober look at the Pearson legacy reveals, but at least Trudeau wasn't a xenophobe.

Harperian semantics are still being parsed. One of Trudeau's first calls upon election in October 2016 was to Netanyahu. He explained there would be "a shift in tone, but Canada would continue to be a friend of Israel's." All three parties are now 'friends' of Israel, a term which applies to no other country,[35] and wasn't used before Harper about Israel or any other country. It's as if there is some doubt about whether a country as near to being a pariah state as Israel could ever be befriended by anyone.

Trudeau told reporters in February 2016 that while Israel is a "friend", his government "won't hesitate from talking about unhelpful steps like the continued illegal settlements" and "will continue to engage in a forthright and open way."[36] In his first press conference, after the obligatory 'friend' word, Justin's foreign minister Stephane Dion added: "But for us to be an effective ally we need also to strengthen our relationship with the other legitimate partners in the region."

Then Foreign Affairs Minister Stephane Dion called the expansion of Israeli settlements "unhelpful" and said that they "constitute serious obstacles to achieving a comprehensive, just and lasting peace" in a statement in January. However, when Israel seized 579 acres – the largest land grab in recent years – in the West Bank a few weeks later, while the European Union released a statement criticizing Israel, saying it violated international law, Canada remained silent.

The 'friend' wind continued to blow.

- Dion urged the United Nations Human Rights Council to "review" its appointment of law professor Michael Lynk as Special Rapporteur on human rights for Palestine after UN Watch and the Centre for Israel and Jewish Affairs claimed Lynk was "anti-Israel".
- Canada voted against a UN Social, Humanitarian and Cultural Committee resolution in support of Palestinian self-determination.
- Ottawa also joined Israel, the US, Marshall Islands, Micronesia, and Palau in opposing motions titled "Israeli settlements in the Occupied Palestinian Territory, including East Jerusalem, and the occupied Syrian Golan" and "persons displaced as a result of the June 1967 and subsequent hostilities." 156 countries voted in favor of the motions while seven abstained on the first and six on the second.
- These votes followed on the heels of Dion attacking UNESCO for defending Palestinian rights. The UN cultural body had criticized Israel for restricting Muslim access to the al-Aqsa Mosque compound and recognized Israel as the occupying power. "Canada strongly rejects UNESCO World Heritage singling out Israel & denying Judaism's link to the Old City + Western Wall," Dion tweeted.

Particularly chilling to Canadian activists was Trudeau's support for a Harper plan to demonize pro-Palestine activism at home, in particular, support for the **Boycott, Divestment and Sanctions (BDS)** movement. The BDS campaign, now in its eleventh year, cites UN resolutions on Israeli violations of international law, and echoes the anti-apartheid campaigns against white minority rule in apartheid era South Africa, calling for "various forms of boycott against Israel until it meets its obligations under international law".

One of Justin Trudeau's first thrusts into foreign affairs was to support a Conservative private member's bill condemning Canadian organizations which support the "boycott of Israel", though, to its credit, it fell short of Harper's vow last year to label such criticism of Israel as a "hate crime". The motion is reminiscent of the Conservative government's "memorandum of understanding," signed with Israeli leaders in 2014, which called the BDS movement "the new face of anti-Semitism." Harper didn't survive long enough to criminalize criticism of Israel, but the US Senate came perilously close, with the US Anti-Semitism Awareness Act of 2016, and Trudeau has a nice precedent for his own version.

Canadians were hoping for a change of government policy by voting Liberal. But during the election campaign, Trudeau told *Canadian Jewish News* that BDS was "an example of the new form of anti-Semitism in the world," and worried that "when Canadian university students are feeling unsafe on their way to classes because of BDS or Israel Apartheid Week, that just goes against Canadian values." And he petulantly tweeted at the time of the parliamentary debate: "The BDS movement, like Israeli Apartheid Week, has no place on Canadian campuses. As a @McGillU alum, I'm disappointed." (March 15, 2015.) The parliamentary motion condemning BDS passed (229 to 51). While it has no legal impact, it will, as intended, have a chilling effect on free expression. Of the 10 sitting Muslims Liberal MPs, eight did not vote at all, afraid to offend no matter what they did.

NDP leader Tom Mulcair and NDP MPs voted against the motion, purely on freedom of speech grounds, loudly asserting that they do not approve of BDS. Even Green Party leader Elizabeth May, who voted against it in line with the NDP, denounced a Green Party BDS policy approved at their convention in 2016, threatening to resign.

By pushing the campaign to prevent BDS, Trudeau and the other pro-Zionists merely called greater attention to it, and to

Israel's crimes, while providing a platform for angry activists to fight on, proving to them that their efforts must be effective. Yet another example of how Zionists shoot themselves in the foot with their own hate/terror campaign against effective, peaceful criticism. The BDS movement has some of its strongest support from within Israel itself. In his acceptance speech in Berlin, Israeli film director, Udi Aloni, winner of the top audience at the Berlin Film Festival for his film, Junction 48, labeled the Israeli government "fascist" and urged Germany to cease its military support of the Jewish state, calling Israel a "democracy of white people".[37]

There was one bright spot. After months of lobbying, Canadians for Justice and Peace in the Middle East (CJPME) congratulated the Canadian government's decision to renew funding to the United Nations Relief and Works Agency (UNRWA) – the UN aid agency for Palestinian refugees. Canada's Minister of International Development, Marie-Claude Bibeau, announced that Canada is contributing $25 million to support the organization's work. "The Trudeau government has finally differentiated itself from the Harper government in regard to the Middle East," declared Thomas Woodley, president of CJPME.

CJPME notes that the Trudeau government distinguishes itself from Harper in several key ways on UNRWA funding. First, Canada restarted aid to UNRWA after Harper ended it three years ago. Also, Canada is now giving to UNRWA 'permanent' development programs. Prior to ending funding, Harper was giving to only 'emergency' UNRWA programs. "It was as if Harper thought the Palestinians had been hit by an earthquake," explained Woodley, "rather than being dispossessed of their land as an indigenous people." UNRWA provides the foremost health, education and development programs for Palestinian refugees in Gaza, the West Bank, Jordan, Syria, Lebanon and elsewhere. In recent weeks, the organization has been cutting staff and services because of budget shortfalls. Prior to this announcement, Canada was the only G7 country that was not contributing to UNRWA. Historically, prior to the Harper years, Canada had been a faithful donor.

Cultural battles

Israel in Canada: Promised lands

A textbook case of the 'new hasbarah' was the Toronto

International Film Festival's **"City to city Spotlight on Tel Aviv"** in 2009, in cooperation with the Israeli Embassy and the Canada-Israel Cultural Foundation. Along with the Royal Ontario Museum exhibition of the Dead Sea Scrolls, this PR scheme was to be the centerpiece of Israeli Consul Gissin's special Canadian "Brand Israel" campaign, dreamed up in 2008 on his arrival in Toronto. Using the same mass marketing techniques of The Israel Project launched in 2002 in the US, it was intended to present a more "benign" vision of Israel to the Canadian public.

The Israel Project uses "grassroots" encounter groups to hone their propaganda efforts. Canadian partners in the Project's Canadian spin-off included Sidney Greenberg of Astral Media and David Asper of CanWest Global Communications, arguably the most powerful media magnates in Canada, who were funding a million-dollar media and advertising campaign aimed at changing Canadian perceptions of Israel. "Brand Israel" is intended to take the focus off Israel's treatment of Palestinians and refocus it on its achievements in medicine, science and culture. In "The Israel Project's 2009 Global Language Dictionary", Frank Luntz explains: "Americans want a team to cheer for. Let the public know GOOD things about Israel ... The language of Israel is the language of America: 'democracy', 'freedom', 'security', and 'peace'". Fleshing out how to rebrand Israeli atrocities, Gissin made it clear that his mission was to "make Israel relevant" to Canadians and use Toronto as a test market for the Israel brand during his term.

The lessons learned from Toronto would inform the worldwide launch of Brand Israel in the coming years, Gissin said. Official Brand Israel logos and advertising could be found across Toronto in bus shelters, on billboards, on radio and TV. Gissin said the ad blitz was to be "an attack on all the senses." The idea of the TIFF 'City to city Spotlight on Tel Aviv' was to see "how to introduce a brand into Toronto" with emphasis on "grassroots" exposure, to promote Tel Aviv as a city of peace, untouched by the wars Israel has waged since 1948, despite the fact that many Palestinian communities were destroyed and adjoining Jaffa annexed to make way for the emergence of modern-day Tel Aviv.

Despite Israel's invasion of Gaza, killing more than a thousand Gazans in Operation Cast Lead, just months earlier, TIFF made no move to cancel the Spotlight. Toronto artists were incensed. They used contacts on the internet to expose this idea of Tel Aviv as a city of peace, which quickly went vial and blew up into an international incident, bringing 1,500 signatures from prominent Israeli public figures and the likes of

Jane Fonda, Julie Christie, Alice Walker, Naomi Klein, Guy Maddin, Walter Bernstein, and Harry Belafonte to the "Toronto Declaration" criticizing Israel *and* TIFF. It was a huge embarrassment, a sign that Israeli propaganda is becoming harder to swallow, even by devotees of Hollywood. Canadian filmmaker John Greyson, the catalyst for the declaration, refused to screen his latest film *Covered* in protest. Egyptian director Ahmad Abdalla withdrew his feature film debut of *Heliopolis*, as did Ahmed Maher of *The Traveller*.

The protesters were denounced in the mainstream media, called "opportunists, hypocrites, fascists, censors, storm-troopers, apartheid-supporters, intolerant totalitarians, a mob of homophobic anti-Semitic terrorist regime supporters" acting "effectively [as] Mahmoud Ahmadinejad's local fifth column" by Canadian film producer Robert Lantos. Greyson condemned the opportunism of TIFF for its complicity with the Israeli consulate's "Brand Israel" campaign. "I'm reminded of last year, when the opening night party for *Passchendaele* featured real soldiers posing on a Canadian Armed Forces tank. Many of us were disturbed by this uncritical collaboration with the Canadian army, currently fighting in Afghanistan. So I have to ask: who is politicizing TIFF? Why hasn't TIFF explicitly explained and repudiated the perceived Brand Israel connection, beyond vague disavowals? What's the extent of Israeli sponsorship, beyond airfare, receptions, and the Mayor's presence? Why an exclusive program of Israeli state-sponsored features, when shorts could have provided critical alternative voices?"

The incident was again a classic example of foot shooting by trigger-happy Zionist hasbaristas, exposing Israel's deep and pervasive cultural and political connections in Canada. Opponents of Greyson wrote to York University, demanding that he be investigated, fired, even deported. In a nice irony, the second Toronto Palestinian Film Festival opened just a few weeks after TIFF closed.

Harper gave the lie to the Teflon cloak Israel tried to wrap itself in since the invasion of Gaza in December 2008. "Canada is so friendly that there was no need to convince or explain anything to anyone. We need allies like this in the international arena," gushed Israeli Foreign Minister Avigdor Lieberman in July as the Spotlight was being installed at TIFF.

Amid the scandal, Toronto's new Israeli consul, Amir Gissin, announced his Toronto staff would be expanded, despite the fact that Canada already has more Israeli diplomatic staff per capita than any other country in the world, due to "the city's large Israeli population" and the fact that Toronto is "an arena for Israel from a PR, cultural and commercial point of view". He also said it "reflects the importance of the Toronto Jewish community" in supporting Israel. Indeed, there are at least 100,000 Israelis Torontonians (who knows?) who prefer the joys of living in Toronto to facing the violence-charged daily life of Tel Aviv.

Just a few blocks from TIFF was the exhibition "Dead Sea Scrolls: Words that Changed the World," at Toronto's Royal Ontario Museum (ROM) June 2009 to January 2010, a joint project with the Israel Antiquities Authority (IAA), funded by the Toronto Tanenbaum family dynasty, who coincidentally were instrumental in the creation of Canada Park in Israel. This exhibition provided a fitting gala premier for the museum's ultra-modern wing designed by Israeli-American Daniel Libeskind.[38]

The Dead Sea Scrolls, regarded as one of the greatest archaeological discoveries of the 20th century and including what is purported to be the oldest known version of the Old Testament (150BC–70CE), were found by a Bedouin shepherd in caves of Qumran, and later by the Palestine Archaeological Museum (also known as the Rockefeller Museum) in a joint expedition with the Department of Antiquities of Jordan and the Ecole Biblique Française between 1947 and 1956. The Scrolls were displayed at the Palestine Archaeological Museum in East Jerusalem until 1967, when they were seized and relocated to the Shrine of the Book at the Israel Museum in West Jerusalem. Since 1967, additional (illegal) excavations and findings by the Israel Antiquities Authority (IAA) took place in Qumran and the surrounding area, and artefacts continue to be (illegally) appropriated by Israel, under the auspices of the IAA.

Under international law and in accordance with Canada's and Israel's obligations as signatories to the 1954 UNESCO protocol for the Protection of Cultural Property in the Event of Armed Conflict, Israel is not entitled to these artifacts. The repatriation of the Scrolls and millions of other artifacts to Palestine remains a key issue for those seeking peace and justice in the Middle East. In 2005, Canada signed other UNESCO conventions and protocols specifically aimed at preventing the removal and the exhibition of illegally removed artefacts from occupied territories, and adopted domestic Canadian legislation – the Cultural Property Export and Import Act – which makes it a criminal offense to import cultural property in violation of the conventions.

In April 2009, before the ROM exhibition opened, Harper and executives at the ROM were sent letters of protest from senior officials of the Palestinian Authority, including PA President Mahmoud Abbas, declaring that the scrolls were in fact illegally seized by Israel following its occupation and annexation of the West Bank in 1967 and calling for their repatriation. The ROM exhibition inspired a campaign of protest led by the CJPME trying to get ROM officials to adjust the display of the artifacts to reflect the fact that the Scrolls were confiscated from East Jerusalem during Israel's 1967 invasion and occupation of the Palestinian West Bank, to use "West Bank (Israeli-occupied)" and East and West Jerusalem with 1948 Armistice borders on maps. CJPME's Thomas Woodley said, "We would like there to be a balanced narrative. The ROM is presenting the scrolls entirely from the Israeli perspective. There's no discussion about what happened between their discovery and their exhibition today."

The ROM, for its own part, is a member of the Canadian Museums Association whose Ethics Guidelines states that "museums must guard against any direct or indirect participation in the illicit traffic in cultural and natural objects that are: stolen, illegally imported or exported from another state, including those that are occupied or war-stricken." The 1954 Convention clearly requires Canada to "take into custody cultural property imported into its territory either directly or indirectly from any occupied territory" and "return, at the close of hostilities, to the competent authorities of the territory previously occupied, cultural property which is in its territory."

Israel not only continues to illegally excavate in occupied Palestinian territory but dismisses international law altogether (despite its UNESCO pledges), using archeology and discoveries such as the Dead Sea Scrolls to reinforce the Zionist national narrative and the colonial project upon which the state was founded. Supposedly a science removed from political, religious, or ideological bias, archeology under the IAA is the very antithesis of this, being rooted in Biblical mythology. Artifacts like the Scrolls are, according to Amos Elon, "almost titles of real estate, like deeds of possession to a contested country". Like British, French, and German imperialist functionaries before them, Israeli archeologists sift through the many layers of historical evidence in search of what will prove their beliefs, ignoring or rather destroying the intervening layers and interpreting finds to suit their needs. The thousands of years of non-Jewish Arab civilization don't matter. Historian Keith Whitelam says in *The Invention of Ancient Israel: The Silencing of Palestinian History*

(1997), the modern state of Israel has "cast its shadow of influence backwards to claim previous periods as its 'prehistory'."

The Israel Antiquities Authority is just as much a steamroller in its own way as the IDF, by obliterating indigenous Palestinian history. Committee Against Israeli Apartheid (CAIA) activist Ali Mustafa writes that Israeli archeology is explicitly categorized by the IAA as either Jewish/Israeli or Arab/Muslim in a process whereby ancient artifacts that supposedly belong to the Biblical era are actively sought after, while supposedly encouraging Palestinians to do the same concerning later Islamic periods. Following the Oslo peace process, Israel claimed it was prepared to assign jurisdiction of all "Arab" and "Muslim" archeological sites in the West Bank over to the PA; however, the offer was flatly refused, and the PA instead demanded control over all sites, as well as an immediate return of artifacts seized since 1967.

The Israeli logic is simple: conflate all Palestinian history as Islamic (openly disregarding Christian and other pre-Islamic influences), and apply these reductive and simplistic binary terms to all artifacts, ignoring the region's shared past and overlapping cultural heritage. Despite the overwhelming evidence that the Scrolls should have been seized by ROM and the Canadian government, under their international obligations, and held or handed over to UNESCO until their ownership is determined, the CBC concluded in June 2009 that "the museum feels the scrolls are legally held and both the federal and provincial government have expressed their support of the exhibition."

ROM met with CJPME members and initially agreed to make changes and even distribute an additional leaflet to be inserted into the museum's brochure. Friday pickets were held throughout the summer to inform the public about the theft of the Dead Sea Scrolls. No such changes were made, and the history of their discovery in Jordan and seizure in 1967 was finessed. According to CJPME's Thomas Woodley, "Tens of thousands of innocent schoolchildren are being respectfully shepherded through subterranean, darkened halls, and left with the impression that the ancient 'Israelis' inhabited the kingdom of 'Judea', that their 'descendants' heroically prevented the 'pillaging of the Scrolls by Bedouin', and are the rightful owners. The mythical kingdoms of 10th–3rd century BC Palestine—for which there is no conclusive evidence—are carefully delineated and explained in commentaries as if they are actual history. A dazzling success story for Gissin's 'Brand Israel'".

The dust-up, however, provided a platform for activists to educate Canadians and empowered demonstrators at the nearby Israeli consulate. It provided a 6-month platform for *re*-rebranding Israel as the center of 21st-century Apartheid. And no amount of slick PR can undo the fact that merely by continuing to exist, despite all odds, Palestinians provide enduring testimony to the injustice of The Israel Project in all its manifestations. Palestinians only have their survival itself as proof of the crimes committed against them, choosing to maintain traditional dress, religious faith (both Christian and Islamic), and the historical memory of the Nakba as their most meaningful and durable expressions of resistance. Though former Israeli Prime Minister Golda Meir notoriously declared that "there is no such thing as Palestinians," Palestinian academic Edward Said more accurately explained that, "In the case of a political identity that's being threatened, culture is a way of fighting against extinction and obliteration." The battle being waged over the Scrolls was not so much about any particular ethnic, religious, or even cultural-based claim, but more importantly a means of opposing Zionist colonial discourse.

Even as Torontonians marveled at the Dead Sea Scrolls and filmmakers rallied to protest TIFF's Spotlight on Tel Aviv, Canadian Ambassador to Israel Jon Allen was honored at **Canada Park**—built on occupied Palestinian land in violation of international law—as one of hundreds of donors who helped establish the park on the ruins of three Palestinian villages. Just north of Jerusalem, it was founded in the early 1970s following Israel's occupation of the West Bank in the 1967 war. It is hugely popular for walks and picnics (or was, until ravaged by wild fires in 2016) with the Israeli public, who are by and large unaware that they are in Palestinian territory that is officially a closed military zone.

Former Israeli parliamentarian Uri Avnery has described the park's creation as an act of complicity in "ethnic cleansing" and Canada's involvement as providing "cover to a war crime". About 5,000 Palestinians were expelled from the area during the war. A plaque bearing Allen's name is attached to a stone wall constructed from the rubble of Palestinian homes razed by the Israeli army. The Jewish National Fund, treated as a charity for tax purposes, establishes and manages such parks on behalf of Jewish people worldwide. Uri Davis, an Israeli scholar and human rights activist who has co-authored a book on the Jewish National Fund (JNF) calls Canada Park "a crime against humanity that has been financed by and implicates not only the Canadian government but every taxpayer in Canada." Canada Park is particularly sensitive for Israel because it lies outside the country's internationally-recognized borders. Canada Park is believed to be the only example, outside East Jerusalem, of the JNF becoming directly involved in managing land in the Occupied Palestinian Territories.

The Palestinian inhabitants' expulsion, Eitan Bronstein, director of the Israeli NGO Zochrot (Remembering), said, was a premeditated act of ethnic cleansing of villagers who put up no resistance. "We have photographs of the Israeli army carrying out the expulsions," he tells tourists, holding up a series of laminated cards. According to Zochrot, 86 Palestinian villages lie buried underneath JNF parks. Zochrot activists regularly select a destroyed village, taking Palestinian refugees with them as they place a handmade sign detailing the village's name in Arabic and Hebrew. Within days, the signs are removed. Bronstein said he believes signs erected by official bodies may have a greater impact in opening Israeli minds. "In a recent newspaper interview, a senior JNF official admitted that it would be hard to stop our campaign," he said. "Slowly we believe Israelis can be made to appreciate that their state exists at the expense of another people. Only then are Israelis likely to be ready to think about making peace."

Allen's support for Canada Park, implicitly condoning Israel's ruthless ethnic cleansing of Palestinians, landed him in hot water. As ambassador to Israel, he had to deny any personal contribution to Canada Park, which is tax deductible, as the JNF is considered by Revenue Canada to be a charity, and insist that his name had been included as a benefactor only because his parents gave a contribution. With Zochrot's efforts in mind, Uri Davis joined in an application to the Canadian tax authorities to overturn the JNF's charitable status. The Green Party actually had this demand in the draft program at their 2016 party convention, but the resolution was watered down to avoid direction mention of the JNF. Davis said attempts to rename Canada Park "Ayalon Park" over the past decade suggested that the Canadian authorities were already concerned about the prospect of the country's involvement in the park coming under scrutiny.

The Power of the Jewish Lobby in Canada

Wealth, Mining, Media

Jews constitute 20% of the wealthiest Canadians. Canadian Jews are better educated, richer, and have great political influence in the

Canadian parliament.[39] Prominent Canadian Jewish families such as the Batas, Bronfmans, Belzbergs, Reichmanns and Munks have created their own family foundations, museums and university chairs for Jewish (and Israeli) studies. The 2011 *Forbes* list of billionaires in the world listed 24 Canadian billionaires. Among the 24 billionaires listed, 25% are Jewish. Immigrant Jewish males earn $7,000 a year above the Canadian average.

The hegemony of the Anglo-Canadian establishment is no longer, replaced by families like the Bronfmans, Reichmanns, Munks, who "represent just the tip of a growing and extremely affluent segment of Jewish society in Canada. According to *Forbes*, Jews are 40% of the top 40 richest Americans."[40] Diana Francis's *Controlling Interest: Who Owns Canada? (1986)* lists wealthy identifiably Jewish dynasties (i.e., possibly there are more, as some names are not clear, due to intermarriage, or conversion, such as the Bentleys of BC who became Anglicans). It's not clear about wealth concentration Canada-wide, but in Quebec, one-quarter of the 66 largest fortunes were Jewish in 1997.[41]

There is a much greater concentration of Jewish wealth in Canada than the US, and none of these billionaires are anti-Zionist; rather, they are supporting Israel, exerting pressure on Canadian foreign policy. At the Munk conference, it was concluded that "the decisive challenge for Canadian Jews in future will be on the posture Canada adopts on matters relating to Israeli security and Middle East peace, and possible roles of Canadian Jews in shaping, supporting or challenging those policies."[42] There is also more wealth than top CEO positions among Jews, suggesting modesty or a preference for behind-the-scenes power, ensuring bonding with Gentile society, assimilating *them* to the Zionist cause, which is important in ensuring acceptable government policies. The leading role in mining played by Munk has been noted elsewhere, as has the consolidation of much of popular media by Israel Asper and CanWest/PostMedia, and the dominance of Jewish interests in US media and entertainment.[43]

Dual Loyalty

Dual loyalty is a problem endemic to human relations. What is your first loyalty? Are you a Jew in Canada, a Jewish Canadian, who sees Canada as homeland #1, or a Canadian Jew, whose real homeland, according to Israel and Zionism is, since 1948, Israel?

Canadian Communists, like Bill Walsh in the 1930s, when asked about Zionism, rejected it, saying "We want to make things better *here*." His priority signifier was as a communist, following his revolutionary gene. He was a Canadian Communist. His loyalty was to a socialist Canada.

This issue of dual loyalty was the basis of McCarthyism. In Canada, where the Communist Party was made illegal, communists like Bill Walsh were jailed from 1939–42 until the Soviet Union was an ally. In 1945, when the Soviet Union was branded as Canada's enemy, this led to the arrest of Montreal MP Fred Rose and denial of his parliamentary immunity, when he was found guilty of conspiring to turn over information about the explosive RDX[44] to the Soviets. The Soviet defector Gouzenko had stolen documents from the Soviet embassy, and alleged that Rose was leading a spy ring of up to 20 Soviet spies.

The issue of dual loyalty of Zionist Canadian Jews is much less cut and dried.

For Canadian Jews, "The old country is not their homeland. ... the homeland—in the abstract as well as in reality—is Israel. This is the place where most relatives are found."[45] That refers not just to Jews emigrating to Israel, abandoning their homelands, but to Canadian Jews, who left, say Poland, became Canadian citizens, but still identify with Israel at a deeper level than with Canada. Weinfeld calls Canadians "highly Zionistic", admitting that "the classic anti-Semitic stereotype that Jews are 'clannish' is true. Such a clear pattern is just not found for any other European immigrant group. Perhaps for Quebecois ... Perhaps for First Nations."[46]

Weinfeld recalls as a child asking his father two questions: "If there was a war between Canada and Israel, who would win? And which country would we support?" He answers "The first: I know the answer to that one. The second: That remains a tough question."[47]

Weinfeld's tone is flippant about a serious charge against Canadian Jews–Canadians who put Israel first–as opposed to Jewish Canadians, who put Canada first. His text is peppered with jokes celebrating Jews' concern with money and wealth, about Jewish holidays being centered mostly on massacres and survival against the ever-present enemy (Passover, Hannukah, Purim vs Christian holidays of love and redemption).[48] He makes light of the otherness unique to Judaism as a religion, making it, in its tribal form, the engine of anti-Jewish prejudice.

As discussed above, enlightened Jewish thinkers such as Spinoza, Marx, Arendt and Slonim rejected this tribalism and were ostracized by Jews (but celebrated by Gentiles) as a result. The battle for Jewish 'hearts and minds' is at the heart of the battle against anti-Jewish prejudice. An end to anti-Jewish prejudice can't be enforced by bullying and legalism. Weinfeld and others who are devoted to 'fighting antisemitism' would probably admit: You can lead a horse to the trough but you can't make it drink.

Suppose in a war against Israel Canada won, as part of a world movement to end Israeli Apartheid? And Israel, as a nuclear power, was willing to go the full mile rather than admit defeat? Weinfeld probably had something else in mind, relying on the Jews' ancient pact with YHWH. Weinfeld isn't worried about the possibility that Israel might lose. The nuclear threat is the perfect Zionist defense – no need for god, just technology and smarts.

The issue of dual loyalty lies at the heart of the Canadian Jewish experience.

Ezekiel Hart's refusal to swear an oath based on the Bible or to swear on the Sabbath lost him his elected post in 1807. Fred Rose was convicted of spying for the Soviet Union in 1945, though not for Jewish dual loyalty, but as a communist intent on "making things better here," which he insisted wasn't really treachery. He was never allowed to clear his name, and all evidence of the affair disappeared, so the matter is lost to history. As Ginsberg states, "'apartness' gives Judaism a revolutionary impulse with regard to state power, active in political mobilization and opinion formation,"[49] which made dual loyalty a boon for those who wish to reform Canadian society, attracting many Jews in the 19th–20th centuries to communism, more easily than non-Jews, who do not have that 'revolutionary gene'. Nothing to be ashamed of if used in the interests of humanity.

When Dual Loyalty Got the Wink and the Nod

Despite protestations of innocence, dual allegiance is proudly embraced by serious defenders of Israel. **Ben Dunkelman** (1913–1997) was a Canadian Jewish officer who served in the Canadian Army in WWII and the Palmach (elite forces of Haganah, the Israel Defense Forces) in the 1948 Arab-Israeli War. In Israel, he was called Benjamin Ben-David. His memoirs, *Dual Allegiance: An Autobiography* (1984), show him unapologetic in his allegiances, with Israel trumping Canada as the occasion demands. "Being a Canadian citizen never stood in the way of my duties to the Jewish people."[50]

Dunkelman commanded the 7th brigade that "carried out atrocities in Safsaf, Saliha, Sasa and Jish." All Arab villagers then in northern Palestine were expelled from territory desired by the Zionists as part of Eretz Israel. In the village of Jish, "soldiers robbed several of the houses and stole 605 [British] pounds, jewelry and other valuables. When the people who were robbed insisted on being given receipts for their property, they were taken to a remote place and shot dead."[51]

Dunkelman's comrade, Montrealer Sydney Shulemson, was dubbed the "father of the Israeli Air Force", and made aliyah, rather than returning to his Canadian motherland.[52] Duneklman wanted to stay but his business proposals were spurned by Histadrut, and he took his Israeli bride to Toronto. A *Globe and Mail* tribute to Dunkelman in 1999 called him a "Canadian and Israeli war hero". All this – far different from the case of Fred Rose at the same time.

While the Foreign Enlistment Act[53] prohibits Canadians from recruiting for a foreign army, it is somehow acceptable for Canadians to fight for Israel. To buttress Israel, at the same time as CSIS hunts down Canadians hoping to fight for their world caliphate, other Canadians buy their El Al tickets, packing their military togs, and make for Israel to fight these rebels or just Palestinians, whatever, with Canadian government complicity. Of the 2,500 "lone soldiers" serving in the IDF in 2014, 145 were from Canada, participating in the "lone soldier" program. In addition, each year, 20 young Canadian men and women visit Israel on the Garin Tzabar program, which prepares them for active duty. Many others arrive on their own. Canadians joined the IDF in its invasion of Gaza in 2008. Thousands of Canadians have fought for Israel since 1948 without sanction. For those who 'make aliyah', they automatically are conscripted into the IDF (service expires only at 49). Jews around the world have the option of supporting Israel's jihad against its Muslim neighbors. The US forbade Americans fighting in foreign armies until 1967. Now there are over a thousand in the IDF. They and their Canadian cousins are needed because Israel is at war with its citizens, has no agreed borders, and Eretz Israel is still expanding,[70] years after it was founded. No one monitors Canadians who are devoted to Israel, whether or not they are Jewish or even dual Israeli-Canadian citizens. Thousands of Canadian Jews have served in the Israeli army, tens of thousands of Israelis have emigrated or returned to Canada after emigrating to Israel. No one keeps track of them or even knows how many there are. Are they all potential *sayanim?*

CSIS and Mossad

The issue of *sayanim* is never talked about, but it is the most serious security problem Canada has. Right from the start of **CSIS** in 1984, it has had secret agreements with Mossad and the CIA to share information. Mossad shares but only filtered through the CIA to determine what Canada needs to know.

CSIS's kowtowing to Mossad exploded in its face over the case of Mahmoud Mohammad Issa Mohammad, an ex-member of the Popular Front for the Liberation of Palestinian, who carried out an embarrassingly inept terrorist act in 1968, when he and a friend attacked an El Al Boeing 707 in Athens, inadvertently killing one Israeli passenger. He was sentenced to 17 years and pardoned a few months later along with six other Palestinian terrorists in a hostage exchange.

In 1987, he came to Canada as a business-class immigrant, neglecting to reveal his membership in the PFLP and his bungled terrorist act, jail term and pardon in Greece. Mossad immediately alerted CSIS, saying he had been a senior PLO member before he quit the PFLP in 1972, though this was never proven and seems unlikely considering his rash, unapproved act at the age of 25. CSIS tried unsuccessfully to 'turn' him as an informer in Canada, then panicked, worried Israel could assassinate or kidnap him. CSIS wanted him to leave immediately (illegally, with no drawn-out deportation procedure), leaving his wife and son in Toronto, and reapply, and handed him over to the RCMP.

The RCMP arranged for his secret exit, but CSIS agents found out and showed up at the airport when Mohammad was about to leave, which meant that Mossad knew, which meant they could assassinate him on his way to Algeria. Worse yet, the sensational news was leaked to the press, and Mohammad was swamped by reporters at the London airport, and was refused passage by Air Algeria, fearing an Israeli attack. He was forced to come back to Toronto on the same airplane on which he had left.

CSIS insisted it was not responsible for the leak, but as CSIS was working with Mossad, 'sharing' information, that claim was bogus. The source of the leak was tracked down by the press. Gilbert Zamonsky, a high-living, self-styled independent security professional for synagogues, Israeli delegations, and what-not, was the culprit, though he refused to say who told him. He claimed he was not in the pay of Israel, but Israelis preferred him to the RCMP for their needs, and they told Zamonsky to cause Mohammad trouble. "I must have caused him half a million dollars in legal fees," Zamonsky boasted.[54] CSIS's reputation was in ruins even as it was starting out, exposed as a Mossad lackey. Mohammad was not deported (legally this time) till 2013. Without the attempt to spirit him out of Canada illegally, and without Mossad breathing down CSIS's neck, he would have left without problem in 1988.

Zamonsky is the classic *sayan*, working with other *sayanim*, some in CSIS, others across Canada, living the high life with no obvious source of income. Mossad has 'offices' in every major city, and close ties with Jewish groups. Israel is the biggest supplier of MP junkets, keeping track of all current MPs both to pressure them and to seduce them, aided by its Canadian helpers.

Norman Spector was appointed ambassador to Israel in 1992 by Mulroney. He was a political appointee rather than a seasoned career diplomat, the norm for such a sensitive post, the first Canadian Jew appointed ambassador to Israel. The appointment was condemned by Canadian Arab Federation president James Kafieh, who called Spector "a Zionist, who was close to the Bronfmans."[55] Spector was not unaware of *sayanim*-like activity going on.

The most serious instance made public was the use of **false Canadian passports** by Mossad 1997 in a botched assassination attempt in Jordan. Prime minister Netanyahu tried to kill Hamas leader Khalid Meshal. CSIS met with Mossad days before the assassination attempt. When the scandal erupted in the media, Spector admitted that CSIS gives passports when requested as *quid pro quo* for information on Arab immigrants.[56] Foreign Affairs Minister Lloyd Axworthy was unaware or playing dumb. He should have called for an investigation, as this was illegal and being done without explicit government approval. But Israel (and CSIS) are off limits in such matters, and ambassadors don't mess with such things.

Chretien was not amused, and recalled David Berger, Spector's successor as ambassador to Israel (also Jewish). Spector admitted that cooperation between Israeli and Canadian intelligence "goes well beyond information sharing to include some operations worthy of a James Bond thriller."[57] He relates in *Chronicle of a War Foretold: How Mideast Peace Became America's Fight* (2003) how a CSIS operative was working for him at the embassy, and the "very close cooperation" between the Canadian and Israeli spy agencies.

As the story unfolded, a number of Jewish Canadians reported being approached by Israeli officials seeking to 'borrow' their passports.[58] Leslie Lewis, a Canadian living in Israel, told Ottawa he was contacted in 1999 by the "Bureau of Immigration Affairs", a presumed Mossad front, asking for his expired passport. Suspicious when asked for his new one too, he refused to hand it over. The Bureau pressed his daughter, Devora, to apply for a Canadian passport and then return to Israel where she would be handed it by the Israelis. Ottawa launched an investigation.

Israel piously promised not to do this anymore (no apology necessary), but continued to use Canadian passports under Prime Minister Harper, who even went further. One of the 27 Mossad agents who assassinated Palestinian Hamas member Mahmoud al-Mabouh in 2010 in Dubai escaped to Canada, where he was given a new name. This was revealed by a honeypot security officer working for Canadian immigration, romancing an Iranian-Canadian businessman Arian Azarbar, who, being an Iranian patriot, let the cat out of the bag in January 2014.[59] Who needs John le Carre? The smitten Canadian, Trina Kennedy, a senior national security investigator at Passport Canada, revealed all to a tall, dark and handsome Arian about the latest intrigue involving Israeli assassins, Canadian officials and another false Canadian passport.

This is old hat, it turns out. Canadian passports have been used by Mossad many times:

- In 1973 in a botched assassination in Norway by Mossad, the agent was using a Canadian passport.[60]
- In 1974 50 blank passports disappeared from the Canadian Embassy in Vienna. The next year, a Mossad agent with a Canadian passport in Cyprus was seized after a hotel bombing killed a Palestinian guerrilla leader. Canadian passports are "still the favorite of the Mossad", according to ex-Mossad agent Ostrovsky.[61]
- Canadian UN peacekeeping officers (*duvshanim*, literally "honey pies") transport messages and packages across the border to Syria and Lebanon.[62]
- Israel also used Canadian passports in 1999 to help its Lebanese Maronite allies escape as Israel withdrew.

Little New Zealand was furious when it was discovered Mossad was trying to use the identity of a New Zealander with cerebral palsy to obtain a passport in 2004. Prime Minister Helen Clark suspended diplomatic relations until Israel issued an apology. An official inquiry revealed that an Israeli passport factory had been issuing New Zealand passports. The culprits served three months in a New Zealand jail and were deported. Israel finally apologized and relations were resumed in 2005. Canada, on the other hand, clearly doesn't take such violations seriously.

The violation of Canadian sovereignty is so common, there seems to be no need to even think about dual loyalty. Anything Israel does is fine by Ottawa.[63]

Harper and the JDL, Attias

2014 was a low point for Canadians not enamored with Israel. The over-the-top Canadian parliamentary junket to Israel in January 2014, just as Trina was wiping egg off her face, was the straw that broke the camel's back. Among the 208 Canadians who traveled with the PM were 77 Conservative donors, 21 rabbis, a handful of influential evangelical Christians, 32 registered lobbyists and JDL Canada's 'event co-ordinator' Julius Suraski. How did a member of the Jewish Defense League, an organization labeled "violent extremist" by the FBI, get on this junket? Explains JDL Canada head Meir Weinstein, "Julius knows some people in the Conservative party." Could the JDL's event co-ordinator Suraski have anything to do with banning Galloway in 2009 as a "security risk", the decision to cut diplomatic relations with Iran, or helping an accused assassin get a new Canadian identity? Could it be that JDL Canada is the real security risk? After all, there's the arson attack against Zundel in 1995.[64] In 2011, the RCMP launched an 'investigation' against at least nine members of JDL Canada accused of plotting to bomb Palestine House in Mississauga.

Even the ultra-Zionist Canadian Jewish Congress was not big on 'events' organized by JDL Canada, such as their "support rally" in 2011 for the neo-fascist English Defence League at the Toronto Zionist Center. CJC leader Bernie Farber said he was "disappointed" and accused the EDL of "violence and extremism". An 'event' Suraski 'co-ordinated' in 2013 was a Toronto speech by American Pamela Geller, founder of Stop Islamization of America, who was earlier prevented from entering the UK to address a rally of the same EDL. The British government ruled that her presence in the UK would "not be conducive to the public good".[65]

Eden Attias, appointed as Canada's first Israel military attaché in 2012, undermines the potential *sayanim* workforce in Canada. Attias was intimately involved in both the invasion of Gaza in 2008 and the assault on the Turkish boat Mavi Marmara in 2010 in which nine Turkish citizens bringing aid to besieged Gaza were killed by Israeli troops. Attias's actions were condemned by a group of remorseful ex-Israeli Defense Force members, and Turkish investigators charged him with murder. When Attias arrived in Ottawa, freshly promoted, he remarked: "Israelis are starting to understand that Canada is a separate entity from the US." Sounds good. Appeal to Canadian nationalism. But the subtext is something else entirely.

This issue of dual loyalty was the basis of McCarthyism, seeing all communists as potential spies for the Soviet Union ('guilty until proven innocent') and it meant jail both in the US and Canada for communists, insofar as the Communist Party was made illegal. (Communists were also jailed in Canada from 1939–42 until the Soviet Union was an ally.) This led to the arrest of Montreal MP **Fred Rose** and denial of his parliamentary immunity of 1945.

Rose did not see sharing RDX information at the time as spying, as the Soviets were allies, doing most of the fighting against the Nazis, but he was quickly convicted. When released, his health broken, abandoned by his wife while in prison, he was unable to work, hounded by the RCMP, and finally emigrated to Poland. In later years, Rose admitted his error, saying, "I made one mistake in my life and I paid for it," but he was denied the chance to clear his name of spying, as his Canadian citizenship was revoked in 1957, and his appeal was denied. Too late to matter, in 1958 Minister of Citizenship and Immigration Ellen Fairclough amended the Citizenship Act with the "Fred Rose amendment" so that such a removal of Canadian citizenship could never happen again.

Years later, former federal cabinet minister Allan MacEachen acknowledged the pages of Prime Minister William Lyon Mackenzie King's diary dealing with Rose had gone missing, as had most of the other records dealing with his case. Rose was not just another Pollard, as Pollard had no interest in his spying in 'making things better' in America.

The issue of dual loyalty of Zionist Canadian Jews is much less cut and dried than for Rose, the one Jewish Canadian convicted of spying. This issue of tribe vs nation is what Goldwin Smith feared in the 1880s, long before Herzl created the official Zionist Organization in 1897, intent on creating a tribal homeland for the world's Jews. He criticized Jews both for their tribalism and for their revolutionary potential, before the days of Zionism or communism. Weinfeld dismisses Smith who "raised the canard of Jewish dual loyalty", who influenced Vincent Massey and Mackenzie King, and who gave "such views a gloss of respectability".[66] Smith argued in "Can Jews Be Patriots?" that the Jewish God is "not the Father of all, but the deity of His chosen race,"[67] and concludes that the Jews' "only country is their race, which is one with their religion."[68] Many conservative Jews such as Slonim reject this distortion of Judaism, insisting that God is universal, and become vocal anti-Zionists, calling for civil rights for all Arabs and Jews in Israel, and an end to the occupation. Like Smith, they are pilloried. This dilemma lies at the heart of Israel today.

Trudeau's legacy is to add multi-culturalism to Canada's bi-nationalism (French-English),[69] with a view to putting all post-settler immigrant ethnicities on the same basis—Jewish Canadians, German Canadians, what have you. Jews celebrate Israel's independence day in Canada, give modern Hebrew more emphasis in Jewish schools than liturgical Hebrew, even use modern Hebrew for prayers. They take free junkets courtesy of Bronfman's Birthright Israel, etc. to their other homeland. Some go the whole hog and make aliyah (keeping their Canadian passports just in case).

They are not just celebrating a heritage, but a dual nationality. "Many of us around the [Passover seder] table have lived in Israel, plan to live in Israel, want to live in Israel, or believe they ought to live in Israel," reflected Ruth Wisse.[70] Some are less starry-eyed. Mordechai Richler, after his 1992 trip, reflected on his experiences in Israel: "All at once, I was fed up with the tensions that have long been Israel's daily bread ... [a] boring country so short on history, victim of its contrary mythologies. I considered the watery soup of my Canadian provenance a blessing."[71] A Jewish Canadian. Trudeau Sr would be happy.

He would also feel honored if his own vision for Canada could help in modeling a Palestine-Israel, with two founding nations—Arab and Jewish.

The upshot is still in the air. There is the Two States One Homeland proposal by Meron Rapoport, Awni al-Mashni, with support among Palestinians and Jewish Israelis, not all that far from Trudeau's vision for Canada. It envisages "two states within a single geographical space and a movement toward simultaneous sharing and separation. The blueprint speaks of two independent polities with Jerusalem as their capital, freedom of movement and even freedom to settle on both sides of the border, a Joint Court for Human Rights, a Joint Security Council, and other common institutions functioning alongside the institutional structures of each state."[72] But it is still a long way from the bargaining table.

On the home front, Jewish Canadians have accommodated themselves to Canada's multiculturalism, and are solidly behind keeping Canada united. They are less into assimilation than their American cousins, less into the US-style patriotic imperial stuff, less likely to move to settlements in the West Bank. But for both groups, Zionism is more 'checkbook Zionism', spectator sport, study and frolic in Israel, and there's as much yerida (leaving) as aliyah.

Approaching 70, Israel is feeling the effects of age, its international image increasingly one of a pariah state, its population aging, many of its citizens—especially the youth—are moving abroad. The heroic age of Zionism is over. The 1956 *Ten Commandments* is far more popular than *Exodus*. People like the legends, because they know they are legends, not some blueprint for war and violence in the real world. There will be no *Exodus* Part II. At least not one with a happy ending. Increasingly, it is the hardcore Zionists and religious fanatics who are left manning the fort. And what are all the nuclear arms for anyway? Afraid of a 'doomsday gap'?[73]

Endnotes

1. Canada does not celebrate the formal date of its accession to independence, which legally occurred on December 11, 1931 through the adoption of a British law called the Statute of Westminster. Canadian citizenship did not appear until 1947.
2. Think of Esau vs Jacob—the older, more traditional, naive son tricked by the younger, wilful son, with the help of a scheming mother(land) Rebeccah. Think also of Ishamel vs Isaac, the older, servant's son usurped by the younger, legal son, taking Eretz Israel, again with the help of the doting mother(land) Sarah, making a sacred pact with God as the 'chosen people'. The Zionists snatched their prize with the unwitting endorsement of the less demanding older brother.
3. Engler, op.cit. 25.
4. Eliezer Tauber, *Personal Policy Making: Canada's role in the adoption of the Palestine Partition Resolution*, Greenwood Press, 2002, 94.
5. Yves Engler, *Canada and Israel: Building Apartheid*, Fernwood, 2010, 26.
6. Ibid., 38.
7. Yves Engler, "What explains Harper's slavish support for Israel?" *yvesengler.*

com, September 23, 2011.
8   Engler, *Canada and Israel*, 94.
9   Stefan Christoff, "Yves Engler's *Canada and Israel: Building Apartheid*: Close relations", *hour.ca*. March 11, 2010.
10 "Canadian Media Giant Censures Editorials Deemed Critical of Israel", *Arizona Daily Star*, December 29, 2001.
11 <http://gilad.co.uk/writings/jon-stewart-on-jewish-power.html>
12 Noam Chomsky, Foreword to Yves Engler, *Lester Pearson's Peacekeeping – The Ugly Truth May Hurt*, RED Publishing, 2012.
13 Tulchinsky, op.cit., 435.
14 "Canada-Israel Relations" <http://www.jewishvirtuallibrary.org/jsource/myths/canada.html>
15 Robinson, op.cit., 164.
16 Ibid.,164.
17 See Chapter 7.
18 Tulchinsky, op.cit., 463. A Latvian camp guard was deported in 1997, and in 2007 two accused Nazi Ukrainian war criminals were stripped of their citizenship.
19 Yves Engler, "Explaining Canada's unconditional support of Israel", www.redressonline.com, July 30, 2013.
20 Margaret Wente,"Harper and the Jewish vote", *Globe and Mail*, January 28, 2014.
21 Yves Engler, "The Real Reason Why Harper is So Gung-Ho on Israel", *Canadian Dimension*, May 10, 2010.
22 Yves Engler, "Harper's Love Affair with Israel", *Canadian Dimension*, September 1, 2011.
23 John Mearsheimer and Stephen Walt, *The Israel Lobby and US Foreign Policy*, 2008.
24 See Chapter 5, endnotes 1 and 2.
25 Evidence given by senior police officers and university administrators to the inquiry held by the CPCCA refuted its claims that Canada is experiencing a surge of antisemitic incidents, and that Jews (especially those supportive of Israel) are routinely persecuted and harassed on Canadian campuses. The CPCCA, which had initially had all-party representation, lost its Bloc Quebecois members, who resigned over the CPCC refusal to give space in its hearings to human rights groups whose views differed from those of its principal organizers. The CPCCA final report was delayed for many months due to dissension prompted in part by the Conservative Party's disgraceful attempts (for which Jason Kenney refused any apology) to undermine Liberal Irwin Cotler in his own riding with robocalls and a whispering campaign that charged him, ironically, with being insufficiently supportive of Israel. And although the CPCCA took pains not to accept any submission to its inquiry that was critical of its own announced presuppositions, eighteen of those submissions were published in a book that appeared many months before the CPCCA's own belated report, and that was recommended in the *Globe and Mail* as late-summer reading for Tories willing to learn. Gerald Caplan, "Mideast reading list for Tories willing to learn," *Globe and Mail* (27 August 2010, updated 15 November 2010).
    Antisemitism Real and Imagined: Responses to the Canadian Parliamentary Coalition to Combat Antisemitism, contains in the first of its three parts eleven submissions by scholars and human rights activists (a majority of them

Jewish), and in its second part, the rejected submissions by seven human rights organizations; the third part consists of three essays by the editor (whose submission to the CPCCA had also been rejected).

26 Harper cancelled Canada's participation in the Kyoto treaty on the environment in 2011, cutting his own miserly promise to reduce CO_2 emissions by 2020 from 20% to 17%, and then doing nothing to implement even that. Canada is 15th out of the 17 largest countries in terms of CO_2 emissions.

27 Yves Engler, "UN vote reveals what world thinks of Canadian foreign policy", *yvesengler.com*, October 20, 2010.

28 In the 2013 UN Human Rights Council's Universal Periodic Review, Canada was criticized to such an extent that the Council decided to send the Special Rapporteur on the Rights of Indigenous Peoples, and representatives of the Committee on the Elimination of Discrimination Against Women and the Inter-American Commission on Human Rights, to investigate. citing "the persistent insecurity faced by women and girls, the urgent need for a public accounting of what has gone wrong for so long, and a robust national plan for addressing it going forward."
In February 2013, Human Rights Watch released "Those Who Take Us Away: Abusive Policing and Failures in Protection of Indigenous Women and Girls in Northern British Columbia, Canada." The report documents the failure of the Royal Canadian Mounted Police (RCMP) in British Columbia to protect indigenous women and girls from violence. It also documents abusive police behavior against indigenous women and girls, including excessive use of force, and physical and sexual assault. The report also found that Canada has inadequate police complaint mechanisms and oversight procedures, including a lack of a mandate for independent civilian investigations into all reported incidents of serious police misconduct. <https://www.hrw.org/news/2013/04/30/canada-safety-indigenous-women-under-un-scrutiny>

29 Nour Samaha, "JDL and far-right parties find common ground", *Al Jazeera*, December 29, 2011.

30 She was accused of being "a spy who had entered the country undercover as a journalist." She refused to hand over her camera during mass demonstrations outside the Evian prison, was arrested along with hundreds of demonstrators, lost her diplomatic status in the upheaval, as she was traveling on her Iranian passport, and died in prison – a case of 'dual loyalty' gone bad. Shirin Ebadi, *Iran Awakening: One Woman's Journey to Reclaim Her Life and Country*, 2007, 197.

31 The Commission on the Intelligence Capabilities of the United States Regarding Weapons of Mass Destruction, set up in 2004 concluded that the United States Intelligence Community was wrong in almost all of its pre-war judgments about Iraq's alleged weapons of mass destruction and that this constituted a major intelligence failure.

32 The 52 hostages were flown to Algeria January 20, 1981, twenty minutes after Reagan concluded his inaugural address, the first move in what came to be known as the Iran-Contra affair. Reagan's foreign policy team had secretly agreed to exchange arms-for-hostages with the Iranians, now at war with Iraq.

33 When 14 women were shot at Montreal's École Polytechnique in Canada's worst mass shooting.

34 Murray was probably denied his US visa at the same time for his own role in getting the Podesta files to Wikileaks, though, like the Canadian refusal, the

	denial was not explained. To add fuel to the US fire, Murray was on his way to chair the presentation of the Sam Adams Award to CIA torture whistleblower John Kiriakou and to speak at the World Beyond War conference in Washington DC. Robert Parry, "A Spy Coup in America?", *consortiumnews.com*, December 18, 2016.
35	Under the leadership of former Spanish Prime Minister José María Aznar, a high level political group, including Harper, met in Paris in 2010 to launch the Friends of Israel Initiative, a new project in defense of Israel's right to exist. In Britain, there are now friends for all the major parties—Labour Friends of Israel, Conservative Friends of Israel and Liberal Democrat Friends of Israel, where virtually all MPs have been pressured to join.
36	"Canada Won't Hesitate to Criticize Israel, Says New Prime Minister Justin Trudeau", *Haaretz*, March 8, 2016.
37	"Israeli filmmaker tells Germans: Don't sell submarines to 'fascist' Israel", *jpost.com*, February 20, 2016.
38	Libeskind, whose parents were Polish Holocaust survivors, and who also designed the Berlin Jewish Museum, the Felix Nussbaum Museum in Osnabruck, Germany, and the Danish Jewish Museum in Copenhagen.
39	Mark Avrum Ehrlich, *The Encyclopedia of the Jewish diaspora: origins, experiences, and culture* (2008), Nadav Aner, *The Jewish People Policy Planning Institute Planning Assessment* (2004).
40	*Forbes* 1982 in Weinfeld, op.cit., 105.
41	Ibid., 106.
42	Derek Marrus Penslar (ed), *Contemporary Antisemitism: Canada and the World*, 2005, 49.
43	See "Munk Heads Up Mining Top 10", *Mining Journal*, http://www.mining-journal.com/world/north-america/munk-heads-canada-mining-top-10/
44	A more powerful explosive than TNT, used widely in World War II. Rose was given the maximum sentence of 6 years "plus a day", enough to override parliamentary immunity.
45	Weinfeld, op.cit., 34.
46	Ibid., 177-8.
47	Ibid., 257.
48	Jewish holidays can be described in nine words: They tried to kill us. They failed. Let's eat. Ibid., 281.
49	See Walberg, *Postmodern Imperialism*, 166-7.
50	Ben Dunkelman, *Dual Allegiance: An Autobiography*, 1984, 159.
51	Engler, op.cit., 34. In his defense, he refused the order to expel Nazareens, preserving one of the few communities of Muslims and Christians in what is now known as "the Arab capital of Israel".
52	David Bercuson, *The Secret Army*, Lester and Orpen Dennys (1993), 52.
53	The 1870 Act made it a crime for any citizen of the United Kingdom of Great Britain and Ireland to enlist themselves in the military of any foreign power at war with any state with which the UK was at peace.
54	It was in fact Canadian taxpayers who had to pay. Richard Cleroux, *Official Secrets: The story behind the Canadian Security Intelligence Service*, 1990, 21-8, 278.
55	Weinfeld, op.cit., 259.
56	Engler, op.cit., 55.
57	Weinfeld, op.cit., 261.

58	Weinfeld, op.cit., 261.
59	Eric Walberg, "Diplomacy Canadian Style", *ericwalberg.com*, February 17, 2014.
60	Engler, op.cit., 53.
61	Viktor Ostrovsky and Claire Hoy, *By Way of Deception*, St. Martin's Press, 1990, 74.
62	Engler, op.cit., 162.
63	Canadian companies operate in the Occupied Territories with the approval of Ottawa. The 1997 free trade agreement includes the West Bank, based on areas Israel maintains territorial control over, not the international recognized borders (vs the EU). There are more than 300 charities with ties to Israel, some sending money to settlement construction. The Toronto Zionist Council's charitable status was revoked in 1996 when it was proven that funds were going to settlement construction. Revenue Canada revoked the Toronto-based Press Foundation in 1999. 10% of Israel's Jews live on territory occupied since 1967 so it is difficult to follow all the trails. Most violations of boycotting settlements avoid detection. There has been no censure of the separation wall. 25 Torontonians took part in the assault on Gaza 2008–09, with the full knowledge of CSIS. Ibid., 69.
64	See Chapter 7.
65	Geller and Spencer, co-authors of *The Post-American Presidency: The Obama Administration's War on America* (2010), are the most prominent organizers of the campaign to stop the building of a mosque at "Ground Zero" in Manhattan (in fact, the Park51 Islamic Community Center). They were refused entry under pressure from anti-racist groups such as Hope not Hate. "The UK should never become a stage for inflammatory speakers who promote hate," reads the decision by the British Home Office, a ruling which will remain in effect for three years. Geller shot back: "In a striking blow against freedom, the British government is behaving like a *de facto* Islamic state." The news came on the same day that a mosque in Redditch was broken into and had Swastikas and the letters "EDL", as well as other racist messages, daubed on it guests at the Markham event featuring Geller paid $500 a head in order to attend a pre-lecture cocktail party. This was Geller's second talk that year in Toronto. Her May event was a "huge success" according to JDL Canada, though it almost didn't take place at all, as the synagogue that offered to host her got cold feet and backed out, and the Toronto Zionist Center had to come to the rescue.
66	Weinfeld, op.cit., 325.
67	Davies, op.cit., 72.
68	Goldwin Smith, *Guesses at the Riddle of Existence*, 1897.
69	Whether Canada should be described as "multinational" is an ongoing topic in academia and popular discourse. The current policy of the federal government is that Canada is bilingual—English and French are both official languages—and multicultural. In 2006, the House of Commons of Canada voted in favor of Government Business No. 11, which states that the Québécois "form a nation within a united Canada," which makes it binational.<https://en.wikipedia.org/wiki/Multinational_state>
70	Tulchinsky, op.cit., 439.
71	Ibid., 440.
72	David Shulman, "Israel's Irrational Rationality", *The New York Review of Books*, May 24, 2017, <2states1homeland.org/en>.

73   Dr. Strangelove: The whole point of a Doomsday Machine is lost, if you *keep* it a *secret*! (1964).

PART III
ANTISEMITISM WACK-A-MOLE

| Chapter Seven |

THE LONE RANGERS

Who are the heirs to the Nazis? There never were more than a handful of card-carrying fascists in Canada, though the rise of the far right in Europe and now in the US means at least more 'lone wolf' type violence, directed now more against Muslims, who, though mostly model immigrants, are rarely white. Despite protestations by B'nai Brith, the total number of hate crimes around the country continues to drop, though the number targeting Muslims has increased.[1] Fascism in Canada peaked in the 1930s, and went into sharp decline with the outbreak of WWII. Neo-fascist groups have come and gone without much effect since then, though they need monitoring. The state's own focus on Islamic terrorism means that the activities of the more numerous and dangerous far right groups such as Blood and Honour, Aryan Guard, La Meute ("Wolf Pack") and neo-Nazi skinheads are given far less attention.

Muslim banner[2]

Racism has been benign in Canada compared to in the US. Anti-Jewish prejudice peaked with the large immigration of east European Jews at the beginning of the 20th century and the Depression of the 1930s, but also abated with the outbreak of WWII. Lloyd George, Clemenceau and Hitler, in retrospect, were the Zionists' best friends; without the Treaty of Versailles, which led to the rise of Hitler, the assimilationist Jews would have prevailed, there would have been no Israel, and no need to fret over anti-Jewish prejudice today.

Hitler caused a mass exodus of European Jews not only to Israel, but to North America after the war, where they quickly rose to prominence in economics, politics and culture, based on the solid foundations laid by the first wave of immigrants in the late 19th century. Hitler's attempt to cut short the feared Jewish hegemony in the western world backfired, even accelerating it. This is the backdrop to the battle that took place in the 1980s, and the belief that WWII was really about saving the Jews rather than a 'fight for democracy'.

The battles of the 1980s were against the so-called "Holocaust deniers" among the anti-Zionists, a category where mainstream media dumps many of those critical of the Zionist narrative, even if the victims make it clear they don't deny the genocidal campaign against the Jews in WWII. Their prey are automatically, using Humpty Dumpty logic, antisemites (i.e., the word means exactly what I want it to mean). The ones the Zionists took on—Keegstra, Zundel and Topham—insisted there were no gas chambers, and that far fewer than 6 million Jews died, mostly from sickness and starvation. Mistaken in their amateur reading of the literature, but in retrospect, not a real threat, given their obvious bad homework, not worth the upheaval and angst that the trials created.

Their real danger lay in exposing the Zionists as following the Nazi praxis—racism and imperialism—which angers not only their victims, the Palestinians, but anyone with a conscience. *They* (the Zionists) are the ones stirring up anti-Jewish prejudice, accusing the so-called deniers falsely of 'antisemitism' and even crafting spectacular false flag antisemitic threats. An Israeli-American 19-year-old was arrested in Israel in March 2017 for making hundreds of bomb threats against Jewish centers, mostly in the US, over the past three years, even forcing a Delta airplane to land. The investigation was conducted by US and Israeli security forces, but no motive was suggested.[3] These 'false-flag' threats and actual attacks are old hat for Zionists, especially once Israel was a fact in 1948, and were carried out wherever Jews were in significant numbers (Egypt, Iraq, Morocco) and have led to bizarre results.[4]

The 'deniers' argue that both Nazism and Zionism were founded by those who saw themselves as a 'chosen people',[5] with a world-historic destiny,[6] demanding an aggressive expansionist policy, where camps for the dispossessed (for the Nazis—Jews, for the Zionists—Palestinians) were the first step in a policy of expelling and/or killing them. Both are militaristic and violent. Both Nazism and Zionism have been the bane of world's Jews—despite the Zionists' claim that they are protecting Jews. Both are racist, imperialist conspiracies. Largely true, but not something the Zionists appreciated being said publicly.

Why did this happen in the 1980s? In the ADL's Global 100 survey (2015), half the world has actually heard of "the Holocaust" (94% in western Europe, 77% in the US/Canada), but 32% believe the numbers are exaggerated (11% in western Europe, 21% in US/Canada), rising to 40% among young people (18–34). Only one in five Asians—and one in ten Middle Easterners and Africans—knows of and believes in "the Holocaust". In other words, Canadians are among the most skeptical of westerners, and most people are no longer interested. This is seen by the ADL as alarming, particularly in Canada, requiring yet more efforts at educating about "the Holocaust" and eradicating any disbelievers. Bringing attention to the Holocaust had morphed into a mission.

Originally, it was considered distasteful to talk about the mass slaughter, where the Jews were portrayed as going like a 'lamb to the slaughter', as wimps. Interest in Nazi crimes as a centerpiece of Jewish ideology started with the 1960 kidnapping of Eichmann in Argentina, his trial in Jerusalem in 1961, and execution in 1962. Arendt saw through Ben-Gurion's insistence on staging the trial for political reasons. He wanted "to prove conclusively that the Holocaust had been the largest anti-Semitic pogrom in history, a means of creating a sense of national unity among a mass of demoralized new immigrants." And to force more reparations money out of the German government ($737 million by 1961).[7]

The 1967 war was a dilemma for Jews outside Israel, as it was both a source of pride and interpreted as some kind of divine payment for past suffering—but also potential evidence of Israel as an expansionist aggressor, requiring justification of the conquest. It sparked the most (in)famous work of Holocaust denial, *The Myth of the Six Million* (1969), unattributed, but revealed to be by a WWI revisionist historian, David Hoggan (1923–1988) who taught at the University of California at Berkeley, the Massachusetts Institute of Technology and other universities.[8] As Israel began its vicious circle of seeking greater security through ever greater expansion and aggression, inducing ever greater hostility, a powerful 'soft power' hasbarah attack was needed in the West. "Holocaust remembrance" became the "Holocaust industry", originally to extract reparations from Germany, now mobilized to cover Israel's further expansion. Hence the fanaticism with which Zionists have pursued those questioning the official Holocaust story. And the chipping away at "the Holocaust" by critics, genuine or otherwise, interested in pursuing the 'facts'.

The inherent injustice of the Zionist project took on new urgency after 1967, when Israel's aggression could no longer be ignored, and the tide of anti-war sentiment in Canada/the West peaked during the Vietnam war. Israel's self-image as the plucky underdog, taking a justified pound of flesh (Arab land) as payment for the persecution of Jews (by Germans) in WWII, lost whatever caché it had. It was never embraced as part of the agenda of youthful supporters of third world liberation, yearning to create a new world. Israel was 'apart' from this.

The public image of the Jewish Zionist folk hero in *Exodus* (1960) could no longer be sustained. No self-respecting anti-imperialist—Jews included—could argue this any longer. The heroic days of the Palestinian hijackings of airplanes to gain attention and release some of their thousands from Israeli jails is best remembered through the iconic image of Leila Khaled, whose 2016 interview shows her unflagging spirit and calm analysis of struggle, which she vows will never end until some modicum of justice is achieved. "We have internalized a culture of resistance. The Arab national question is not a matter of a single generation."[9]

The Zionists have good reason to fret about the "new anti-Semitism", which is not new, nor is it arising from some primordial 'goy' instinctual bigotry. It arises from the accusation that all the responsibility for age-old anti-Jewish prejudice is the fault of bigoted Christians (after the rise of Zionism, include Muslims). Most Joe Canucks sense that it is wrong to conflate Jewish with 'lover of Israel, right or wrong', but Israel and Jewish organizations in Canada insist on conflating the two, as the change of name of the Canadian Jewish Congress to the Centre for Israel and Jewish Affairs emphasizes.

Joe Canuck fears the 'antisemite' slur, so the house of cards stands, and dead anti-Jewish sentiment gains new life out of disgust with the "Jewish state". "The Holocaust" became the new silver bullet to keep people in fear, but it needs constant burnishing, ever new "Holocaust museums" and obligatory school trips. Just as important, it needed careful gatekeeping in the mainstream media and specialized departments of Jewish and Israeli history and politics at universities.

Which brings us to Canada's colorful array of "antisemites", as christened by Canada's Zionist thought police. All three Canadians depicted here—Keegstra, Zundel and Topham—are somewhat like Don Quixote, convinced of the nobility of their cause, not bad people by any means, just simple fellows, unlettered in comparison with their scholarly opponents, not 100% correct in their analysis of world events, but refusing to accept what they see as a one-sided interpretation of what's going on around them.

They are all died-in-the-wool anticommunists, and insist that Jews both 'created' communism and unceasingly promote it (long after the Soviet Union collapsed and communism died), in the same way as Winston Churchill and many other prominent politicians and businessmen did in the 1920s.[10] Henry Ford even serialized the *Protocols of the Elders of Zion* in his *Dearborn Independent* until a lawsuit, boycott and media campaign against him forced him to formally apologize and to close the newspaper in 1927. All except Churchill are despised now as anti-Jewish bigots and ignored, and Churchill's position is buried and if seen, dismissed as an anticommunist peccadillo.

They're really just recycling Goldwin Smith and Churchill, but without the former's intellect and the latter's PR skills and social standing, and now in a tightly controlled media. Smith's *Telegram* is now the *Sun*. Its leading op-edder, Ezra Levant, has been one of Canada's loudest promoters of Zionism, and anti-Zionists are caricatured and slandered there, and in the mainstream press generally. The role of Jews in western society, let alone of communism, is not discussed seriously in the mainstream media or intellectual discourse. The fact that the Zionists launched their Orwellian attack against Keegstra and Zundel in 1984 is an eerie coincidence.

None of the offenders are denying that many Jews died in WWII, along with many other innocent victims of war. What they are denying is that Jewish suffering is worth more respect—the cult status of capital H holocaust—which no other groups merit, that 'the Holocaust' justifies the creation of a special Jews-only country, Israel, and the expelling and killing of the inhabitants to make way for all the world's Jews. They are suspicious that the tribulations of Jews in WWII might be exaggerated as part of the Zionist agenda to condone the creation of a Jewish state, and its unending persecution of the native Palestinians.

By framing all such critics as "Holocaust deniers", a not-so-subtle sleight of hand takes place. Yes, they deny the use of the term "Holocaust", some of them even denying (wrongly) the use of gas chambers to systematically murder millions, but they do not deny the tragedy of persecution of Jews by Nazis itself. The difference is lost, as governments, including the world government, the UN, pass laws criminalizing questioning not only the denial of WWII Jewish suffering, but also the mere denial of the validity of the term Holocaust, as a "hate crime". Jewish organizations, with B'nai Brith at the helm, have managed to convict hundreds of people around the world, not just high school teachers (Keegstra) or populist writers (Zundel), but historians and intellectuals like Faurisson and Irving, making them pariahs, getting them fired, beaten up, removing their books from libraries wherever they can, burning or pulping them. People who question what actually happened—suggesting that numbers might be exaggerated, that not all Germans were blood-thirsty, evil murderers, that most might not have been aware of what was going on or were just blindly following orders—have been labeled "Holocaust deniers".

The 'deniers' write about these important questions clumsily, seeking to at least have raised the issues, in a truly Quixotic way, sacrificing themselves before their altar of Truth. They see something very suspicious behind world events as portrayed in the mass media, and put some of the pieces of the puzzle together, but jump to conclusions where they see gaps in information, something we all do every day, mistakenly interpreting the hidden truths behind what looks innocuous. Your wife knows you're lying, thinks you're betraying her with another woman, but maybe you really just like drinking with the boys, or maybe you're doing something illegal and must keep this under wraps at all costs. What is the real story?

Keegstra, Zundel, Topham

The real story began in Long Beach, California, in 1981, with a lawsuit by Mel Mermelstein against the Institute for Historical Review (IHR).[11] The newly formed IHR immediately launched a competition with a reward of $50,000 to anyone who "could prove that the Nazis operated gas-chambers to exterminate Jews during WWII." Both Mermelstein and Simon Wiesenthal took up the challenge. Wiesenthal suggested Mermelstein leave the attack to his Simon Wiesenthal Center, founded in 1977 in Los Angeles, but Wiesenthal's terms were rejected by the IHR (Wiesenthal demanded that a California Supreme Court preside over the case), and Mermelstein decided to go it alone.

Mermelstein submitted a notarized declaration of his experiences at Auschwitz, along with a warning that he would institute civil proceedings to enforce the contract if he didn't get a response. He didn't, and filed a lawsuit. The prosecutor was clever, and requested "judicial notice of the fact" (acceptance that the facts are so well-known "in the community" that they cannot "reasonably be questioned" and therefore need not be produced). Judge Thomas Johnson accepted this argument, and summarily dismissed defense attempts to debate the validity of the Nazi crime: "It is simply a fact," he declared, stopping discussion and refusing any testimony. He declared Mermelstein the winner by default, and awarded him $90,000 ($40,000 "for pain and suffering"), insisting on the defendants signing a letter of apology "for the emotional distress they had caused him and all other Auschwitz survivors."

This success for the 'deniers of the deniers' was too tantalizing to pass up, and prompted the trials of Keegstra and Zundel, both of which were launched in 1984, hoping to put a stop to gas chamber denial in Canada. Rumors of gas chambers had been around since long before the Nazis began their 'Final Solution' in 1942. They were in use in the US for executions until 1990, and mass gassing was a monstrous crime in WWI. By 1933, with the declaration of war against Germany by world Jewry, fearing Nazi plans to suppress Jews and force them to emigrate, there was talk of an impending mass murder. The campaign of mass extermination, even the 6 million estimate, was assumed to be true before the war was over. The small 'h' holocaust term was used by the end of the war, and the first notable Canadian to deny this "holocaust" of Jews was Adrien Arcand, who began denying that 6 million figure as soon as it was proposed, before the war was over. Though interned as a fascist during the war, he was never tried on charges of Holocaust denial or hate speech. The time was not ripe.

Until 2017, Keegstra's case was largely forgotten. (See Chapter 9 - Muslim Activism). James Keegstra (1934–2014) was respected as a charismatic and articulate public school teacher and popular mayor in Eckville, Alberta (population 1,125). He was charged and convicted of hate speech in 1984. He appealed and the conviction was overturned. The Crown appealed again and the conviction was reinstated by the Supreme

Jim Keegstra

Court of Canada in 1990. He was stripped of his teaching certificate and charged under section 319(2) of the Criminal Code with "willfully promoting hatred against an identifiable group" by teaching his social studies students that the Holocaust was exaggerated and criticizing Jews for being tribal. He was originally fined $5,000. A subsequent decision by the Alberta Court of Appeal reduced that to a one-year suspended sentence, one year of probation, and 200 hours of community service work. While the Supreme Court upheld the original conviction and the constitutionality of the law, they did not restore the original sentence.

The complaints came, not because of his Jewish comments, but from a student's mother, Marg Andrew, whose father had been in the IRA, and who took offense when Keegstra told the class the IRA was Marxist (true). Keegstra was a shop mechanics and social studies teacher, intelligent and well read. Originally, he was more concerned with Catholics, communists and then blacks. His views were typical of SoCred Alberta, of a devout Christian, sensing a conspiracy underlying the mainstream, complacent news. By 1980, this was formulated as bankers, Jews (he estimated 7% of Jews were the problem) and communists, and the Jews "created the Holocaust to gain sympathy for their cause and, especially, for the state of Israel."[12] He pointed to the declaration of war against Germany by world Jewry in 1933 as a serious mistake.[13] This would not have been a problem a few decades earlier, but by the 1970s, education about the Holocaust had become an important item in the Zionist agenda, a key plank in turning attention from their plan to colonize all of Palestine. The Israel lobby would soon be lobbying to introduce classes in the Holocaust to all schools, and policing to make all public discourse politically correct from their point of view. An Irish Catholic mom fighting for her son was a great foil.

The school superintendent, a Catholic like Andrew, was reluctant to take harsh measures against the popular Protestant teacher, who was only telling an uncomfortable truth about the IRA, but when the new superintendent, R.K. David, took over in 1979, the backlog of complaints pushed him into action. He came to Eckville, found that Keegstra, while intelligent and well read, was teaching about a world Jewish conspiracy, and that he indeed was popular and would be hard to dislodge. He was also defiant, arguing the other teachers gave the mainstream interpretation of history, and that the students gained from hearing another view. Students would discuss the topic of world history outside of class, even as they fixed cars in Keegstra's shop class. "Students apparently would leave Keegstra's class and make a bee-line for the [socialist] teacher, to see if he could refute Keegstra's interpretations of history." Even the left-wing teacher supported Keegstra. High school principal Olsen was against firing him, telling Stanley Barrett when interviewed that he "had been especially pleased when his son, under Keegstra's influence, began for the first time to take an interest in world events."[14]

The vice-principal testified to the Lacombe school board, "He is a man whose morals are beyond doubt ... a most respected member of his community, in and out of school." The members of the board voted against firing Keegstra despite the pressures on them. Supervisor David insisted that the Jewish conspiracy lectures had to stop. But in October 1982 another parent, Susan Maddox, sent David a two-page letter revealing that Keegstra was "teaching creationism, dismissing evolution and the metric system as communist, that all bankers are crooks and judges corrupt."[15] Neither Andrew nor Maddox were liked by the Eckvillers that anthropologist and author Barrett interviewed; Maddox in particular was called "aggressive, dogmatic".

Keegstra was fired. The high school students petitioned to reinstate him, but were ignored. His fellow teachers were solidly on his side. One teacher told Barrett, who covered the incident, about "a former member of the staff who advocated premarital sex, pornography, and drugs. In her judgment, that teacher, and not Keegstra, posed a danger to the students."[16] The Alberta Teachers Association supported Keegstra, but their appeal was dismissed in Edmonton. The wheels were in motion and Keegstra was served a warrant in 1984. His case brought offers of financial support from white supremacist groups. "He replied he could only accept money on a no-strings-attached basis, because he can't interpret the scriptures and Christianity the way they do. When they start equating Christianity with racism, 'I can't go along with that'." "To me, they're just Judaism tipped upside down, meaning people who considered themselves superior to all others."[17] He said he didn't hate anyone, that the hatred he witnessed was from "parents out to get him, and Jews gleefully backing them up." Keegstra defined "Zionism as atheism," saying that for Zionists "the Messiah is the Jewish people collectively."[18]

He was found guilty of hate and fined $5,000. He could have demurred, saying the conspiracy was only a theory, and got off, but the man believed what he taught and refused to compromise his beliefs, and though his arguments were about a *systemic* conspiracy, not intended to harm anyone in particular but not provable, he was charged with a hate crime. (Zundel was acquitted at the same time of "spreading false news" precisely *because* he believed there were no gas chambers, which was provable, but false) Keegstra, father of four, a first-rate teacher, was condemned for believing, stripped of his job after 15 years, and turned into a national pariah. Eckville was swamped by national media blasting innuendo and gossip on national media front pages. It was turned into a warring camp, the old timers backing their boy, vs the minor hockey and figure skating crowd, the transients (the doctor, nurses, the Presbyterian minister in the Dutch Reform community). Finally, they voted him out as mayor but he still got a third of the vote. The local economy was depressed, several businesses had folded, residents, previously vibrant and friendly, became dull and sullen. Some of the students cracked under the pressure of the court experience, bursting into tears, traumatized by the ordeal.

No one involved approved of the court case, not even Andrew and David. Maddox told the *Red Deer Advocate*[19] the RCMP investigation and legal charge were just a political maneuver of the Alberta government to demonstrate (after the fact) its concern. Canadian Civil Liberties Association general counsel Alan Borovoy spoke out strongly against Keegstra's conviction, arguing the law was vague and the precedent a serious threat to freedom of speech.[20]

On the other hand, B'nai Brith hailed it for breaking "the log-jam. The legal charges as precedent would give the courts the opportunity to prosecute under the anti-hate laws,"[21] unlike the more problematic 'false news' law that would let Zundel off, as we shall see next.

Keegstra appealed this conviction to the Court of Appeal of Alberta, claiming that it was in violation of Section 2(b) of the Canadian Charter of Rights and Freedoms, guaranteeing "freedom of thought, belief, opinion and expression, including freedom of the press and other media of communication." Keegstra's appeal ultimately reached the Supreme Court of Canada, in the case of *R. v. Keegstra* (1990). While the Supreme Court upheld the original conviction and the constitutionality of the law, they did not restore the original sentence.

In effect, he fought the Zionists to a draw, neither serving prison time nor paying "blood money", but banned from teaching, emerging battered and vilified. Keegstra was a minor critic to be quashed, not a public icon to be politely ignored or tolerated, as was Goldwin Smith (or, for that matter, Churchill[22]). He said much the same as they did, but was an obscure, small-town teacher in Alberta, and refused to observe the new political correctness. He told his students, "Look, I'm teaching you stuff that others have been crucified for, smeared beyond imagining, so if it happens to me one day, it won't surprise me."[23]

The question of the precise number of Jews that died under the "final solution" was not part of the trial. This and the gas chambers were the main issues in the subsequent trials of Zundel, and outside of Canada, of David Irving.

The ongoing war against anti-Zionists is a stark reminder of the Jewish tragedy throughout history that Ginsberg so starkly pointed out in *The Fatal Embrace: Jews and the State*: rising meteorically to dizzying heights, becoming over-confident, and then risking all, plunging down, losing everything. Jews have reached the top of the pecking order in North America, with Canada the most open country in the world, but resentment seethes, occasionally boiling over. Critics are labeled dangerous racists and persecuted.

The critics keep popping up, and are ruthlessly hounded by angry, strident Zionists, giving a cruel face to Judaism in as much it is identified with Zionism in today's world. The trials of Zundel, the most spectacular attempt to squash the 'deniers', ended up a fiasco, a blow to what looked like a victory streak after the Mermelstein and Keegstra trials, creating a historic precedent, encouraging the critics of Zionism and creating new ones.

Ernest Zundel (1939–2017), an immigrant to Toronto from Germany in 1958, especially frightened Zionists because he was/is so articulate, and so prominent, speaking defiantly from the very heart of Canada. Like Keegstra, he was tried in 1984, in his case as author and publisher of his own "The West, War and Islam" (1980), and *Did Six Million Really Die? The Truth At Last*, (1974) by Richard E. Harwood. Harwood was a pseudonym for Richard Verrall, at the time a member of the British National Front.[24]

Ernest Zundel

The antics and trials of Ernst Zundel are the stuff of legend. During the 1960s, Zundel came under the tutelage of Adrien Arcand (1899–1967). French Canadian nationalist Arcand was impressed with his

German fascist acolyte, and bequeathed his library to Zundel.[25] Zundel set up his own Samisdat[26] publishing house, reprinted Verrall's polemic in 1974, and went on to issue his own "The Hitler We Loved and Why". In September 1981, he published an ad in the *Toronto Star* classifieds "Happy New Year to all our Jewish Friends".

But Zundel's travails began not as a result of the Harwood pamphlet, first published in Britain in 1974, when the official story of the persecution of Jews in WWII was being consolidated in the 1970s, and the far right National Front was growing in popularity.[27] The suit against Zundel was sparked by his own 1980 work, "The West, War and Islam", where he argues that the Muslim world should stop wasting their petrodollars on outmoded western military hardware, and use their money to finance a campaign "centered on Revisionist findings ... to achieve liberation through information by peaceful, democratic means."[28]

The wealthy Toronto Holocaust survivor Sabina Citron had succeeded in getting a postal ban on Zundel in 1981, preventing him from mailing his 'revisionist' pamphlets (primarily to Germany where they were illegal), but it was repealed in 1982. Impatient with the dawdling Ontario attorney general Roy McMurtry, she decided to lay a private charge under the hate section of the criminal code, which spurred the Ontario government into action. Despite his not unjustified misgiving about the wisdom of this, McMurtry joined her cause, charging Zundel with "spreading hate" for authoring and mailing out "The West, War and Islam", and "false news" for reprinting the Harwood pamphlet, under section 181 of the Criminal Code "spreading false news". Harwood/ Verrall (b 1948) upset the Zionists, because his "J'accuse!" pamphlet is on the whole well-written and documented, unlike most "Holocaust denials". Verrall had a first-class honors degree from Westfield College, now part of Queen Mary, University of London. Zundel relished the battle, as if he had snagged a big fish and was determined to reel it in, undeterred by the Mermelstein victory down south.

He was able to mobilize Keegstra's civil rights lawyer, Doug Christie. The one journalist willing to join the fray, Doug Collins, a WWII hero, joined the battle for freedom of speech. Keegstra flew in from Eckville to testify, but he was not much help. Zundel was found innocent *and* guilty in a jury trial—innocent for his own pamphlet, guilty of spreading false information for republishing the Harwood pamphlet, and sentenced to 15 months.

But the appeal court accepted Christie's submission that the judge had been wrong on 16 points of law, and ordered a retrial, which took place in 1988. Zundel was happy, if only because the trials gained him publicity, on the principle that any attention is better than none at all. The whole point of his own essay was to alert the world to the dangers behind Zionist manipulations. The Holocaust Historiography Project lists 500 newspaper articles on Zundel from 1981–97. Almost all are negative or just reporting on the trials.

The Crown applied for "judicial notice of the fact" as had the 1981 case in Long Beach, hoping to cut the trial short and sweet, but the judge rejected the application, believing that taking notice would hinder a proper defense and let the prosecution off easy.[29] Zundel marshaled his forces for the attack. He commissioned what he thought was a first-time scientific report on Auschwitz for his retrial, the so-called Leuchter Report, on the urging of his fellow Zionist critics, Faurisson and Irving, but it blew up in his (and later Irving's) face.

Fred Leuchter[30] went to visit the Auschwitz and Majdanek concentration camps, to surreptitiously take some samples of the alleged gas chambers, and test them, producing "The Leuchter Report: An Engineering Report on the Alleged Execution Gas Chambers at Auschwitz, Birkenau, and Majdanek, Poland", which Zundel published at his Samisdat Publications (1988). The report was discredited by the prosecution's evidence that other tests in 1945[31] attested to cyanide traces, and that there was lots of evidence of the existence of crematoria, and that most of the facilities for gassing and cremation had been destroyed by the Nazis. Leuchter's testimony as an expert witness was accepted by the court, but the Leuchter Report was excluded, based on his lack of engineering credentials.

The conviction in 1985 had been overturned on a legal technicality, but the false news conviction was confirmed in the retrial in 1988, despite the testimony of Joseph Burg, himself a Holocaust survivor, and fellow doubter of the '6 million'. In both trials, the court found that Harwood's work had "misrepresented the work of historians, misquoted witnesses, fabricated evidence, and cited non-existent authorities." Zundel appealed.

But third time lucky. In 1992, *R v Zundel* became a landmark Supreme Court of Canada decision where the Court struck down the provision in the Criminal Code that prohibited publication of false information or news, on the basis that it violated the freedom of expression provision under section 2(b) of the Canadian Charter of Rights and Freedoms. Justice Beverley McLachlin, writing for the Court, found that Zundel did violate section 181. The book was examined, and the court concluded that it "misrepresented the work of historians, misquoted witnesses, fabricated evidence, and cited non-existent authorities." However, section 181 violated section 2(b) of the Charter. The Justice noted that section 2(b) protects all expression of a non-violent form, and as such, the content itself is irrelevant (section 2(b) is content neutral). The protection provided by the Charter includes expression of minority beliefs even where the majority may find it false (Morais 2001). The imposition of imprisonment for expression has a severely limiting effect on freedom, beyond reason.

Not one MP or politician had spoken out in defense of freedom of speech, despite the judges' waffling on the dangerous precedent of targeting people based on a subjective criteria of "false news". Instead, the cries in mainstream media and in parliament were for Zundel to be deported. Just as disappointing for Zundel, opinion polls showed there was no increase in "Holocaust denial" as a result of the publicity.

The silence on the Canadian left, including the communists, was shocking, but the slur of antisemite was feared, and Zundel was a rightwing buffoon, however well-meaning. Only Judge McLachlin and Alan Borovoy (1932–2015), general counsel of the Canadian Civil Liberties Association (1968–2009), and lifelong member of the community relations committee of the Canadian Jewish Congress, dissented. "I think it was unwise from square one to prosecute this kind of thing," Borovoy said in 1985. He told Zionists they were "foolish" to try to use a law to censor free speech as a way to prove 6 million was the definitive number of the Holocaust death toll.

Justice John Sopinka, in the 1992 ruling, went the furthest: "Certain segments of society who are justifiably seeking equality for their particular interests have extended their demands so far that they threaten the freedom of others. They not only criticize the expression of views that do not accord with their own, but demand that contrary views be suppressed."[32]

No one had time nor interest in 1980s Soviet-style *glasnost* (openness) in Canada. Other than Iran, there was no governmental anti-Zionist voice by the mid-1980s. The Soviet Union was making friends with everybody under *perestroika* (rebuilding), opening the Jewish floodgates at last. The world was never more pro-Zionist. Zundel and Keegstra were genuine Lone Rangers against the world.

Besides Zundel, his lawyer Doug Christie and journalist Doug Collins, were pilloried for their efforts. (See below.) Together, these three Musketeers paved the way for more reputable critics of the Holocaust such as the Jewish academic Norman Finkelstein, who borrowed Zundel's characterization of the official narratives of the Zionists embodied in the Holocaust as a "hoax"[33] and the manipulation of the Holocaust as a "racket". Of course, Finkelstein was helped by having both parents *bona fide shoah* survivors, and none of Zundel's nostalgia for the third Reich. In Finkelstein's polemic with Alan Dershowitz, Dershowitz cracked in frustration, "He's only Jewish on his parents' side."

The "false news" section of the criminal code was discredited. Canada's Supreme Court ruled that you can question the veracity of the official Holocaust narrative. (No one has been prosecuted for this or any other free speech issue since based on "false news".) Zundel's victory put a lid, at least temporarily, on the Zionists' attempt to muzzle all dissenters from the official line, and paved the way for the more timid to take on the Zionists. A victory for free speech.

In 2011, Shimon Fogel, CEO of CIJA, said "What was intended as a shield against hate has become a sword ... What it has really done is create difficulties for those who might legitimately want to raise questions that are in fact a threat to the Jewish community or Israel ... like radical Islam."[34]

So Zundel's ultimate triumph was seen as likely, right from the start. It took him seven years to land his prize-winning catch. A classic case of Ginsberg's 'fatal embrace' and the Zionist penchant for foot shooting. Zundel's muddled free speech became a legal precedent *safeguarding* free speech.

A quarter century later, the whole saga emerges as a victory for Zundel, despite his unapologetic love of Hitler. He has gained his place in history for stripping the aura of invincibility from the Zionists, pricking the bubble of their ideology, with "the Holocaust" at its heart. An unapologetic defender of his beliefs, all unpopular and some very flawed, he was willing to defy the powers-that-be to defend them, risking his personal freedom and indeed his life. In 1995, Zundel's Toronto residence was the target of an arson attack resulting in $400,000 in damage.

A group calling itself the "Jewish Armed Resistance Movement" claimed responsibility for the arson attack; according to the *Toronto Sun*, it was a front for the Jewish Defense League and Kahane

Chai. The leader of the Toronto wing of the Jewish Defense League, Meir Weinstein (known then as Meir Halevi), denied involvement in the attack; however, five days later, Weinstein and American JDL leader Irv Rubin were caught trying to break into the Zundel property (again), where they were apprehended by police. No charges were ever filed in the incident. Weeks after the fire, Zundel was targeted with a parcel bomb that was detonated by the Toronto Police bomb squad.

A 1985 poll found support for "Holocaust denial" had declined, but that half of Canadians doubted the '6 million' and, more disturbing, that 16% believe the Holocaust was partly the Jews' fault. Zundel's strategy of 'any news is good news' failed, but Canadians were still skeptical of what half saw as an exaggeration.[35]

As a denouement, Canadian Jewish groups promptly responded by demanding that Zundel be tried again for the same "crime", this time under Canada's "hate law" that bans willful incitement to hatred. In 1992, Bernie Farber, national director of the Canadian Jewish Congress, filed a formal complaint against Zundel with the "Pornography/Hate Literature Section" of the Ontario Provincial Police in Toronto.

But the provincial government had had its knuckles rapped first time around. The Jews' embrace by the state is not unconditional, as Ginsberg warned. In a letter of March 5, 1993, Ontario Provincial Police Staff Sergeant Robert E. Matthews responded to Farber's complaint about Zundel's interview on CFRB: "In the above letter of complaint [of Sept. 9], you [Farber] allege that Mr. Zundel is willfully promoting hatred toward an identifiable group, that being the Jews, when he makes statements through the media in which he denies the Holocaust. ... The statements made by Mr. Zundel on that data do not constitute an offense contrary to ["hate law"] Section 319(2) of the Criminal Code."

Zundel responded to Farber's 1992 move by filing a complaint of his own on September 3, 1993 with the Ontario Provincial police. In his formal protest, he cited a statement by Elie Wiesel in *Legends of Our Time*: "Every Jew, somewhere in his being, should set apart a zone of hate—healthy, virile hate—for what the German personifies and for what persists in the German." In his letter to the Provincial Police, Zundel commented: "I know of no other clearer invitation to hate in any book or publication I have seen."

What about the book that set the whole process going?

Verrall's book was published under the pseudonym Richard E. Harwood. When he was 'outed', Verral denied he wrote it, for good reason, considering the wrath it incited. Intriguingly, he himself was never prosecuted and did not testify at Zundel's trial. Despite his legendary status, he is completely absent from the internet except for a terse Wikipedia entry that abruptly ends in 1980, the only citation of any activity post-trial, a bogus url,[36] a nonexistent or irrelevant external references. Though it can be purchased at Amazon[37] and downloaded for free, there is no deconstruction of Verrall's work anywhere, and only superficial references to it in Zundel's trial. Perhaps Verrall didn't write it after all? Perhaps he doesn't exist? A veritable who-dunnit.

Harwood/Verrall argues that:

> 1. there was no final solution to kill all Jews, that the scale of the Holocaust had been exaggerated by the Allies to hide their own guilt over such things as the atomic bombs dropped on Japanese cities, the air raids of predominantly civilian towns such as Dresden, and the Allies' own human-rights abuses,
> 2. it is used as a pretext for the establishment of the state of Israel and as a free pass for atrocities against the Palestinian population,
> 3. it is fuel for the extraction of "restitution" payments to victims.

Compelling arguments. Not at all over-the-top, though he went on to deny the gas chambers based on a misreading of Red Cross statistics.

The book, a classic polemical pamphlet by a hot-headed 24-year-old, full of passion, but well-argued and with hundreds of footnotes, made some false statements, which the Zundel trial prosecutor pointed out, such as a supposed memorandum from Joseph Goebbels that purportedly showed that the Final Solution was never more than a plan to evacuate Jews to Madagascar.[38] He misread and/or misquoted some statistics. But nothing willful (who knows?) like in David Irving's writings. He was never taken to court in Britain.

Colin Wilson (1931–2013) published the only sympathetic review of Harwood/Verrall's *Did 6 Million Really Die?* in the mainstream press, though it was not a formal review, merely a PS to his review of Joachim Fest's biography of Hitler in *books and bookmen*.[39] While writing his review in 1974, Wilson had received the Harwood book hot off the press in its first edition in Britain. He had a few years previously sent for a free copy of the unattributed *The Myth of the Six Million* (1969).[40] Wilson wrote a lot about conspiracy and mysticism, and he was intrigued by the coincidental mailing as he prepared his article on Hitler, and the topic.

Wilson figured Harwood's claim made sense—that Hitler had no reason to murder Jews when he needed them for forced labor. He was intrigued by Harwood's denial of the existence of extermination camps (as opposed to concentration work camps) and was also suspicious of memoirs about the camps, which had too often been exposed as "journalistic forgeries, churned out like pornography for an audience that revels in horrors." He didn't believe that the Holocaust was "all an invention", but he was suspicious of the figure of 6 million, and whether claims might be true that it was an "emotional historical distortion". "Some time over the next ten years or so, an Israeli historian is going to write a book called *The Myth of the Six Million*. It will cause a tremendous scandal; he will be violently attacked—and will become a rich man. And no one will be able to accuse him of being anti-Jewish."

Deborah Lipstadt was aghast that Colin Wilson would say anything positive about the Harwood work, jumping to the conclusion in *Denying the Holocaust* that Wilson had come to doubt the 6 million after reading Harwood, that his protestations of objectivity "are reminiscent of deniers' claims", inferring that Wilson has "sympathies toward Nazis" and "antipathies toward Jews". Very close to calling the popular Wilson a denier and antisemite. Lipstadt says Wilson described Harwood's tone as "reasonable and logical" and "devoid of hysteria or emotional antisemitism", was "generally rather pedantic", and attacks his willingness to take Verral seriously as "evidence of why the new pseudo-academic style adopted by deniers in recent years is so dangerous. Their packaging, which mimics legitimate scholarly research, ... confuses consumers. Readers are more susceptible to being influenced by an academic style than by poorly printed extremist and racist publications."[41]

Translate: Only universities are legitimate as authorities, where, of course, "Holocaust deniers" are *verbotten*. Lipstadt touched a sore spot with this swipe at Wilson, as Wilson had never gone to university, was a self-made intellectual, famous at the age of 25 for *The Outsider*, still a classic of disaffected youth. He also presciently predicted the work of Norman Finkelstein, whose *The Holocaust Industry: Reflections on the Exploitation of Jewish Suffering* (2000) caused a "tremendous scandal", and for which he was denied tenure and refused entry into Israel. And which, like Wilson's *Outsider* (and Harwood's *Did 6 Million Really Die?*) has sold far more copies than Lipstadt in all her writings.[42]

Harwood/ Verrall zeroes in on serious flaws in the official account of the Holocaust, in particular the coincidence of key Nurenburg witness Hoettl's testimony about Eichmann in 1945, the only real source for the '6 million'.[43] According to *Haaretz*,[44] 6 million is based mostly on word-of-mouth from Wilhelm Hoettl (1915–1999), an Austrian Nazi Party member, and SS major. He served in the Security Service, and by 1944 was acting head of Intelligence and Counter Espionage in Central and South East Europe.

Hoettl figured prominently as a prosecution witness at the Nuremberg trials. In an affidavit dated 25 November 1945, the thirty-year-old Hoettl described a conversation he held with Adolf Eichmann in August 1944 during the closing months of the war. The meeting of the two men took place at Hoettl's office in Budapest. Recounting a conversation with Eichmann, Hoettl told his US captors: "Approximately 4,000,000 Jews had been killed in the various concentration camps, while an additional 2,000,000 met death in other ways, the major part of whom were shot by operational squads of the Security Police during the campaign against Russia." Hoettl later wrote that "6 million had become the magic number," that Chaim Weizmann had mentioned it first in 1942 (calculating 2 million already murdered and 4 more to come), and *Reader's Digest* in 1943 suggested that Eichmann had probably picked it up from the BBC broadcasts that he listened to regularly. SS General Erich von dem Bach-Zelewski claimed that his units exaggerated their figures by up to 25%, and Auschwitz Commandant Hoss was clearly exaggerating when he claimed 2.5 million had been killed by 1942.[45]

As the Nazis began the invasion of the Soviet Union in 1941, their Jewish policy changed from emigration to extermination. To co-ordinate planning for the genocide, Hoettl and Eichmann's SS boss Reinhard Heydrich hosted the regime's administrative leaders at the Wannsee Conference on 20 January 1942. Eichmann collected information for Heydrich, attended the conference, and prepared the minutes. Eichmann and his staff became responsible for Jewish deportations. Eichmann also reportedly stated in 1945 that, "I will leap into my grave laughing because the feeling that I have 5 million human beings on my conscience is for me a source of extraordinary satisfaction."[46] Eichmann escaped to Argentina after the war, was captured by Mossad, and hanged in 1962, after preparing his diary in an Israeli prison.

But Hoettl escaped any punishment and was snapped up by the fledgling CIA in 1948, as part of the new Cold War against the Soviet

Union, working for the US Counter Intelligence Corps in Cold War espionage operations MOUNT VERNON and MONTGOMERY, one of many Nazi war criminals who were welcomed with open arms by the US. (See Chapter 6.) Some speculate that he was already in the pay of the Americans by 1944.

Harwood was making telling points, blowing the cover of the US and its murky prosecution process at Nuremburg. His doubts about the gassing seem genuine. Leuchter's report came a decade later, and seemed to confirm doubts for a while, but then was discredited. Nothing more was heard from 'Harwood'. Maybe he just decided to move on.

As a militant nationalist, Harwood/Verrall admired the chutzpah of the Zionists and the Jews through history: "No one could have anything but admiration for the way in which the Jews have sought to preserve their race through so many centuries, and continue to do so today. In this effort they have frankly been assisted by the story of the Six Million, which, almost like a religious myth, has stressed the need for greater Jewish racial solidarity. Unfortunately, it has worked in quite the opposite way for all other peoples, rendering them impotent in the struggle for self-preservation."

He argues that the declaration of war against Germany, made in the name of world Jewry in 1933, was a big mistake, or at least a gift to the Nazis, making all Jews traitors of Germany by definition. The US and Canada interned Germans and Japanese during the war, also considering them potential traitors. So again, in Harwood's view, a case of 'shooting themselves in the foot'.

The Crown stressed that Verrall/Zundel misrepresented the work of historians, misquoted witnesses, fabricated evidence, and cited non-existent authorities, that the pamphlet was littered with errors and exaggerations, that indeed there was a 'Final Solution' by 1942. Verrall cites Red Cross witnesses who testified that they saw no evidence of gassing and mass cremation when they visited the camps in 1944, and the statistics they had do not confirm mass killings. But he was selectively choosing his quotes. Also in the Red Cross report is their report that Jews are "outcasts condemned by rigid racial legislation to suffer tyranny, persecution and systematic extermination ... [They] formed a separate category without benefit of any Convention."[47] The Red Cross "repeatedly attempted to refute the deniers' claims."[48] Radu Ioanid, the US Holocaust Museum's specialist on survivors said of Red Cross documents only released in 1996, that the Red Cross had rescued thousands of Jews in Hungary and Romania and had assisted Jews at a concentration camp in Ravensbruck, Germany.[49]

There has been genuine confusion and exaggerations about numbers. Auschwitz revised the numbers of deaths from 4 million to 1.5 million in 1992.[50] Wikipedia states that in 1939, the core Jewish population reached its historical peak of 17 million (0.8% of the global population). Due to the Holocaust, the number was reduced to 11 million in 1945, citing "World Jewish Population: Latest Statistics".[51] Nizkor, sponsored by B'nai Brith, is a site dedicated to Holocaust information, and cites the Anglo-American committee for studying the Nazi genocide inflicted on the Jews of Europe, which came up with 5,721,500, based on registration records pre- and post-war. Poland (3,271,000) and USSR (1,050,000) are the venues of the bulk of deaths. University of Minnesota's Center of Holocaust and Genocide Studies suggests 5.2 million.[52] Yad Vashem's project to compile names of victims came up with 4 million. Many of the Jews were communists, certainly among the Soviets, so it's a moot point whether they were killed as communists or Jews.

There is still a hot debate among WWII historians about what the Nazis had in mind, which eventually crystallized in two factions by the 1970s: the intentionalists and the functionalists. The former insist that the Nazis intended to exterminate the Jews as early as 1933. This ignores Hitler's attempt to get Britain and France to agree to deporting Germany's Jews (those who didn't leave on their own accord) to Madagascar. (See Chapter 5.) The functionalists argue that the intent to exterminate only came about after it was clear in late 1941 that Britain and the Soviet Union would not capitulate, like France. That the war would be long or lost, and there was nothing to do with 'the enemy within' but use the able bodied as forced labor and kill the rest.[53]

Still a war crime, but not evidence of Germans' innate evil, as intentionalists such as Daniel Goldhagen argued, and whose *Hitler's Willing Executioners: Ordinary Germans and the Holocaust* (1996) became a bestseller. Goldhagen wrote his anti-German polemic in response to the functionalist Browning's *Ordinary Men: Reserve Police Battalion 101 and the Final Solution in Poland.*[54]

Browning's study showed that the guilty draftees, simple working-class men not fit to fight, were ordered to transport Jews or, if there was not enough room, to shoot them. Shocking from our peacetime perspective, but they were not sadistic murderers, just following orders. The men of Unit 101 killed out of a basic obedience to authority and peer pressure, not blood-lust or primal hatred. Browning cites the Milgram experiment on obedience to authority figures, which was first carried out in 1961, three months after Eichmann's trial started in Israel, and showed that experiment subjects were easily convinced to kill people under stress, merely following the orders of their controller.[55]

The most telling proof of the mass exterminations, especially of Jews, is the testimony of those guards who survived, escaped punishment, later felt remorse and spoke out. Such voluntary testimonies of guards and witness are compelling proof, vs the memories of the victims (we always inflate our unreliable memories), but the guards were caught, convicted or confessed and wanted to atone. One who that has become a sort of icon of truth-telling is Oskar Groening.

One of the few Germans to voluntarily speak out about their role in the genocide as an Auschwitz guard, Oskar Groening (b 1921), finally decided to speak out in the 1980s, when he saw the "Holocaust deniers" denying the gassing took place. "I saw the gas chambers. I saw the crematoria," he told the BBC in the 2005 documentary "Auschwitz: the Nazis and the 'Final Solution'". He described standing with another guard as he dumped the poison Zyklon B into a panel above a mass "shower room" and how he could hear the screams diminish after that. He talked about how, upon arriving to work at Auschwitz-Birkenau for the first time, he was informed that a large part of the camp was devoted to "discarding" the arriving Jews deemed unfit for slave labor. He was sentenced to 4 years at the age of 93.[56]

More Foot Shooting

The most detailed sympathetic account of Zundel's trial is Michael Hoffman's *The Great Holocaust Trial: The Landmark Battle for the Right to Doubt the West's Most Sacred Relic.*[57] He recounts how in a startling reversal, the 'survivors' who had appeared in court in order to send him to jail, had to submit their testimony to scrutiny, the rules of evidence and cross-examination, something that had never happened before and has never happened since. Canadians grew ever more surprised and shocked at the contradictory admissions which the defense team elicited from the supposed eyewitnesses to the homicidal gas chambers. As a result, television reporters and print journalists who covered the 1985 trial produced broadcasts and news reports that turned Canada upside down. Coincidentally, the fake

Holocaust memoirs were already coming off the press at this point,[58] compounding the Zionists' embarrassment.

Zundel was absolved, but the attempt to deport him to Germany—which was happy to do the Zionists' dirty work—were stymied. After 8 long years in the courts, Zundel was free by 1992. Worse yet, by putting all this before the world in a kind of show trial, Zundel playing the spirited little David fighting the grim Goliath, he was able to bring to public attention the very important but uncomfortable points: the *shoah* was and is being used by both the US and the Zionists to further their aims, and the bigger the number of deaths, the better for both. Arendt had exposed this in 1964 and Finkelstein would do it again in the 2000s. Gruesome, but true.

After 1992, the witch hunt against anti-Zionists around the world has continued apace, most famously with the defeat of David Irving in his in 1996 Deborah Lipstadt, the subject of *Denial* (2016), with Canada playing a supporting role. Irving had instigated the discredited Leuchter Report for Zundel, had been convinced by it, and was destroyed when he was convicted, finally seeing his errors, repenting, but never forgiven. This should have been the last word on the gas chambers, but there are still stubborn disbelievers, BC farmer **Arthur Topham** (b 1948) in particular, whose crime is "hate speech" but, like Zundel and Keegstra's trials, resulting in muddled rulings and long, drawn-out court appearances.

Topham's real crime is his devastating use of the anti-Zionists' two weapons—the internet and chutzpah. Like Zundel, he has snagged a big fish, and is still in the process of trying to reel in his catch. He is a more difficult adversary for the Zionists than Zundel, without the flimsy "false news" law to call on, without Zundel's eccentric nostalgia for Hitler, which made him a buffoon, and happily married to a Jewish wife, with 4 Jewish kids to boot. The Zionists managed to stamp out Keegstra, Zundel was eventually deported to Germany, but their ongoing persecution of Topham added fuel to Topham's fire, creating powerful theater, appealing to all those Canadians fed up with Zionist propaganda overkill at home.

Topham, publisher of *Radical Press,* woke up on May 16, 2012, to the ominous 'knock on the door'. "I was arrested and jailed and my home was entered illegally by the RCMP's 'Hate Crime Team' who then proceeded to steal all of my computers and electronic files." He was charged on two separate occasions using the same strategy used against Keegstra: Criminal Code Sec. 319(2) willfully promoting hatred against "people of the Jewish religion or ethnic group". "Since that date I have been involved in a protracted and onerous legal battle, first with the British Columbia provincial court and now with the British Columbia Supreme Court." *R v Roy* charged Topham with "hate crime" (2007) and "hate propaganda" (2012) under new Criminal Code "Hate Propaganda" legislation. Harry Abrams, a businessman and B'nai Brith volunteer from Victoria, launched the complaint that led to the charges against Topham.

Topham had to wait 3 years for the trial. After a jury trial he was found Guilty on the first charge of "hate crime" and Not Guilty on the second charge. He immediately launched a challenge to the Constitutional legitimacy of Sec. 319(2), which, if it fails, will lead to an appeal and sentence.

Such was the combined power of the state and the Canadian Jewish lobbies (CIJA, Bn'ai Brith, JDL) against a penniless backwoods farmer, a family man with a Jewish wife to boot. The new Ontario Civil Liberties Association (OCLA) director, Joseph Hickey, is not, like Borovoy (during Zundel's travails), a member of the community relations committee of the Canadian Jewish Congress (now Centre for Israel and Jewish Affairs). On the contrary, Hickey sent a strongly worded defense of Topham's free speech rights[59] to the presiding judge in the October 2016 trial. It is hard to imagine if a CIJA member as OCLA head could have written so eloquently in Topham's defense, considering they are also part of the prosecution.

Zionist theatre: The evidence[60]

As evidence of hate, in Topham's trial in 2015, Len Rudner (standing in for Bernie Farber) presented Topham's political poster which truthfully (if provocatively) shows the theatrical state of Canadian-Israeli relations today, depicting the leaders of Canada's political parties as puppets guided by a Zionist puppet master.

Then the trial turned to *Israel Must Perish!*, Topham's parody based on a now forgotten book *Germany Must Perish!* (1941) by Theodore Kaufman. As the US WWII effort began and the evidence against Nazi crimes mounted, pacifist Kaufman drew inspiration, and wrote his startling book *Germany Must Perish!*, advocating the sterilization of all German males. Kaufman's book was ignored in the US. 1941 was not a good year for civil rights advocates, especially of

German rights. Americans of German descent were being herded into prison camps along with Japanese Americans and communists.

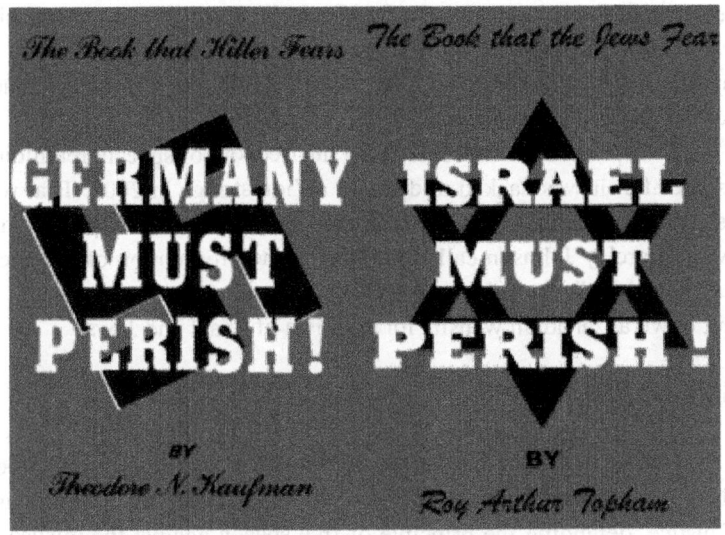

1941 Jewish book precedent for Topham parody

Nazi Propaganda Minister Joseph Goebbels read the book and immediately grasped its value, writing in his diary: "This Jew did a real service for the enemy [German] side. Had he written this book for us, he could not have made it any better." Under Goebbels' direction, *Germany Must Perish!* became a staple of German radio and press, convincing wavering Germans that killing Jews was necessary and justified, till the last Jewish death was registered as the Reich collapsed.

In his defense, Kaufman's plans for Germany were not so different from FDR's (Jewish) Secretary of the Treasury Henry Morgenthau, who advocated dismantling postwar Germany's industrial base, turning it into a harmless (destitute) rural nation. Luckily for the Germans, the US occupational forces did not follow directions for large-scale destruction of mines and industrial plant, giving wide-ranging discretion to the military governor and Morgenthau's opponents at the War Department.

The trials and tribulations of Arthur Topham reveal details about the penchant of Zionists for conspiracy even in the minutest details. In addition to *Israel Must Perish!*, the tired, old *Protocols of the Elders of Zion* were trotted out as evidence. Officially the Protocols were declared a forgery in a Swiss court in 1935, though no one ever made clear just what they were a forgery of, and the ruling was overturned in the Appeals Court in 1937. Like *Did Six Million Really Die?*, it is easily available on the internet, so what makes Topham particularly guilty of anything in regards to *Israel Must Perish!* remained a mystery (much like the *Protocols* themselves).

Topham's sin was exercising his freedom of speech, rebuilding his site after it was hacked to death in a Zionist rage in 2006. That was his crime. Refusing to yield. In final arguments at the 2015 trial, defense lawyer Barclay Johnson called the hate crime prosecution of his client "an inquisition" by "lobby groups for a foreign government trying to shut down a Canadian website for criticism of Israel and Jews."

The Lone Rangers' Tontos

There are two more actors in this drama, battle-scarred heroes, who made sure that Zundel and many other 'black sheep' had a modicum of justice, defending the principle of free speech against the misuse of "hate speech" laws, even though they didn't share their views. (Neither denied the tragedy of WWII, but were loudly pilloried as Holocaust Deniers.)

Doug Collins (1920–2001) is one of Canada's WWII heroes, unjustly forgotten, a victim of Zionist vengeance for his unflinching defense of free speech. He finally achieved some grudging public respect, but only in his obituary, "Death of a True Radical".[61] His one-time employer, the *Vancouver Sun*, now a part of Israel Asper's media consortium, now called Postmedia Network, disowned him in an editorial the day after he died: "Even when Mr. Collins was right, he was wrong, because all he did with his bellicose approach was stoke the unconstructive anger of his supporters."

Collins reported on the Zundel trials for his community paper *North Shore News,* calling the trials a travesty. He was now blacklisted from his beloved *Vancouver Sun*, which eventually became a Zionist mouthpiece with the increased 'consolidation' of Canada's media.

Collins began his own court nightmares in 1997 after he wrote several columns, both about *Schindler's List*, predicting it would win all the Oscars, and criticizing Jewish hegemony in Hollywood and the use of the *shoah* to make profit, distort history, and justify Israeli atrocities.[62] He and his shoestring community paper *North Shore News* had to defend themselves against a Canadian Jewish Congress complaint in November 1997 before the BC Human Rights Commission, which, in the end, ruled in his favor, after his paper spent more than $200,000 and Collins spent $50,000 of his own money. No payment of court costs.

Barely had he won the case when he was re-charged—for the same column, along with three others.[63] Interestingly, a Filipino comedy "Swindler's List" came out in 1994.[64] This time the big guns were brought in. B'nai Brith Canada used fall guy Harry Abrams of Victoria (who was also their frontman against Topham) to lodge a complaint. Victoria is nowhere near North Vancouver, so Abrams would not even have seen the offending article on his doorstep, but 'his' complaint was upheld.

The Zionists had snagged their prey, thanks to the BC courts, and had done their homework after the Zundel-Imre Finta[65] disasters. They succeeded in driving Collins into bankruptcy and unemployment, expunging him from Canadian memory even for his wartime heroism. His crime? His zeal in defending free speech, and criticizing the Zionist slant on WWII, which he witnessed both on the front lines and as a POW, escaping Nazi persecution time and again. Telling truth to power.

Even Conrad Black, himself a WWII history fan, but an even bigger fan of Israel, spoke out after Collins died, along with Allan Fotheringham, who paid tribute to "a complex guy whose whole life was about fighting for the freedom to say something that other people thought was wrong." Fotheringham criticized "the bullies, the new Politically Correct who now ruled the roost, [but who] were the most intolerant of all, those who could not abide a true radical who listened only to his own inner drum and didn't give a damn for those who disagreed. He had been through a mill that his opponents could never imagine." Fotheringham carefully avoided any mention of just who the "new Politically Correct" were.

Even as he lay dying, Collins was shooting such deathbed barbs as:

- "There were so many Jews in the Clinton administration that the Israeli embassy would know about American policies before most members of the administration." (March 2001)
- "Groups who claim to speak for Jews are the biggest single threat to free speech in Canada." (May 2001)
- "No judge, British or otherwise, was about to take on the world-wide Jewish Establishment."[66]

- "I will conclude by saying that ... I defended freedom in the 1940s when Hitler was on the loose, in the 1970s when the federal hate laws were passed, and in the 1990s when those idiots in Victoria passed their misnamed Human Rights Act, and that I shall go on defending freedom until the day I die."[67]

As the Holocaust came to be institutionalized in the 1970s, Collins saw it as yet another distortion of WWII history and his instinct as war hero and journalist brought him into the heart of the battle for truth. He was the only public figure who supported Zundel, despite having to hold his nose on Zundel's love of Hitler. Though misguided, Zundel wasn't lying, like Dupre,[68] and the negative role of Jewish power in post-WWII western society increasingly alarmed Collins. Collins saw fascist revanchism entering our lives via Zionism, and his WWII fighter instincts clicked in. Collins' own works, his wartime memoir, *POW: A Soldier's Story of His Ten Escapes from Nazi Prison Camps* (1968), *Immigration: Parliament versus the People* (1986), *The Best and Worst of Doug Collins* (1988), and *Here We Go Again* (1998), were not so lucky. They all disappeared from Canadian public libraries.[69]

The other Sancho Panzo, really a Don Quixote in his own right, is **Doug Christie** (1946–2013), a Canadian lawyer and political activist based in Victoria, BC, who was known nationally for his defense of Zundel, Doug Collins, but also less noble scrappers, like former Nazi prison guard Michael Seifert[70] and white nationalist Paul Fromm. He was a friend and admirer of Collins, and his defender in court. "He was one of the most courageous men I ever knew," he said of Collins.

He first came to national attention as a lawyer in 1983 when he became James Keegstra's attorney, and then Zundel's lawyer in 1984. Christie would act as Zundel's attorney in several cases over the subsequent two decades up to Zundel's deportation from Canada in 2005. Christie's advocacy on behalf of Keegstra and Zundel led to him acting as legal counsel in a number of notable cases involving far-right figures.[71] He also represented numerous individuals in civil actions against the police, in an effort to ensure police accountability, and in 1987 successfully represented Gary Botting[72] in a defamation suit against the CBC.

Reflecting on the Zundel trial in 1988, Collins congratulated Christie: "The greatest credit is Mr. Christie, who never gave up even in the face of vilification. It takes guts to keep going for years in an unpopular issue of this sort. Most lawyers would have withdrawn. But

Christie had the last laugh when the appeal court accepted his submission that the judge had been wrong on 16 points of law. Hence the second trial. If freedom of speech has received a bit of a fillip we owe it not to Canadian liberals but to a German who salutes the late Adolf Hitler. A pox on Hitler. But supporting tyrants, fools and saints—and spreading false news—is what freedom of speech is all about."[73]

Another notable Canadian who suffered from the Zionists' scourge and turned to Christie for help was David Ahenakew (1933–2010) a prominent native leader, who had served in the army in Germany in the 1950s and picked up his ideas there.[74]

Zundel's ability to taunt and infuriate Zionists reached a zenith with the trial of alleged war criminal **Imre Finta** (1911–2003), which started in 1987. Zundel took a break from his own ordeal to give testimony which apparently was credible and helped clear Finta's name.

Imre Finta was the first person prosecuted under Mulroney's Deschênes war crimes legislation. He was charged in 1987 as a commander of the Gendarmerie in Szeged, Hungary, who had immigrated to Canada in 1948 and settled in Toronto in 1953. Unlike Zundel, he was fortunate to gain his Canadian citizenship in 1956. He was accused of committing manslaughter, kidnapping, unlawful confinement and robbery in relation to his alleged activities as a police officer assisting the Nazis in the forced deportation of 8,617 Jews from Szeged during the Holocaust. Defended by Doug Christie and Barbara Kulaszka, his defense was based on the argument that he had only been following orders and was only responsible for transporting Jews.

Finta was acquitted in 1990, after a six-month jury trial upheld by the Ontario Court of Appeal in 1992 and the Supreme Court of Canada in 1994. Justice Peter Cory, writing on behalf of the Supreme Court, said "Even where the orders are manifestly unlawful, the defense of obedience to superior orders and the peace-officer defense will be available in those circumstances where the accused had no moral choice as to whether to follow the order." The Milgram experiment (see above) was filtering into the justice system, much to the Zionists' chagrin. The Supreme Court also ruled that the use of the Criminal Code to prosecute Finta was unconstitutional.

The decision brought to an end prosecutions under the Commission of Inquiry on War Criminals under Justice Jules Deschênes in 1985, a smart election ploy for Mulroney, but all it showed was that the Canadian justice system had worked just fine on its own. Thereafter, the government attempted to deal with alleged war criminals by stripping them of their Canadian citizenship and deporting them to the country in which the alleged crime occurred.

Sabina Citron, from the Holocaust Remembrance Organization, who had started the Zundel fiasco, finally got a bit of revenge, winning a civil lawsuit for libel against Finta, after Finta accused her of being a liar for saying that he had committed war crimes. Slim pickings for the Zionists. Ironically Imre lived his life in Canada in a predominantly Jewish neighborhood. "I never was an anti-Semite, I never was a Nazi," an exonerated Imre Finta said after a long and emotional court struggle.

Justice Minister Ray Hnatyshyn was leading the charge under the Deschênes Commission, himself of Ukrainian heritage, and his pursuit of alleged war criminals was not appreciated by Ukrainian Canadians. Ukrainians suffered not only under the Nazis but under the Soviets, both during collectivization in the 1930s and when the Germans retreated as the war was lost, now suspected of collaboration. "I suffered like Jew did. I was twice under gun, to be shot. Only God saved me," Walter Marko, editor of the *Ukrainian Herald* in Winnipeg, told CBC in 1987. "I feel very, very bad when I hear them say, 'All Ukrainian people are criminal.' Ukrainian people were killed in concentration camps, in Babi Yar, all around. But they don't think about it. One Jew is killed and the whole world is crying."

Up to that point, there had been only two German Canadians tried and convicted of war crimes. German SS Major-General Kurt Meyer was accused of "direct or indirect responsibility" in the execution of 48 Canadian prisoners of war and became the first war criminal to be tried by Canadian military authorities. He was convicted and sentenced to death, but ended up serving nine years in prison, part of it in a New Brunswick penitentiary, and then he was deported for a trial in Germany. He died in 1961.

Helmut Rauca, a master sergeant who served in Hitler's SS, came to Canada in 1950 and was granted citizenship in 1956. In 1961, West Germany issued an arrest warrant for Rauca, alleging he murdered 11,500 Jews, and in 1972, asked the RCMP to help locate him. In 1982, he was extradited to West Germany, but died in 1983 awaiting trial. It was following the Rauca case that the government of Canada had established the Deschênes Commission.

What had the Zionists' sudden decision in the 1970s to find 'justice' achieved? The real offenders in Canada—Meyer and Rauca—had long been tracked down and dealt with. Inspired by the *Hitler's*

Willing Executioners-type 'intentionalists', the Zionist witch hunts did manage to show their own bigotry, and inflame relations between ethnic communities.

The real war criminals, the useful Nazi elite (scientists and the secret service, especially the anticommunist intelligence operatives) had been spirited into the US and Canada, on orders from the US and Britain, the pretext being to keep them out of Soviet hands, but really to work in the new Cold War, continuing their wartime criminal acts, now under US patronage, escaping retribution. "Operation Paperclip" was the United States Office of Strategic Services (OSS) program in which more than 1,500 Germans, primarily scientists but also engineers and technicians, were brought to the US and put into government employment starting in 1945. They were "bleached" of their Nazism, the scientists were granted security clearances, their new identities bearing lots of 'paperclipped' amendments.[75]

This started to come to light in the 1960s, primarily due to a Jewish communist journalist, Chuck Allen, writing in *Jewish Currents*, looking for war criminals still at large, and discovering they were working under new identities for the US government.[76]

US adoption of Nazi war criminals was already old news by the time it became public knowledge. It was justified in the 'fight against communism'. It's touching that by this time Hollywood could fete some of its own casualties from the McCarthy communist witch hunts, but that's because communism was on its last legs, and political films really don't cut it in the real world anyway. Lots of Holocaust films, but still no accounting for the Nazification that embedded itself in the West's foreign policy.

Jewish organizations such as B'nai Brith, Wiesel and Weisenthal's institutes for Holocaust studies were still finding war criminals in the 1980s, though not many. After Klaus Barbie, Demjanjuk[77] was the most celebrated. Small potatoes. They moved on to "Holocaust deniers" and the "new antisemitism" as their line of defense for Israel, character-assassinating any sufficiently prominent person for criticizing Israel.

Even offspring of victims of the Holocaust like Norman **Finkelstein,** who argues that "the allegation of a new anti-Semitism is neither new nor about anti-Semitism: it is, rather, an ideology formulated in the early 1970s for the explicit purpose of deflecting pressures on the state of Israel to end its occupation of the Palestinian territories of Gaza and the West Bank that had been captured by Israel in the 1967 Six Days War, classic 'hasbarah'."[78]

In 2006, the ADL repeatedly accused Norman Finkelstein of being a Holocaust denier,[79] despite the fact that Finkelstein's mother survived the Majdanek concentration camp, his father survived the Auschwitz concentration camp, and most of his family died in the Holocaust. Middle East Media Research Institute skirted around the accusation, arguing that "because Israel has misused the Nazi holocaust, exploited the Nazi holocaust, they [anti-Zionists] have decided to deny the Nazi holocaust ever happened."[80] That is true for the Zundels and Tophams, whom Finkelstein dismisses as idiots, and even for Finkelstein in the sense of "the Holocaust" as the quasi-religious totem that the Zionists have made out of the tragedy of Jewish suffering. But by trying to smear someone with the credibility of Finkelstein, the Zionists again shot themselves in the foot.

Finkelstein

They couldn't take Finkelstein to court for "antisemitism" or "Holocaust denial" but their smear helped made sure his tenure at DePaul University, originally granted, was denied after petitioning by Alan Dershowitz.[81] In 2008, he was deported from Israel and banned from entering it for 10 years.

Zundel, much less of a threat, was jailed (briefly) in 1988 for publishing literature "likely to incite hatred against an identifiable group" as a threat to national security, before the Supreme Court freed him. He had lived in Canada from 1958 to 2000 but was denied citizenship. In 2007, he was deported to Germany, convicted and sentenced to the maximum term of five years in prison for "inciting racial hatred" (released in 2010). He was prevented from making any public statements until his death in 2017.

What is shocking, even frightening, through all these trials, and pervasive in the Zionist narrative, is the obliviousness to a major cause of anti-Jewish prejudice, increasing with every bomb that Israel drops, every acre of land that 'settlers' steal. Critics are now deemed "subtle, sophisticated, devious",[82] calls for objectivity are antisemitic, criticism of Jews is always and everywhere suspect, Jews share no responsibility for prejudice against them in history, only the bigoted gentiles who act without reason. Any suggestion that banking, entertainment, media are dominated by Jews is antisemitic. Holocaust studies professor Deborah Lipstadt would do well to look in the mirror when she asserts: "Demonology, common to virtually every denier, is an affirmation of Nazi ideology."[83]

But who is demonizing who? Christians are bigots for calling Jews "Christ killers", but the Talmud and Jewish lore accepts that Jews were responsible for his crucifixion under Roman rule. While the Church has apologized for holding Jews responsible for Christ's death, and the mayhem against them that resulted,[84] the Jews have not revised their commentaries nor apologized in turn.

Zundel goes down in history as the most notorious victim of what Finkelstein dubbed "the Holocaust industry", though the confusion and indecision of the judges and the legal system made him as much a victor, when his case was finally thrown out. The Simon Wiesenthal Center, whose reports are accepted as the authority on the scholarly study of the *shoah*, including *Nazi Germany and the Final Solution, 1933-1945* and *Post-war trials and modern anti-Semitism*, took a beating. The precedent meant that it was okay to question the number of those who died in Nazi concentration camps, though at one's peril. Others elsewhere, such as David Irving and Robert Faurisson were not so 'fortunate'.

Investigating the conspiracies

Whatever the worth of Topham's own writings (his graphics are striking), he provides sources at his site, long repressed or forgotten, that both intrigue and expose the agenda and thinking of Zionists, and documents their activities in Canada for all to see. All three of these Lone Rangers—Keegstra, Zundel, Topham—insist that Jews both 'created' communism and unceasingly promote it even today. Thus, they are easily caricatured and despised in the mainstream press, and by left wing intellectuals, for whom it is politically incorrect to even broach the important topic of Jewish influence in politics, economics and culture, except for a small but growing movement, led by anti-Zionist Jews (who can get away with it).

The role of Jews in western society is far more complex than the black and white analysis of these 'revisionists' allows, colored as it is by Cold War bigotry, and limited by their lack of 'higher education'.

There *are* Jewish conspiracies, just as there are conspiracies of merchants (Adam Smith), British and other schemes for world domination (Hobson's imperialism), the pretexts that led to wars in Vietnam (Tonkin), Gulf War I (incubator babies), Afghanistan/GWOT[85] (9/11), Iraq 2003 Weapons of Mass Destruction, the creation of Israel (Herzl, Jabotinsky, Ben-Gurion), the invasion of Egypt in 1956,...There are conspiracies appearing and disappearing every day—you and your mates (it takes three for a legal conspiracy) decide to rob the corner store owner, one distracting him while the till is open. Even if the authorities don't know whose hand was in the till, if they can prove you 'conspired' then that can be prosecuted.

By definition, a tribal people is always conspiring together against the larger society, as indeed are sections of that society's elites. Not everyone is privy to the plot, but that doesn't mean it's not happening. What the larger society does to that small minority is rarely a conspiracy, as whatever is done is hard to hide when most people are privy to it. Hitler's 'final solution' was not a conspiracy, much as the language in German documents avoided the 'gas' and other words, using euphemisms which fooled nobody. The trick is to recognize the real conspiracies and expose them. The best defense is bringing them to light. They are only considered conspiracies *ex post* if we never find out who did them. If they succeed, like Pearl Harbor or Greater Israel, and are accepted, then the earlier, conspiratorial part is airbrushed out of history. Uncomfortable facts are dismissed as irrelevant.

Benjamin Disraeli wrote, in 1852: "Persecution, in a word, although unjust, may have reduced the modern Jews to a state almost justifying malignant vengeance. They may become so odious and so hostile to mankind, as to merit for their present conduct, no matter how occasioned, the obloquy and ill-treatment of the communities in which they dwell, and with which they are scarcely permitted to mingle... They may be traced in the last outbreak of the destructive principle in Europe. An insurrection takes place against tradition and aristocracy, against religion and property. Destruction of the Semitic principle, extirpation of the Jewish religion, whether in the mosaic or in the Christian form, the natural equality of man and the abrogation of property, are proclaimed by the secret societies who form provisional governments, and men of Jewish race are found at the head of every one of them. The people of God co-operate with atheists; the most skillful accumulators of property ally themselves with communists; the peculiar and chosen race touch the hand of all the scum and low castes of Europe! And all this because they wish to destroy that ungrateful Christendom which owes to them even its name, and whose tyranny they can no longer endure."[86]

While this sounds much like the later discredited *Protocols of the Elders of Zion*, it was the work of the future prime minister of Britain, of Sephardic Jewish descent, hailed for his brilliant foreign policy in the service of British imperialism, though today mostly forgotten. And armed with the knowledge of Rhodes' secret society[87] and the later incorporation of much of the communist social policy into the imperial conspiracy, we can take his words as an appropriate (if creepy) introduction to the role of Jews in all the 20th century conspiracies. Yuri Slezkine's *The Jewish Century* (2006) refers to the three 'promised lands' of 20th century Jewry—the US, the Soviet Union and Israel—putting Jews at the heart of all three conspiracy factions, in line with Disraeli's musings. With the Balfour letter and the Russian revolution in 1917, and the collapse of the Ottoman Caliphate the next year, it looked like the Jewish bankers and Zionists had hit the jackpot, but Ginsberg would only shake his head, contemplating where that soaring to the heights of wealth would lead.

There are really three Zionist conspiracies in recent times, with Canada playing a key role in all of them, if only because of the large Jewish immigrant community and lack of a Canadian foreign policy, leaving it to act as a handmaiden, a foil for Israel and the US. All three have to some degree come to fruition, but the cauldron of world politics continues to boil. There is no happy ending in sight.

Conspiracy #1

The first is the one directed against the Arabs, the now open conspiracy to take over all of Palestine as 'belonging to the Jews from biblical times', the so-called Promised Land, promised in Genesis 15: "The Lord made a covenant with Abram, saying, Unto thy seed have I given this land, from the river of Egypt unto the great river, the river Euphrates." The land was actually given to all of the children of Abraham, including Hagar's son Ishmael, and Abraham's six sons by Keturah, whom he married after Sarah died (Zimran, Jokshan, Midian, Ishbak and Shuah), but that got lost in the translation.[88]

This was not really a conspiracy at all, at least among the cognoscenti. Wrote Ben Yehuda, who settled in Jerusalem in 1881 in a letter: "The thing we must do now is to become as strong as we can, to conquer the country, covertly, bit by bit ... We will not set up committees so that the Arabs will know what we are after, we shall act like silent spies, we shall buy, buy, buy."[89] Whether or not it was made explicit, the Arabs were aware of this plan and resisted it fiercely, but without the sophistication and resources that the Jews had.

This conspiracy (against the native Palestinians) was heartily supported by British imperialists and Christian literalists. Canadian Henry Wentworth Monk (1827–1896), Christian Zionist, mystic, Messianist, and millenarian, was convinced that Revelation foretold the establishment of Palestine as a sort of global capital, which would serve to settle all nations' disputes via a permanent international tribunal, and secondly, as a safe haven for the beleaguered Jews of the world. The "great light" that would "overwhelm Christendom" was the return of the Jews to Palestine, and its establishment as a world capital. The industrial revolution was in full swing, with gas lighting, and his vision was that the science of the day would be the shining light of the world, bringing about the "new dawn." The nations of Europe and North America would be atoning for all the injustices they had perpetrated on the Jewish people over the centuries. Abraham Lincoln, not long after signing the Emancipation Proclamation, showed sympathy for Monk's pleas to end the suffering of Russian and Turkish Jews by "restoring" them to Palestine.

Herzl acted as a catalyst, touring Europe and America, targeting the rich Jews through the burgeoning Zionist organizations, a process which culminated in the monolithic Jewish lobbies of today, which effectively keep western Middle East policies in line with Israeli requirements, despite occasional squawks. From the start, Herzl's plan was to dispossess the native Palestinians "covertly, bit by bit": "We must expropriate gently the private property ... We shall try to spirit the penniless population across the border ... in transit countries, while denying it employment in our country ... We are not going to sell them anything back."[90]

Only the Arabs were alert to the Balfour letter's implications, but they were dismissed as barbarians, "antisemitic". The plan to seize Palestine went through various metamorphoses—the declaration of war by world Jewry against Germany in 1933[91] while urging European Jews to emigrate to Palestine, collaboration with the Nazis until the very end to buy Jewish prisoners to go to Palestine, terrorist acts against the British in Palestine (to force them out quickly before any accommodation with the natives could be made), and against Arabs in north Africa and Iraq (to encourage anti-Jewish mini-pogroms,[92] encouraging their Jews to emigrate to Palestine-Israel).

It went into high gear after 1967, with all of Palestine now 'liberated', and has accelerated since the 1980s with the illegal settlements, all in broad daylight. It was then that "the Holocaust" became the new meme in western culture—"the Holocaust ideology", as Finkelstein coined it in *The Holocaust Industry,* a quasi-religious cult idolizing Jewish suffering in WWII. The religious connotation made secular Jews, even some Zionists, uncomfortable, but it became the lynch-pin allowing the Zionist dream of a Jewish homeland from the Nile to the Euphrates to proceed without opposition.

Because it is taking place so boldly, it isn't really a conspiracy. When you accept something as fact, and make sure no one questions it, it is no longer a conspiracy. But no one knows what the final borders of Eretz Israel will be—Israel has not yet constitutionally defined its borders—and the seizure of Palestinian lands proceeds apace. Daniel Pipes dismisses the "conspiracy mentality", and the boasts of Herzl, Jabotinsky and Dayan,[93] as of "limited importance" (see map next page).

This is the context of the bold, spontaneous counter-attack by anti-Zionists, so-called "Holocaust deniers". Keegstra, Zundel, Topham et al, acting independently, were perceptive and surprisingly uncowed, willing to sacrifice themselves to persecution by Zionist thought police to fight this open conspiracy. They saw there's 'something rotten in the state of Denmark', involving Zionism, Jews, world politics, economics, mass media, and Canadian leaders like Pearson. It's a complicated conspiracy, full of twists and turns, shifting political currents, communism, fascism, liberalism, mass murder ... Almost none of the co-conspirators, even Pipes, are aware of the overall plan and how the many elements work (or don't work) together. After Herzl's death, there has been no master conspirator.

Each of the dissidents documented here fashioned a story that fit the pieces together, not necessarily logically, given that none of them has a PhD in WWII history, Marxism or Jewish studies. Indeed, it is impossible to put the pieces together if one is narrowly specialized in one obscure aspect of the issue, or too beholden to mainstream academia. But creative, curious souls use their "social brain" to create a story that fills the many gaps in their knowledge and in the facts.[94] The conspiracies conjured up over the past century to make sense of what's going on are many (Freemason, Illuminati, comunism, Judaic, Pentagon,...). Pretty well all of them contain shreds of

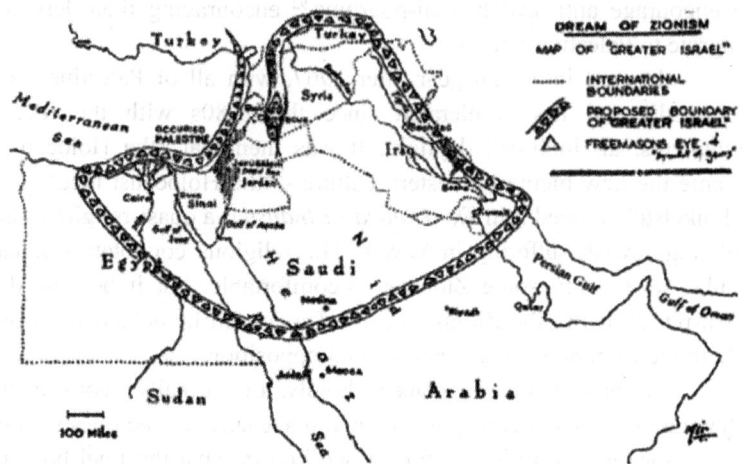

Conspiracy # 1 - 'A light unto nations': Moshe Dayan in the Golan Heights: "We have established Israel within the 1967 borders; and you have to establish a Greater Israel from the Nile to the Euphrates."

truth. The conspiracy is happening on different levels at the same time, with actors playing certain roles, almost oblivious to, or uninterested in other parts of it.

On the one side, the collective force of world Jewry and Israel, on the other, the motley group of dissidents and figures from the shattered Middle East and world Islam, using whatever means they have to try to open minds and discussion, before, as they see it, it is too late. But even if the Zionists are able to fulfill their dream of Eretz Israel (whatever its borders), there is still the greater 'motherland', world Jewry wherever it is found. (See conspiracy #3.)

Conspiracy #2

There was another conspiracy, or rather a sub-conspiracy, a corollary to conspiracy #1. Unlike the other ones, it has been achieved. The conspiracy to foment anti-Jewish sentiment in the Soviet Union, to create a pretext to gain special treatment for Soviet Jews, pushing them (and many non-Jewish Soviets masquerading as Jews) to abandon their prosperous but slightly boring lives in their 'motherland' to go to

Israel. The Zionists made clever use of the Cold War rivalry, adding their own antisemitism weapon to the US arsenal, to 'liberate' a million Jews, intended for illegal settlements in Palestine.

In the 1980s, at a time of confusion and crisis in the Soviet Union, the country was flooded with propaganda, mass mailings, *sayanim*, western intelligence, and western-backed NGOs, using the so-called Helsinki Accords[95] to promote a tendentious western idea of "human rights", employing the full range of world Jewish power. All efforts were mobilized to bring the Soviet Union down. Jews, the most productive and well-educated Soviet minority, were suddenly perceived as a possible traitor class, giving rise to anti-Jewish resentment and mistrust, and in the end helping to shatter the Soviet Union itself. This resentment was called "new antisemitism" (not to be confused with Harper's "new antisemitism"), an essential part of the conspiracy. So what if anti-Jewish prejudice was fomented—*inter alia* by Jews? So what if non-Zionist Soviet Jews, many of them communists, suffered (and still suffer) from resentment at the role of the genuinely traitorous Jews in the collapse of their beloved Soviet Union?

At the time, Forrest (see Chapter 5) opposed Soviet Jewish immigration to Israel "on the grounds that it was part of a sinister Zionist plot to expel the Palestinians."[96] Zionists proudly acknowledge this particular conspiracy,[97] claiming it as *their* victory (though Forrest was vilified as an antisemite for daring to expose it, viewed in a different light). The difference with most past Jewish conspiring with the state was, in the 1980s—they won. Unlike the conspiracy for Greater Israel, this exodus of Soviet Jews was highly popular all round, East and West. Even Soviet citizens were seduced by western consumer 'culture' into abandoning their hard-earned social system, counting on the empty promise of prosperity American-style. The world's Zionist Jews were the lynch-pin in destroying the Soviet Union, in league with their real motherland, US-Israel, chalking up points for new billions in pay-off for Israel from the US motherland, in gratitude for their subversion of the 'enemy' (who was only trying to make friends at the time).

Between 1989 and 2006, about 1.6 million Soviet Jews and their non-Jewish relatives and spouses, as defined by the Law of Return, emigrated from the (now former) Soviet Union. One million, or 61%, migrated to Israel. Another 325,000 migrated to the US and Canada, and 219,000 migrated to Germany, East and, after 1990, West.[98] At least 100,000 eventually returned to a Russia, where they now had nothing and had to start from scratch a second time.[99]

But the conspiracy was shoddy at best. The supposed Jews in the Soviet Union were mostly assimilated, many had only Jewish fathers, virtually none had any religious inclination or knowledge of Jewish history or even traditions. They included some who managed to forge the necessary 'proof' of their Jewishness, and virtually all were actually *conspirators within the conspiracy*, only wanting to get the precious exit visa to leave the Soviet Union, where cynicism had come to reign, faced with the remorseless Cold War and the lure of the West as projected by Hollywood. When they got to Austria, they went immediately to the US, Canadian and Australian consulates and applied there for refugee status or merely immigration. Israeli officials saw what was happening and finally pushed Austria to allow the 'refugees' to go only to Israel. An Israeli joke goes: Q: Who is Israel's biggest enemy? A: Los Angeles (even more popular than Toronto).

The ones who stayed in Israel were treated with hostility. From 1992–95, 4,000 Soviets applied to come to Canada from Israel as refugees, insisting they were suffering racism in Israel for not being sufficiently 'Jewish'. Hundreds were accepted before a 1995 ruling stopped this—even if they could prove that they had arrived in Israel under false pretenses. It's estimated that up to half the Soviet 'Jews' are not really Jews at all. Many Russians had obtained phony proof of their Yiddish heritage. More than 300,000 of the Russian-speaking immigrants were simply classified as non-Jews, because Rabbinical law says that Jewishness passes through the maternal line. The Soviets had been sold a false bill of goods. There are no civil marriages in Israel. If Russian Israelis defined as non-Jews wish to marry, they must go abroad or convert. Conversion to Orthodox Judaism is not an easy or a popular option. Hence Los Angeles or Toronto.[100] In contrast with the previous immigration waves to Israel, many from this wave kept their culture and language, without trying to blend their customs with their new lives in Israel. They were largely secular, and critical of Israeli society, which snubbed them, where they couldn't marry normally, where they were forced to be part of the persecution of Palestinians.

Despite the hemorrhage, the Israeli economist Shlomo Maoz said about the Russian aliyah: "The Russians saved Israel, big time. The aliyah improved our situation almost on every parameter."[101]

What happened in the 1980s Soviet Union was really a kind of tragic echo of 1920–40s Germany. Zionism made Jews appear as a menace to both states, as they had come to be at crucial moments in the past—their 'fatal embrace' with the state. From the 1920s on, Zionism established itself as a political quasi-religious ideology and allegiance for all Jews, which was, as always, a danger to both them and their countries of residence, putting them at odds with same. Yakov Rabkin documents how Zionists early on made it a practice to "cultivate the myth of a world Jewish plot"[102] to incite anti-Jewish sentiment in Russia, Britain and Germany (and later, Egypt, Iraq and other Middle East countries with large, assimilated Jewish populations) precisely to encourage emigration to Palestine. The anger among first north African and Iraq citizens and later Soviet citizens who saw their Jewish neighbors one day, and then—poof!—gone the next, without warning, leaving a yawning gap in Soviet science, medicine, education and the arts, was understandable.

In both the 1930s and 1980s, the Zionists got their wish, succeeding in their conspiracy—the creation of a Jewish state, with a steady inflow of immigrants and cash to keep it afloat, though at a terrible cost. Hitler won the battle (ridding Germany of Jews), but lost the war. And by 1991, though the Soviet Union imploded, Germany opened its borders to Jews again. The Zionists also won, but in the case of WWII, at a terrible cost. Many Jews found Israel was not the 'promised land', and made their way instead to fraternal Canada, 'Israel without the war, and with lots of beautiful scenery', keeping the Jewish Diaspora alive and well, and/or working to help the Jewish state achieve ever greater power.

Consider the Soviet-era anecdote:

Q: What is the greatest tragedy that Russia experienced? A: The birth of Lenin.
Q: What is the 2nd greatest tragedy? A: The death of Lenin.

And its post-Soviet version:
Q: What is the greatest tragedy that Russia experienced? A: The incorporation of the Pale into the Russian empire.
Q: What is the 2nd greatest tragedy? A: The mass emigration of the Jews after the founding of Israel and the collapse of the Soviet Union.[103]

Zundel et al had no qualms about destroying the Soviet Union. He was a true Hitlerite. So that conspiracy was applauded by him as well as his Zionist foes. The Zionist conspiracy that Zundel et al were/are investigating is the #1 above and #3 below. He could have made the link between #1 and #2, and seen how both were two sides of the same coin, but that's not so easy. Few people at the time saw the significance of it, and no one listened to them. This conspiracy was taking place unnoticed as Zundel went to trial.

Conspiracy #3

Zionism, now established in Israel, almost immediately became a potent, even overwhelming, new force in Jewish life, and increasingly, the life of non-Jews, seeming to incarnate the classic debunked "Jewish conspiracy" for world domination, the *Protocols of the Elders of Zion*. But decades before the *Protocols* burst on the world in 1905, Karl Marx the communist, and Goldwin Smith the liberal, were warning in a scholarly way that the tribal nature of 19th century Jewish culture had become lethal. Both urged, pleaded, for Jews to wake up to the apocalypse that both Marx and Smith, in their own ways, foresaw coming, and to assimilate, cleanse themselves of tribalism in the modern world, where it was already proving, in Smith's words, poisonous.

Marx said 'we are all Jews in capitalism' by which he meant secular materialists, and advocated overthrowing capitalism, to free everyone from feudal cobwebs, carrying the Enlightenment to its natural fulfillment. Smith, the liberal, rejected revolution. Like Marx, he saw that the coming catastrophe was not only for Jews, but for the whole of western society, but as a liberal, and broadly religious man, he foregrounded the problem as a weakening of Christian morality, confronted by a Jewish tribalism that was vigorous and increasingly powerful in secular capitalist society. Neither were heeded. Only Marx's romantic idea of revolution seemed to hold any real hope. Tragically, neither Cassandra was able to avert the coming catastrophe of WWI and II, and the disaster of Israel-Palestine.

Israel's latest Basic Law proposal (2011) defines Israel as the Nation-State of the Jewish People, i.e., world Jewry. But there really is no reason for the Jews of the world to migrate to Israel. Even in the late 1940s, once the Nazis were dethroned, Jews were able to stay in Europe. Many did, and prospered, though the first decade was rough, requiring the reconstruction of their devastated homelands. But it was rough for everyone. By then, civil rights were institutionalized, and Jews were already respected as survivors of the genocidal Nazis. Israel, constantly at war with its neighbors, was hardly a safe place. Immigrants to Israel today similarly have no pressing need to abandon their birth homelands (unless they are fleeing the law in their real 'homeland'). The fears of French Jews are only because of the scurrilous *Hebdo* affair[104] and the French anger against Israeli persecution of Palestinians.

Beware: the passport comes with a price, a soldierly one. I recall a friend, Yuri, in Tashkent who was on the lam. Seduced by the promise of an easy exit visa, he had emigrated to Israel (his father's father was Jewish), and was faced with conscription.[105] He had no desire to fight Muslims, having grown up in Uzbekistan. He wanted help to go to Canada, but those doors were already closed.

It turns out the 'conspiracy to end all conspiracies', *The Protocols of the Elders of Zion*, that we have all been warned against, from Churchill and Henry Ford on, has more or less come to pass. Perhaps it could have been written with a little less bile, but satirists get carried away. Look at the evidence. The 'elders' are not so much an actual people, but the logic of history (capitalism, Jewish relations with the sovereign and control of money), a ruling elite that uses social forces to promote its own agenda. Soften its tone and replace "neocon" for "Jew" and it looks like it could have been written yesterday, as a satire on the current economic system and the globalization drive for western hegemony. Jews have been central to capitalism (and its critique, thanks to Marx) from the start. Israel has just added another layer of conspiracy to the earlier imperial one already at work when Lord Shaftesbury called for 'a people without a land' to head to that 'land without a people' in 1839.

Should the Jews have their own go at world empire? The Brits did, the Americans too. Why is the issue *Jewish* Empire, and not Empire (the domination and exploitation of other peoples) itself?

But this is a problematic which cannot be addressed. It is unacceptable for public figures to even hint that Jews were once the backbone of both (the British) empire, and communism, that today "international bankers", among whom Jews hold pride of place, are too powerful,[106] that Jewish capital and smarts dominate the US and Canadian economies and media.[107] Or that Jews are the most privileged group in the West in all areas of life today. Such prominence is a tribute, *inter alia*, to *Yiddishkeit*, but has its negative side, as does any attempt to control others, as Ginsberg warned.

Keegstra's claim to his students in the 1960s–80s that "the Jews believe that by the year 2000 they will control the world ... They want to set up their new world order with the headquarters in Israel" is dismissed, indeed prosecuted as hate propaganda, despite being based on the actions of Israel. He could take comfort from the travails of Hannah Arendt for her comments with regard to Eichmann's trial. She saw it as an attempt to "put anti-Semitism through history on trial. Bad history and cheap rhetoric." She was in turn accused of making "Eichmann look like the innocent executor of some mysteriously foreordained destiny, or even of anti-Semitism," which perhaps was "necessary for ... 'the bloodstained road traveled by this people' to fulfill its destiny." During the trial, she read that an Egyptian MP told the National Assembly: "Hitler was innocent of the slaughter of the Jews; he was a victim of the Zionists, who had 'compelled him to perpetrate crimes that would eventually enable them to achieve their aim-the creation of the State of Israel.' "The trial put History in place of the Elders of Zion."[108] She was denounced, effectively being called a 'denier' before the cliché set in, even though her work is a devastating expose of the tragedy of Nazism.

An arresting image of this conspiracy coming into its own is the Israeli Supreme Court Building (below), with 33 steps at the entrance, recalling the stages in Freemasonry, that lead to the base of the "Illuminati" Pyramid atop the Israeli Supreme Court (aka the Sanhedrin). It stands next to the Foreign Ministry and the Central Bank.[109] The Rothschild family designed and paid for the construction of the building, inaugurated in 1992, described by Paul Goldberger of *The New York Times* as "Israel's finest public building," achieving "a remarkable and exhilarating balance between the concerns of daily life and the symbolism of the ages."[110]

Criticism of Israel "to delegitimate Israel itself" is made illegal.[111] There are ever new words to incorporate in our lexicon—Zionophobia, Israelophobia. Globalization concerns give new life to "traditional antisemitic tropes" such as the "canard" of dual loyalty. Such now largely accepted statements as "the Bush government's hostility to Iraq was driven by a cabal involving the Israeli government and hawkish American Jews" are seen as having "moved from antisemitic websites to respected newspaper columns and television opinion shows." *Globe & Mail* journalist Jeffrey Simpson is criticized for "glibly referring to 'Likudniks' in the Bush Admin."[112] At the Contemporary Antisemitism: Canada and the World conference at the Munk Centre of University of Toronto in 2005, it was concluded that the "decisive challenge for Canadian Jews in future will be on the posture Canada adopts on matters

Israeli Supreme Court Building   **Masonic Pyramid**

relating to Israeli security and Middle East peace, and possible roles of Canadian Jews in shaping, supporting or challenging those policies. Antisemitism today acts and flows through Israel, and reflects global forces and ideologies."[113] There is no room any longer for voicing the idea that Zionism is in violation of international law. The Basic Law of Israel—that Israel is "the Nation-State of the Jewish People," i.e., world Jewry—is a form of racism, as the UN acknowledged in 1975, only to reverse itself after the collapse of the Soviet Union, under US pressure. (Were it to read that Israel is the nation-state of the Israelis—just as Canada is the nation state of the Canadians, thereby including all the disparate immigrant ethnicities—that would be in accordance with norms.)

Israel is not just an independent offspring of a mother country, as was the case with British imperialism in Great Game I, when Britain was the motherland of its colonies. As Shahid Alam put it in *Foreign Policy Journal*, "By winning over the Jews in the western Diaspora, and galvanizing them to use their wealth, intellect, and activism to promote Zionist causes, the Zionists succeeded in substituting the West for the missing natural mother country."[114] Indeed, without the unswerving support of the West and the Jewish Diaspora, Israel would quickly have collapsed. And though it is defiantly following its own policies in many countries around the world these days, operating as a *modern* state, both above-board and in the shadows through its mercenaries and mafia,[115] its most important role is still within the establishment in the US, on the left and the right, both in and out of power, its adopted 'mother country', which it dare not abandon completely.

But Alam's hypothesis suggests something more. World Jewry itself is in a sense the "missing natural mother country", and given the leverage it has in the US through its 'fatal embrace', and the leverage the US has in a world of predominantly *postmodern* nations, that gives the Zionist project far-reaching power, with the 'mother country' in a sense world Jewry, as diaspora leaders publicly assert.[116]

Zionism became the ruling ideology of the neocon Great Game III precisely because the 'embrace' was not just an informal understanding between monarch and banker (which can be discarded), but is now formalized in the Jewish state which, arising out of the fatal embrace of yore, has secured itself a place at the heart of the new empire's financial and military-political strategies. For what is Zionism but a specifically Jewish form of imperialism? A colonial venture based on tribal legends and employing the skills honed over the centuries which fit so well the economic system now ruling the world.

Throughout history, Jews and Christians were enemies in Christian Europe, tolerating each other. Jews were merchants and bankers for all sides in the many wars among 'Christian nations', profiting, but also in fear of the other side moving in and killing them for helping 'the enemy'. There was never any serious schism among Jews, but rather tribal solidarity and a honing of money and then banking skills. When the warring 'Christians' finally exhausted themselves and embraced capitalism and the Jews, it only made sense for the Jews to take advantage of the opportunity.

An Ontario Jewish MMP stated in the 1930s: "No fire is so easily kindled as anti-Semitism. The fire is dormant in Canada, it has not yet blazed up, but the spark is there. Germany is not the only place with prejudice. Look at Quebec."[117] So is that accusation supposed to make Quebecois love Jews, or at least be cowed into suppressing their "antisemitism"? Will all the Holocaust museums, antisemitism institutes, university programs in Israel and Jewish studies be able to stamp out anti-Jewish sentiment once and for all, to make Canada and Israel the 'safe havens' for the world's Jews?

"The sheer complexity of the factors involved in the nature of the anti-Zionist phenomenon makes Canadian scholar Michael Marrus argue for a careful, nuanced examination before deciding definitively whether anti-Zionism and antisemitism are one and the same phenomenon."[118] Nothing like a claim of complexity to hide the obvious.

A short course on Israel-Jewish studies searching out the elusive 'spark' that lights the ever-smoldering flame of 'antisemitism', should use Occam's Razor, which in a nutshell, states: Don't make things unnecessarily complicated. Israel cheats, steals, lies, kills. Jews are conflated with 'lovers of Israel'. This is the 'spark' that kindles anti-Jewish prejudice.

A 1937 CJC report compared Canada at that moment to "the situation of Germany in the early years of the Nazi movement."[119] That dire warning proved wrong. Canada has always been a good place for Jews, even when they couldn't drink cocktails at the Granite Club. But if Israel continues on its present path, and if all Canadian Jews don't stand up and criticize it openly, it could become germane today, where anger at Israel and Canada's shameful kowtowing to Israel can't help but foment anti-Jewish sentiment.

It is no coincidence that such groups as the Illuminati and the satirist who wrote the *Protocols* devised their fantasies when they did. The institutions governing western civilization today were taking shape in the 18th–19th centuries, as capitalism began to transform society, at a time when individual players had greater systemic import. Today, the 'elders' are merely window dressing for the relentless grinding of an economic system which is much more mundane, and includes us all, Jew and Gentile, in as much as we obey the rules of the capitalist game.

The Unknown Holocaust

Just how seriously one should take the Illuminati/Freemason symbolism,[120] is a moot point. The bottom line is that the Final Solution was mercifully halted, and many Jews (and the other potential traitors and 'undesirables') survived. And it was a *communist country* that defeated fascism. Despite that, the US and Britain immediately launched the Cold War to destroy communism, which had been their agenda all along, inducing them into letting Hitler rearm and launch what they expected to be a German-Soviet war.

The Russian revolution of 1917 was the first communist revolution, not a conspiracy at all. The communists proclaimed themselves the enemy of capitalism and aimed to overthrow it. Unfortunately for

Lenin, the rest of the world stayed in thrall to the capitalist conspiracy against the working people, and, after a valiant go at it, communism, the antidote to capitalism, failed to take. Few outside the ex-communist countries seemed to mourn the demise of Soviet communism or to be interested in documenting how many communists were killed in Great Game II. No museums or monuments to those fighters for a better future for all—many of them Canadian, many of them Jews, quite a few of them Jewish Canadians, some of them Israelis and Palestinians. The Nazis treated Jews and communists as if they were one-and-the-same, and the slightest suggestion of communist sympathies led to execution, the same fate as for racial 'traitors' or sexual deviants. But many Jews were communists, or at least socialists, so the reason was for their execution was often moot.

Recently, an exhibition by the Topography of Terror Foundation opened in Berlin exploring the mass executions after the Nazi invasion of the Soviet Union, focusing mainly on Jewish victims, but recognizing the special vindictiveness of the Nazis with respect to the Soviet Union, where mass shootings were carried out nonstop as soon as Operation Barbarossa began on June 22, 1941, reaching 2 million before the Nazis had to find a less messy way of killing and disposing of bodies.

The savage annihilation of Soviet civilians, all assumed to be communists and/or Jews, in WWII is not even acknowledged, especially by the Holocaust deniers, who are all militantly anti-communist. True, many Soviets were not convinced communists, but they still fought for the Motherland, and accepted that the communists were the force directing this fight. There was no hint of insurrection against Stalin. Call them reluctant communists, but the Nazis didn't mince words and killed anyone who resisted as 'communist'. While "antisemite" is thrown at people as the ultimate slur, "anticommunist" is still considered a positive term. It's as if it was okay for Hitler to murder every last communist; the problem was that he focused on Jews. Our history of WWII crimes is a kind of politically correct, airbrushed holocaust, with no hint of the real 'good guys' of WWII, those who fought for the Russian Motherland and/or for socialism, the great enemy of fascism, and died in the millions for their efforts.

Many of the 'good Jews' were indeed communist, having embraced secular socialism as their 'promised land', abandoning any claim to being a chosen tribe. This meant that in Canada, in the 1930s–50s, they became fair game along with their non-Jewish comrades for persecution as communists rather than as Jews. No communists could teach at universities, as one of Canada's greatest historians, Stanley Ryerson, learned. Fred Rose, a sitting MP, was victimized for helping our Soviet communist ally in the war.

"The myth of Jew as Bolshevik...became central to the Nazi program of ideological anti-Semitism, and helped inspire the collaboration of non-Germans throughout eastern Europe in that program's murderous execution during WWII."[121] How many of those gassed or shot by the Nazis were actually killed for being communists? We will never know, as no one seems to care. This overlap of signifiers that led to persecution in Canada and throughout the West of Jewish communists,[122] became, in the Cold War, persecution now only for communists, who may or may not be Jews, and no public acknowledgment of the important link between Jews and communists was ever made. Communism was the acceptable villain, Jews—no longer.

Communists were fair game, and anticommunists were respected. This was because the US claimed it had won WWII, which we in Canada have also been taught. But the Soviets were the ones who beat Hitler, and should have been honored and helped to rebuild their devastated country. Instead war was declared against them. In 1948, the Jews, now with their own state, joined forces with the US empire in a new 'fatal embrace', this time against the communists. Israel was key to the destruction of the USSR and was lauded and well rewarded for its performance in the service of empire, with Canada the head cheerleader.

This anticommunist bigotry is more than just a minor distortion of WWII history. It covered up the ultimate 'crime against humanity'—the tens of millions killed in the past century for fighting the imperial conspiracy against humanity. Communists have been the primary fighters against imperialism worldwide, recognizing the inherently genocidal nature of the beast. And imperialism has responded in turn, most graphically forecast in Jack London's *The Iron Heel*.

The US and Israel won the Cold War. Both came out on top as their ascendancy from 1991 on shows, though the victory for both was dear, creating a world obsessed with 'security', awash in arms and death. The US justifies itself as the world's policeman, and the Zionists are at the heart of this agenda. Israel Shamir conflates the imperial and Zionist conspiracies, arguing that the world is currently dominated by a largely Jewish-run United States, provoking wars around the world in pursuit of total control of the world's resources and people's minds.

With respect to the US and Israel, it is neither 'the dog wagging the tail' nor 'the tail wagging the dog', but rather "the US Zionist financial and economic elite that control both the dog and the tail. They make sure Israel gets its $3 billion a year (and much more on the side) and conducts its unending wars, as a symbol, a unifying force for American and European Jews, their *raison d'etre,* to keep them and their *shabbas goy* allies true to 'the faith'." In effect, both the US and Israel are pawns on their world chess board.

Shamir refers to the little known Mega Group of the 50 richest and most powerful Jews in the US and Canada, founded in 1991 by Jerrold Wexler and Charles Bronfman as an informal but all-powerful policy-making group to add greater clout to the Israeli lobby. "Indeed, the Megabucks crowd, represented at the Bronfman gathering, influence us [Israelis] more than they influence the US. Our politicians are just as weak and corrupt as America's, but they are easier to swing and cheaper to buy. Consider that California bingo-parlor owner Moskovitz could push our ex-prime minister Netanyahu to open the tunnel near the Mosques, causing major bloodshed. That is why, in Israel, we have a parody of democracy instead of a democracy."[123]

Shamir's conflation makes sense. Zionism, gaining its toe-hold in 1917 and becoming a powerful movement by the 1920, paralleled the rise of Nazism at precisely the same time. Both Hitler and Herzl were founders of an expansionist ideology based on race, which became more and more fanatical, violent and murderous, culminating in a state based on race, destruction of the people on its territories, *lebensraum*, and bent on world domination. We can forgive the Zionists for negotiating with the Nazis before[124] and during WWII to buy up healthy Jews before slaughter, even as the Nazis were killing the weaker, older Jews who would make poor settlers. Ruthless, but at least saving some lives.

But Zionism then hitched a ride on US imperialism, and adopted the Nazis' more virulent version of capitalism/imperialism, with the neoconservatives drawing US-Israel into unending war in the Middle East. Has the death toll of the US/Zionism reached the '6 million' mark yet? Is that an exaggeration? Perhaps it's only 4 million. There's no denying the ongoing slow-motion holocaust against the Palestinians, but now it is engulfing the Arab world as well.

Endnotes

1. Safiah Chowdhury, "Why the Quebec mosque shooting happened", *Al Jazeerah*, February 1, 2017.
2. Andrea Iorga Curpan <http://rabble.ca/blogs/bloggers/raluca-bejan/2017/01/muslim-new-jew-and-were-not-even-moved-it>
3. A few days prior to this sensational arrest, David Schraub denounced Trump for suggesting attacks on Jewish sites—bomb threats, vandalism, and otherwise—were false flag attacks designed to discredit the right. He was shamed into publishing an apology. David Schraub, "Yes, the Jew Who Called in Bomb Threats Was Anti-Semitic", *tabletmag.com,* March 2017 <http://www.tabletmag.com/scroll/228149/yes-the-jew-who-called-in-bomb-threats-was-anti-semitic>
4. See Chapter 3 re the Lavon affaire. In a bizarre coincidence, three weeks earlier, Juan Thompson, a 31-year-old Afro-American journalist, son of Hunter S. Thompson, was arrested in Missouri for such threats made in his ex-girlfriend's name to frame her as part of a revenge scheme. Thompson had tweeted his opposition to President Donald Trump several times. He has also ranted about white people on his Twitter account, calling them "trash", suggesting his motive was not to target his girlfriend or Muslims, but right wing whites. Melissa Chan, "What to Know About Juan Thompson, the Man Accused of Threatening Jews to Frame His Ex-Girlfriend", *Time*, March 3, 2017.
5. Anthropologists regard claims of chosenness as a form of ethnocentrism. Christian denominations believe the church has replaced Israel as the People of God. The British had their version, as Goldwin Smith argued (see Chapter 5), as did the Germans. American "exceptionalism" is in a similar vein.
6. Arendt, op.cit., 19-20.
7. Arendt, op.cit., xiv, 13.
8. According to Lucy Dawidowicz, published without his permission. "Lies About the Holocaust", *Commentary*, Volume 70, Issue # 6, page 33.
9. Dimitris Konstantakopoulos, "Leila Khaled on ISIS and Islamism, Syria and the Palestinians", An Interview of Leila Khaled to the Athens-Macedonian News Agency, defenddemocracy.press, August 9, 2016.
10. Winston Churchill, "Zionism vs Bolshevism: the struggle for the soul of the Jewish people", *Illustrated Sunday Herald*, 8 February 1920, and Jeffrey Wallin and Juan Williams, "Churchill's Greatness", Fox News, September 2001. <http://web.archive.org/web/20031216033237/http://www.winstonchurchill.org/i4a/pages/index.cfm?pageid=282>
11. Founded in 1978, an organization which Wikipedia dismissed as "primarily devoted to publishing and promoting pseudo-historical books and essays concerning the Nazi genocide of Jews," which its current director denies: "Every responsible scholar of twentieth century history acknowledges the great catastrophe that befell European Jewry during World War II. All the same, the IHR has over the years published detailed books and numerous probing essays that call into question aspects of the orthodox, Holocaust-extermination story, and highlight specific Holocaust exaggerations and falsehoods." In January 2009, Weber, the IHR's director, released an essay titled, "How Relevant Is Holocaust Revisionism?" In it he noted that Holocaust denial had attracted little support over the years: "It's gotten some support in Iran, or places like that, but as far as I know, there is no history department supporting writing by

these folks." Accordingly, he recommended that emphasis be placed instead on opposing "Jewish-Zionist power". (Mark Weber, "Real Politics Is Not a Game: The Stubborn Reality of Jewish-Zionist Power", *ihr.org*, October 2016, <http://www.ihr.org/other/oct2016webertalk>)

12. David Bercuson, Douglas Wertheimer, *A Trust Betrayed: The Keegstra Affair*, Doubleday, 1989, x.
13. Jewish leaders formally issue a "Declaration of War" against Germany. On March 23, 1933, 20,000 Jews protested at New York's City Hall. Rallies and boycotts were directed against German goods. The front page of the March 24, *London Daily Express* carries the headline: "Judea Declares War on Germany".
14. Stanley Barrett, *Is God a Racist? The Right Wing in Canada*, 231.
15. Ibid., 220.
16. Ibid., 231.
17. Ibid., 248.
18. Ibid., 250.
19. *Red Deer Advocate*, January 14, 1984.
20. *Toronto Star*, 29 July, 1985.
21. Barrett, op.cit., 256.
22. See Chapter 5, endnote 23.
23. Ibid., 246. Another teacher fired for similar views as Keegstra's was Malcolm Ross in New Brunswick. His trials started in 1991 and continued to 2000. He was fired from teaching but allowed to be the school librarian.
24. Founded in 1967, eclipsed by the British National Party, which in turn was eclipsed by UKIP, both of which now support Israel, and are only concerned about keeping out blacks and Arabs.
25. Gabriel Weiman, *Hate on Trial*, Mosaic Press, 2007, 13.
26. Russian for "self publishing", mimicking the dissident publishing in the Soviet Union in the 1980s.
27. Lipstadt claims a million copies were distributed between 1974 and 1984. Lipstadt, *Denying the Holocaust*, 1993, 104.
28. Excerpt: "In Germany alone, over 5,800 people have been prosecuted and fined in the last few years. We see the results of this massive deceit—that is, that Zionist interests are identical to western interests—in the many publications and pronouncements of organizations such as the 'Councils of Christians and Jews' ... Western Christians have become circumcised mentally by this incessant yet false propaganda! ... Pat Boone, a Christian, says that there are really only three kinds of Judaism: Orthodox, Reformed, and Christian—saying that Christianity is just another form of Judaism!" Ernst Zundel, "The West, War and Islam", 2005 [1980]. <http://vho.org/aaargh/fran/livres5/zunwestwarislam.pdf>
29. Alan Davies, ed., *Antisemitism in Canada: History and Interpretation*, 1992, 251.
30. Leuchter was recommended to Zundel by Bill Armontrout, warden for Missouri State Penitentiary in Jefferson City, Missouri, responsible for carrying out executions by the use of cyanide gas, though he had no formal training in toxicology, biology or chemistry. Gas chambers were used in 11 states, the last time in Arizona in 1999.
31. The debate prompted further tests in 1990.
32. Doug Collins, "The Zundel affair: A national legal disgrace", *North Shore News*, September 2, 1992.
33. Most famously, targeting Alan Dershowitz's *The Case for Israel* (2003).

34 <http://www.cija.ca/cija-to-consult-community-on-hate-law-stand/> Journalists worried about the implications when courts, already armed with a battery of slander and libel laws, would now be required to judge truthfulness, always an elusive quality. "It gives me a bit of a pause having the courts decide, really, on one's thought processes," George Bain, a journalism professor at King's College in Halifax, said. Robert Fulford, editor of *Saturday Night*, said, "This law should be wiped from the books." Douglas Martin, "Anti-semite is on trial, but did Ontario blunder?", *The New York Times*, February 15, 1985.
35 Robinson, op.cit., 143.
36 Rita Carter, "When the tenant refuses to go" (*The Independent*, October 2, 1996) links to an article "Technology brings a new dimension to the Glastonbury experience on 3D disco" (May 3, 2009).
37 "This hard to find, extensively referenced publication is an essential addition to the library of anyone with an interest in WWII history." It has become a collector's item, with used copies, presumably the first edition, going for $130.
38 The Madagascar plan dates from Zionist Organization founder Chaim Weizmann, and was mooted by Hitler in the 1930s up until the Germans occupied France in 1940. See Chapter 5 endnote 41.
39 Colin Wilson, "The Fuehrer in Perspective: 2", *books and bookmen*, November 1974.
40 By David Hoggan. See endnote 5 above.
41 Lipstadt, op.cit., 120.
42 Lipstadt's works include *Beyond Belief: The American Press and the Coming of the Holocaust* (Free Press/Macmillan, 1986, 1993), *Denying the Holocaust: The Growing Assault on Truth and Memory* (Free Press/Macmillan, 1993), *History on Trial: My Day in Court with David Irving* (Ecco/HarperCollins, 2005.)
43 Six million is actually a kind of sacred number for Jews. It was first used in Europe to describe age-old Jewish ghetto suffering, quoted frequently in *The New York Times* concerning Jewish suffering from the 1880s ("Rabbi Gottheil says a word on the persecution of the Jews ... about six million persecuted and miserable wretches." *NYT* 26/1/1891) and also attributed to Tsarist Russia, ("Russian imperial leaders had long been suspicious of the Jews. Beginning in the 1880s western media issued exaggerated reports of slaughters ... whose aggregate numbers were always recorded—astonishingly—as 6 million." (*NYT* 25/3/1936). It is most likely that Nazi officials specialized in Jewish matters well knew this. Was Eichmann's purported estimate of 6 million just coincidentally the 6 million of Jewish historical lore? The fact that the actual number indeed approached 6 million is a gruesome denouement to this long history of the 6 million.
44 "Holocaust facts: Where does the figure of 6 million victims come from?", *Haaretz, August* 11, 2013.
45 In spite of the exaggerations and the source of the number, Hoettl accepted it. Hoettl, *Secret Front*, 320.
46 David Cesarani, *Eichmann: His Life and Crimes*. London: Vintage, (2005) [2004], 300.
47 Lipstadt, op. Cit. 115.
48 Ibid., 117.
49 Irving Molotsky, "Red Cross Admits Knowing of the Holocaust During the War", December 19, 1996.

50 Dan Stets, "Fixing The Numbers At Auschwitz", *Chicago Tribune*, May 7, 1992.
51 <http://www.pewresearch.org/fact-tank/2015/02/09/europes-jewish-population/,https://www.washingtonpost.com/news/worldviews/wp/2015/02/09/chart-the-decline-of-europes-jewish-population/>
52 <http://chgs.umn.edu/museum/memorials/auschwitz/>
53 Christopher Browning, *The Final Solution and the German Foreign Office: a study of Referat D III of Abteilung Deutschland, 1940–43*, 1978.
54 Christopher Browning, *Ordinary Men: Reserve Police Battalion 101 and the Final Solution in Poland*, 1992.
55 Milgram devised his psychological study to answer the popular question at that particular time: "Could it be that Eichmann and his million accomplices in the Holocaust were just following orders? Could we call them all accomplices?" The experiments have been repeated many times in the following years with consistent results within differing societies. In Milgram's first set of experiments, 65% (26 of 40) of experiment participants administered the experiment's final massive 450-volt shock, resulting in the supposed victim's death (there was no real victim, only a confederate who screamed and finally stopped reacting, indicating death). University ethics boards outlawed such experiments in the 1980s.
56 "Auschwitz guard trial: Oskar Groening admits 'moral guilt'", BBC, April 21, 2015. <http://www.bbc.com/news/world-europe-32392594 > Other powerful witnesses include Wilhelm Cornides (1920–1966), a Wehrmacht sergeant serving in the General Government territory (Poland). He kept a diary during his service which was published as the Cornides Report, which contains his account of the extermination of Jews at Belzec during the Holocaust. Among those Nazis arrested, the best known for confessing are Kurt Gerstein (1905–1945), a German SS officer and member of the Institute for Hygiene of the Waffen-SS and Head of Technical Disinfection Services. He witnessed mass murders in the Nazi extermination camps Belzec and Treblinka. He gave information to the Swedish diplomat Goran von Otter, as well as to members of the Roman Catholic Church with contacts to Pope Pius XII, in an effort to inform the international public about the Holocaust. In 1945, following his surrender, he wrote the Gerstein Report covering his experience of the Holocaust. He died, an alleged suicide, while in French custody. Pery Broad (1921–1993) also confessed, but was only a translator and stenographer at the Auschwitz headquarters; he was released in 1947, and sentenced to 4 years in 1965. Rudolf Hoess, the longest-serving commandant of Auschwitz, tested and carried into effect various methods of gassing, confessed to his role and was hanged in 1947.
57 Michael Hoffman, *The Great Holocaust Trial: The Landmark Battle for the Right to Doubt the West's Most Sacred Relic*, Independent History and Research, 2010. None of Hoffman's books are in public or university libraries in Canada.
58 The fake Holocaust memoir is by now a genre of its own, the most famous (that has been exposed) is Jerzy Kosinski's *The Painted Bird* (1965). Also Joe Corry's *005: Ian Fleming's Last Agent* (1990) reissued in 2014 by Simon & Schuster, Benjamin Wilkomirski's *Fragments: Memories of a Wartime Childhood* (1995, 1996 National Jewish Book Award for Autobiography and Memoir), Misha Defonseca's *Misha: A Memoir of the Holocaust Years* (1997). She had to repay her publisher $22 million. Also Herman Rosenblat's Oprah-endorsed *Angel at*

	the Fence (2009).
59	<https://www.change.org/p/hon-suzanne-anton-attorney-general-of-bc-jag-minister-gov-bc-ca-hon-suzanne-anton-retract-your-consent-for-the-criminal-proceedings-against-mr-arthur-topham>
60	For a detailed analysis of Topham's trials, see "From Zundel to Topham: Zionist theatre" and "Topham, Zionist Elders and their Trial Protocols" at *ericwalberg.com*
61	Alan Fotheringham, "Death of a True Radical", *MacLean's*, October 15, 2001. <http://www.orwelltoday.com/dougcollins.shtml>
62	"Hollywood Propaganda", *North Shore News,* March 9, 1994.
63	All three articles, including "Swindler's List" are posted here <https://freespeechtwentyfirstcentury.com/2016/02/19/swindlers-list-movie-review/>
64	<https://www.youtube.com/watch?v=NcKPy1Bet7g>
65	See below concerning Imre Finta.
66	Explaining why David Irving lost his case. Robert Fulford, "Robert Fulford's column about Doug Collins & Allan Fotheringham", *National Post,* November 3, 2001.
67	Fotheringham, op. cit.
68	He had won the National Newspaper Award in 1953 for his report on George Dupre, a popular wartime journalist, who falsely claimed to have been a Special Operations Executive operative during World War II.
69	Many "remaindered from library" copies are still available at Amazon.
70	Michael Seifert (1924–2010), an SS guard in Italy, convicted in absentia in 2000 by a military tribunal in Verona, Italy, sentenced to life in prison and extradited in 2008, buried in a cemetery near Caserta after his body went unclaimed by friends and relatives.
71	Terry Long, former leader of the Aryan Nations in Canada; Malcolm Ross of New Brunswick who, like Keegstra, was a teacher fired for antisemitic activity; Three alleged leaders of the Ku Klux Klan in Manitoba; Rudy Stanko of the World Church of the Creator; John Ross Taylor of the Western Guard Party and Aryan Nations; Imre Finta who was alleged to be a Nazi war criminal and collaborator (see *R. v. Finta*); Doug Collins, accused by the British Columbia Human Rights Commission of antisemitic and racist comments; Paul Fromm, head of "Citizens for Foreign Aid Reform" and "Canadians for Freedom of Expression", fired from his job as a teacher; Lady Jane Birdwood, a British follower of Oswald Mosley; Wolfgang Droege of the Heritage Front
72	Canadian legal scholar and criminal defense lawyer as well as a poet, playwright, novelist.
73	Doug Collins, *North Shore News*, September 2, 1988.
74	See Chapter 8.
75	"The Nazis Next Door: Eric Lichtblau on How the CIA & FBI Secretly Sheltered Nazi War Criminals", *democracynow.org*, October 31, 2014.
76	J. Edgar Hoover ordered Allen to be wiretapped for a number of years.
77	The American John Demjanjuk (1920–2012) was a Soviet Ukrainian soldier, and a POW during the Second World War, called Ivan the Terrible, making news headlines for 30 years, starting in 1975, shuttling back and forth from the

US to Israel, to the US and finally Germany, before he finally died of old age there, still a 'free' man.
78 Norman G. Finkelstein, *Beyond Chutzpah: On the Misuse of Anti-Semitism and the Abuse of History,* 2005, 21 ff.36. "Hasbarah" literally means "explanation" but is used to refer to Zionist propaganda for non-Israelis.
79 Powell, Michael. "In N.Y., Sparks Fly Over Israel Criticism", *Washington Post,* October 8, 2006.
80 <http://normanfinkelstein.com/2006/10/23/how-memri-doctored-finkelsteins-interview-to-portray-him-as-a-holocaust-denier/>
81 Dershowitz carried on a vicious campaign across the country to prevent the publication of *Beyond Chutzpah,* appealing to California Governor Arnold Schwartzenegger and comparing the critique to the notorious *Protocols of the Elders of Zion.* He also worked to undermine Finkelstein's tenure appointment, even pursuing him in an op-ed in the *Wall Street Journal.* Finkelstein finally managed to publish the scathing critique but was denied tenure and fired from DePaul.
82 Lipstadt, op.cit., 123.
83 Ibid., 125.
84 See Chapter 5 endnote 154.
85 Global War On Terror.
86 Benjamin Disraeli, *Lord George Bentinck: A Political Biography* (Archibald, Constable & Co. Ltd., London, 1905, 318-324 .
87 By the time of the outbreak of WWI, Britain controlled the Suez Canal, strategic ports in Kuwait, Oman, Bahrain, and both the Atlantic and Pacific oceans. The Round Table plan of conquest, which the "war to end all wars" was supposed to realize, was to link the Rhodes-Rothschild South African gold fields northward, through a predominantly British colonial Africa, through the Suez Canal to Mesopotamia, Kuwait and Persia into India, based at each stage on divide-and-rule. With this solid imperial core, the rest of the world would come into line either as friend or subordinate. Walberg, *Postmodern Imperialism,* 41.
88 Currently, the most common definition of the land encompassed by the term is the territory of the State of Israel together with the Palestinian territories. The biblical 'definition' comprises all of modern-day Israel, the Palestinian Territories, Lebanon, Syria, Jordan, and Iraq, as well as Kuwait, Saudi Arabia, UAE, Oman, Yemen, most of Turkey, and all the land east of the Nile river. A survey of the various versions of Greater Israel are at https://everipedia.org/wiki/Greater_Israel/
89 Kovel, op.cit., 45
90 Ibid., 48. Theodore Herzl *The Complete Diaries,* June 12,1895. The US had dispossessed the natives the same way, 'selling' land where the concept of private property was nonexistent or unsophisticated, and then forcing out or killing the natives, which perhaps accounts for the lack of Canadian protest against Israel's ongoing theft.
91 The boycott did nothing to stop the harassment of Jews in Germany. Pious claims that the boycott was motivated by purely moral reasons were made by Jewish leaders such as American Reform rabbi Stephen Wise, who along with Supreme Court Justice Louis Brandeis, Felix Frankfurter, and others, had laid the groundwork for a democratically elected nationwide organization of 'ardently Zionist' Jews (American Jewish Congress), 'to represent Jews as a group and not as individuals'. ("Religion: Jews v. Jews", *Time,* June 20, 1938.). "We must

speak out," and "if that is unavailing, at least we shall have spoken." <https://en.wikipedia.org/wiki/Anti-Nazi_boycott_of_1933>) The public avowals are belied by the Haavara Agreement, which had by 1937 largely negated the effects of the Jewish boycott on Germany.

This duplicity by the Zionists shows the conspiratorial nature of the relations with the Nazis, intended to promote the creation of a Jewish state, using the Nazis.

92   For example, the Lavon affair. See Chapter 3.
93   Vladimir Jabotinsky, the founder of Revisionist Zionism, was quoted in 1935 stating "We want a Jewish empire." Moshe Dayan's visit to the Golan Heights soon after its capture by Israeli troops in 1967 has become the stuff of legends. According to Hafiz al-Asad, Dayan announced that "the past generation established Israel within its 1948 borders; we have established Israel within the 1967 borders; and you have to establish a Greater Israel from the Nile to the Euphrates." The map is cited at Daniel Pipes, "Imperial Israel: The Nile-to-Euphrates Calumny", Middle East Quarterly , March 1994, and is from Kayhan International , May 30, 1991.
94   See, for instance, Matthew Lieberman, *Social: Why Our Brains Are Wired to Connect*, Crown, 2013. The famous shovel-chicken split brain experiment shows how the right hemisphere will jump in when the normal left brain understanding is contradictory. <https://en.wikipedia.org/wiki/Split-brain> Some of the 'facts' are simply not available, others actively suppressed.
95   Signed in 1975, intended to promote peaceful reconciliation between the West and the Soviet Union
96   Tulchinsky, op.cit., 436.
97   American Zionists lobbied presidents Johnson and Nixon intensely on behalf of Israel and its demands for Jewish emigration from the Soviet Union. "Ultimately the Israeli voice would prevail, and during the 1970 a noticeable trickle of Soviets emigrants to Israel would begin. This is perhaps to be expected, as every Prime Minister Israel has ever had was either born in the Russian Empire or born to parents born in the Russian Empire, thus the connection to the region's Jewish population runs deep among Israel's elites." Michael Dorman, "American Zionism and Soviet Jews", notevenpast.org/, May 4, 2016.
98   The US and Canada no longer accepted Soviet Jews as refugees after 1989, but Germany did.
99   Henry Kamm, "Evolution in Europe; Soviet Jews in East Berlin Tell of Intolerance," *The New York Times*, June 25, 1990, Michael Mainville, "100,000 Former Soviet Jews in Israel Return To Russia," *Toronto Star*, May 4, 2005.
100 Philip Weiss, "The latest existential threat to Israel? Those Russians the world was implored to free", *mondoweiss.net*, January 26, 2013.
101 Tani Goldstein, "Did Russians save Israel?" Ynet.co.il, July 2, 2010.
102 Rabkin, *A Threat from Within*, 34.
103 Once Jews had their own state in 1948, many Soviet and eastern European Jews abandoned Communism, leading to the "refusenik" campaigns of the 1960s-80s. The dissident movement in the Soviet Union and eastern Europe from 1956 on was led by returnees from prison and the labor camps, and of course supported heartily by western media and intelligence organizations. Many of the returnees were Jewish, part of the intelligentsia purged in the 1930s and contributed to the conspiratorial dissident movement of the 1960-80s. This corresponded to the (also subversive) western Jewish-led Trotskyist radicalism

in western universities in the 1960s, which rejected capitalism and 'real existing socialism'.

104 See "*Hebdo* vs *Al Jazeera:* A tale of two journalisms", *ericwalberg.com*, January 11, 2015. The *Hebdo* incident—though not directed specifically at Jews like the Lavon affair and other bombings in the early 1950s in Egypt, Iraq and Morocco, which incited anti-Jewish anger and forced Jews to emigrate to Israel—was nonetheless picked up by the Israeli leadership and used to the same effect. Like Sharon's comment on 9/11 ("It's very good"), Netanyahu then exhorted French Jews to make aliyah ("Israel is your home").

105 All Israelis are conscripted and expected to serve 3 years, men before the age of 40, 45 for officers, and 49 for reservists who perform certain specific duties. Women serve two years and are on call until they have a child, with the exception of women in combat roles. Recently the age for males making aliyah to be conscripted dropped from 30 to 24, recognizing that most foreigners won't come if they are immediately forced to serve 3 years in the IDF.

106 Donald Trump was loudly castigated during the election campaign in 2016 for saying he is only being accused of sexual assault because he stands in the way of Clinton's plan to sell America to "international bankers."

107 In 2002, Israel Asper who owned some 60% of Canada's media outlets through CanWest, issued a written directive instructing his newspapers that they must not print anything critical of Israel or Zionist policies. CanWest is now Postmedia.

108 Arendt, op.cit., 19-20.

109 <https://www.youtube.com/watch?v=AXdPkH2cQGY>

110 "Paul Goldberger, "Architectural View: A Public Work That Ennobles As It Serves", *The New York Times*, August 13, 1995. Serious interpretations of the symbols built into the Supreme Court are at <http://thegoldenreport.net/the-roots-of-evil-in-jerusalem/>

111 Penslar, op.cit., 46.

112 *Globe & Mail*, March 4, 2003, Penslar, op.cit., 48.

113 Ibid., 49.

114 M Shahid Alam, "Zionist Dialectics Past and Future", *foeignpolicyjournal.com*, September 21, 2010.

115 Piracy was transformed by capitalism into various mafia groupings in the Great Games, the latest and most powerful being the Russian mafia or Kosher Nostra. (Walberg, *Postmodern Imperialism*, 27.)

116 "Jerusalem belongs to all Jews, and they must play a role in its future and Israeli policy in general, said US and European Jewish leaders, including former presidential adviser, Elliott Abrams; Malcolm Hoenlein of the Conference of Presidents of the Major American Jewish Organizations, former US ambassador to Israel, Daniel Kurtzer, head of the Anti-Defamation League Abraham Foxman, senior vice president of B'nai Brith International, Daniel Mariaschin, French leader Pierre Besnainou, in a conference in Jerusalem in November 2010 organized by the Jewish People Policy Planning Institute." ("World Jews must play role in future Mideast peace talks", *Haaretz*, 21 October 2010.)

117 Robinson, op.cit., 97.

118 Ibid., 150.

119 Ibid., 97.

120 Washington DC was also built according to Freemason principles. See <http://www.freemasonrywatch.org/washington.html>

121	Jerry Muller, *Capitalism and the Jews*, Princeton, 2010, 133.
122	'Communist Jew' was never used. Communism is in a sense tribal and cancels out Jewish as primary signifier.
123	Shamir, *Masters of Discourse*, 2008, 531. Also Scott Thompson and Jeffrey Steinberg, "Did 'Mega' Bucks Help Sharon Steal Israeli Elections?" <http://www.informationclearinghouse.info/article1113.htm>
124	Kovel, op.cit., 57. Chaim Arlosoroff went to Berlin in 1933 to negotiate over the transfer of German-Jewish assets to Palestine and was assassinated in Tel Aviv shortly afterwards, probably by more radical Jabotinsky Zionists who were against any negotiations.

| Chapter Eight |

NATIVE NATIONS / CANADA AND PALESTINE/ISRAEL

> "An Indian is either friendly (assimilated) or savage, instinctively, reiterating the basic propagandas that the British would use to justify their subjugation of India, or that the Germans would employ in their extermination of Jews, or that the Jews would utilize to displace Palestinians, or that the US military and media would craft into jingoistic slogans in order to make the invasions of other countries—Grenada, Panama, Afghanistan, Iraq— seem reasonable, patriotic and entertaining to television audiences."
> Thomas King, *The Inconvenient Indian* (2012)

Submit to us or be against us and face the consequences, has been the alternative posed by colonialism, though it takes different forms for Canadian and Palestinian natives. "Friendly" meant natives in Canada were offered assimilation as a captured people dispossessed of their lands, vs "savage" which meant hanging on to native identity and facing a quick or slow death. In a famous anecdote, Justin Trudeau's father, Prime Minister Pierre Trudeau, told Marlon Brando when the American actor wanted to discuss native rights. "There are differences in the way we treated our natives," he said. "You hunted them down and murdered them. We starved them to death." Trudeau meant actual physical starvation, as opposed to cultural starvation, echoing what the Canadian historian James Daschuk has called "the politics of starvation."[1]

In the past, Canada appeared to stand apart from such settler colonies as the US and Australia in dealing more fairly with its natives.

John Ralston Saul argues for the "originality of the Canadian project", that contained elements of a rejection of the Enlightenment project of Europe/the US, which was based on secular rationality and liberal revolution. Canada was never a monolithic nation state, but rather based on consensus, incorporating the native philosophy of man as part of nature. In *A Fair Country: Telling Truths About Canada* (2008), he argues that Canada is a "Metis civilization", not a European one. "We are a blend of Aboriginal and non-Aboriginal, but the driving ideas underneath are the Aboriginal ones."[2]

Saul argues that Canada was 'founded' as a modern nation not in 1867 but in 1701 with the Great Peace of Montreal between New France and 40 First Nations of North America. This treaty, achieved through negotiations according to Native American diplomatic custom, was meant to end ethnic conflicts. From then on, negotiation would trump direct conflict, it was thought, and the French would agree to act as arbiters during conflicts between signatory tribes. The paradigm is a confederation of tribes, consensus, the Aboriginal circle, "eating from a common bowl". The treaty is still valid and recognized as such by the Native American tribes involved.

French Canadians are generally of pre-French revolution immigrant stock. Similarly, Anglo-Canadians were against the American revolution (seen as a merchants' revolt against the crown). The downside of this "Metis civilization" is Canada's enduring colonial mentality, the constant reassertion of conservative elites (Confederation, Borden, Mulroney, Harper) kowtowing to the British/US imperial center. There has never been any genuine meeting of minds with the natives, despite 1701. The attempts to force natives into multicultural Canada as 'native Canadians' (like French or Ukrainian Canadians)—the First Nations moniker mere words—have not succeeded.

Things looked better with the arrival of Justin Trudeau. In his victory speech following the 2015 election, he vowed to form a "renewed nation-to-nation relationship with Indigenous Peoples that respects rights and honors treaties". He is the first prime minister to acknowledge, in his/her victory speech, the "nation-to-nation" relationship which dates back to 1763 when the Royal Proclamation was signed by King George III. He stated: "Now that the federal government has moved to embrace Indigenous and all of its legal ramifications by recognizing First Nations, Inuit and Metis as Indigenous Peoples, the government is implicitly acknowledging their internationally legal right to offer or withhold consent to development under the United Nations Declaration of the Rights of Indigenous Peoples."[3]

Facts on the ground, like Alberta's tar sands and Labrador's Muskrat Falls, belie this nice story. This failure has important repercussions for Canada's relationship with its "best friend" (or Trudeau Jr's less effusive "friend"), Israel. Their common tragic history with their natives continues to haunt them both. Natives in Canada have a different colonial heritage from those to the south. They are more prominent than their American counterparts as a 'nation within the nation', closer to the Palestinians in significance to Israel. More and more frequently, public meetings in Canada begin with honoring the tribe on whose land the meeting is being held, echoing the Israeli Zochrot activists, who regularly place handmade signs detailing the village's name in Arabic and Hebrew where Canada Park now stands. The JNL vowed to stop Zochrot's postings. Canada's natives are more respected than Palestinians, but then, there is in effect a truce with Canadian natives. Treaties and a nominal First Nations status are grudgingly honored, and native culture is increasingly respected, studied and encouraged.

Canada's uniqueness in world culture is thanks to its natives, who are regularly trotted out in ceremonies related to international events such as the Olympics, and now featured in the composition of the new Canadian ten dollar bill.[4] But they remain at the bottom of the mainstream pecking order economically.

Terminology is not nit-picking. Natives, First Nations, indigenous, aboriginal all come without the 'Canadian' as primary signifier. It can be 'natives in Canada', 'Canadian natives', but not native Canadians. Reversal of signifier logically changes its importance. 'Canadian Jew' would make Jew the primary signifier, i.e., special status as the chosen people. No Ukrainian immigrant calls him/herself a Canadian Ukrainian. Natives in Canada hold a different place that do Ukrainian Canadians, Jewish Canadians, and even French Canadians.

As promoters of their own tribal special status, Canadian Jews consider themselves a 'nation within the nation', making them a kind of rival to First Nations, much as they face(d) a kind of rivalry with French Canadians, who come second after the First Nations, despite Harper's "two-founding nations" acknowledging parity between English and French. Unlike the natives, Jews are at the top of the pecking order. So relations between Canadian natives and Jews, as the most privileged white Canadians, are delicate. In native eyes, even the richest whites are still below First Nations.

As critics of Zionism, Zundel et al, with their flawed anti-imperialist message, were a problem for Zionists in the 1980s as discussed in Chapter 7, but were more or less quashed. Canada's natives have their own very good reasons to be anti-imperialist and anti-Zionist, and have faced some of the same persecution as Zundel, but also a concerted soft power hasbarah campaign to try to 'correct' native thinking, to Zionize it, so that it would recognize the affinity between First Nations and Jews everywhere as a 'nation within a nation', with mixed success. The native time bomb still ticks.

Both Harper and Justin Trudeau made public gestures of reconciliation with the natives. Trudeau even attended the Assembly of First Nations General Assembly during his election campaign and accepted the recommendations of the Truth and Reconciliation Report. Nonetheless, Trudeau's record by 2017 is not encouraging.

For a half century now, the Canadian government has tried to whitewash its exploitation of natives. New Democratic Party MP and Justice Thomas Berger wrote in 1966: "They began by taking the Indians' land without any surrender and without their consent. Then they herded the Indian people onto reserves. This was nothing more nor less than Apartheid, and that is what it still is today." On almost all counts, the Canadian government has been unwilling or unable to find a healthy relationship with the First Nations.

- Aboriginal people were deprived of their land and cultural traditions. Children were removed from their families and forcibly sent away to residential schools where many were sexually abused by their white teachers.
- Aboriginal people are three times more likely than non-Aboriginals to be victims of violent crime, and at even higher risk of sexual assault.
- Aboriginal people are six times more likely to be in prison. Only 2.8% of the Canadian population, natives account for 18% of federal prisoners. In the Prairies, 50% of prisoners are Aboriginals.
- First Nations children in western countries live in Third World conditions, with an estimated 80% of urban Aboriginal children under the age of 6 living in poverty.[5]

All of these points hold true for the Palestinians, except for the terrible situation of native women. Islam remains the moral compass of Palestinians, prohibits alcohol and protects women. The pseudo Christianization of Canadian natives and then the rapid decline of Christianity as the moral compass in Canadian society has left the natives prey to the same moral decline that mainstream Canada suffers, deepened by their marginalization. There are no residential schools to assimilate Palestinians but just as Canada's prisons are the 'new residential schools',[6] tens of thousands of Palestinians, many children, have languished in Israeli jails for long periods merely for modest acts of resistance.

Harper refused approval of the **UN Declaration on the Rights of Indigenous Peoples** (UNDRIP) in 2007. Canada's ambassador John McNee complained at the time that the UN declaration gives "Indigenous peoples the right to the lands and resources which they have traditionally owned". He said this language was too vague, leaving the government open to expensive law suits. Harper finally was shamed into signing it in 2010, but with the proviso "in accordance with the Constitution", gutting the sense of the UN declaration. Trudeau claimed he was going to improve on Harper's dismissal of UNDRIP, but used his minister of justice—the first indigenous person named to that post in the country's history—Jody Wilson-Raybould,[7] as a foil to neuter UNDRIP (See Chapter 1), leaving the proviso in place. Canada's land claims and self-government policies are far below the international standards set out in UNDRIP.

However, there's a confusion in UNDRIP. While Article 6 states that "Every indigenous individual has the right to a nationality", this is often enthusiastically misinterpreted by indigenous persons as a right to their own respective tribal nationalities. Rather, Article 6 concerns a right to a *state-conferred* nationality, e.g. Canadian, which can be an issue for stateless indigenous persons—such as Palestinians. As UNDRIP says in summation in Article 46:1, none of the foregoing UNDRIP rights are to "be construed as authorizing or encouraging any action which would dismember or impair, totally or in part, the territorial integrity or political unity of sovereign and independent States"—in this instance, Canada. So the state nationality may leave native nations' tribal nationality as a hyphenated affair at best: as [tribe]-Canadians.

UNDRIP at least gives a platform for indigenous peoples in North America, supporting their rights, making their struggle the same as the Palestinians',[8] despite Israel denying that UNDRIP has anything to do with them. Israel absented the ratification of UNDRIP. The Israeli Supreme Court ruled ruled in 2015 that Bedouin have no rights as indigenous people.[9]

On the contrary, there are concerted hasbarah attempts to seduce Canadian native leaders, trying to justify Israeli acquisition by force, writ and theft of Palestinian land as age-old Jewish rights to their 'promised land'. The UN ruled that at least Bedouin have rights under UNDRIP.[10]

Natives are slowly gaining recognition as the founding peoples in the US and Canada, as citizens with claims to the land based on treaties, land which they consider holy, their own Jerusalem. Their status is complicated, as both are recognized as citizens of capitalist states, where private property rules, whereas their treaties recognize ancestral collective property rights. Maintaining their rights requires living or at least registering as aboriginals on the remaining lands that were still accorded them. A delicate dance, which still goes on.

Land and Resource Rights

Pipelines

The big issue in both Canada and Israel is land and resources. Natives in Canada have an edge on Palestinians, at least those who have treaties. The best Palestinians could do is to keep tattered personal/ family property records from before they were driven off their lands, and even keys to their doors (the 'key people'), much as European Jews and others who fled the Nazis kept records of their confiscated homes, in order to someday redeem them. Justin Trudeau made support of native rights a key electoral platform in 2015, and became the first prime minister in Canada's history to vow to provide justice to them. The litmus test will be the Alberta tar sands and pipelines. Trudeau's hurried approval of the Kindle-Morgan pipeline and insistence that the tar sands will be around "for decades" is a bad start.

Natives on both sides of the US-Canada border are fighting not only for their own remaining rights, but now in alliance with environmentalists, who are concerned about oil pipelines, fracking, and the broader issue of global warming. The natives are adamant that environmental issues know no boundaries, and North American natives are increasingly working together, as well as with nonnatives on these issues. The new respect for native history and traditions of harmony with nature resonate with mainstream youth, looking for allies in fighting the destruction of nature.

Israel has discovered gas offshore, the Tamar and Leviathan gas fields on the border with Lebanon. Tamar production began in April 2013. In 2015, Russian President Putin and Israeli Prime Minister Netanyahu agreed to allow major concessions for Gazprom to develop the Leviathan reserves. All of the coastal waters are under Israeli jurisdiction (as are all Canadian coastal waters under Canadian jurisdiction). At the same time, Israel is the biggest polluter in the eastern Mediterranean, dumping over 140 tons of heavy metals into the sea every year with government approval, according to Zalul, an Israeli environmental organization.[11]

Unlike Palestine-Israel, Canada is blessed with more **fresh water** than any other country. Canadian natives have had to yield to environmentally destructive hydroelectric dams at every step when it is considered in the 'national interest', but at least now there are negotiations, recognition of basic human rights, and some form of long term compensation. Domestic opposition (both native and non-native), the World Commission on Dams, UNDRIP, Amnesty International and, increasingly, social media[12] do not let up. As environmentalism continues to gain momentum, the fate of what's left of the world's wildernesses is increasingly an international concern.

Water Use

Canada is the world's second largest producer of hydroelectricity after China, and generates almost two thirds of its electricity from hydroelectricity. Hydroelectricity is touted as clean and environmentally sound, but the reality is that it is dirty and environmentally destructive, just in its own way. The culprits are mainly BC, Manitoba, Ontario, Quebec and Labrador, and all of the earlier dams have been built on native lands, until recently without their approval, though compensation has been offered, sometimes long after the fact. The natives are being given some recognition, even if their lands are destroyed in the interests of 'clean' energy for non-natives. Protests, demands for more rigorous environmental studies, and UNDRIP mean that fewer dams are expected in future.

A turning point came in 2004 with the court case, *Haida Nation v. British Columbia* (Minister of Forests), where the Supreme Court of Canada decided that full consent of a First Nation must be given for resource claims by developers over indigenous lands. This seminal case began to alter the way hydropower companies in Canada negotiated with First Nation communities. One such example was the Wuskwatim Dam on the Burntwood River, which was being developed by Manitoba Hydro for $1.24 billion. After nine years of negotiations, the company finally agreed to enter into an equity partnership with the Nisichawayasihk, the first case of its kind in Manitoba. Community leaders were able to significantly change the utility's original plan and reduce the dam's impacts, including alterations to its design, construction and operation. As part of this equity partnership, the Nisichawayasihk would own a third of the Wuskwatim generating station.

The Minashtuk project commissioned by Hydro-Quebec in 2000 with the Innu people allowed the Innu to become the majority shareholder with a 51% stake in the project. Hydro-Ilnu, a general partner of the limited partnership responsible for designing the station, is entirely Innu-owned. Hydro-Québec also committed to buy all of the electricity generated by the project under a 20-year contract, which provided the necessary conditions for the local community to invest. The Innu were able to design and develop the project to best meet their needs, as well as receive a share of the profits that they plan to invest in employment initiatives.[13]

Hopes for a more sympathetic government under the Liberals have been dashed. A global campaign launched by Amnesty International in January 2017 called on the federal government and BC to withdraw all permits and approvals for the Site C hydroelectric dam, a $9 billion project that will see more than 5,000 hectares flooded in north-east British Columbia. Despite protests by several First Nations groups, the project was approved by provincial and federal authorities in 2014, allowing preparatory work to begin in 2016, under Trudeau. Construction was held up by a protest camp set up by indigenous activists but the protesters were removed. "We seem to have gone backwards with this government," said chief Roland Willson of West Moberly First Nations, one of the communities most affected by the construction of Site C. A complicating factor is that most major hydro project proponents in Canada are provincial Crown corporations: BC Hydro, Nalcor (Newfoundland and Labrador), Manitoba Hydro, Yukon Energy, Hydro-Quebec. Because the state owns the projects, environmental review processes often look to be "rigged in advance" given that environmental reviews are conducted by government agencies.

Much of the power generated is exported to the US. In 2009 this earned Canada $2.38 billion. This is convenient for the US, as the US has stronger environmental protection laws and more powerful pro-environment groups, and the same destructive dams have been stopped in the past. Dams such as Labrador's Muskrat Falls not only destroy wildlife, but release toxic methylmercury in fish and mammals from rotting dead trees, poisoning the remaining wildlife that natives hunt and live on, reminding us of Trudeau Sr's flippant sound byte with Brando about Canada starving natives, mentioned earlier. Like the Alberta tar sands, Labrador's Muskrat Falls dam should be stopped, despite the billions poured into these crimes against nature. This is the native position, but Trudeau Jr supports both projects, despite his solemn vow at election time to respect native views. Muskrat Falls has been plagued with disaster, as if the Great White Spirit is angry. It was supposed to open in 2016, but its massive retainer wall collapsed in 2016 and now no proposed date has been set. $5 billion has been spent and the original $6.2 billion estimate is now closer to $10 billion, to be spent to provide mining companies with 'cheap' electricity, leaving a trail of devastation for eternity.

Given their desert climate, the worst resource danger Palestinians face is theft and depletion of **ground water**, and prevention of use of the Jordan River. Israel has been using ground waters without any regard for international law since 1948. The violations are painful to read:

- Of the water available from West Bank aquifers, Israel uses 73%, West Bank Palestinians use 17%, and illegal Jewish settlers use 10%.
- While 10-14% of Palestine's GDP is agricultural, 90% of farmers must rely on rain-fed farming methods. Israel's agriculture is only 3% of their GDP, but Israel irrigates more than 50% of its land.
- Each Israeli consumes as much water as four Palestinians.
- Israel consumes the vast majority of the water from the Jordan River despite only 3% of the river falling within its pre-1967 borders. The National Water Carrier channels water from the Jordan River, but for Israelis only. Only with Jordan was Israel able to reach an agreement on the sharing of water resources in 1995 as part of the Israel-Jordan Peace Treaty.

- Under international law it is illegal for Israel to expropriate the water of the Occupied Palestinian Territories for use by its own citizens, and doubly illegal to expropriate it for use by illegal Israeli settlers. Nonetheless, "There is no reason for Palestinians to claim that just because they sit on lands, they have the rights to that water," said Katz-Oz, Israel's negotiator on water issues and minister of agriculture from 1988 until 1990.
- Israel does not allow new wells to be drilled by Palestinians and has confiscated many wells for Israeli use. Israel sets quotas on how much water can be drawn by Palestinians from existing wells.
- When supplies of water are low in the summer months, the Israeli water company Mekorot closes the valves which supply Palestinian towns and villages so as not to affect Israeli supplies. This means that illegal Israeli settlers can have their swimming pools topped up and lawns watered while Palestinians living next to them, on whose land the settlements are situated, do not have enough water for drinking and cooking. Israeli settlers have no restrictions on water use.
- Israel often sells the water it steals from the West Bank back to the Palestinians at inflated prices. During the war of 1967, 140 Palestinian wells in the Jordan Valley were destroyed to divert water through Israel's National Water Carrier. Palestinians were allowed to dig only 13 wells between 1967 and 1996, less than the number of wells which dried up during the same period due to Israel's refusal to deepen or rehabilitate existing wells.
- The Gaza strip relies predominately on wells that are being increasingly infiltrated by salty sea water because Israel is over-pumping the groundwater. UN scientists estimate that Gaza will have no drinkable water within fifteen years.
- Vandalism by settlers is rampant. In Madama village 50km north of Jerusalem settlers from Yizhar settlement have repeatedly poured concrete into the villagers' only source of water, vandalized the connecting pipes and even dropped disposable diapers and other hazardous waste into the springs. Three villagers have been attacked by settlers while trying to repair the water source.
- Many of the most important underground wellsprings in the West Bank are located just to the east of the Green Line

dividing Israel from Palestine. Israel has built the Wall not only to annex land but also to annex many of these wells in order to divert water to Israel and illegal West Bank settlements. Some of the largest Israeli settlements are built over the western mountain aquifer, directly in the middle of the northern West Bank agricultural districts. In the West Bank, around 50 groundwater wells and over 200 cisterns have been destroyed or isolated from their owners by the Wall. This water was used for domestic and agricultural needs by over 122,000 people. To build the Wall, 25 wells and cisterns and 35,000 meters of water pipes have also been destroyed.[14]

Parks

Israel's Canada and other Parks on stolen land are similar to, but far worse than, Canada's policy of establishing national and provincial parks on native lands, as hundreds of thousands of Palestinians were robbed of their lands and killed, with dozens of their villages obliterated, without even the pretense of treaties or even IOUs. Canada was more respectful than Israel, mostly negotiating treaties for land use, though not above resorting to open theft and violence. The Canadian government is also more respectful these days, though the policy of confiscating land to build pipelines and extract resources on native lands continues apace. Natives have struggled to gain some control through the courts, but, with rare exceptions, the Canadian legal system does not take account of the very different needs of First Nations. And as in Israel, establishing parks isn't just a matter of whatever advantages the seizing government wishes to reap from them, so much as of establishing a blockage to dispossessed indigenous peoples' ownership and use of territories that rightfully belong to them. Typically, if there's a problem about tar sands or whatever, 'Canadian sovereignty' pre-empts native rights.

The same violation of native rights goes on around the world; mostly glaringly at present the pipelines through Azerbaijan, Georgia, Turkey, which have meant loss of sovereignty, confiscation of the land of hundreds of thousands of nationals, and massive destruction of the environment. At present, a new pipeline, the Kinder-Morgan will cut a 150 metre path through the Rocky Mountains delivering toxic tar sands oil to Chinese supertankers on the Pacific coast, and a massive dam, Site C, will flood native lands in northern BC on the Peace river.

Because Palestine is resource poor and tiny, those kinds of confiscation aren't such a problem so far, but Palestinian land and homes are regularly confiscated "for security reasons" and converted to Jewish use. Settlements are constructed on Palestinian lands in increasing numbers, much as the choicest native lands in Canada were taken in various ways and converted to settlers' use.

Education

Native education in Canada from 1960s on has been more integrated, promoting assimilation for off-reserve natives in cities, though attempts at wholesale assimilation have been reduced. In 1972, the National Indian Brotherhood (the Assembly of First Nations) produced a policy on Aboriginal education called "Indian Control of Indian Education." The policy was subsequently adopted by the Department of Indian Affairs and Northern Development (now Indigenous and Northern Affairs Canada) as an unofficial education policy. It identified the importance of local community control to improve education, the need for more native teachers, the development of relevant curricula and teaching resources in native schools, and the importance of language instruction and native values in native education. Teacher education programs to increase the number of native teachers have been established in several universities in Ontario, Manitoba, Saskatchewan, Alberta, British Columbia, Nova Scotia and New Brunswick.

Indigenous and Northern Affairs Canada (INAC) is responsible for schools on First Nations reserves. Off-reserve First Nations children receive the same education as non-natives, which is better than on-reserve education, but leaves no room for native languages or a strong native component in social studies. Half of First Nations students drop out before finishing Grade 12, 60% of on-reserve students, 40% of off-reserve students. As well, INAC underfunds First Nations post-secondary education. There are about 27,000 First Nations post-secondary students. In 2009, more than 5,000 eligible First Nations students were denied post-secondary funding.[15]

In 1969, Trent University in Peterborough became the first Canadian university to establish a Native Studies program. Most colleges and universities now offer similar programs or departments across Canada. In 1973, the Saskatchewan Indian Federated College (SIFC), part of the University of Regina, became the first Aboriginal-controlled degree-granting post-secondary education institution in Canada, since 2003, the First Nations University of Canada. There are several First Nations community colleges throughout Canada. The creation of Nunavut in 1999 has led to an Inuit-controlled government that is working to achieve an education system that is more Inuit-based and Inuit-defined.

The 2016 Liberal budget included $8.4 billion over five years for indigenous community infrastructure, including $2.6 billion for education and $1.2 billion for infrastructure improvements such as housing and clean water, in order to bring "transformational change" in reserves across the country. It was generally greeted with approval by native leaders, reversing the budget-cutting of the Harper years. But Canada has a long way to go, and it looks like assimilation is coming whether the natives want it or not. The Inuit population ranked 63rd in a federal government study comparing Aboriginal communities to the United Nations' Human Development Index, while First Nations reserve communities ranked 72nd.[16]

Palestinians face an education system that is completely segregated in Arab-only schools with an Israeli-approved curriculum, with all that implies for studies of history, literature, even sciences. Arabs can study at post-secondary institutions with Jews, but all university classes are in Hebrew, and few Arab Israelis are fluent, much as most Canadians outside of Quebec cannot speak French. That recalls the pre-1960s Canadian education of natives, when schooling was more or less segregated, poorer, with used, white man's textbooks. But at least Palestinians have kept their native language and no attempt was made to eradicate their culture. On the contrary, they were meant to keep separate and not learn Hebrew as part of a policy not to integrate them into Israeli society. Their education funding is at a lower level than in Jewish schools—in Arabic, but with mandatory Hebrew. (In Jewish schools, Arabic is optional.)

In terms of performance up to the secondary school level, Palestinians in both the Occupied Territories and Israel have 98% literacy. In the territories, there are 11 universities (10 private and one public), 11 technical colleges (4 Palestinian Authority, 2 UNRWA, 4 public and 1 private), and 19 community colleges (1 Palestinian Authority, 9 public, 2 UNRWA, and 7 private)—all Arab-language.

Arab Israelis face an uphill battle, surrounded by better funded Hebrew schools, and forced to study in Hebrew (but never speaking it) at the post-secondary level.[17] And their situation is getting worse, unlike the improving situation of Canadian natives, who have a handful of native colleges, and native study programs at universities. Arab Israelis comprise 20% of Israel's population, 50% of them are under the age of 20, but account for only 12% of students pursuing undergraduate degrees in Israel. Only 65% of Arab youngsters, compared to 92% of Jews, reach the 12th grade. Only 23% of Arabs meet the rigorous admission standards for an Israeli university. Among Jews it is 47%. A 2009 report showed that obstacles to Arab students participating in higher education resulted in over 5,000 moving to study in nearby Jordan.

Arabs can study the Palestinian Authority curriculum to reinforce their national identity as Palestinians, or the Israeli one to ensure them access to Israeli universities and job prospects in the Israeli world, the latter omitting any Palestinian or Muslim content. The Israeli authorities "don't only want to occupy the land, they want to occupy the minds of the people – like a brainwashing," director of the parents' association in East Jerusalem, Abdul-Karim Lafi said. In 2014, Israel revised the Palestinian Authority textbooks for over 32,000 Palestinian children who study under Israeli control, taking out parts that the government believes incite violence. Jibril showed a *New York Times* reporter a copy of a 2012 Palestinian history textbook for third grade students in Arabic, alongside a revised edition from this year. The differences were glaring—large sections of text and several images had been removed from this year's edition, including the Palestinian flag, text from the Quran and information about the late Palestinian leader Yasser Arafat.

UNRWA runs several schools in East Jerusalem. UNRWA spokesman Chris Gunness said inequalities between schools there were vast. "Schools administered by Israelis are mostly built as schools, while the other schools are operated in rented houses which results in a lack of specialized rooms and labs. There is overcrowding in Palestinian schools and the jobs and salaries for teachers are higher in Israeli schools and this impacts recruitment for Palestinian schools."[18] Palestinian university degrees are not recognized in Israel, and all jobs require fluency in Hebrew, which means those studying in Jordan can only work in the territories. Palestinian students can apply to study at Israeli universities but must study an additional year before entering university to show they have adequate Hebrew skills. Even if they pass through all the hurdles, Arab Israelis face open discrimination in hiring, preference being given to Israeli

Jews and even new arrivals making aliyah. The law grants preference to army veterans, which again means Jews.[19] Though Canadian natives also face discrimination, the situation is clearly worse for Palestinians.

The Laws and Courts

The legal framework for natives in Canada is still not clear. Canada's colonial legacy meant that native legal traditions were suppressed and even forgotten. Canada has only a common civil legal system, not recognizing native or religious legal systems for Jews and Muslims. Natives must abide by the civil justice system, with special provisos based on treaties, and some autonomy on reserves. This is in contrast to some acceptance of both Jewish and Muslim courts in the US,[20] though attempts to follow suit for Jewish and Muslim religious courts in Ontario were quashed by Islamophobes.[21] In the Muslim and Jewish traditions, religious law still takes precedent in family matters. This is the case in Israel, with Jewish, Muslim and Christian courts regulating marriage and family matters, though Jews have the option of using civil courts on matters of custody, support or equitable distribution of property. Economic issues are all dealt with in the civil legal system.

There are no First Nations courts in Canada, unlike in the US, where 145 American tribes operate their own courts, including Traditional or Customary Courts, Courts of Indian Offenses, and Tribal Courts. The traditional courts operate by virtue of American Indian Nations having been declared "domestic dependent nations" by the American Supreme Court in the 1820s, and in the absence of any federal legislation to expressly remove them. The Tribal Law and Order Act of 2010 gave them further authority over sentencing.

Now that a more just relationship with the natives is becoming a part of Canadian tradition, there are attempts to undo the legal straitjacket, but they have stalled.[22] The alternative is to continue using civil law courts, which promotes **assimilation**. Assimilation is not a threat for Palestinians, but is for Canadian natives, who are still rebuilding their culture, their communities and family traditions, and need to do so by reviving their lost legal traditions. So First Nations will look to US precedents and ways to enhance tribal governance. Incidents like the Oka, Ipperwash and BC crises (see Chapter 1) could then be resolved without recourse to violence and the imprisonment of natives simply for observing their religious celebrations. These frictions with the dominant capitalist society can be dealt with much better if natives have councils with legal authority within the broader Canadian legal system.

The major difference between the fate of Palestinians and natives in Canada is the ongoing state policy of continued isolation (apartheid) for the Palestinians and assimilation for the natives. Christianity is a universal religion, welcoming (sometimes forcibly) all. 'We are all one before God.' Judaism is a tribal religion, which does not promote mass conversion. The Christian idea in colonizing America was assimilation of everyone, on the colonizers' terms, natives and immigrants, into a 'melting pot', now deemed a 'multicultural' one, guaranteeing equal rights for all. Though a two-edged sword, natives in Canada have contested assimilationist policies and Canada has, to a degree, responded, allowing for revival of native cultures as 'nations within a nation', Canada's multicultural masses also benefit from this native revival, promoting both the rich traditions the natives have and the spirit of reconciliation that no nation can do without. It might be argued that this is 'good assimilation', two-way assimilation which meets the specific context—if it were not for the ongoing discrimination in social and economic life.

Things are clearer in Israel. Arabs are Arabs (Muslim and Christian), Jews are Jews. Period. No assimilation. A recipe for ongoing colonialism, apartheid, a broken society. No society only consists of one ethnicity, one tribe. No society can survive without accommodation for its various ethnicities/tribes. An Israeli nationality, the basis for Israel's survival and integration into the world polity as an accepted member, requires a similar two-way accommodation. Arab Israelis benefit from Israel's undisputed technical and intellectual dynamism, and most do not want to leave, despite their inferior status and the racism they experience every day. (Of course life is worse in the Occupied Territories.) They are waiting and hoping that the Jews will recognize the inevitable and learn from Israel's older sibling, Canada, hopefully learning the right lessons, and not repeating Canada's mistakes.

Arab *Jews* in Israel are in much the same boat as their Muslim cousins. Even though more than three million or about 61% of Israel's Jewish population are of north African and Iraqi Arab descent,[23] they are classified simply as Jews, downplaying their Arabic background. Not surprisingly, they have suffered discrimination from the start, though at least they have the same legal status as European Israelis. Israel is a very complex mix of white and brown colony. The fact that the majority of Israelis now have some Arab 'blood' also suggests an evolutionary path out of Israel's colonial dead end, at least the possibility of some kind of reconciliation between Jew and Arab, if ever the Zionist militancy wears down, Saul's 'Metis civilization'.

Native culture has always had a fascination for English and French Canadians, some of whom went 'native' in the 18th–19th century, living as natives themselves, learning their language and working as trappers, captivated by the mystique of Rousseau's "noble savage". Similarly, some Israeli Jews learn Arabic and respect local Muslim and Christian heritage, as well as the rich heritage of the Mizrahi, despite pressures to maintain the apartheid Israeli culture.

Ultimately the same logical conclusion to our colonial venture lies in store for both Canada and Israel. The problems of resource management, property rights and education highlight Israel's dilemma: justice demands equal rights before the law, in education and a concerted effort at bilingualism, whether or not there is a Palestinian state. As with native, French and English Canadians, this will mean the Arabs must be bilingual in the first place. But most of Israel's Jews have Arabic heritage, and it is only natural to embrace this Arab heritage as part of the Arab Middle East, so Jews must learn Arabic to live a full life in Israel. For Israel, this extends beyond its as yet nonexistent borders: there can be no peace until Israel also honors its neighbors.

Native Canadian languages will never fully revive due to Canada's 19th century forced assimilation policy and 20th century Residential Schools, but then, Hebrew was a dead language and was revived by political passion (and state endorsement). Canadian programs to revive at least a few native languages are active and their popularity growing. Accommodation will mean different things for Canada and Israel, but the cultural legacy of indigenous peoples in both Canada and Israel includes a yearning for a simpler past more in touch with nature and with the land. Just as Jews must embrace and absorb Arab culture, so Canadians must honor the First Nations, who are the conscience of modern society, and who have profound wisdom to share.

Idylls

Imagine a Canada with no walls separating the still more-or-less pristine nature of the mountains, forest and tundra. With less energy consumption and more efficient and diverse sources of energy, the era of damming rivers, clearcutting forests and creating inferno-like desolation of yawning tar pits is over. Natives have both the advantages of urban civilization and wilderness living, attracting all Canadians and many fans of native life from all countries to explore with them their beloved lands, sharing the secrets of sacred nature.

Imagine an Israel with no walls, no bombing, no intifadas, no Apartheid, where Muslims, Christians, and the few observant Jews shared their holy sites without violence, where archeological digs employ scholars and workers of all faiths, objectively sifting through remains for hints of the common past. Jerusalem as the symbolic 'world's capital', the Zionist dream, but without the hate and murder that is daily fare there now.

Just as the Canada-Israel nexus of 2017 is one of torment and hypocrisy, money and racism, both within each country and between them, that nexus could be one of solidarity and justice for all. Cultural sequestration in the age of globalism is impossible. Its negative opposite, assimilation, has already happened, but in a chaotic, disruptive way. Integration can be shaped to preserve cultures, the point of 'multiculturalism'. The global environmental crisis forces us to bury our hatchets and work together.

Native vs Judeo-Christian theology

Thomas King sees in the Genesis story the source of the West's hierarchical, martial religion, the triumph of egotism and self-interest. We cut forests not to enrich the lives of animals but to make profit. We tolerate poverty not because we believe adversity makes you strong, but because we're unwilling to share. In King's telling, the Native vision of creation has much more in common with the Quran than with the Old Testament:

- Satan (a kind of Trickster, part of Creation) did not come to Adam and Eve in the form of a snake and can never be totally defeated, though he must be resisted.
- Like Charm in the Native story, Eve in Islam is by no means weaker or less important than Adam, and is not guilty of tricking man into disobeying God.
- In the Quran, eating the fruit of the tree was a mistake committed by both Adam and Eve. They bear equal responsibility. And it

- was not the "original sin" spoken about in Christian traditions, resulting in expulsion into a world of chaos.
- The descendants of Adam are not being punished for the sins of their original parents. They made a mistake, and God, in His infinite wisdom and mercy, forgave them both. 'I love you,' God said, 'but I'm not happy with your behavior. Let's talk this over. Try to do better next time.'

The attempts to lure natives with 'Canadian culture' and now Zionism and 'Israeli culture' have been mixed at best. Once the element of forced assimilation was abandoned, tribal cultural life rebounded and continues to do so today, with at least some native languages surviving. The process of cultural assimilation continues now, passively, relying on the lure of western mass culture, but the beauty of native culture, including its spirituality, is increasingly honored. The natural affinity between native struggles and those of Muslims[24] was caught by the slogan at the demonstration in Toronto following the mass murder of Muslims at the Quebec City mosque in January 2017: *No Muslim ban on stolen land!*, protesting in addition Trump's ban on Muslims and decision to proceed with the pipeline through native lands, thus emphasizing the enduring dual legacy of oppression, and necessary solidarity, of Canadian and Palestinian native peoples.

Israeli/Zionist soft/hard power with First Nations

Jews traditionally had little interaction with North American natives. A popular vaudeville skit in New York in the 1920s was fashioned on an old tale of Jews disguised as Gypsy bands, as a "conflation of Indian tribes with the tribe of Moses in tasteless comedy sketches which created a template for later depictions on television from vaudeville to television" showing "the nimbleness with which the ever adaptive Jewish entertainer would embrace alternative identities ... with more contemporary artistic desire to transform and adapt materials than to understand them intellectually."[25] But it led to no real affinity, as appeared between natives and say, Germans and French, who developed an enthusiastic cult of the 'noble savage'.[26]

In the 18th–19th centuries there were never any Jewish *couriers du bois,* who loved native culture and intermarried, their offspring metis, now a third of Canada's native population. The closest Jews came to any contact with the natives was as merchants with the Hudson's Bay Company or its rival the Northwest Company, possibly in Fort William on Lake Superior, but more likely in Montreal or London, buying their furs without any direct contact. By the time the Jewish mass immigration started in the 1880s, the reserves were mostly in place and again there was virtually no contact between Jews and natives. Jews were fighting their own battles with the rival 'white' colonists in the big cities, demanding equal rights, especially property rights, learning the hard way in western commercial practices. As masters of the commercial and financial world, Jews lived a rarefied life, unknown to the natives, rapidly growing rich and into leading positions in Canadian society.

When Zionists became prominent in Canadian society, they had a conundrum. The natives in Canada were much more prominent than in the US, much stronger in defending their heritage. Much less assimilated, and still (rightly) suspicious of the 'white man'. They could not be ignored if Canadians were to be onside with the Zionist plan to erase the Palestinians as a people, and steal their land. That would touch a very sore spot with the natives, and complicate their PR tasks. Zionist interest in the native peoples in Canada arose as part of the broader hasbarah campaign from the 1970s onward to justify the occupation of the entire Palestinian territory.

The Palestinians' natural allies in the conspiracy against them are those very natives, who had likewise been dispossessed of their lands in bloody wars and forced resettlements. As part of the assimilation effort, the natives in Canada had largely been Christianized—initially—forcibly, but now accepting the new Christian religion, merely adding it to their own—and the Zionists capitalized on this, portraying the Old Testament Israelites, with their chief, Moses, returning to a 'promised land' of yore, as a *common* bond between persecuted peoples, Jews and Indigenous. Their point that natives in North America were persecuted by Gentiles, *not the Jews*, did not really resonate as, for the natives, Jews and goys were both simply Europeans taking their lands. That goys may have persecuted the Jews unjustly for thousands of years over in Europe was not part of their worldview. In any case, natives were Christianized, and would see the Jews as rejecting the white man's Jesus, whom they had embraced and loved. Another white man's trick?

A few native leaders have succumbed to this hasbarah, but most ignore the Zionists' tortured analogies. 'History' means Palestinians losing their land to colonial invaders. Ancient history is legend. 'Chosen' is Jewish legend only. Natives don't demand resurrecting ancient empires of their own, only wanting some restitution of what they had lost when the white man invaded in the 16th century.

Until the 1970s, there was virtually no interest or contact between Jews or Jewish organizations and natives in Canada, except for business purposes, such as providing legal counsel in the natives' continuing and now multiplying legal processes concerning land claims. Canada's natives held no real interest for the Zionists until the 1970s–80s, when they were fashioning their new "Holocaust" ideology to be eternally the world's victim people, meriting Israel as their 'safe haven'. Suddenly, in Zionist eyes, the natives became possible allies— they were also victim nations, struggling to gain their rightful heritage, their historic legacies. For outsiders, it is hard to accept this logic unless you are a biblical literalist, and see no real difference between, say, 100 years and 10,000 years in terms of 'rightful heritage'. Yet what is one to say of the Doctrine of Christian Discovery to which Canada turns even now, in an effort to justify its dispossession of native lands and imposition of Canadian citizenship, and similarly religion-based justifications in Israel, put forward by Jews determined to take over all the Old Testament biblical sites?

The Knesset established the **Christian Allies Caucus** in 2004 to facilitate the growing Christian Zionist-indoctrinated tourism along with tourism for "indigenous peoples" from around the world. But participants in the 2005 conference "Contemporary Antisemitism: Canada and the World" at the Munk Centre for International Studies agreed that it is hard to make common cause between Jews and visible minorities, that the type of racism was different, Jews being white, more established, and economically successful, attacked for their perceived power and suspect loyalties. Visible minorities experience more overt and systemic racism, and suffer from poverty and their perilous immigrant status. These Canadians (immigrants and natives) resent both Jews and whites.[27] The Zionists hadn't pondered the issue of natives. So it is bizarre that Zionists would approve of victimizing leading native figures, as happened in the case of Chief Ahenakew. (See below.)

In their own defense (addressing white critics), the Zionists like to flaunt America and Canada's genocidal treatment of the natives. 'You did worse things to your natives.' They have a point, but don't take it far enough. The real comparison is indeed between the natives in Canada and the natives in Israel, the Palestinians, and the parallels between the timelines and the mechanics of their dispossession by the colonial masters, the British and Israel, as Elias Sanbar noted.

The Zionist hasbaristas ignore the fact that the occupiers actually signed treaties for at least some of the land, and that North America is still occupied territory in the eyes of the natives. Furthermore, the occupiers have matured somewhat, honoring the natives now, helping them revive their cultures and build meaningful lives whether on reserves or in the broader society. It's not the full UNDRIP model but it is at least the UN "minority rights" model, giving them not just full citizenship rights but a special status as genuine 'nations within nations', as would be agreed upon by a nonracist society. (Canada is much closer to that description than it was 50 years ago. Israel has moved even further from it.) This indeed could be a responsible template for overcoming Zionism, just as it was the way to overcome the genocidal racism of the early settlers.

The hasbaristas use WWII memes to gain sympathy, calling the Palestinians "fascists" for supporting Hitler, ignoring the context of the British Mandate and the fact that WWII had no significance for the Palestinians. They point to Palestinian and Egyptian sympathy with Nazi Germany in WWII, though this was perfectly natural, as the British were the occupiers of Palestine, and hence enemies by definition of the Arabs, who could hardly do worse than accept German promises of some kind of independence after the war. It wasn't the Germans who issued the Balfour letter, after all. It is easier to ignore such inconvenient truths and just change the topic.

The Zionists seek to pervert the native genocide in North America as reflecting their own history of unjust persecution over the ages. There are even eccentrics who claim an Indian tribe has Jewish genes (from a Jewish settler in the 16th century), establishing the "10th lost tribe", an idea which had been around since the 18th century.[28]

In July 2013, Canada's media solemnly admitted "the sad truth that the country engaged in a deliberate policy of attempted genocide against First Nations people,"[29] referring to government-sponsored abuse of native children a century ago, which Canada's Chief Medical Officer Peter Bryce exposed in 1907, but which was hushed up. Whistleblower Bryce was fired and the post of chief medical officer abolished in 1919. This was a terrible crime, coming to public attention only in 2013, though the facts have long been known (the study referred to was published in 2006). An earlier study published by Ian Mosby in May 2013 added fuel to the fire, revealing that from 1942–1952, the government conducted "nutritional experiments" on native children in the residential schools, where milk rations were halved for years, essential vitamins not issued, and dental services withheld as gum health was a measuring tool for scientists and any care would distort research.

But the media breakthrough was made not just by Phil Fontaine, former chief of the Assembly of First Nations, but by Bernie Farber, senior vice-president of Gemini Power Corporation and former head of the Canadian Jewish Congress (now CIJA), indicating just how advantageous such a linkage could be. This is not the first time that CIJA has expressed 'support' for beleaguered natives. For years now, just as hundreds of Canadian MPs, MPPs, police officials, what-have-you are invited regularly on junkets to Israel by CIJA or other pro-Israeli groups, CIJA self-proclaimed "social activists" are now courting local native groups with similar free trips. For instance, Winnipeg CIJA official Shelley Faintuch organized a 10-day Cree Youth Leadership Development Mission to Israel in 2012 and 2013 with the support of Norway House Cree Nation Chief Ron Evans "to develop the next generation of First Nations leaders by looking through the lens of Israel's inspiring story."

Why would Canadian Jewish leaders suddenly take such an interest in natives? Is it altruism, because of the Jewish tradition of being 'a light unto peoples'? This is what CIJA would have us believe, with its claims to "profound cultural and historical similarities," "striving for acceptance, equal rights, rights to their own land." There is another, very different explanation. The native resistance movement has continued to grow in the past half century. The increasing awareness in Canada and internationally of how natives in Canada were dispossessed and abused by colonial settlers leads automatically to the parallel between Canada's natives and the Palestinians, who have suffered a century of identical treatment by Jews immigrating to Palestine, which the latter arbitrarily renamed 'Israel' in 1948.[30] Israel's founder, David Ben-Gurion, admitted this when he stated in 1936, "Were I an Arab I would rise up against [Jewish] immigration," for Arabs are "fighting dispossession." As natives become more aware of their common struggle with other aboriginal peoples around the world, they can't help but identify with the Palestinians. So it makes perfect sense for Canada's Zionists to be proactive, to try to convince Canada's natives of the counter-intuitive narrative that it is the European and American Jews who are indigenous to Palestine, not the native Arabs. The story the Cree are told on their Youth Leadership Development Missions is that Israelis, like the natives, are merely trying to reassert their legitimate indigenous rights to their land.

The headlines about the Canadian government's "genocide" against the Natives a century ago just happens to be accompanied by self-serving lectures about the Nazi Holocaust, the 'Final Solution', and even allusions to the infamous Dr. Mengele experimenting on Jewish victims. This shameless manipulation of events surrounding a genuine human tragedy is despicable, as Arendt argued in 1961 at Eichmann's trial as did Finkelstein in *The Holocaust Industry*. It was also a direct slap in the face for Harper as head of government, despite his fawning allegiance to Israel. Does Bernie Farber, former chief executive officer of the Canadian Jewish Congress, have no allegiance to Canada's prime minister? Is this sudden embrace of native resistance a *sayanim* thrust?

Gemini Power's VP is a self-proclaimed "social activist" who according to Wikipedia "works in partnership with First Nations to help develop sustainable business." A cynical view of this translates into: convince the natives to sell out to resource-hungry corporations like Gemini Power and their government lackeys, intent on building such wonders as liquefied natural gas terminals on the west coast, chromite mining and smelting projects in the James Bay, and tar sands oil production in Alberta.

Is it possible that hat this apparent sympathy is all part of a larger win-win plan to defraud the hapless natives in both countries of their resources?

However, the bulk of the native community is supporting not Israel, but Idle No More, which has declared war on the Conservatives' attempt to replace the government's treaty obligations with market mechanisms in Bills C-45 and C-38. Farber failed to mention the fact that Israel itself conducted Dr. Mengele-type experiments on its own Jewish citizens—north African and Ethiopian Jews, who swallowed the Zionist propaganda and fled their traditional homes and cultures to live in the 'Jewish state'. According to the documentary "100,000 Radiation" *shown on Israeli TV in 2003*, starting in 1951, the American army paid the

Israeli Health Ministry to radiate children to test for side effects of radiation. An entire generation of Mizrahi youths were unwittingly used as guinea pigs. Yet another Israeli TV documentary aired in 2012 revealed that until recently, Ethiopian Jews were forcibly injected with Depo-Provera, a drug to make them sterile, before they were allowed to immigrate to Israel. Cree Chief Ron Evans personally suffered under the 'Dr. Mengele' experiments, which were conducted on the Norway House and Le Pas Cree beginning in 1942.[31] But instead of putting two and two together, Evans was coopted by CIJA's Winnipeg affiliate to sponsor the Cree 'Missions to Israel', where he pronounced the Jewish people "the true, historic indigenous people of Israel". Evans was not the only one coopted.

- Reverend Raymond MacLean founded the First Nations Family Worship Centre (Winnipeg) and **World Indigenous Nations for Israel**. He has visited Israel 16 times since 2003 and was part of the Indigenous Tour to Israel in February 2012 billed as bringing together "Original peoples from both the northern and the southern ends of the earth", including Greenland, Fiji, Samoa, New Zealand and Australia. More than 300 natives visited Israel from 2004 to 2013. When his group demonstrated to support Israel's bombing of Lebanon in 2006 in Winnipeg, they were criticized "from all sides, both people from the streets and from the media." As an evangelical Christian, MacLean sees Zionist claims to Palestine as "the inheritance of the land by the ancestors," that it is wrong to see the conflict as "the Colonizer occupying land and kicking out the First Nations to live in poverty and in refugee camps. ... Our conflicts are not the same." He told the Sderot Media Center, "There were Arab nomads who lived in the Holy Land prior to the establishment of the State of Israel in 1948 who were hired by the new Jewish settlers." Sderot was built in 1951, after the Palestinians there were expelled to Gaza and their village Najd was razed, far from any "nomads".[32]
- Ryan Bellerose described himself, on *Arutz Sheva* (Channel Seven), as a "Zionist Metis from the Paddle Prairie Metis settlement in Northern Alberta, an organizer and participant in the Idle No More movement in Calgary, and founding member of **Calgary United with Israel**." He writes for *Arutz*

Sheva, a news service of religious Zionism and the settlement movement, a counterbalance to "negative thinking" and "post-Zionist attitudes." "Israel is the world's first modern indigenous state. Those who are arguing for Palestinian 'indigenous rights' are usually those who have little grasp of the history, and no understanding of the truth behind indigenous rights."[33]

- In 2006, Phil Fontaine, then National Chief of the Assembly of First Nations, visited.
- In 2008 a delegation of native women went to the Golda Meir Mount Carmel International Training Centre.

Such hasbarah attempts have fallen flat in the US,[34] and gained only the support of evangelical Christian natives as in Canada, derisively called "Uncle Tom-Toms" by the broader native community. Natives see the current reality of oppression, reserves, murder and despair in both Canada and Israel, and see the 'whites', including the Jews, as the oppressors. It is the Palestinians who are struggling to get their land back. Face with overwhelming military force, the natives can only get rights over their land by mounting substantial political pressure domestically and internationally. They know peaceful resistance and negotiations are their only hope, just as negotiations and substantial international political pressure are the only hope of the Palestinians, a peaceful settlement of past injustices. The Zionists have nothing to offer the natives except junkets to the holy land and some scholarships to study hasbarah, or charity projects to help individual reserves.

The most outstanding casualty of Zionist wrath was **David Ahenakew** (1933–2010), a Canadian First Nations politician, and former National Chief of the Assembly of First Nations, who served in the Canadian Forces from 1951 to 1967, during which time he was stationed in Germany, Korea during the Korean War, and Egypt, in Gaza as a UN peacekeeper, witnessing Israel's daily persecution of Palestinians. He saw Israeli atrocities first hand and was appalled.

Ahenakew received the Order of Canada in 1978. His citation read: Member of a United Nations committee and of the World Indigenous Peoples Council. His many years of service to Indians and Métis in Saskatchewan culminated in his election as Chief of the Federation of Saskatchewan Indians, which has revolutionized Indian education in his province.

In 2002, Ahenakew gave a speech to a Federation of Saskatchewan Indian Nations group, which was attended by James Parker, a reporter from the Saskatoon *StarPhoenix*. He made references to "goddamn immigrants" in Canada during his speech. "The Germans used to tell me, and I got to know them well because I played soccer against them and with them. They used to tell me that you guys are blessed. What we know about the Indians in Canada. They are blessed. But that blessing is being destroyed by your immigrants that are going over there. Especially the Jews, they said. And look what they're doing now, they're killing people in Arab countries. I was there [Gaza] as well."

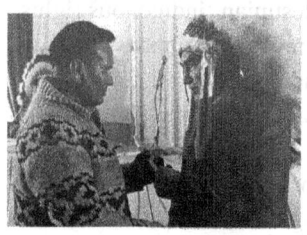

Chief Ahenakew (right)

During an interview following his lecture, Parker asked Ahenakew what he thought of Hitler. Ahenakew said that Jews were a disease in Germany and that Hitler was trying to "clean up Europe" when he "fried six million of those guys. The Second World War was started by the Jews and the Third World War, whatever it is, is between Israel and the Arab countries. But there's going to be a war because the Israelis and the "Bushies"—you know, the bully, the bigot in the United States—tells you that if you're not with me you're against me."[35] Ahenakew was so shocked by what he had seen in Gaza that he in turn went to an extreme—Israeli policy brought that of the Nazis to mind, prompting him to attempt to justify the Holocaust. He was speaking to a reporter, not giving a public formal address, and had drunk some wine. It was a cheap scoop for an ambitious journalist, if not an entrapment. Parker hounded Ahenakew and wrote up a piece of yellow journalism, vilifying him. In June 2003, Ahenakew was formally charged by the Saskatchewan Justice Department with promoting hatred. The remarks had been recorded on tape, and the prosecution was allowed to use them.

Ahenakew had to face two trials—in 2005 and 2008. His lawyer, Doug Christie, revealed that Parker was taking revenge against the Federation of Saskatchewan Indian Nations' Christie for complaints over earlier reporting, and that it was Parker who should be charged with promoting hate.[36] To no avail. In 2005, Ahenakew was found guilty of inciting hatred, fined $1,000, and stripped of his Order of Canada. His sentence was overturned by the Saskatchewan Court of Queen's

Bench on the grounds that the judge had failed to properly take into account the context of Ahenakew's statements that came out in an angry confrontation with a reporter, and therefore may not have constituted willful hatred. He was tried again in 2008 and acquitted again in 2009, "because his statements, while "revolting, disgusting and untrue" did not "show an intent to incite hatred." He was never reinstated as a member of the Order of Canada.

National Chief of the Assembly of First Nations Matthew Coon Come condemned Ahenakew, but former Roseau River chief Terrance Nelson accused the Canadian government of attempting to commit genocide, asserted Ahenakew was a "victim of Jewish-controlled media". Why didn't the judge just throw the whole thing out and ask the native leaders to deal with it?

Native control of their own affairs should be part of any 'grand bargain' with the state, something that has been sorely lacking in Canada's relations with its First Nations. Justin Trudeau promised to rewrite government relations with the natives, but has done nothing much, beyond throwing some money at education, health and investigations into rape, suicide and murder of women, an easy cynical photo op.

Native Political Resurgence

Among the highest profile native activist leaders is **Terrance Nelson**, vice chair of the American Indian Movement, former chief of Manitoba's Roseau River First Nation. He says, "The First Nations still don't seem to understand how we finance all Canadians. Unless the Defenders and Idle No More develop a strategy based on economics there will be no change of government policies. I have been called an 'economic terrorist' since 1993 because I used the Bond Rating Agencies to pressure government on the Treaty Land Entitlement and Land Claims issue." He criticized the Museum of Human Rights[37] for its huge expense, an albatross for the government donated by Asper, "inviting the world to view the sins of Germany and the holocaust. In the meantime, the denial of the North American holocaust, the Genocide of the indigenous people of the Western Hemisphere continues to be ignored."

No junkets to Israel for Nelson. Instead, he went to Tehran in October 2012, shortly before Harper severed diplomatic relations with Iran in December 2012 and was received by high level officials who offered help getting Canada's natives a seat at OPEC and to discuss resource development and human rights abuses in Canada. Harper shut down the Iranian embassy in Ottawa because they met with us. Nelson said Iranians and Canada's natives have a lot in common as victims of European colonialism.

Nelson explained to the Iranians that at the same time that Canada was establishing independence at Confederation in 1876, the less celebrated Indian Act was passed, confirming the expropriation of native lands that had taken place since the first white settlers came, and the relegation of natives to reserves under the federal government's authority. His Iranian colleagues told him how in Iran at that time, British capitalists were bribing the corrupt Nasser al-Din Shah to allow them to control the entire Persian economy. Britain and Russia occupied Iran during both WWI and WWII, and Britain and the US orchestrated two regime changes—in 1941 and 1953—to make sure Iranian oil was in their hands. A century of invasion, subversion and rule by more western-backed shahs finally ended in 1979, when Khomeini brought western domination to an abrupt end, but in the process turned Iran into the West's *bête noire*, demonized in the mainstream media ever since.

According to APTN (Aboriginal Peoples Television Network), Nelson and former Dakota Tipi chief Dennis Pashe were told at meetings with government officials and academics that the Iranian government is willing to back First Nations leaders if they want to address OPEC, to get a better deal on the 2.5 million barrels a day of oil that is pumped from Indigenous territories and sent by Canada to the US each year. Nelson plans to tell OPEC that the native people of Canada are the true owners of Canada's petroleum resources. "We call upon the government of Canada to consider the experiences of other countries regarding fair distribution of the natural resource income. The OPEC nations have had a similar history in dealing with colonial powers." Nelson met with Mohammad Larijani, Iran's secretary for the High Council for Human Rights, who told him, "As we defend the rights of people in Bahrain, Iraq, Afghanistan and Palestine in the international organizations, we will also defend Canada's Aboriginal population. Canada has exploited and even committed genocide against the Aboriginal people rather than investing in their treasure of cultural and civilization wealth."

The only Canadian public response to Nelsen's efforts to help his people was to accuse him of treason, of consorting with the enemy, an 'enemy' which has never threatened Canada, the US or any other nation with aggression. The First Nation leader was grilled by the *National Post* in a joint interview with Iranian-born anti-Iran activist (former Miss World Canada) Nazanin Afshin-Jam, who also just happened to be the wife of Defence Minister Peter MacKay. She called Nelson's trip "a real insult to Iranians, Canadians and the entire international community" and accused Iran of wanting "to use him for the purposes of demonizing Canada in forums such as the UN Human Rights Council". When asked to condemn Iran on human rights abuses, Nelson pointed out that there are serious human rights abuses in Canada which are not given prominence in the mainstream media. He complained that the hysteria in the media made it very difficult for him to pursue his efforts to gain recognition for Canada's native people. "What the western media says is not always true. Nobody gave a damn about half-a-million children dying in Iraq in 1998. Harper shut down the Iranian embassy in Ottawa because they met with us. I asked them in an email 'Was the decision to shut down the Iranian embassy made by caucus or in Peter MackKay's bedroom?'" Nelsen told me.[38]

When it was suggested that the Iranian government would enlist First Nations to perpetrate violence against Canada, he laughed. "When have First Nations people ever bombed anything? The worst we've ever done is make the white man late for lunch when we do our protests in the city street." He accused the West of perpetrating insidious violence against countries it victimizes through sanctions, including against both Iraq in the 1990s and Iran today. He said his hope was to break down the unjustified bias against Iran. "We know what demonization is all about because we've been demonized in our own land." Nelson praised Tehran for raising the human rights issues of indigenous people in Canada and called for the Non-Aligned Movement, which Iran presided over at the time, to address the plight of Canada's aboriginal population. As for Afshin-Jam's claim that the Iranian government was using native Canadians to blacken Canada's reputation at the UN, there is no need, as there was lots of evidence of Canadian government neglect of human rights under the Harper regime. At the top of the list he brought to Tehran was Harper's defunding of five human rights NGOS—the International Centre for Human Rights and Democratic Development, the Canadian Human Rights Commission, KAIROS, Status of Women Canada and the Court Challenges Program—addressing issues affecting tens of thousands of Canadians and victims of violence around the world.

"We were warned not to go to Iran, and western media have consistently tried to dehumanize and demonize the Iranian people. The people of Iran are nothing like the lies told in western media," said Nelson on Iran's PressTV. The Iranian NGO Peace Lovers Society agreed to provide university scholarships to 10 First Nations students to study in Iran in the area of oil and gas, medicine and economics. Iranians have a lot to teach Canadians about oil and imperial greed.

The ongoing **Idle No More** movement of Canada's natives was sparked in 2012 by a new stage in the government's 'final solution' of assimilation of the natives—the Harper government's omnibus bill C-45, passed in 2012, which abrogated the Indian Act, ending native sovereignty. Canada's natives desperately need a genuine 'new deal' to overcome centuries of abuse to reconstruct some semblance of the multicultural nation that 'North America' once was. But twisting compliant Native leaders' arms to allow corporations to build, say, liquefied natural gas terminals on the west coast, chromite mining and smelting projects in the James Bay "Ring of Fire", not to mention the tar sands, paying off natives with dollars, is not the answer. What benefits are there for people who revere Nature, in oil exploration, coal mining, dam construction, clear-cut logging, and nuclear waste storage?

Founded by four native women in Saskatchewan, Idle No More's catalyst was Attawapiskat Chief Theresa Spence's month-long hunger strike near Parliament Hill in December 2012, spearheaded by native activists, and joined by other Canadians opposed to the agenda. It was hailed by similar groups in the US who are opposed to the neoliberal agenda. The "Forward on Climate" march in 2013 in Washington DC gave Obama the courage to cancel the Keystone pipeline (since renewed by Trump). But there are other pipelines in both the US and Canada planned and underway. The one at Standing Rock, North Dakota, was delayed by protests, but approved by Trump as soon as he took power. And Trudeau Jr approved the Kinder-Morgan pipeline through the Rocky Mountains, despite opposition by close to half of Canadians and 2/3 of BC residents.[39] The new environmental awareness in the face of the corporate agenda on both sides of the 'border' is bringing natives and non-native activist together.

In Ontario, former NDP premier Bob Rae, a strong supporter of Israel whose wife was a vice president of the CJC, is now the natives' negotiator with the mining interests in the James Bay 'ring of fire'. However nice elder statesman Rae may be, his common interests—economic and political—with Farber and Harper remained. Clearly, the natives need a new deal with corporate Canada, but the option of "No!"

must be on the table, not just the flimsy right to be consulted, and some form of payoff. So far the natives have not been able to prevail when the state decides a pipeline or dam is "in the national interest". There are hints of what a new dispensation might entail, and the suddenly pro-native Zionist supporters like Farber and Rae have nothing to contribute to it. An example of a new approach is the 1987 Gwaii Haanas National Park and Haida Heritage Site, which allows Haida to regulate logging and maintain their sacred forests, permitting sustainable use of some natural resources. Thomas Berger called for re-tribalization of lands: "As long as the land is a corporate asset, it will be vulnerable."[40]

Idle No More speaks for all Canadians against the 1% who so eagerly sell out Canada's resources and smirch its reputation in the world. As Naomi Klein pointed out, "The greatest blessing of all is indigenous sovereignty itself. If Canadians have a chance of stopping Harper's planet-trashing plans, it will be because these legally binding rights–backed up by mass movements, court challenges, and direct action–will stand in his way."[41] Not only do Canada's natives empower all Canadians against the 1%, they also help us understand the injustice of Canada's actions in Palestine and Iran, countries whose peoples love Canada and root for our natives, whose struggle against the imperial order is their struggle too. At the end of Amy Goodman's video of Stand Rock protesters in 2016 that electrified the world, an unknown man with a raw voice and pained face poignantly says it all, "No one owns this land. This land belongs to the earth. We are only caretakers. We're caretakers of the earth."[42]

Natives in Canada fought for their land once they understood what the friendly new immigrants had in mind by the term 'ownership', but were overwhelmed by the wily and land-hungry colons, and today represent only 3% of Canada's population, living for the most part short, bleak lives in dire poverty on the dregs of land allotted them by the victors. But resistance is alive and well. Idle No More has swept Canada since Spence pitched her tent near Parliament Hill.

The Middle East also has seen resistance. Egyptians have risen up four times since Disraeli's coup in 1878, eventually taking back the Canal and, at least for a few years following the 2011 Arab Spring, were fashioning a new political order inspired not by western imperial dictates, but by the Quran. Iran finally had its revolution in 1979 and has been affronting the imperial monster ever since, telling truth to the world's would-be masters. Palestinian resistance is legendary, but so far has had primarily diplomatic triumphs, few actual territorial successes.

The Berger Report recommended that, "on environmental grounds, no pipeline be built and no energy corridor be established across the Northern Yukon" and that any pipeline construction be postponed until native claims could be settled. For Berger, Canada is divided into two parts: Indigenous nations and everyone else. In his speech to Citizens for Public Justice in June 2005 "My Idea of Canada" he states:

> I think diversity has become the essence of the Canadian experience and it is our strength. It's not a weakness. We're not addicted to bogus patriotism. We believe in diversity. We believe in being a good citizen of the world. Canada "could be the prototype nation state of the 21st century in which a citizen's identity does not have to be authenticated by a spurious nationalism."[43]

This is something that Zionists will cringe reading, as it applies equally to their proposed "Jewish" state of Israel and those Canadians who look to Israel as their chief homeland.

Endnotes

1. In *Clearing the Plains: Disease, Politics of Starvation, and the Loss of Aboriginal Life* (2013), James Daschuk argued that famine was a conscious settlement strategy to "create ecological conditions in which disease exploded."
2. Kate Fillion, "Maclean's Interview: John Ralston Saul", *Maclean's*, September 25, 2008
3. Bob Joseph, "Indigenous or Aboriginal Which is Correct?", www.ictinc.ca/blog/, January 5, 2016. and "Back to the Future: PM-Designate Trudeau Evokes the Royal Proclamation", www.ictinc.ca/blog/, October 26, 2015.
4. < http://www.bankofcanada.ca/ banknotes/banknote150/>
5. <http://www.ccsd.ca/resources/CrimePrevention/c_ab.htm>, <http://www.justice.gc.ca/eng/rp-pr/cj-jp/victim/rd3-rr3/p3.html>
6. Nancy Macdonald, "Canada's prisons are the 'new residential schools'", Macleans, February 18, 2016.
7. Wilson-Raybould was regional chief of the British Columbia Assembly of First Nations.
8. According to the UK-based Minority Rights Group, the most prominent organization addressing international law and minority rights, the Palestinians are indeed indigenous. World Directory of Minority and Indigenous Peoples: Palestine, <http://www.refworld.org/docid/4954ce4d23.html> See also, *inter alia*, Hazem Bazian, "The Indigenous Palestinians," *Harvard International Review*, March 23, 2014. <http://hir.harvard.edu/article/?a=3234> It is a view hotly denied by Israelis, whose perspective has found its way into an article in *Indian Country Today* by Ryan Bellerose, "Don't Mix Indigenous Fight with

	Palestinian Rights," January 11, 2014, countering the earlier December 31, 2013 article "'Redwashing' Panel Follows Academic Associations' Boycott of Israel" on *IndianCountryTodayMediaNetwork.com*
9	The court rejected a petition filed by the Al Uqbi family to recognize its ownership over a large plot of land in Israel's Negev/Naqab Desert. The land also includes the unrecognized village Al Arakib, which is still in its own legal battle for recognition from the state. According to Attorney Michael Sfard, who represented the Ul Uqbi family, no one is arguing with the fact that the family has been living in this area for centuries. However, the ruling does not recognize the family's ownership of the land. Mairav Zonszein, "Israel Supreme Court: Bedouin have no indigenous rights", *https://intercontinentalcry.org/*, June 9, 2015.
10	UNSG, Report to the GA, A/67/372, 14 September, 2015. 2012, par. 55.
11	Tova Cohen, "Israel's Mediterranean a "septic tank?"", Reuters, October 17, 2007.
12	Labrador's Muskrat Falls was able to gain national attention despite being very "out of sight and mind for a lot of the Canadian public" due to an effective harnessing of social media. (James Wilt, "How 22 Hydroelectric Projects in Canada Put First Nations Communities at Risk", *vice.com*, Nov 28, 2016.)
13	Katy Yan, "Canada's Hydro Partnerships No Panacea for First Nations", *World Rivers Review*, June 9, 2010.
14	<http://www.ifamericansknew.org/cur_sit/water.html>http://www.palestinecenter.org/
15	Robert Laboucane, "Canada's Aboriginal education crisis", Aboriginal Multi-Media Society, *Windspeaker*, Vol. 28, number 7, 2010. <http://www.ammsa.com/publications/windspeaker/canada%E2%80%99s-aboriginal-education-crisis-column>
16	<http://www.statcan.gc.ca/pub/89-645-x/2010001/education-eng.htm> and <http://www.statcan.gc.ca/pub/89-656-x/89-656-x2015001-eng.htm>
17	There are several Arab-language teacher training colleges, including in Haifa.
18	Kate Shuttleworth, "For Arabs in Israel, Curriculum Choice Is Politically Charged", *New York Times*, January 19, 2014.
19	Kenneth Bandler, "On My Mind: Tackling Israeli-Arab education", *jpost.com*, February 18, 2013. A handful of Arabs go through the hurdles to join the IDF, but even if they survive what for them is at best an unpleasant experience, their service record is of little real help. See Introduction, endnote 7.
20	The US federal arbitration law, passed by Congress in 1925, allows religious tribunals, and their judgments are given force of law by state and federal courts. US Jews have had their *beth din* religious courts for more than a century, and there are now Christian conciliators for those Christians who prefer canon law to the secular law of the land. US courts "have been positively encouraging [its] use since the 1980s" for inheritance, business, and matrimonial disputes, sorted out by Islamic scholars according to the sharia. "The precepts of Islamic law, like those of other religious codes, therefore have judicial force in the US already." (Sadakat Kadri, *Heaven on Earth: A Journey Through Sharia Law from the Deserts of Ancient Arabia to the Streets of the Modern Muslim World*, New York: Farrar, Straus and Giroux, 2012.)
21	The introduction of sharia law in Ontario, Canada, was effectively recommended by a 2004 report. Family faith-based tribunals had been set up by Catholic and

	Jewish communities following the passing of the province's Arbitration Act in 1991. The move, intended to lighten the overloaded civil courts, was quashed, and all religious courts were annulled.
22	The Aboriginal Justice Implementation Commission formed in 1999 in Manitoba issued its last report on 2001 without implementing any changes. <http://www.ajic.mb.ca/implementation.pdf> The BC Ministry of Children and Family Development issued "The Road to Aboriginal Authority over Child and Family Services Considerations for an Effective Transition" (2008) which states its intent to implement indigenous self-determination and control over family law. But it was not serious about adjusting legal rights, and was never followed up. <https://ihraamorg.files.wordpress.com/2016/12/the-road-to-aboriginal-authority-over-child-and-family-services-ccpa_bc_aboriginal_authority.pdf> At the National Aboriginal Law CLE Conference March 4-5, 2005, it was recognized that the government pledges that "matters relating to traditional land holding, the role of elders in the administration of customary practices, legal proceedings and leadership authority have been explicitly provided for in legislation and constitutional provisions." But it is admitted that "Indigenous legal traditions on customary Indigenous governments and leadership processes, their decisions and decision-making processes, and traditional Indigenous dispute resolution processes" have not been seriously addressed. "Canada acknowledges Indigenous peoples' inherent rights to govern themselves in relation to matters that are internal to their communities, integral to their unique cultures, identities, traditions, languages and institutions, and with respect to their special relationship to their land and resources. What is required is acknowledgment and acceptance of these practices and values as Indigenous legal traditions having a legitimate place within Canada's juridical system." (Lisa D. Chartrand, "For the Indigenous Bar Association in Canada", March 2005. <http://www.indigenousbar.ca/pdf/Indigenous%20Legal%20Traditions.pdf>) In Manitoba in 2003, the Child and Family Services Authorities Act created a new child welfare system in Manitoba. This law allows authorities for the Northern and Southern First Nations and a Metis authority to develop and deliver Aboriginal child welfare services for their own people. Aboriginal Justice Inquiry - Child Welfare Initiative website at: www.aji-cwi.mb.ca. <http://www.gov.mb.ca/justice/family/law/pubs/familylawbooklet2014.pdf>
23	At Abuse Wiki, "Jewish exodus from Arab and Muslim lands", <http://abuse.wikia.com/wiki/Jewish_exodus_from_Arab_and_Muslim_lands#cite_ref-Bermani_19-0> citing Bermani, Daphna, "Sephardi Jewry at odds over reparations from Arab world". November 14, 2003. <http://wings.buffalo.edu/academic/department/law/jlsa/jews_arab_lands.htm> Wikipedia's entry looks lower: 859,100 (15.53%) from Africa, 681,400 (12.33%) from Asia, 1,939,400 (35.11%) from Europe/ America, but includes 'father born in Israel' 2,043,800 (37%). <https://en.wikipedia.org/wiki/Demographics_of_Israel>
24	This affinity is most visible in political terms. For affinity between native spirituality and Islam, see the writings of Frithjof Schuon. An important documentary source on native spirituality is by Joseph Brown, *The Spiritual Legacy of the American Indian*, World Wisdom, 2007. Also my *From Postmodernism to Postsecularism*, 200.
25	Buhle, op.cit., 4-5.

26	Red Haircrow, "Germany's Obsession With American Indians Is Touching—And Occasionally Surreal", <https://indiancountrymedianetwork.com/>, March 24, 2013.
27	Penslar, op.cit., 47.
28	One of the foremost proponents of the belief that the American Indian is descended from the Ten Lost Tribes was the trader James Adair (c.1709–1783). In 1775 he wrote *The History of the Indians*. Some of his proofs include: Their division into tribes. Their worship of J-hov-h. Their notions of a theocracy. Their language and dialects. Their change of names adapted to their circumstances and times. Another proponent of this theory was William Penn (1644–1718), the founder of Pennsylvania. Geneticists at an Israeli hospital said they have found a unique Jewish genetic mutation among an American Indian tribe, indicating that they are descendants of Jews expelled from Spain 600 years ago. The findings of the study, conducted at the Sheba Medical Center near Tel Aviv, show that a group of Indians from the State of Colorado bear the so-called "Ashkenazi mutation," on the BRCA1 gene—a marker unique to European Jews. (*Haaretz*, May 30, 2012)<http://www.vosizneias.com/107039/2012/05/30/israel-researchers-find-american-indians-with-jewish-genetic-markers/>
29	Phil Fontaine, Michael Dan, Bernkie Farber, "A Canadian genocide in search of a name", *Toronto Star*, July 19, 2013.
30	See Introduction endnote 9 and citation.
31	James Craven, Indians, Jews, Palestinians and Zionists, https://www.linkedin.com/pulse/indians-jews-palestinians-zionists-james-craven-1 , July 9, 2015.
32	Noam Bedein, "Canadian First Nations To Stand With Israel Against IAW", *SderotMediaCenter*, February 13, 2012.
33	"Israel: The World's First Modern Indigenous State", *Arutz Sheva*, January 14, 1014.
34	In 2008, the Sovereign Nation of the Coushatta Indiana Tribe of Louisiana was the first Native American tribe to establish a formal relationship with Israel, The following year the tribe took a delegation to Israel which resulted in their first Israel-related venture, becoming the exclusive distributor of Aya Natural, an Israeli skincare company based in the Druze community of Beit Jann in the Galilee. David Sickey, the head of the tribe, has made a number of visits there, as has Navajo Nation President Ben Shelly. But the visit created a torrent of letters to the *Navajo Times* against President Shelly's visit and an op-ed in *Indian Country Today* opposing Joy Harjo's visit, sponsored by supporters of the BDS movement. Janene Yazzie from Lupton, Arizona, writes: "It should not shock or surprise us that our Navajo Nation President Ben Shelly has taken an unexpected trip to visit Israel, a government that has committed itself to carrying out genocidal practices against its population of indigenous Palestinian peoples. To hear that our president believes the apartheid government of Israel has more to offer than the Dene people in his homeland fighting against his policies is hurtful and unbelievably ignorant. I stand in solidarity with the people of Palestine and those indigenous nations and non-indigenous peoples fighting against continued corporate, religious, and political exploitation." Dina Gilio-Whitaker in *Indian Country Today*: "This week Muscogee Creek scholar and literary diva Joy Harjo ignited a firestorm of controversy when she announced on Facebook that she was leaving for a trip to Israel where she was scheduled to perform on Monday, December 10, at Tel Aviv University. The

controversy came when friends and fans challenged her decision to go in light of the US Academic and Cultural Boycott of Israel (USACBI) and the Palestine Campaign for the Academic and Cultural Boycott of Israel (PACBI), as part of a larger boycott, divestment and sanctions (BDS) movement. The problem with someone as high profile as Joy Harjo collaborating with an institution like Tel Aviv University (which is built on top of an ethnically cleansed Palestinian village) is that it sends a message that she as a Native American represents all Native Americans in support of apartheid Israel's domination of Palestinians. I, for one, don't want to be associated with that."

35   Robinson, op.cit. 146, <http://www.cbc.ca/news/canada/charge-reporter-with-hate-crime-ahenakew-s-lawyer-1.561003>

36   Even as the trial was in progress, Parker was hired for a senior communications job with Indian and Northern Affairs Canada, and promptly launched a suit against former Saskatoon-Humboldt MP Pankiw for defaming him by saying this was a reward for years of praising the government's race-based agenda while at *The StarPhoenix*. He didn't win, but had the RCMP probe Pankiw for defamation and for threatening him, leaving a further legacy of anger and hate.

37   See Chapter 5.

38   The reference is to the US-instigated UN sanctions policy applied to Iraq, leading to even greater deaths among the population as a whole. The reference to MacKay's bedroom concerned Nelson's jab as he was being interviewed in the *National Post* along with MacKay's Iranian wife who was a former Miss Universe Canada. < http://nationalpost.com/news/canada/concern-that-first-nations-will-be-used-as-pawns-as-former-chief-to-meet-iranian-leaders/wcm/7031e8d7-3d1a-4ddb-a020-097b430eeac6>

39   <https://www.burnaby.ca/Assets/TMEP/Public+Opinion+Poll.pdf>

40   "Natives and Israel: Manipulating genocide", *ericwalberg.com*, July 27, 2013.

41   Naomi Klein, "As Chief Spence starves, Canadians awaken from idleness and remember their roots", *Globe and Mail*, December 24, 2012.

42   <http://www.defenddemocracy.press/amy-goodman-faced-jail-time-reporting-dakota-access-pipeline-scare-us/>

43   <https://cpj.ca/thomas-berger-my-idea-canada>

| Chapter Nine |

THE NEW ANTISEMITES: TARRING ANTI-ZIONISM

Harper talked about a "new anti-Semitism", as if bigotry just naturally wells up in Gentiles every generation and must be fought remorselessly to keep the innocent Jews safe. But there is no 'new' 'bigotry'. Anti-Jewish prejudice increased in Canadian history due to clear causes: the sudden deluge pre-WWI of poor immigrants with foreign ways, gravitating to the large, overwhelmingly Christian cities, demanding special treatment, then disproportionately outperforming at universities. After 1948, just as these immigrants were being fully accepted by Canadian society, large numbers among them suddenly began embracing a dual nationality with another newly-emerged state that was engaged in willfully violating the rights of the natives, then started promoting that state stridently in Canadian politics and through media where it had achieved outsize corporate control.

Most of the non-Israeli catalysts for anti-Jewish prejudice are gone. Until the 1950s, the non-Jewish majority tried to implement restrictions on education and property ownership, accepting that Jews were masters of scholarship and commerce, and would on average outperform non-Jews. But in our postmodern multicultural mix, many ethnicities now vie for first place and these restrictions are a thing of the past. It is no longer taken for granted that any ethnicity stands above any other anymore except for the special place First Nations should be entitled to hold (but do not), and all are expected to be first and foremost Canadians, with no dual loyalty. The claim by Zionists that the motherland of all Jews everywhere is Israel is like a red alert.

This is happening at a time when Canadians are learning more about their own historic sins against Canada's native peoples, and the native peoples in turn are becoming more aware of the unfinished decolonialization struggles of other indigenous peoples around the world. They all cry out for social justice, and Canadians, with their large and increasingly prominent Jewish minority, expect those Jewish Canadians and the Canadian government to also be on the forefront of those struggles, which means as critics of Israel in the first place. Jewish Canadians can best fight residual anti-Jewish prejudice in Canada by fighting for justice for those oppressed by the State of Israel. Some view it as not merely a choice, but an obligation, an essential part of the struggle against any residual anti-Jewish prejudice in Canadian society.

Secular Activists

That is the '**new anti-Zionism**', one that brings Jewish Canadians, Muslim/Arab Canadians, all Canadians together. It embodies the 'good Jew', the universalism of conservative and reform Judaism (the Reuben Slonims, Satmar,[1] International Jewish Voices), the secular communists (the Bill Walshes, David Nobles, Anton Kuertis), those who genuinely belong in Canada and the world's progressive elite. Not the Bronfmans or Munks, their eyes on Eretz Israel, with a third temple arising in Jerusalem,.

Universities have traditionally been the hotbed of idealism and concern for social justice, where youthful energies, passions and intellectual curiosity at times explode in defiance of established truisms, looking for ways to make the world better. The struggles were solidly left-wing a century ago, with the communists at the forefront. Then, only the communists clearly stood against all forms of racism and exploitation, challenging the ethnic and class rigidities of the imperial order. They had no use for Zionism, which rapidly gained ground in the 1930s with the very real threat of Nazism to Jews, and the refusal of the anticommunist elite to fight it, but communists like Bill Walsh stuck by a Canadian identity, counting on socialism to eradicate all forms of prejudice. Their mantra was: "We want to make things better *here.*"

Those days are gone. Communists served their immediate purpose, helping to bring unions and universal health care. The Soviet Union was their foil, pushing the Canadian government to enact reforms, but it was never their motherland. And then, the communist experiment failed to achieve 'peace on earth'.

Most Jews turned to Zionism after World War II. Other groups also found their activist niches, with the era of "identity politics" replacing class politics. From the 1970s onward, advances were made in civil rights for all social groups—ethnicities, women, gays. As environmental concerns increased, Greens seemed to take the lead in the struggle for social justice.

Now Israel has become a major concern on campuses, with Muslims outnumbering Jews in the population, some of them Palestinians, putting their sad plight directly in front of Canadians. As Islam is universalist, they easily make alliances with other students seeking social justice by appealing to universally-accepted values. Zionist tribalism can never be a passion for more than a tiny minority of Canadians, nor urge its case within a universalist framework. With today's international problems mostly coming from the Middle East, all of them touching Israel and its ongoing, illegal colonization of Palestine, students naturally try to do something to address the underlying issues. They have found the best avenue to be the Boycott, Divestment, Sanctions (BDS) movement against Israel.

Despite federal and Ontario provincial motions condemning BDS, students are defiant, disappointed that Canada's supposed democratic politicians support not the victim, but the aggressor. The motions changed no one's mind. If legal prohibitions have any effect, it is to increase Israel's status as a pariah state, and anti-Jewish prejudice, as the prohibitions are seen to be the result of vigorous Jewish lobbying, and negatively highlight Jewish power in Canada. More foot shooting.

But this attempt to legislate a ban on boycotting Israeli goods is not new. The **Arab boycott of Israel** began in 1948 and took a quantum leap with the 1973 oil crisis, when the members of the Organization of Arab Petroleum Exporting Countries (OAPEC)[2] announced an oil embargo, when the US supplied arms to Israel during the 1973 Yom Kippur War. The OAPEC embargo targeted Canada, Japan, the Netherlands, Britain and the US.[3] The Zionists lobbied federal and provincial governments to pass laws preventing Canadian companies from complying with the Arab boycott. Trudeau Sr waffled, as he was trying to promote better ties with Arab countries while keeping out of Israeli sights. Ontario premier Bill Davis was more amenable and passed a flimsy bill to mollify the Israel lobbyists, which was ignored. BDS was still only a glimmer in the as yet nascent pro-Palestinian movement.

The old anti-boycott law is still on the books, and Ontario Premier Wynne's bill against BDS, hot on the heels of Trudeau's, merely dusted it off. It still is not such a threat, more a finger-wagging, yet further proof of how monolithic (at least on paper) the Israel lobby is. Canada currently has sanctions against 19 countries, including Iran, Russia, and Zimbabwe.[4] It is fine for the government to impose sanctions, but for some reason, it is considered wrong for citizens to be able to boycott. Canadians disagree. Already two-thirds of all Canadians say it is time not only for citizens, but for the government to impose sanctions on Israel.[5]

The Jewish lobby in Canada lobbied in league with Israel. The **Green Party**, which finally adopted a BDS policy, was pushed to withdraw it. The lobby managed to get the leadership to make a compromise approved by 84% of members, but couldn't force the grassroots party to back down. The compromise "calls for consumer boycotts, institutional divestment and other sanctions to pressure Israel over Jewish settlements in occupied territories."[6] In February 2017, the Greens defiantly adopted a stronger resolution, including a call for an arms embargo, for the Canadian government to recognize the state of Palestine, and for the International Criminal Court to prioritize its investigation into potential Israeli war crimes. The Green Parties (England and Wales, Scotland) have been more resolute.

The holes in the dyke are multiplying. The Israeli Knesset passed a strong anti-BDS law in March 2017 to stop the leaks, but the Israeli desperation did not play well in the US, prompting leftist US Jewish groups, including J Street, Americans for Peace Now, Ameinu, the New Israel Fund and T'ruah, a rabbinical human rights group, to condemn it. Even the American Jewish Committee and Anti-Defamation League joined the chorus. AJC CEO David Harris said that "barring otherwise qualified visitors on the basis of their personal views will not by itself defeat BDS, nor will it help Israel's image as the beacon of democracy in the Middle East it is, or offer them opportunities to expose them to the exciting and pulsating reality of Israel."[7]

In 2014, the Canadian Federation of Students' Ontario branch, representing 300,000 students, joined BDS. The latest student campaign was in Trudeau's Montreal, where McGill BDS was formed in February 2016. The anti-BDS parliamentary motion made it easy for the Board of Governors' Committee to Advise on Matters of Social Responsibility to reject the student-led motion. The new 'law' against BDS did not stop Israeli Apartheid Week events across Canada in March. The University of Toronto Divest Campaign in 2016 featured presentations by Kwara Kekana (BDS-South Africa) and Amanda Lickers, activist at Reclaim Turtle Island.

The churches are less cowardly than university administrators and politicians. The United Church and the Quakers both refuse to invest their funds in Israel. The Postal Workers' Union, Canadian Union of Public Employees (Ontario branch), the Confédération des syndicats nationaux in Quebec, all voted to join BDS including an end to trade in military goods and a boycott of Canadian firms such as Indigo/Chapters[8] that support the Israeli military occupation. The boycotts around the world extend to academicians and entertainers, including Pink Floyd singer Roger Waters and writer Alice Walker. Canadian celebrity boycotters face greater pushback compared to British and American performers, given the more conservative Jewish community and the more powerful Jewish lobbies in Canada. So far, few Canadian artists other than Anton Kuerti have spoken out strongly against Israel and refused to perform there.

Neither the Conservatives nor the Liberals have dared make support of BDS a criminal activity, which could ignite mass civil disobedience, resulting in hundreds of political prisoners. Canadians for Justice and Peace in the Middle East President Thomas Woodley countered that possibility with a "Go Ahead, Make My Day, Condemn Me" country-wide flash campaign, inviting Canadians to sign up for a packet of free "Boycott Israel" sticky notes to post at local stores on Israeli merchandise. Finally, the West is joining—with great resistance—the Muslims in their 70-year old boycott campaign.

There are dissenting voices among leading anti-Zionist critics from the US and Britain about the value of BDS:

- Finkelstein and Chomsky: Its "hypocrisy is so transparent ... why not boycott the United States? ... Israeli crimes [are] a fragment of US crimes, which are much worse."[9] While Finkelstein possibly sought balance, it's impossible to boycott the US in a world of globalization dominated by the US. Chomsky argued that the Palestinian people don't support boycotting Israel and that the BDS movement is run by "one man NGOs", who falsely claim to represent the Palestinian people.[10] Finkelstein might be forgiven for wanting to target the US after all that he has suffered, but Chomsky has long served as head goose well able to veer the flock off into directions less harmful to Israel. You can't fight the dragon in its den. Israel is the offspring of US imperialism, and an excellent place to start educating people as to the wider enemy. It is above all necessary to mobilize US public opinion on mistaken US foreign policy, where Israel stands out as contrary to US professed beliefs in evenhandedness and accepted international standards on human rights. Chomsky would leave critics with nothing.

- Gilad Atzmon, who on the other hand criticizes the BDS movement from a radical anti-Zionist position, complaining the BDS movement limits debate among supporters of the Palestinians due to their concern about alienating Jews who still support Israel as a *Jewish* state.[11] This is indeed a dilemma, as many (most?) Jews still maintain 'Jewishness' as their primary signifier, and aren't ready to fully reject Zionist ideology. Such a radical stance implies abandoning the notion of a special ontological status and a unique history of victimization, and even critiquing Jewishness and Judaism itself as stumbling blocks to dismantling Israeli Apartheid. "Even the Palestinian solidarity movement is shy of the topic. Why? Because the Palestinian solidarity movement is also dominated," says Atzmon, "by similar Jewish institutions such as Jewish Voices for Peace, JFJFP [Jews for Justice for Palestinians] etc. In other words, the voice of the oppressed is shaped by the oppressor and oppressor's sensitivities."[12]

As both Chomsky and Atzmon are Jewish, their polemic itself is a reflection of the Jewish traditional dual role as social critic within empire, unafraid to criticize the Jewish elite role within imperialism. As such, they stimulate further debate, sharpening the skills of those who want direct action against Israel now.

The debate around the BDS parliamentary motions was lively in the mainstream press, mobilizing commentators who otherwise wouldn't touch Israeli matters. The public groundswell and the Green Party head Elizabeth May's threat to resign galvanized NDP ex-candidate Linda McQuaig to risk her party links with an eloquent op-ed in the *Toronto Star*.

She appealed to May to stay the course, emphasizing Canada's complicity in Israeli crimes, and the need to take a controversial stand when justice demands it. "Back in the 1980s, it was divisive when Prime Minister Brian Mulroney imposed sanctions against the white-minority regime in South Africa. Today, everyone agrees that Mulroney's stance was laudable. But at the time it was highly controversial, with Mulroney acting in defiance of business leaders, members of his own cabinet and caucus, as well as British Prime Minister Margaret Thatcher and US President Ronald Reagan. Some consider it unfair to compare Israel with South Africa. But Archbishop Desmond Tutu considers the comparison valid."[13]

The debate was heartening to BDS activists, as it proved they were having an impact. 2016 saw a surge of successes:

- French telecom giant, Orange, pulled out of Israel.
- Four UN agencies in Jordan and one in Lebanon ended their contracts with the British security giant G4S, pushing it to sell its operations in Israel.
- In Britain, a test case for banning BDS campaigning failed in the high court.
- More than 50 cities across Spain now declare themselves "Apartheid-free zones", free of all Israeli products, in a campaign that began in July 2014, at the height of Israel's invasion of Gaza.
- Norwegian cities voted to boycott Israeli goods and services produced in settlements inside occupied Palestinian territory.
- US Presbyterians reaffirmed their previous commitments to divestment. Lutherans voted to call for an end to US aid to Israel. Other Christian denominations less boldly call for "economic leverage" against businesses or governments that violate human rights.
- In Massachusetts, an anti-boycott amendment was withdrawn in the state senate in July following a campaign by Palestine solidarity groups.

BDS is having an impact. A 2014 UN report found that foreign investment in Israel had dropped almost by half from the previous year, partly because of the campaign.[14] But there's been huge push-back. US casino billionaire Sheldon Adelson brought 50 groups to Las Vegas last year to organize a strategy for fighting BDS.[15] The Zionists have been much more active in the US, working at state and federal levels. After the American Studies Association (ASA) became the second academic association (after the Association for Asian American Studies) to pass a resolution endorsing the academic boycott of Israel in 2013, US Congress, New York, Illinois and Maryland state legislatures introduced bills to defund colleges/universities that subsidize groups that boycott Israel.

Israel lobbyists mounted waves of **legislation** in local, state, and federal legislatures in 2014–15. Eighteen states have passed motions condemning BDS.[16] In June 2015, Obama got "fast track" authorization that would have charged US trade negotiators of the Trans-Pacific Partnership to ensure that anti-BDS provisions are included, targeting European and Asian countries. "This is an historic milestone in the fight against Israel's enemies, as American opposition to insidious efforts to demonize and isolate the Jewish state is now the law of the land. The bipartisan bill enacted today conditions any free trade agreement with the European Union on its rejection of BDS," said Republican Peter Roskam, who, together with Republican Juan Vargas sponsored one of two anti-BDS provisions. This law died with TPP, but like Canada's anti-BDS resolutions, emphasizes the clout of the Israel lobby.

The battle continues. The pro-Israel crowd are on the defensive. In August 2016, Israeli Strategic Affairs Minister Gilad Erdan, the Israeli official in charge of combating the BDS movement, and Interior Minister Aryeh Deri, formed a task force to prevent the entry of foreign activists into Israel affiliated with organizations that support BDS, and to expel those already there. "This is a necessary step, given the evil intentions of the delegitimization activists working to spread lies and distortions about the reality in our region."[17]

Since **Israeli Apartheid Week** (IAW) began in Toronto in 2005, it has spread to at least 55 cities around the world. It is especially strong in the US. It is picketed by the JDL and Hillel groups, but is also attracting the support of some Jewish Canadians. The events are normally held in February or March. According to the organization, "the aim of IAW is to educate people about the nature of Israel as an apartheid system and to build BDS campaigns as part of a growing global BDS movement."

Zionist students attempt to outlaw it (McMaster University and University of Toronto in 2008, Carleton, University of Ottawa, Trent, Wilfrid Laurier in 2009) but the majority of students are only challenged by such moves. The term Israeli Apartheid was actually coined by Israel Prize laureate and former Minister of Education, Shulamit Aloni,[18] and adopted by Jimmy Carter in his 2006 *Palestine: Peace Not Apartheid.* In 2010, former executive director of the American Jewish Congress Henry Seligman described Israel in the *Nation* as having morphed from "the only democracy in the Middle East into the only apartheid regime in the western world."[19] The UN was forced, kicking and screaming, to reaffirm its 1975 resolution condemning Zionism as racism with the publication of the UN Economic and Social Commission for Western Asia report in March 2017 calling Israel an apartheid state.

Pro-Palestinian student activism in Canada finds its strongest support in Quebec. Quebec's campaign for independence in the 1980s did not embrace Israel as an example of creating a national state based on ethnicity, and was opposed by the Montreal Jewish elite.[20] FLQ militants even trained with Palestinian militants briefly in the 1970s. Those heady revolutionary 1970s are history, but the embers of liberation live on and provide inspiration for pro-Palestinian activism, resulting in occasional hostile encounters with JDL and Hillel activists, even a mini-riot at Concordia in 2012, when Netanyahu was forced to cancel his speech. Canada is too much of a 'friend' to arrest Israeli politicians accused of human rights crimes, as is the case in some European countries, but even 'best friends' have limits to their hospitality.

York University Intifada

Not surprisingly, anti-Zionist activism has increased most where there are more Muslim students, and Zionist activism where there are more Jewish students: Montreal (Concordia and McGill) and in Toronto (University of Toronto, Ryerson and York). York University has seen the most turmoil. The fight that erupted in 2016 is a classic case of Zionist blackmail and student courage.

Students were emboldened by **David Noble** (1945–2010), a professor of history of science and technology at York, who became an outspoken anti-Zionist with his *Beyond the Promised Land: The Movement and the Myth (*2006). He also published a flier in 2004 for his students, "The York University Foundation: The Tail That Wags the Dog (Suggestions for Further Research)", accusing the university fundraising body of being "biased by the presence and influence of staunch pro-Israel lobbyists, activities and fundraising agencies," and naming members of the group who had ties to Jewish organizations.

York University, the York University Foundation, and two

student groups—Solidarity for Palestinian Human Rights (sic) and Hillel at York—jointly issued a press release strongly condemning "this highly offensive material." The Canadian Jewish Congress also released a media statement calling Noble's actions "appalling". CJC spokesman Joel Richier called the flier "anti-Semitism, vaguely disguised as anti-Israel rhetoric." But the Zionists had gone too far. Noble, who was Jewish, sued the school (ignoring the CJC, the spurious SPHR and Hillel) for defamation, and won, the first professor in Canada to be paid a cash reparation ($2,500) for a violation of academic freedom.

This legacy ensured vibrant, genuine Palestinian support among students, erupting again in 2016 in another battle. Prominent donor Paul Bronfman, a relation of Samuel Bronfman (head of the CJC from 1939 to 1962), objected to a painting "Palestinian Roots", displayed on campus. Bronfman is the head of film equipment supplier Comweb Group Inc. He was planning to endow the William F. White Center. "York is going to lose thousands of dollars of television production equipment used for emerging student filmmakers, and access to technical people. ... York University will be *persona non grata* at William F. White International until they take that poster down."[21] In January 2016, he ended his donations to York when his threat was not heeded.

Another case of targeting an anti-Zionist university professor is that of Lethbridge University history professor **Anthony Hall**. Suddenly, there appeared on Hall's Facebook page a doctored photograph with the caption "Kill all Jews now", which was immediately followed by a complaint to the Calgary police. Hall had nothing to do with the offensive image, which was posted by Facebook user "Glen Davidson" as a comment on a story at Hall's Facebook page. Facebook initially refused to remove the image, prompting a watchful B'nai Brith to immediately complain to the police and publish an article attacking

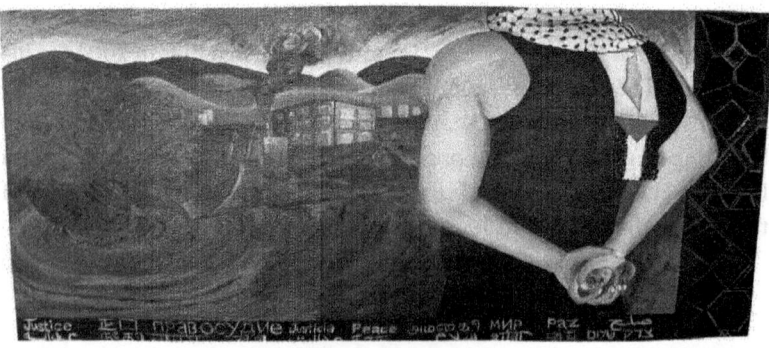

Palestinian Roots

Hall, stating Tony Hall "is well-known for using academic credentials to deny the Holocaust." B'nai Brith stated it will "monitor the police investigation."[22]

Hall was suspended. Supporters of Hall did their own snooping and discovered that the photoshopped image was created several years earlier by a 20-year-old Jewish man Joshua Goldberg, who was arrested by the FBI in 2015 for sending bomb-making instructions to what he thought was a Muslim terrorist—instead it was an FBI undercover agent. Goldberg is now pleading mental illness, but "for years he was allowed to stir up trouble from his parent's basement in Florida. For some reason he enjoyed targeting me and he's the one who created that image as well as many other hate screeds."[23] Hall appealed and eventually received his back pay in full but was not reinstated.

Another incident highlighting CIJA and B'nai Brith's relentless campaign of intimidation is that of **Nadia Shoufani**, a teacher in Mississauga, who was suspended after their complaint for addressing an Al-Quds Day rally in Queen's Park in 2016, calling on the public to "support the resistance [against Israel] in any form." "We applaud the Dufferin-Peel Catholic District School Board for taking decisive action by suspending Shoufani," said CIJA spokesman Berl Nadler. "It is disturbing to think that someone who is entrusted with the responsibilities of a teacher would be among the leading voices at a toxic, anti-Semitic event like Al-Quds Day."[24]

A women's flotilla to Gaza was launched by Canadian activists, in September 2016. Two ships, Amal (Hope) and Zaytouna (Olive) attempted to defy the blockade. On board were Nobel Peace Laureate Mairead Maguire, Green Party New Zealand MP Marama Davidson, other European parliamentarians, a decorated US diplomat, journalists, an Olympic athlete, and a physician. A former New Democratic Party MP and clergyman, James Manly, was on the 2012 flotilla and was briefly arrested by the IDF when the boat, the *Estelle*, was seized. The flotillas have been taking place every year since 2003. When asked why they are going, the women gave a variety of responses. Mairead Maguire notes that "they say that 'silence is golden', but, regarding the plight of Palestinians in Gaza, the silence of the world, especially concerning their little children, shows a lack of moral and ethical leadership from the international community. Why has it lasted so long?"[25]

For two of the women, their countries' own historical struggles for human rights played an important role in their decision to join the

Women's Boat to Gaza. Leigh-Ann Naidoo, an Olympic volleyball player from South Africa, feels that "South Africans understand the importance of international solidarity in fighting regimes that practice segregation." Marama Davidson, a Maori native, carries with her a strong personal connection to Palestinian women in Gaza. "As an indigenous woman myself, I want to stand alongside the women of Gaza and to draw attention to the ongoing humanitarian crisis there."[26]

There have also been relief convoys from Europe and even India, though Israel has seized every one. Despite mobilizing its powerful international resources, its hard and soft power, Israel has not been able to stop such efforts, exposing Israel's inability to control the narrative concerning Palestine.

Canadians for Justice and Peace in the Middle East (**CJPME**), founded in 2002 in Montreal, is the most active Palestinian support group with branches across Canada. It produces informative videos, monitors the mainstream press for biased coverage of Palestine, arranges speaking tours and exhibits, and helps organize public meetings and rallies.[27]

The efforts to co-opt other minorities in the West to the Zionist cause have continued to stall. While Tel Aviv is touted as the gay capital of the Middle East, Canadian gays have never mobilized to defend Israel, but they have done so to defend Palestine, despite knowing that gay liberation is not acceptable in the Muslim world. The Toronto-based **QuAIA** (Queers Against Israel Apartheid) was formed in 2008 as a member of the Coalition Against Israeli Apartheid. The group was involved in Israeli Apartheid Week as well as Pride Week and spoke out against "pinkwashing", the use of gay rights as a propaganda tool to justify Israel's policy toward Palestine.

In 2010, the group was initially banned from marching in the Pride Toronto parade, despite receiving statements of support from queer organizations within and outside Canada, including the three major Palestinian queer rights organizations. However, following a backlash from the local queer community, Pride Toronto reversed its decision to ban the words "Israeli Apartheid" in 2010. Yakov Rabkin, professor of history at the Université de Montréal, stated, "One may sympathize with Israel fans in this country who find it hard to present the state of Israel in an attractive light. By campaigning to ban the QuAIA, they only confirm what many have long suspected: that Israel is indeed an apartheid state. Wise men of South Africa extricated their country from a violent conundrum. This should show Israel and its supporters a way to lasting peace. A prohibition of the QuAIA will be remembered as a ridiculous and irrelevant act."[28] Shortly before QuAIA dissolved in 2015, then-mayoral candidate John Tory said Pride should be denied funding if QuAIA marched. Tory went on to be elected. QuAIA saw the writing on the wall, and finally decided it was better for activists just to join mainstream Palestinian support groups, keeping in mind that actively identifying as gay and trying to help gays in the Middle East was actually much like the foot-shooting that the Zionists do. The purpose of the organization had been more to inform Canadian gays, than to do outreach to Middle East gays.

Queer Arabs of Halifax sought community support to oppose the presence of an Israeli table at the annual Halifax Pride community fair with propaganda about Israel as the "gay capital of the Middle East". The Nova Scotia Rainbow Action Project (NSRAP) supported them, but Halifax Pride refused to act on their concerns, pressured by a Zionist evangelical organization which, while it opposes homosexuality, supports the state of Israel, and packed the gay pride meeting to vote down the motion. In other words, policy for LGBTQ Pride in Halifax was decided mostly by homophobes.[29]

Jewish, Muslim Activism

Israeli Peace Now is Israel's leading grassroots (Zionist) movement (1978), supported by Canadian/US Friends of Peace Now (1981) (600 members in Toronto, 200 in Montreal and a few other cities), but with no activism, no critical newspaper ads as in the US. It fits perfectly Atzmon's criticism of Jewish peace groups who try to control the agenda of dismantling Israeli apartheid.

The United Jewish People's Order[30] continues its critical approach to Israel, trying to maintain ties with the larger Jewish community.[31] **Independent Jewish Voices** (IJV, 2008)[32] supports both BDS and the campaign to end the Jewish National Fund's tax-exempt status as a charity, and was excluded from the CJC. Ex-CJC head Farber dismisses IJV as a "fringe group" that spews "vile, anti-Zionist rhetoric".[33] Its members perform a vital task, weathering the Zionist rhetoric hurled at all pro-Palestinian activists, in the name of Judaism. Jewish tribalism prevents Farber from demanding that Jewish critics be persecuted as he does the non-Jewish Halls and Shoufanis. Sid Shniad of IJV accused the CJC of "playing the anti-Semitic card ... because they don't have a lot else. They want to intimidate; they want to shut [the debate] down, a losing game. They're placing themselves on the wrong side of the issue of free speech. You don't win people's hearts and minds by telling them to shut up and go away." He stated that it was "outrageous" that Bernie Farber attended a conference of the United Church of Canada (UCC) "to try to shut down this debate."[34]

IJV sees itself as rescuing the true Jewish heritage—Jewish morals and ethics based in religion—which is now secularized. This puts these Jewish Canadians in line with all those Canadians whose main signifier, after 'Canadian', is a commitment to social justice and universal human rights. IJV has branches in Britain and Australia. It has not adopted a position on the question of a one-state versus a two-state solution, but believes it is crucial for Israelis and Palestinians to have fully equal rights in any solution. Shniad explained, "Shifting the political forces here is the only practical leverage we have. So it is the people of Canada whom we must mobilize."[35]

The main Muslim Canadian organizations include the Canadian Arab Federation formed in 1967, and the National Council of Canadian Muslims (NCCM), which successfully lobbied for a parliamentary motion condemning anti-Muslim bigotry in 2016.[36] The NCCM also brought to light serious cases of racism against Muslims in the North York schools which the Ontario government acted on in 2016. The Islamic Society of York Region carries on the political activism of Kalim Siddiqui (1931–1996), co-sponsoring Al-Quds Day and other Palestinian solidarity actions. In an op-ed in the *Toronto Star*, they pointed to the Keegstra verdict, based on Section 319(2) of the Criminal Code for willfully promoting hatred, as the precedent to convict Kevin Johnston, who was charged with promoting hatred of Muslims with such statements as "Beat the living hell out of these [Muslims]. Pin them down on the ground, and beat them until they pass out. And when they're passed out, you beat them further..."[37]

From Canadian Jew to Jewish Canadian

The secular Ben-Gurions and Netayahus, who have no use for religion, tolerate their pesky Orthodox allies in parliament, whom they need in order to form majorities. They lend a thin veneer of legitimacy to the Israeli line claiming a right to the land based on Judaic/Old Testament sources. The religious types tolerate the secular state because it feeds them and protects them from the wrath of the Palestinians and the entire Muslim world.

Who will blink first? To win, the Palestinians merely have to survive and hold to their identity as such. The Israelis must struggle every day to bully their foes into submission or at least to keep them at bay, all the time fighting within the tribe. Israel has its nationalist heroes, such as Herzl or Ben-Gurion, but the greatest Jews of the past century, such as Einstein and Hanna Arendt, were universalists, Jews who adapted to their societies and assimilated, not losing their Jewish spark, but not becoming slaves to a notion of race above humanity. Jews mentioned here who fit this definition include Slonim and Avnery, one Canadian and the other Israeli, both of whom started out as Zionists and ended as post-Zionists, aware of the crimes committed in the creation of Israel, and both nonetheless striving to hold the Israeli state intact, to finding a way to achieve peace, both calling for Israel to be a state with equal rights for all its citizens, Jewish and non-Jewish.

As for Naomi Klien, Noam Chomsky, David Noble, Yehudi Menuhin, Anton Kuerti, Mordecai Richler, IJV activists – their criticism of Israel comes from the same universalist spirit. Kuerti said after Israel's invasion of Gaza in January 2009, "The unbelievable war crimes that Israel is committing in Gaza ... it makes me ashamed to be a Jew. The servile way in which Canada is supporting the US position— basically it's all Hamas's fault because of missiles that they throw over in desperation—I think this reluctance of Canada to use its influence makes me ashamed to be Canadian."

The invincibility of the Zionists is paper thin. Religious Jews from the start felt that it was for God, not for the Jews themselves, to fulfill his intention of bringing them back to Jerusalem. Many came to Israel, but continue to denounce the secular state and refuse to support it by joining the IDF or having any truck with the secular establishment. The bottom line for them is: Israel should be a religious state, run— like Islamic states Saudi Arabia and/or Iran—according to religious law. Ironically, it is Israel's Muslims and Christians who are the secularists' real allies in promoting a vision of Israel as a secular state abiding by international law. Together with secular Israeli Jews, they are would be a majority if they had the courage to unite, which is what the Zionists dread. Over half of Arab Israelis polled said they were content with living in Israel.[38] Give them full rights and this will jump to 100%. Ditto

Christian Israelis. How the Palestinian right of return would be realized is not clear given this scenario, but it is a possibility that the Zionists have to deal with eventually. Just as most Jews don't yearn for aliyah, far from all Palestinians abroad will want to return to Palestine, but the right will have to be faced some day.

The religious Jews, who are divided on the legitimacy of Israel as a secular state, were, are, and always will be a minority, unless they manage to breed themselves into a majority, outpacing the family-centered Muslims. Even with dozens of children, there's no guarantee that the next generation will buy into the ongoing state of war. Islam and Christianity are universal religions, welcoming one and all, unlike the tribal Zionist version of Judaism. The odds are in favor of the universalists, just as they have been for two millennia. The Palestinians, to 'win', merely need to survive. The Zionists must fight and scheme with their soft power lobbies and hard power to keep a racial, secular Jewish state alive.

The new anti-Zionism comes in different shapes and sizes. The most universal term is **post-Zionist**, a term popularized by Avnery and others such as Canadian Reuben Slonim, though that can mean different things to different people. In Israel, there are also **'revisionist/ new' historians** like Benny Morris,[39] Ilan Pappe, Shlomo Sand, Uri Avnery, even "liberal Zionist" Ari Shavit, coiner of a new definition for the acronym WASP (White Ashkenazi Supporter of Peace). There are countless Jewish non-Israeli secularists like Canadians Richard Noble, William Schabas, Americans Richard Falk, Chomsky, Finkelstein, Joel Kovel, Philip Roth. What unites post-Zionists is that Palestinian dispossession was central to the creation of the state of Israel, and owning up to this is a start to unlocking peace.

Deconstructing Jewishness

The final frontier in the new anti-Zionism is one that zeroes in on Jewishness itself, an existential dilemma for Jews who are struggling to determine what it means to be a Jew in today's world. If you are religious, there is no question. You believe in God and in the religious texts of the Jewish bible, the Torah. Some Orthodox Jews stop there. Most include the Talmud, the medieval exegetical texts, where the 'proof' that 'the Jews killed Jesus' is mentioned, though it is not a central text.[40] Then there are various strains of reform

Judaism, whose proponents revise their interpretation of the texts to make them relevant to society as it appears three millennia later. There are many versions of Judaism, but Jewishness has traditionally meant some variant of this religious faith. About half of Israelis are not religious at all, and half of those are outright atheists. So for them, Jewishness means being a citizen of a tribe, now a state. But this is a racial basis for statehood, which is outside the parameters of international law. A dead end.

The Israeli passport recognizes this by omitting any reference to Arab or Jew. Israeli nationality is by definition, 'a citizen of Israel'. But that definition has no actual standing in the domestic law of Israel. It is only a subterfuge to allow citizens of Israel to travel. The underlying reality is a two-tier citizenship, which most Israeli Jews will hotly deny, but which is a fact observed and felt every moment.

Brave Israelis like Shlomo Sand, ex-Israelis like Gilad Atzmon, who got fed up and went into exile, have dared to breech this last frontier, rejecting the very concept of Jewishness as irrelevant in a secular society. They substitute Israeli (or British or Canadian, etc.) as their primary signifier. The irony is that Zionism, by creating a *de facto* secular state for Jews, without having fashioned any identity other than race as justification for being Israeli, may simply vanish from the historical stage. Israelis increasingly ignore the 'Zionist' label. They are simply Israelis living in Israel much as the descendants of Canadian settlers view themselves simply as Canadians living in Canada, the rights and territories of the indigenous peoples only intermittently coming to mind. Many no doubt are genuine racists, even proud ones, but even they do not relish living in a state of Permanent War. Zionism lives on more in the minds of Jews in the West, routing for Israel as if it were a soccer game at the World Cup, trouncing the bungling, fractious Arabs. A spectator sport.

What Atzmon and Sand are doing is helping shift the signifier for diaspora Jews away from identity with Israel. What these 'deniers' want is to change the identity away from 'Canadian Jew' to 'Jewish Canadian'. Zionism revived and cultivates the archaic Jewish tribalism that in the 21st century is poisonous. It no longer has value once anti-Jewish bigotry is gone, and it is gone, especially in Canada—as long as Jewishness is not equated with Zionism. The anger that continues is not directed against an ethnicity, but on the contrary, against injustice. Anyone who loves Hollywood loves *Yiddishkeit*.

For such radical critics as Atzmon and Sand, to reject the Zionist agenda in effect requires rejecting secular ethnic Jewishness itself, which Marx was the first to address, critiquing 19th century Jewishness as "the practical spirit of the Christian peoples,"[41] an existential crisis which Zionism, a 19th century secular movement, put at the heart of 20th–21st century Judaism. Jewish students who have joined the IJV, participate in Israeli Apartheid Weeks and BDS activities or Al-Quds marches, make a clear break with the Zionist narrative and, if they still think of themselves as Jewish, think of themselves as part of the traditional Jewish view of their obligation to be a 'light unto nations', a spiritual role deriving from Judaism. Secular Jewishness, *Yiddishkeit*, is part of all of us now via American culture.

For the Israeli Sand, the only viable Jewish identity is a religious one, and as a nonbeliever, he logically concludes, "Cogito, ergo non sum." Gilad Atzmon takes Sand's logic further in *The Wandering Who?* (2011). He tore up his Israeli passport, becoming an ex-Israeli as well as an ex-Jew. What's so wrong with a secular, ethnic Jewish identity? Well, it can be based on only one of two things: persecution (being "forced" into being a Jew whether one likes it or not, as in the Nazi's racial laws) or being "born" into the Jewish people. The former is no longer an issue and the latter is full of holes, based on a dangerous myth. The current secular Jewish identity is a variant of the fashionable identity politics that replaced class politics beginning in the 1960s, a liberal facade to balance Zionist crimes. Atzmon argues that, "The Jewish Diaspora is there to mobilize lobbies to recruit international support. The Neocons transform the American army into an Israeli mission force. Anti-Zionists of Jewish descent (and this may even include proud self-haters such as myself) are there to portray an image of ideological plurality and ethical concern."[42]

Sand asks: when was the Jewish People invented? "At a certain stage in the 19th century, intellectuals of Jewish origin in Germany, influenced by the folk character of German nationalism, took upon themselves the task of inventing a people 'retrospectively', out of a thirst to create a modern Jewish people." For Jews, this required a homeland, and the westernized Jewish elite were able to provide this. As the West suffered one mortal blow after another (WWI&II), Zionism took on a new meaning, leading to the creation of Israel.

But the Jewish exile legend is a myth, at best, a legend, like Moses and the Red Sea. Sand is a historian and couldn't find any

Shlomo Sand

historical texts supporting it. The Romans did not exile peoples. "Judaic society was not dispersed and was not exiled." Jews continued to live in the Holy Land through thick and thin, freer under Muslim rule than Christian, but even the latter never "ethnically cleansed" them. Most Jews converted to Christianity or Islam, creating the (Christian, Muslim) Palestinians. However, a tiny core stuck stubbornly to the original monotheism, nurtured by the Babylonian exile in the 6th century BC, from which they returned. Jews are not a race but rather a collective of many ethnic groups, united only by the Torah, who were hijacked by a late 19th century 'national' movement. There is no direct racial or ethnic Jewish lineage running from the Holy Land for any other than those descending from Jewish communities historically and still living there before the tidal wave of aliyah starting in the late 19th century. The great majority of those who today consider themselves Jewish are descended from converts in Central Asia, eastern Europe and north Africa, not from ancient Hebrews expelled from the Holy Land by the Romans. They are not ethnic "Semites", of near eastern origin, or ethnic anything else.

As we saw at the beginning, Jewishness is more a state of mind, the Jungian shadow to mainstream culture, just as mainstream culture is the Jew's shadow. I.F. Stone put it succinctly: "The Palestinians are Israel's Jews."[43] Sand dismisses both religion and nationalism as the basis for his identity. Atzmon argues both are legitimate, though they both are perverted in the case of the Israeli state. Nationalism is an authentic "bond with one's soil, heritage, culture, language", a cathartic experience, not at all "empty" as a signifier. Though nationalism may well be an invention, it is still "an intrinsically authentic fulfilling experience". It can be misused, is often suicidal, but nonetheless, "it sometimes manages to integrate man, soil and sacrifice into a state of spiritual unification."

What is especially moving about ex-Jews like Sand, and ex-Israelis/ex-Jews like Atzmon, is that they are trapped by their own Israeli heritage, whether or not they emigrate. Reading Sand's book in Hebrew, writes Atzmon, "is for me, an ex-Jew and ex-Israeli, a truly authentic experience that brings me closer to my roots, my forgotten homeland and its fading landscape, my mother tongue or shall I simply say my Being." He is confronted not by some "'identity' or politics but rather the Israeliness, that concrete nationalist discourse that matured into Hebraic poetry, patriotism, ideology, jargon, a dream and a tragedy to follow." Israel's present state has "robbed him of that Israeliness which was once to him a home."[44]

Most Jews in the West still yearn to keep a diaspora Jewish identity alive.[45] For Sand and Atzmon, there is no "new Jewish identity" possible, because there is no Diaspora. Secular French-speaking Jews are French Canadians in Canada. English-speaking Jews are English Canadians. It's fine to be a believing 'person of the Book', and even an Israeli, speaking Israeli (really not the former Hebrew but a modern dialect), and being a citizen of a well-behaved multi-ethnic state, based on universal norms, like Canada. It's safe to be a Rathenau or an Einstein now. Assimilation does not lead to physical or spiritual extermination, despite Golda Meir's cries of "Wolf!" Non-religious Jewishness will continue to fade, along with Christian and Muslim identities of those who abandon their faith.

Zionists and anti-Zionists alike realize Israeli policies as rekindling "Judeophobia",[46] because Israel identifies all Jews as a "certain race-based people, and confuses them with Zionists."[47] Besides Jews who renounce secular Jewishness, there are the converts to Christianity such as Mordecai Vanunu, Bob Dylan and Israel Shamir. They give up Jewish tribalism to embrace universalism, like the first Christians or Jewish communists of yore. Such converts are worrisome to both religious Jews and Zionists. Conversion, rejection of your fundamental beliefs, is threatening at a deep level. Yet Jews have always been converting. The first Christians were Jewish converts. Of early Jewish immigrants to Canada in the 18th–19th century, some converted and became members of the British Canadian elite. The wealthy philanthropist Bentleys of British Columbia became Anglicans in the 1950s.[48] These converts are lost to Jewish historians and are not noted by non-Jewish historians of Canada or wherever. Who knows how many Jews convert or just fade into mainstream society after a generation or two?

South Africa and Israel

There is a growing feeling around the world of solidarity and resilience, like in the anti-apartheid movement of 30 years ago. After the Israeli invasion of Gaza in 2008, Canada witnessed the largest pro-Palestinian demonstrations in Canadian history. Ten thousand in Montreal braved the January cold, and 18 other cities had demonstrations across Canada.[49] People are not afraid to recognize allies among the Muslim immigrants to Canada and the West.

In the 1980s, arch-conservative Margaret Thatcher declared the African National Congres a terrorist organization, and in 1987 her spokesman, Bernard Ingham, famously said that anyone who believed that the ANC would ever form the government of South Africa was "living in cloud cuckoo land".[50] Yet three years later Thatcher was urging President Frederik Willem de Klerk to allow just that, to negotiate the handing over of power to their nemesis Nelson Mandela.

Lessons from South Africa:

- Don't be afraid to tell the truth that by demanding to be a Jewish state, Israel is a racist state. If the lie can be maintained in the global public, it will eventually be internalized, and Israel will remain 'secure' from global disapproval, which is the last major guarantee of support for the oppressed Palestinians.
- Don't lose hope when mainstream political forces backtrack.
- Respond to Israeli atrocities with direct action which can gain mainstream media attention (occupying MPs' offices, speaking out at public meetings, picketing)
- Use creative artistic means (satire, color, human interest stories).
- Contrast the humanity of the Palestinians with the inhumanity of the Zionists. Their only weapons are threats and force.
- Criticize Zionist hasbarah in the mainstream media.

In a sense, the struggle today, like the struggle to liberate South Africa, is a struggle to free Israelis from their dead-end Zionism, which long ago lost its progressive aspect. South African Jews largely accepted

Apartheid, and many (but not most) left for Israel, the US, Canada and Australia after its dismantling[51] (just as Quebec Jews left Quebec during the Quebecois independence drive in the 1980–90s). Probably fewer Israelis will emigrate when a peace settlement is reached. Yerida (emigration) is already an Israeli tradition, and accommodation will not be any more of a problem than it has been for South African Jews.

Assimilation is no longer a threat for Jewish Canadians. Just as Canada was a binational British colony, celebrating British and French heritage, with mostly citizens of Anglo-Saxon descent, it is now a multicultural nation, where those with British and French heritage are becoming the minority, though still celebrating that heritage. Even as Canadians have become a complex ethnic mix, no ethnicity is totally erased through assimilation to what is presently called 'Canadian'. French Canadians added a language law to buttress their culture, and flirted with an independent state, but even if they had separated, Quebec would have remained a democracy, where all citizens have equal civil rights. Most countries are multicultural now, with a dominant multicultural culture, where language and history form the bedrock of a unified state, where different ethnicities live on equal terms, one or more being predominant. *Yiddishkeit* is embedded in world culture now, very much so in Canada. It will never disappear, though it too will continue to evolve.

Forced assimilation is still an issue for native peoples in Canada. There can never be real integration for natives as such until they have their lands, and a just resolution to their past injustices, including a rebuilding of cultures forcibly destroyed, including languages and traditions. They need to maintain their 'special status' as First Nations via domestic legal measures, just as has been accomplished for the French. Paradoxically, only this will ensure that 'equal rights before the law' has real meaning for them. Jewish Canadians have achieved that and do not need to fear assimilation into a multicultural society, where ethnic differences are celebrated without any imperialist overtones (either 'Aryan' or Jewish).

At some point, anti-Zionism will become a core mainstream Canadian belief, as did anti-Apartheid before it. [52]

Afterword

The mindset of Jews in North America—American and Canadian—is vital to the survival of Israel. Hollywood is a bellwether for the world's chances to force Israel and its Zionists to change. Israelis—both Jewish and Arab —love Hollywood, watching movies via internet from both sides of Israel's walls, routing for the same Yiddishkeit-inspired heroes. We in Canada do too, and along with the Israelis and Palestinians, are all in the same soft power boat, on board the same US juggernaut.

Who is at the helm these days, under Trump the monarch? We have seen here that the two captains in North America—Ginsberg's archetypes of the Jew as vizier and storyteller—are no longer a happy family (if they ever were).

The struggle to achieve justice in the Middle East has entered a new chapter, where genuine political struggle about it is taking shape outside it. During the January 2017 rally in Toronto[53] to mark the advent of Donald Trump as the world's reigning monarch, the chant was 'No Muslim Ban on Stolen Land'.

In a few short weeks, Trump managed to unite millions of Americans and Canadians behind native rights, and bring the domestic struggles for social justice in line with world struggles against US policies in the Arab world—including Palestine. Interestingly, Palestine was not included in his ban, but that is only because Palestine isn't recognized by the US as a state, and Israel is keeping a watchful eye on its natives.

This new political nexus is taking shape now, bringing together a growing network of protesters, including Jewish Canadians, as well as natives of both Canada and Israel.

Endnotes

1 Satmar, the largest Hasidic dynasty (120,000), mostly in Brooklyn, Montreal, Europe, Australia, Israel, was founded by Joel Teitelbaum (1887–1979) in 1905. Teitelbaum rejected Zionism as a severe heresy and a rebellion against God, said that its pursuit brought about the Holocaust as a divine punishment, and warned that the continued existence of Israel would unavoidably lead to further retribution.
2 Consisting of the Arab members of OPEC plus Egypt and Syria.
3 OAPEC threatened to cut oil production 5% monthly "until the Israeli forces are completely evacuated from all the Arab territories occupied in the June 1967 war." The embargo lasted for about five months. Following the Oslo Peace Accords, the Cooperation Council for the Arab States of the Gulf (GCC) states, ended their participation in the Arab boycott. Companies found ways of bypassing the boycott and managed to trade with both Israel and the Arab world. For example, some firms that did business with Arab countries officially

	complied with the boycott, but in practice subcontracted their trade with Israel to companies already blacklisted, or cultivated good personal relationships with Arab leaders, who would allow them to trade with Israel.
4	<http://www.international.gc.ca/sanctions/countries-pays/index.aspx?lang=eng>
5	30% for Conservatives, 75% for Liberals, 85% for the NDP, 94% for the Bloc Quebec. EKOS survey sponsored by CPJME and IJV, *CJPME.org*, March 2017, <http://www.cjpme.org/survey>
6	The Green Party voted to continue to call for consumer boycotts, institutional divestment and other sanctions to pressure Israel over Jewish settlements in occupied territories — while issuing a statement saying it "rejects the goals of the 'BDS movement' as they do not include supporting the right of the State of Israel to exist." "A ban on the importation into Canada of products produced wholly or partly within or by illegal Israeli settlements, or by Israeli businesses directly benefiting from the illegal occupation;" "Renegotiation of the Canada-Israel Free Trade Agreement (CIFTA) such that it explicitly excludes products produced wholly or partly within or by illegal Israeli settlements, or by Israeli businesses operating within the OPT;" "The strengthening of CIFTA compliance/audit provisions in such ways and clauses as to ensure that imported products labeled 'Made in Israel' are actually produced, entirely and exclusively, within Israel's internationally recognized borders; "The termination and indefinite suspension of all military and surveillance trade and cooperation between, on the one hand, the Government of Canada and Canadian corporations or residents of Canada and, on the other hand, the State of Israel, Israeli corporations or residents of Israel's illegal settlements; "The repeal the House of Commons resolution condemning the BDS movement."
7	"AJC criticizes Israel's anti-BDS law", *JTA*, March 8, 2017.
8	The Heseg Foundation is a charitable foundation created by Canadians Gerry Schwartz and Heather Reisman in 2005 to provide scholarships to former lone soldiers (servicemen and servicewomen without family in Israel) who serve in the Israel Defense Forces. Reisman supervises the chapters and Schwartz, her husband, serves on the company's board of directors.
9	"Chomsky says BDS tactics won't work, may be harmful to Palestinians", *http://www.jpost.com/*, July 3, 2014.
10	Noam Chomsky Interviewed by Frank Barat, on Israel/Palestine (4/4). 2010.
11	BDS calls only for "various forms of boycott against Israel until it meets its obligations under international law". It does not officially refuse to accept Israel as a Jewish state, though its goal of "recognizing the fundamental rights of the Arab-Palestinian citizens of Israel to full equality; and respecting, protecting and promoting the rights of Palestinian refugees to return to their homes and properties," certainly implies that. Zionists online angrily denounce BDS precisely for that reason. Joseph Massad,"Recognizing Palestine, BDS and the survival of Israel", *The Electronic Intifada*, December 16, 2014. The Native American and Indigenous Studies Association (NAISA) and the Association for Asian American Studies explicitly opposed the racist policies of the state of Israel against its own Palestinian citizens. The Palestinian Campaign for the Academic and Cultural Boycott of Israel (PACBI) is clearer on this. The Columbia University Center for Palestine Studies reversed its apolitical position in 2014, inviting Omar Barghouti, co-founder of PACBI, to speak.
12	Gilad Atzmon, "'The Israeli Lobby dominates American, British and French foreign affairs'", www.gilad.co.uk/October 12, 2016.

13	Linda McQuaig, "Elizabeth May shouldn't run away from BDS: McQuaig", *Toronto Star*, August 22, 2016.
14	<http://europe.newsweek.com/foreign-investment-israel-slashed-by-half-329269>
15	Nora Barrows-Friedman, "What were the top 10 BDS victories of 2016?", *Electronic Intifada*, December 30, 2016.
16	<http://palestinelegal.org/righttoboycott> but only three of the bills passed into law (the federal Trade Promotions Authority, Illinois and South Carolina), and all are unconstitutional. Clearly legislatures are too cowed to just tell the Israel Lobby to read their US constitution, its amendments and legal interpretation. Better to blame the constitution. <http://palestinelegal.org/legislation/> Another 'shot in the foot' for the Zionists. Scare people with threats of blackmail, create lots of legal busywork, make lots of noise, all sound and fury, to infringe on American freedoms in the interests of a paraiah state.
17	<http://palestinelegal.org/righttoboycott>
18	Shulamit Aloni, "Yes, There is Apartheid in Israel", *Counterpunch*, January 8, 2007
19	Cited in Keefer, op.cit. 231.
20	See Chapter 5.
21	<http://www.citynews.ca/2016/01/25/paul-bronfman-pulls-support-of-york-u-over-anti-semitic-mural/>
22	Kevin Barrett, "Zionists plant 'hate speech' on professor – then call the police", *Veterans Today*, September 16, 2016, <http://www.bnaibrith.ca/calgary_police_investigating_antisemitic_post_on_facebook>
23	Private letter to Arthur Topham.
24	"Mississauga teacher suspended after concerns raised about conduct", *Canadian Press*, August 10, 2016.
25	"Zaytouna-Oliva departs for Gaza; Amal-Hope II to follow soon", *canadaboatgaza.org*, September 27, 2016.
26	Ibid.
27	<https://www.facebook.com/CJPME/videos/1645395678819772/>
28	"Counterpoint: Yakov Rabkin on Pride parade", *National Post*, May 7, 2010. permanent dead link, quoted from Wikipedia.
29	Ardath Whynacht and Dee Morse Scott Neigh, "LGBTQ+ organizing against racism and pinkwashing in Nova Scotia", *rabble.ca*, November 2, 2016.
30	http://ujpo.org/
31	The Canadian Jewish Congress expelled the United Jewish Peoples' Order and other "left-leaning" Jewish organizations in 1951. It was readmitted to the CJC, expelled again in 1995 but never admitted to the Centre for Israel and Jewish Affairs when the CJC changed its name. <https://en.wikipedia.org/wiki/Canadian_Jewish_Congress>
32	http://ijvcanada.org/
33	<https://en.wikipedia.org/wiki/Independent_Jewish_Voices_(Canada)> IJV was never admitted to either the CJC or CIJA. <https://en.wikipedia.org/wiki/Talk:Independent_Jewish_Voices_(Canada)>
34	Kathryn Blaze Carlson, "United Church, Jewish group try to reconcile", *National Post*, January 29, 2010.
35	Sid Shniad quote at Yves Engler, *Canada and Israel*, 142.
36	An amendment, Motion 103, strengthening the motion to include "Islamophobia" as a hate crime, was tabled by Iqra Khalid, Liberal MP for Mississauga-Erin Mills

in March, following the murder of six Quebec City Muslims in February 2017. It was loudly protested as an infringement of freedom of speech, but passed with 91 dissenting votes.

37 Carko Prodanovic and Essa Abdool-Karim, "Hate laws put reasonable limits on freedom of speech", *Toronto Star,* August 8, 2017

38 Index of Arab-Jewish Relations in Israel 2012 (The Israel Democracy Institute, 2013.)
55.9% of Arabs reconciled themselves to Israel as a state with a Jewish majority.
53.2% as a state with an Israeli-Hebrew culture.
80.5% of the Arabs agreed that among the kinds of relationships "between Arabs and Jews [there] should also be relationships that people voluntarily choose such as personal friendship and activity in joint organizations."
42.4% want to live in Jewish neighborhoods.
48.2% of the Arabs responded that in a public referendum they would vote for a constitution that "defines Israel as a Jewish and democratic state and guarantees full citizenship rights to Arabs."

39 Benny Morris is the only Zionist among the "new historians", concluding, according to Finkelstein, that the ethnic cleansing in 1948, "morally, was a good thing—just as, in his view, the 'annihilation' of Native Americans was a good thing—that, legally, Palestinians have no right to return to their homes, and that, politically, Israel's big error in 1948 was that it hadn't "carried out a large expulsion and cleansed the whole country—the whole Land of Israel, as far as the Jordan" of Palestinians." <https://en.wikipedia.org/wiki/Benny_Morris#Criticisms_of_Morris.27_post-2000_views>

40 See Introduction, endnote 29.

41 I.e., pious claims of the nobility of poverty, disdain of wealth etc., are belied by practical money-oriented life of 19th century secular (Christian) society.

42 <http://www.gilad.co.uk/writings/2016/7/31/renouncing-jewishness-shlomo-sand-and-gilad-atzmon>

43 *The Washington Report on Middle East Affairs,* quoted in Slonim, *Family Quarrel,* 107.

44 Gilad Atzmon, "How Shlomo Sand Ceased to be a Jew – or Did He?", *gilad. co.uk,* October 14, 2014.

45 Judith Butler's *Parting Ways: Jewishness and the Critique of Zionism* (2013) is by a liberal-leaning Jew who feels she must salvage her Jewishness from Israel's nationalism and occupation policies. "A new Jewish identity might emerge that connects Tel Aviv with New York's Upper West Side, Berlin, Paris, London and Buenos Aires -- and all of them on an equal footing," writes Carlo Strener in his review.

46 "As Israel is attacked, Jews are attacked for being supporters of Israel." There is a "chillier climate ahead, despite the objective gains in so many other areas." Penslar, op.cit, 46, 49.

47 Shlomo Sand, *How I Stopped being a Jew,* 94-5.

48 Peter Bentley was born in Vienna in 1930, the son of Leopold Bloch-Bauer and Antoinette Ruth Pick. His family fled Vienna in 1938 after unsuccessfully trying to prevent the nationalization by the Nazis of the family business, one of the largest sugar mills in Austria, later sold to a Nazi sympathizer for a nominal cost. They moved to British Columbia where his father, who changed his name to Leopold "Poldi" Bentley, founded Pacific Veneer, later the Canfor Corporation. In 2005, his family was awarded a portion of $21.8-million in

	restitution payments for the theft of the family's sugar refinery in Austria by the Nazis.
49	"Montrealers march in solidarity with Gaza", *McGill Daily*, January 15, 2009.
50	<https://www.theguardian.com/politics/2006/aug/27/uk.conservatives1>
51	The Jewish community peaked in the 1970s (at around 120,000), 70,000 remaining in South Africa after Apartheid ended. Approximately 1,800 Jews emigrate every year.
52	"CUPE chief apologizes for Nazi comparison", *Toronto Star, January 8, 2009*.
53	The Toronto demonstration attracted as many as 50,000, far larger than any demonstration in recent years. the 2003 demonstration against the US invasion of Iraq attracted 9,000. Tom Clift, "Anti-Trump Rallies Attract Millions Around The World And Inspire Some Truly Excellent Signs", jukee.com, 22 January 2017.
54	Trump's executive order issued January 27, 2017, banned citizens from Iran, Iraq, Libya, Somalia, Sudan, Syria, and Yemen from entering the US, as well as all Muslim refugee claimants. In February, the United States Court of Appeals for the Ninth Circuit blocked key portions of the original travel ban. A new order no longer bans citizens of Iraq, exempts people from the remaining six countries who have a valid American visa, includes no mention of religious preferences, and makes the ban on Syrian refugees temporary. But thousands of Muslims who could in principle still enter the US have cancelled their plans, as the ban signals trouble for them, implicitly condones anti-Muslim prejudice, and could well be lifted, leaving them in danger.

BIBLIOGRAPHY

Abella, Irving, *None Is Too Many*, Lester and Orpen Dennys, 1982.
----*A Coat of Many Colours: Two Centuries of Jewish Life in Canada*, Key Porter, 1990.
----"Never Again May Be None Too Many," Globe and Mail, February 26, 2013.

Alam, M Shahid, *Israeli Exceptionalism: The Destabilizing Logic of Zionism*, New York: Palgrave Macmillan 2009.

Anderson, Benedict, *A Life Beyond Boundaries*, Verso, 2016

Arendt, Hannah, *The Origins of Totalitarianism,* Harcourt, Brace, Jovanovich, [1951] 1973.
----*Eichmann in Jerusalem: A Report on the Banality of Evil,* Introduction Amos Elon, Viking Press, 1963.

Atzmon, Gilad, *The Wandering Who?,* Zero Books, 2011.

Avnery, Uri, *Israel Without Zionists: A Plea for Peace in the Middle East*, MacMillan, New York, 1968.

Barrett, Stanley, *Iis God a Racist? The Right Wing in Canada,* University of Toronto Press, 1987.

Bialystok, Franklin, *Delayed Impact: The Holocaust and the Canadian Jewish Community*, McGill-Queen's University Press, 2000.

Braham, Randolph, *The Politics of Genocide,* Columbia University Press, 1994.

Browning, Christopher, *The Final Solution and the German Foreign Office: a study of Referat D III of Abteilung Deutschland*, 1940–43, New York : Holmes & Meier, 1978.

Buhle, Paul, *From the Lower East Side to Hollywood: Jews in American Popular Culture*, Verso, 2004.
----Ordinary Men : Reserve Police Battalion 101 and the Final Solution in Poland, New York : HarperCollins, 1992.

Cleroux, Richard, Official secrets : the story behind the Canadian Security Intelligence Service, 1990.

Collins, Doug, *POW: A Soldier's Story of His Ten Escapes from Nazi Prison Camps* (New York: W.W. Norton, 1968

Cook, Ramsay, *The Regenerators, Social Criticism in Late Victorian English Canada*, University of Toronto Press, 1986.

Davies, Alan, ed., *Anti-Semitism in Canada: History and Interpretation*, Wilfred Laurier University Press, 1992.
---- & Marilyn Nefsky, *How Silent Were the Churches? Canadian Protestantism and the Jewish Plight during the Nazi Era*, Wilfrid Laurier University Press, 1997.

Delisle, Esther, *The Traitor and the Jew,* Robert Davies, 1993.

Dunkelman, Ben, *Dual Allegiance: An Autobiography*, Goodreads, 1984.

Ebadi, Shirin, *Iran Awakening: One Woman's Journey to Reclaim Her Life and Country*, Random House, 2007.

Engdahl, William, *A Century of War: Anglo-American Oil Politics and the New World Order*, revised ed., London: Pluto, [1992] 2004.

Engler, Yves, *Canada and Israel: Building Apartheid*, RED/ Fernwood, 2010.
----*Lester Pearson's Peacekeeping -- The Ugly Truth May Hurt*, RED Publishing, 2012.

Falk, Avner, *Anti-Semitism: a History and Psychoanalysis of Contemporary Hatred,* Westport, CT: Praeger, 2008.

Finkelstein, Norman, *The Holocaust Industry: Reflections on the Exploitation of Jewish Suffering,* Verso, 2000.
---*Beyond Chutzpah: On the Misuse of Anti-Semitism and the Abuse of History*, University of California Press, 2008.

Fogel, Bryan, Wolfson, Sam, *Jewtopia: The Chosen Book for the Chosen People*, New York: Grand Central Publishing, 2006.

Forrest, A. C., *The unholy land*, McClelland and Stewart, 1971 [1968].

Fraxer, David, *"Honorary Protestants": The Jewish School Question in Montreal, 1867-- 1997*, University of Toronto Press, 2015.

Genizi, Haim, *The Holocaust, Israel, and Canadian Protestant Churches*, McGill-Queen's University Press, 2002.

Ginsberg, Benjamin, *The Fatal Embrace: Jews and the State,* Chicago: University of Chicago Press, 1993.

Hoettl, Wilhelm. *The Secret Front*, Enigma Books, [1954] 2003.

Haultain, Arnold, *Goldwin Smith: His Life,* Cornell University Library, 1910.

Herzel, Theodor, *The Complete Diaries,* ed. Raphael Patai, New York, Herzel Press, 1960.

Keefer, Michael, *Antisemitism Real and Imagined: Responses to the Canadian Parliamentary Coalition to Combat Antisemitism*, Waterloo: Canadian Charger, 2010.

King, Thomas, *The Inconvenient Indian: A Curious Account of Native People in North America*, Doubleday, 2012.

Klein, Ruth and Diomant, Frank, *From Immigration to Integration: the Canadian Jewish experience*, Institute for International Affairs B'nai Brith Canada, 2001.

Knowles, Valerie, *Strangers at our gates: Canadian immigration and immigration policy, 1550-2015*, 2016.

Kovel, Joel, *Overcoming Zionism: Creating a Single Democratic State in Israel/Palestine*, Pluto Press, 2007.

Marianopolis College "Canadian Immigration History", <http://faculty.marianopolis.edu/c.belanger/quebechistory/readings/CanadianImmigrationPolicyLectureoutline.html>

Lipstadt, Deborah, *Denying the Holocaust: The Growing Assault on Truth and Memory*, Free Press/Macmillan, 1993.

Mackinder, Halford, *Democratic Ideals and Reality: a study in the politics of reconstruction*, New York: W.W. Norton, [1919] 1969.

Mearsheimer, John, Walt, Stephen, *The Israel Lobby and US Foreign Policy*, Farrar, Straus and Giroux, 2008.

Mulvany, C., *Toronto: Past and Present*, W.E. Caiger, 1884.

Myers, Peter "Fighting with Words: the word 'Holocaust'", mailstar.net , January 5, 2014, <http://www.mailstar.net/holocaus.html>

Nadeau, Jean-Francois, *The Canadian Fuhrer: The Life of Adrien Arcand*, Lorimer & Co., 2010.

Penslar, Derek Marrus, Michael Stein, Janice Gross (eds), *Contemporary Antisemitism: Canada and the World*, University of Toronto Press, 2005.

Rabkin, Yakov, *A Threat from Within: A History of Jewish Opposition to Zionism*, Zed, 2006.

Richler, Mordechai, *Oh Canada! Oh Quebec! Requiem for a Divided Country*, Penguin, 1992.

Robinson, Ira, *A History of Antisemitism in Canada*, Wilfed Laurier University Press, 2015.

Said, Edward, *The End of the Peace Process: Oslo and after*, Vintage, 2001.

Sand, Shlomo, *How I Stopped Being a Jew*, Verso, 2014.

Shahak, Israel, *Open Secrets: Israel Nuclear and Foreign Policies*, London: Pluto Press, 1993.

Shamir, Israel, *Pardes: An etude in Cabbala*, USA: BookSurge, 2005.
----*Masters of Discourse*, Booksurge, 2008.

Sheffe, Norman, *Goldwin Smith*, Fitzhenry and Whiteside, 1976.

Slezkine, Yuri, The Jewish Century, Princeton University Press, 2006

Slonim, Reuben, *Both Sides Noew: A 25-year encounter with Arabs and Israelis*, Clarke, Irwin & Co, 1972.
----*Family quarrel : the United Church and the Jews*, Clark & Co, Irwin, 1977.
----*To Kill a Rabbi*, WCE, 1987.

Smith, Goldwin, *Lectures on Modern History*, J.H. Parker, 1861.
---- *Essays on the Questions of the Day Political and Social*, Macmillan, 1893.
----*Guesses at the Riddle of Existence*, Toronto, 1897.
---- *Labour and Capital*, 1907.
---- *A selection from Goldwin Smith's correspondence, comprising letters chiefly to and from his English friends, written between the years 1846 and 1910*, Duffield, New York, 1913.

Spector, Norman, *Chronicle of a war foretold : how Mideast peace became America's fight*, 2003.

Speisman, Stephen, *The Jews of Toronto: A History to 1937*, McClelland and Stewart, 1979.

Torrey, E Fuller, *Freudian Fraud: The malignant effect of Freud's Theory on American thought and culture*, HarperCollins, 1992.

Tulchinsky, Gerald, *Canada's Jews: A People's Journey*,University of Toronto Press, 2008.

Vaugeois, Denis, *The First Jews in North American*, Montreal: Baraka Books, 2012.

Wallace, Elisabeth *Goldwin Smith: Vicorial Liberal*, University of Toronto Press, 1957.

Walsh, Bill, Cy Gonick, *A Very Red Life*, Canadian Committee on Labour History, 2001.

Weinfeld, Morton, *Like Everyone Else ... But Different: The paradoxical Success of Canadian Jews*, McClelland & Stewart, 2001.

INDEX

A

Abbas, Mahmoud 16, 212
Abella, Irving 147
Abramoff, Jack 41, 55
ADL   (See Anti-Defamation League)
Afghanistan, Afghan 111, 197
Agudath Israel of America   17
Ahenakew, David 263, 319–321
AIPAC (See American Israel Public Affairs Committee)
Alberta 32, 241–245, 299, 302, 305, 317
Aliyah 60, 61,72, 73, 77, 80, 153,169, 178, 179, 188, 219, 225, 226, 274, 292 308, 346, 349
Al-Aqsa mosque 206
Al-Qaeda 118, 121, 122, 199, 205
Al-Quds 31, 162, 198, 341, 344, 348 (See also Jerusalem)
American Jewish Committee 17, 180, 334
American Israel Public Affairs Committee 121, 157
Anticommunist 94, 105, 110, 186, 239, 282, 283, 332
Anti-Defamation League 157, 170, 182, 183, 237, 266
Anti-Jewish 19, 30, 58, 65–67, 71, 89, 94, 97, 105, 128, 133–139, 147, 153, 155, 157, 160, 168, 171, 189, 217, 218, 235, 236, 238, 239, 252, 266, 270, 272–275, 281, 292 331–333, 347
Antisemitic 21, 27, 29, 31, 155, 161, 162, 170, 172, 175, 227, 236, 266, 267, 270, 278, 289, 355
Anti-Zionism 24, 107, 346, 352
Apartheid 12, 29, 51–53, 71, 115, 126, 138, 160, 169, 207, 210, 213, 297, 309, 311, 329, 330, 335– 339, 342, 343, 348, 351, 357
Arabs, Arab nations 14–16, 22, 31, 54, 57–59, 62–64, 72, 74, 77, 79, 106, 107, 110, 113, 114, 116, 118, 174, 185, 190, 194, 221, 318, 333, 344, 353, 354
Arab Israeli 13, 14, 30, 39, 44, 115, 116, 120, 306, 307, 309, 327, 345, 347, 354
Arab Jews (Mizrahi) 19, 24, 29, 31, 116, 131, 153, 155, 179, 212, 309, 310, 318
Arab Spring 325
Arafat, Yassar 29, 56, 107, 114, 198, 307
Arcand, Adrien 138, 155, 241, 24
Arendt, Hannah 23, 65, 83, 100, 154, 218, 257, 278, 317, 245
Armenia 24, 26, 32, 58, 78
Arms exports, production 53, 62, 65, 73, 77, 79, 89 , 101, 106 , 117, 141, 185, 226, 228, 254, 283, 324, 333
Ashkenazi 86, 133, 153, 155, 329, 346
Asper , Israel 19, 160, 165, 180, 188, 209, 216, 260, 292, 321
Assimilation (Jewish) 350, 352, 67, 68, 83, 92, 95, 103, 130–154, 165, 175, 176, 226, 236
Assimilation (Palestinian, native) 16, 40–54, 116, 130, 131, 294, 305–313, 324, 352
Australia 37, 39, 63, 79, 139, 142, 197, 274, 344, 352, 353
Avnery, Uri 169, 174, 214, 345, 346
Atzmon, Gilad 183, 189, 336, 343, 347–350

B

Balfour, Lord 18, 58–61, 134, 150, 187,

269, 270, 315, 346
Basic Law (Israel) 13, 16, 29, 119, 276, 279
Bata, Thomas 142, 143
Batman 92, 99
Bedouin 29, 38, 52, 58, 115, 119, 211, 213, 299, 327
Begin, Menachem 23, 103, 106, 191
Ben-Gurion 15, 23, 74, 79, 83, 94, 103, 160, 191, 237, 268, 316, 344, 345
Bentley, Peter 216, 350, 357
Berger, Thomas 297, 325, 326
Berlin, Irving 89, 97
Bernadotte, Count Folke 63, 77
Biden, Joe 82, 87, 88
Binationalism 225
Birthright Israel 160, 225
B'nai Brith 125, 153, 157, 161, 162, 167, 170, 171, 174, 193, 235, 240, 244, 258, 261, 265, 292, 340, 341
Boa, Franz 31
Boycott, Arab 333, 334
Boycott, Disinvestment Sanctions (BDS) 12, 53, 126, 161, 170, 190, 191, 207, 270, 330, 333, 334–338, 354
Boycott, Jewish, of Germany 80, 286, 290
Brand Israel 209, 210, 213
Brando, Marlon 294
British Columbia 47, 49, 71, 228, 258, 261, 300, 301, 304, 308, 324, 326, 350, 357
British Empire 22, 23, 58, 69, 120, 130, 165, 167, 184, 277
Bronfman, Charles 159, 160, 181, 221, 225, 284, 332. 340
Bronfman, Samuel 143, 157, 159, 173, 216
Bund, Socialist 169
Bush, George H.W. 108, 111
Bush, George W. 79, 84, 111, 191, 201, 204, 278, 320

C

Cairo 63, 76, 80, 125, 126, 175, 195
Caliphate 58, 60, 66, 112, 113, 202, 219, 269
Campbell-Bannerman Report   59, 113

Canada-Israel Committee 150, 154, 191, 192
Canada Park 9, 211, 214, 215, 296
Canadian Parliamentary Coalition to Combat Antisemitism 196
Canadian Jewish Congress (CJC) 157, 159, 192, 194, 223, 281, 324, 340, 343, 355, 356
Canadian Security and Intelligence Services 125, 202, 204, 219–221, 230
Canadians for Justice and Peace in the Middle East 208, 212, 213, 342
CanWest Global Communications 165, 209, 216, 292
Capitalism 37, 61, 66, 81, 82, 88, 112, 119, 276, 277, 280 –284, 292
Carter, Jimmy 83, 111, 199, 202, 339
Catholic 20, 44, 54, 101, 128, 133, 136, 138, 164, 173, 177, 194, 242, 288, 328, 341,
Centre for Israeli and Jewish Affairs 157, 160, 194, 249, 258, 316, 318, 341
Census 11, 13, 17, 18, 30, 31, 179
Central Intelligence Agency 110, 111, 202, 220, 229, 253, 289
Chabad-Lubavitch 82–85, 173
Charlie Hebdo 153, 277, 292
Chomsky, Noam 189, 335, 336, 345, 346
Chretien, Jean 136, 193, 204, 221,
Christ 20, 96, 137, 147 172, 267
Christian, evangelical 71, 74, 75, 194, 197, 223, 318, 319, 343
Christian Jews 73
Christianity 96, 117, 129, 155, 163, 164, 167, 172, 176, 243, 286, 298, 309, 346, 349, 350
Christie, Doug 246, 247, 249, 262, 263, 320
Christie Pits 133
Churchill, Winston 24, 39, 58, 59, 108, 120, 135, 144, 177, 239, 244, 277, 285
CIA (See Central Intelligence Agency)
CIJA (See Centre for Israeli and Jewish Affairs)
Citizenship 14–16, 24, 29, 44, 54, 70, 107, 115, 119, 129, 150, 152,153,

188, 192, 224, 226, 227, 263, 266, 314, 315, 347, 356
Citron, Sabina 246, 264
Civil rights 14, 30, 41, 53, 79, 155, 225, 246, 258, 276, 333, 352
CJPME (See Canadians for Justice and Peace in the Middle East)
Clark, Joe 191–193
Clinton, Bill 108, 261, 292
Cold War 10, 92, 98, 105, 106, 120, 253, 254, 265, 267, 272, 274, 281, 283
Collective blame 78
Collins, Doug 27, 246, 249, 260, 261, 262, 289
Colony, white settler 37, 39, 42, 52, 53, 55, 60, 61, 127, 141, 145, 184, 197, 322, 352
Colony, brown 58, 112, 309
Committee Against Israeli Apartheid (CAIA) 213
Communism 64, 73, 94, 105, 106, 111, 120, 199, 218, 225, 239, 265, 267, 271, 277, 281–283, 291, 293
Communist Party 10, 93, 136, 217, 224,
Confederation 37, 44, 48, 50, 54, 137, 142, 177, 197, 295, 322, 335
Conservative Party 49, 84, 126, 135, 136, 162, 191, 196, 197, 223, 227, 317, 335
Conspiracy 28, 55, 57, 60, 61, 65, 73, 86, 88, 101, 176, 313 (See Chapter 7)
CPCCA (See Canadian Parliamentary Coalition to Combat Antisemitism)
CSIS (See Canadian Security and Intelligence Services) 125, 126, 202, 204, 219, 220, 221, 230

D

Dayan, Moshe 271, 272, 291
Dead Sea Scrolls 211, 213, 214
Diabo, Russell 52, 56
Diaspora 15, 17, 19, 26, 28, 41, 68, 70, 87, 99, 114, 118, 154, 158, 275, 279, 280, 347, 348, 350
Disraeli, Benjamin 66, 130, 166, 182, 268, 269, 325

Dominion 11, 38, 39, 194
Downton Abbey 66, 73
Dreyfus trial 69
Druze 29, 77, 329
Dual loyalty 7, 61, 70, 95, 149, 151, 192, 216–218, 223–225, 228, 278, 332
Dunkelman, Benjamin 218, 219
Deschênes legislation 192, 263, 264,

E

Egypt 16, 22, 23, 39, 63, 68, 71, 72, 76, 77, 78, 100, 106, 107, 108, 110–116, 120, 125, 127, 168, 175, 179, 185–187, 198, 236, 275, 292
Eichmann, Adolph 23, 25, 80, 83, 145, 159, 178, 237, 253, 256, 278, 287, 288, 317
Einstein, Albert 10, 135, 176, 177, 345, 350
Eisenhower, Dwight 106, 110
English Defense League (EDL) 223, 230
Enlightenment 20, 276
Eretz Israel 10, 219, 226, 271, 272, 332
European Union (EU) 53, 54, 56, 121, 206, 230, 338
Ethnicity 13, 14, 17, 18, 55, 69, 90, 176, 309, 331, 339, 347, 352
Evangelical 71, 74, 75, 96, 194, 197, 223, 318, 319, 343
Exodus (film) 95, 226, 238

F

Farber, Bernie 223, 250, 258, 316, 317, 324, 325, 343, 344
Fatah 114
Final Solution 24, 52, 54, 241, 245, 251–256, 268, 281, 317, 324
Finkelstein, Norman 19, 85, 96, 134, 249, 252, 257, 265, 266, 267, 271, 290, 317, 335, 336, 346, 356
Finta, Imre 193, 261, 263, 264, 289
First Nations 41, 46, 50, 52, 56, 126, 154, 180, 217, 295 –297, 301, 308 –310, 315-331, 352
FLQ   (See Front de Liberation du Quebec)

Forrest, A. E. 168–174, 182, 273
France 32, 37, 42, 55, 59, 64, 79, 81, 110, 119, 127, 140, 144, 149, 153, 158, 170, 173, 178, 185, 187, 200, 255, 287, 295
Friends of Israel (UK parties) 229
Front de Liberation du Quebec 156, 339
French revolution 20, 295

G

Galloway, George 196, 198, 223
Gay 25, 67–69
Genesis 31, 269, 311
Genocide 26, 42, 45, 55, 112, 180, 253, 285, 315, 317, 321, 322, 329, 255, 256, 269
Germany 71, 79, 83, 117, 144, 146, 158, 176, 184, 208, 229, 237, 245, 246, 257, 263, 264, 273, 275, 286, 348
Germany, Nazi 10, 25, 37, 63, 80, 105, 116, 133, 140–142, 176, 178, 184, 185, 196, 241, 242, 254, 255, 258, 259, 270, 274, 275, 281, 286, 315
Gentile 10, 20, 22, 67, 68, 86, 90, 93, 105, 133–135, 140, 141, 149, 160, 165–168, 267, 281, 313, 331
Ghetto 19, 90, 118, 131, 132, 133, 139–141, 167, 174, 176
Globe and Mail 193, 219, 227, 278
Gorbachev, Mikhail 107
Gouzenko, Igor 147, 217
Goy(im) 82, 89, 96, 238, 284, 313
Great Game I (See Chapter 1) 57, 60, 63, 70, 73, 108, 118, 279, 292
Great Game II 57, 63–66, 70, 73, 88, 106, 108, 110, 111, 114, 118, 121, 157, 199, 282
Great Game III 70, 77, 107, 111, 117, 118, 119, 199, 280
Greater Israel 71, 108, 268, 272, 273, 290, 291
Green Party 334, 336, 341, 354, 207, 215
Greyson, John 210
Gaza 190, 195, 197, 208–210, 219, 224, 230, 265, 303, 318–320, 337, 341, 342, 345, 351, 355
Ginsberg, Benjamin 66, 87, 92, 105, 136, 159, 176, 218, 245, 249, 250, 269, 277, 353

H

Haganah 62, 80, 157, 218
Hamas 81, 104, 118, 195, 197, 221, 222, 345
Hard power 61, 65, 77, 96, 160, 187, 194, 199, 312, 346
Harper, Stephen 298, 306, 317–325, 331
Haredi 24, 32
Hart family 128, 129
Harwood, Richard E. 33, 245–255
Hasbarah 114, 117, 159, 160, 180, 208, 237, 265, 290, 297, 299, 313, 319, 351
Hasid 17, 24, 32, 181, 351, 353
Heartland 43, 57, 71, 103, 116
Hebrew 19, 23, 24, 26, 30, 31, 82, 95, 100, 115, 129, 157, 164, 173, 175, 180–182, 215, 225, 296, 306, 307, 310, 349, 350, 356
Herzl, Theodore 15, 71, 74, 76, 101, 180, 187, 268 270
Heuchter Report 33, 104
Himmler, Heinrich 80
Hitler, Adolph 28, 58, 62, 69, 78, 80, 87, 100, 103, 138, 140, 142, 144, 178, 201, 235, 236, 246, 249, 251, 252, 255, 257, 262–264, 268, 275, 278, 281–284, 287, 315, 320
Hizbullah 118
Hoettl 178, 253, 287
Hollywood 26, 65, 85, 86, 89–99, 102, 103, 105, 149, 210, 260, 265, 274, 347, 352
holocaust 24–26, 32, 69, 158, 241, 266, 282, 284, 321
Holocaust 19, 24–28, 32, 33, 69, 74, 80, 85, 96, 97, 103, 104, 148, 154, 158–161, 174, 175, 180, 181, 183, 188, 192, 200, 229, 236–242, 246–260, 271, 280, 285–288, 314, 317, 320,

341, 353
Holocaust denier 19, 27, 28, 236, 239, 252, 256, 265, 266, 271, 282, 290
Holocaust industry 85, 96, 237, 252, 271, 217
Holodomor 25, 180
Holy Land 13, 58, 71, 169, 170, 318, 319, 349
Homosexual 27, 68, 69, 158, 343
Horowitz, David 85, 186

I

Ideology 18, 19, 23, 69, 79, 94, 99, 168, 177, 237, 249, 256, 267, 271, 275, 280, 284, 314, 336, 250
IDF (See Israeli Defense Forces) 29, 52, 62, 96, 119, 213, 218, 219, 292, 327, 341, 345, 354(See Israeli Defense Forces)
Idle No More 317, 321, 324, 325
Ignatieff, Michael 196
IHR (See Institute for Historical Review) 240, 285 (See Institute for Historical Review)
Immigration to Israel 14, 15, 23, 59–61, 77, 80, 112, 112, 120, 147, 153, 169, 273, 274, 313, 316, 318
Immigration to Canada 33, 130–133, 139 –155, 169, 176–179, 222, 224, 262, 263, 274
Imperial Conference (1921) 184
India 31, 38, 39, 64, 290, 294, 342
Indian Affairs and Northern Development, Department of 49, 50, 305
Indigenous and Northern Affairs, Department of 47, 305
Institute for Historical Review 240, 285
Intifada 45, 113, 193, 311, 339
Inuit 41, 295, 306
Ipperwash 46, 47, 308
Iran 17, 31, 67, 79, 81, 101, 108–111, 115, 125, 161, 175, 176, 187, 188, 196, 198–202, 222, 223, 228, 248, 285, 322–325, 330, 334, 345, 357

Iraq 31, 58, 77, 78, 111,115, 116, 118, 119, 176, 179, 188, 193, 197, 199, 201, 202 –204, 228, 236, 268, 270, 275, 278, 290, 292, 294, 309, 322, 323, 330, 357
Ireland 53, 54, 229, 242
Irving, David 27, 104, 240, 245, 247, 251, 257, 267, 289
Islam 30, 31, 54, 67, 68, 82, 111, 117, 118, 173, 185, 198–202, 204, 213, 214, 230, 235, 245, 249, 272, 285, 298, 328, 333–346, 349
Islamic State 67, 118, 199, 202, 230
Islamophobia 31, 85, 158, 197, 205, 223, 308, 311, 327, 356
Israel Project 86, 209, 214
Israeli Defense Forces 29, 30, 52, 62, 97, 119, 213–215, 219, 224, 292, 327, 341,

J

Jabotinsky, Ze'ev (Vladimir) 22, 23, 71, 268, 271, 291, 293
Jewish Defense League (JDL) 74, 85, 157, 158, 196, 198, 223, 228, 230, 249, 250, 258, 338, 339,
Jerusalem (See al-Quds) 12, 21, 22, 28, 29, 31–33, 39, 55, 57–60, 71, 72, 110, 101, 103, 112, 118, 122,145, 170, 179, 183, 191, 206, 211–215, 226, 237, 269, 299, 303, 307, 311, 345
Jesus 20, 23, 67, 73, 172, 173, 183, 194, 313, 346
Jewish Agency 61, 80
Jewish Legion 61
Jewish State 10, 11, 14–18, 22–24, 28–30, 58, 60, 61, 63–65, 69, 71, 80, 82, 84, 88, 94, 96, 106, 113, 116, 120, 135, 145, 151–153, 172, 174, 177, 179, 185, 186, 188, 189, 198, 208, 238, 239, 275, 280, 291, 217, 336, 338, 346, 354
Jewish terrorists 62, 63, 76, 157
Jewry 31, 70, 80, 94, 117, 144, 147, 180, 241, 242, 254, 269, 270, 272, 276,

279, 280, 285, 328
Jews, Russian 17, 19, 107
Jewishness 19, 28, 67, 68, 73, 92–96, 128, 135, 137, 149, 153, 163, 164, 167, 274, 336, 346–350, 356 (See also Yiddishkeit)
Johnston, Kevin 344
Jordan 16, 22, 29, 30, 63, 100, 103, 106, 185, 186, 208, 211, 213, 221, 290, 302, 303, 307, 337
Judaism 15 –21, 30, 54, 68, 69, 81, 84, 97, 105, 127, 140, 163–174, 177, 183, 206, 217, 218, 225, 243, 245, 274, 286, 309, 332, 336, 343, 346–348
Jung, Karl 66, 67, 349

K

Kairos 182, 195, 196, 323
Keegstra, Jim 241, 242, 243, 244, 245
Khaled, Leila 238, 322
Khomeini, Ayatollah 11, 198
Knesset 16, 101, 314, 334

L

Labrador 296, 300–302, 327
Lavon affair 78, 285, 291, 292
Lawrence, T.E. 39, 60
League of Nations 113, 184
Lebanon 29, 63, 77, 112, 114, 118, 152, 185, 191, 192, 195, 208, 222, 290, 300, 318, 337
Lebensraum 117, 284
Lehi (See Stern Gang)
Lenin, Vladimir 103, 275, 282
Liberal Party 45, 47, 50, 56, 84, 126, 135, 136, 138, 162, 181, 189, 196, 198, 200, 205, 207, 227, 301, 306, 335, 354, 356
Liberalism 57, 74, 89, 92, 102, 103, 108, 120, 141, 154, 162, 163, 263, 271, 276, 295
Lipstadt, Deborah 104, 252, 257, 267, 286, 287
Lobby, Israeli/ Jewish 82, 108, 171, 186, 191, 193, 215, 284, 333, 334, 355
Lower Canada 54, 129
Lubavitch (See Chabad-Lubavitch)
Luther, Lutheranism 101, 129, 135, 172, 173, 337

M

Mayer, Louis B. 82, 92
McCarthyism 94, 05, 217, 224, 265
Macdonald, John A. 130
MacKinder, Halford 57, 58, 61, 64, 70, 187
Manitoba 32, 159, 160, 180, 289, 300, 301, 305, 321, 328
Marshall Plan 59, 72
Marx, Karl 81, 88, 90, 99, 101, 167, 182, 218, 242, 271, 276, 277, 348
McGill University 159, 160, 207, 335, 339
Metis 41, 55, 295, 310, 312, 318, 319, 328
Milgram experiment 256, 263, 288
millenarian 59, 270
Mizrahi (See Arab Jews)
Monk, Henry Wentworth 59–61, 270
Montreal 46, 60, 61, 127, 128–141, 147, 148, 155, 156–161, 177, 217, 219, 224, 228, 295, 313, 335, 339, 342, 343, 351, 353
Morocco, Moroccan 17, 77, 179, 292
Moses (Bible) 90, 152, 312, 313, 348
Mossad 110, 157, 220, 221, 222, 253
Mossadegh. Mirza 108, 110
Mulroney, Brian 136, 192, 193, 221, 263, 295, 337
Multicultural 51, 53, 54, 85, 98, 116, 137, 149, 151, 154, 155, 189, 203, 22, 230, 295, 309, 311, 324, 331, 352
Munich (film) 97, 103
Munk, Peter 159, 181, 216, 278, 314
Muslim 13, 19, 30, 31, 58, 60–68, 79, 85, 106, 111, 113, 117, 118, 127, 131, 140 153, 155, 164, 169, 180, 185, 190, 199, 202, 204–207, 213, 219, 229, 235, 238, 246, 277, 285, 307,

307–312, 332–335, 339, 341 –346, 349–353, 356, 357
Muslim Brotherhood 125, 126
Mussolini, Benito 23, 103, 185

N

Nasser, Gamal Abdel 22, 110, 113, 125, 186, 187, 322
National Post 126, 160, 162, 175, 181, 195, 189, 322, 330, 355, 356
NATO (See North American Treaty Organization)
Nazi 17 –21, 24 –29, 52, 62, 68, 80–88, 100, 103, 105, 133, 138, 140, 141, 143, 144, 148, 150, 153, 155, 158, 161, 169, 178, 180, 192, 224, 227, 235–237, 240, 241, 247, 252–270, 276, 278, 281 –291, 299, 315, 317, 320, 332, 348, 357
Nelson, Terrance 176, 321–324, 330
Neoliberalism 125, 175, 198, 324
Neturei Karta 26
New Christians 127, 128, 134
New Deal 44, 94, 98, 324
New Democratic Party (NDP) 47, 52, 69, 84, 90, 181, 200, 324, 336, 354
New Israel Fundm 334
New Zealand 37, 39, 63, 79, 222, 318, 341
Newfoundland 138, 301
NGO (nongovernmental organization) 215, 324
Noahide laws 84
Nobel Peace Prize 13, 63, 100, 107, 110, 187, 189, 197, 341
North Africa 17, 77, 79, 116, 144, 148, 153, 166, 185, 270, 275, 317, 349
NATO (North Atlantic Treaty Organization)65, 11, 186
Nuclear weapons 20, 24, 25, 53, 65, 79, 87, 117, 195, 197, 201, 218, 226, 324

O

Obama, Barak 12, 13, 59, 84, 99, 117, 324, 338
Occupied territories 13, 100, 107, 108, 115, 211. 212, 230, 306, 309, 315, 334, 354
OCLA (See Ontario Civil Liberties Association)
Odigo 102
Oka 45, 46, 308
One state solution 51, 72, 79, 186
Ontario 43, 47, 136–138, 143, 148, 161, 190, 211, 246, 250, 258, 263, 280, 287, 300, 305, 308, 324, 328, 333, 334, 335, 344
Ontario Civil Liberties Association 258,
Operation Cast Lead (2008-9) 209
Operation Paperclip 265
Oscar 95, 98, 104, 200, 260
Oslo Accords 9–11, 16, 49, 175, 213, 354
Ottoman 38, 58, 60, 61, 66, 71, 112, 173, 269

P

Pakistan 31, 64,
Palestinian Liberation Organization 16, 22, 107, 114, 177, 156, 190, 191, 198, 220
Palestinian mandate 22, 37, 39, 60, 62, 70, 76, 112, 113, 120, 185, 186, 315
Partition 16, 64, 78, 108, 186, 226
Passover 32, 217, 225
passport 13, 15, 16, 115, 119, 122, 127, 145, 150, 152, 188, 204, 221–223, 225, 228, 277, 347, 348
Pekar, Harvey 99
Peres, Shimon 12, 13, 59, 72, 200, 248
Peacekeeping, peacekeeper 63, 100, 187, 190, 195–197, 222, 319
Pearson, Lester 77, 100, 110, 186–189, 193, 194, 197, 202, 205, 271
Pipeline 52, 79, 299, 304, 312, 324 – 326, 330, 353
Pipes, Daniel 271, 291
PLO (See Palestinian Liberation Organization)
Poland, Polish19, 32, 90, 103, 144, 106,

167, 168, 201, 217, 224, 229, 247, 255, 288
Postmodern pogrom 94, 105, 194, 280
Postmodern nation 9, 64, 70, 142, 188
Post-Zionist (See Zionism, post-)
Presbyterian 128, 167, 168, 173, 186, 244, 337
Promised Land 22, 28, 60, 65, 89, 97, 98, 135, 148, 150, 152, 158, 179, 298, 269, 275, 282,299, 313, 339
Protestant 44, 54, 59, 130, 133, 136 – 138, 164, 167, 172, 173, 177, 194, 242
Protocols of the Elders of Zion 211, 239, 259, 260, 269, 276, 277, 281, 290

Q

Qana 13
Quebec 45, 46, 54 – 56, 60, 126 – 129, 136 – 141, 147, 153, 154 – 157, 160, 177, 204, 205, 216, 217, 227, 230, 280, 300, 301, 306, 312, 335, 339, 352, 354, 356
Quotas 30, 102, 133, 134, 146, 147, 303
Quran 67, 73, 307, 311, 325

R

Rabin, Yitzhak 29, 53, 79, 117
Race 11, 13, 16–20, 29, 31, 44, 55, 66, 71, 102, 11, 116, 121, 131, 134, 164 – 166, 176, 190, 196, 225, 254, 268, 284, 330, 345, 347 349 350
Racist, racism 10–12, 16, 19, 21, 29, 38, 48, 52, 58, 69, 78, 115, 118, 119, 133, 150, 152, 165, 169, 172, 181, 230, 235–237, 243, 245, 274, 279, 289, 309, 311, 314, 315, 332, 339, 344, 347, 351, 355
Racial 10, 12, 13, 19, 20, 29, 30, 31, 56, 92, 119, 122, 136, 145, 148, 188, 254, 266, 282, 346 – 349
Rathenau, Walther 134, 135, 164, 177, 350
RCMP (See Royal Canadian Mounted Police)
Reformation 59, 173
Refugees 10, 15, 18, 29, 37, 58, 63, 77, 78, 114, 127, 131, 140–148, 150, 151, 153, 169, 172, 174, 175, 186, 190, 191, 199, 208, 215, 274, 291, 318, 354, 357, 357
Religious state 10, 17, 70, 345
Revisionist 27, 237, 246, 267, 291, 346
Reparations 69, 83, 138, 142, 201, 237, 328, 340
Richler, Mordechai 97, 141, 225, 345
Roma 25, 27, 69, 312
Roosevelt, Franklin (FDR) 45, 88, 144, 170, 185, 259,
Royal Canadian Mounted Police 47, 220, 221, 223, 224, 228, 244, 257, 264, 330
Royal Ontario Museum (ROM) 180, 209, 211–213,
Rose, Fred 136, 138, 147, 217–219, 224, 229, 236, 283
Rosenberg 105
Rothschild 59,66, 70, 73, 81, 82, 101, 113, 130, 134, 278, 290
Russian17, 19, 24, 28, 29, 31, 57, 61, 79, 90, 94, 103, 106, 107, 131, 165, 190, 199,200, 253, 269, 270, 273 – 275, 281, 282, 286, 287, 291, 292, 300, 322, 334
Russian revolution 61, 269, 281

S

Sadat, Anwar 125
Samizdat 246, 247
Sand, Shlomo 31, 346, 347, 349
Sandler, Adam 98
Satmar 17, 23, 332, 353
Saudi Arabia 17, 115, 120, 185, 198, 199, 290, 345
Saul, John Ralston 295, 310
Sayan(im) 78, 79, 84, 100, 188, 220, 221, 224, 273, 317
Schindler's List 96, 260
Schneerson, Rabbi Menachem 83, 84,

173
S.C.T.V. 89, 95, 98
Secular 17, 18, 24, 26, 30, 54, 69, 71–73, 74, 81, 82, 89, 96, 99, 101, 108, 110, 114, 116–118, 121, 129, 140, 150, 154, 160, 164, 166, 169, 178, 198, 204, 271, 274, 276, 282, 295, 327, 329, 332, 344–350, 356
Security cooperation partnership 195, 201
Semitic, semite 19, 30, 31, 116, 131, 160, 166, 174, 182, 210, 217, 237, 285, 341, 343
Sephardic 127, 269
Settlements 12–14, 22, 32, 45, 47, 55, 60, 62, 79, 80, 101, 103, 108, 113, 115, 117, 151, 174, 175, 187, 206, 226, 230, 271, 273, 303–305, 313, 318, 319, 326, 334, 337, 352, 354
Shadow 23, 32, 58, 66–68, 82, 93, 95, 105, 138, 166, 213, 279, 349
Shaftsbury, Lord 57, 60, 277
Sharon, Ariel 219, 220, 292
Simon Wiesenthal Center 32, 159, 240, 267
Slezkine, Yuri 267
Slonim, Reuben 19, 31, 119, 152, 171, 173–175, 218, 225, 332, 345, 346, 356,
Shoah 24–27, 32, 249, 257, 260, 267
Smith, Goldwin 57, 88, 147, 162–167, 169, 174–176, 180–182, 184, 224, 225, 230, 239, 244, 268, 276, 285
South Africa 37, 52, 53, 114, 115, 138, 148, 149 157, 169, 207, 290, 335, 337, 342, 351, 352, 357
Soviet Union 64, 65, 83, 88, 103–107, 110, 111, 114, 115, 118, 120, 121, 135, 146, 147–54, 157, 158, 170, 178, 190, 1989, 199, 217, 218, 224, 239, 248, 253, 255, 264, 272 – 275, 279, 281 – 283, 286, 289, 291, 333
Spielberg, Steven 97, 103,
Spinoza, Baruch 167, 218,
Spies, spy 79, 93, 111,147, 188, 217, 218, 221, 224, 228, 229, 270
Spinoza 167, 218,

St. Louis (ship) 140, 142
Stalin, Joseph 25, 94, 106, 107, 115, 210, 282
stateless 15, 16, 144, 298
Stern Gang 63, 76, 80, 157
Stewart, Jon 95, 104,
Storyteller 87, 99, 353
Suez Canal 63, 66, 72, 77, 100, 108, 110, 169, 187, 290
Superman 89, 92, 98, 99, 103
Supreme Court, Canadian 49, 51, 52, 241, 242, 244, 247, 249, 263, 266, 300,
Supreme Court, Israeli 15, 29, 101, 278, 279, 299, 327
Syria 17, 19, 22, 29–31, 63, 77, 78, 106, 118, 119, 121, 175, 185, 186, 200–208, 222, 285, 290, 353, 357

T

Taliban 118, 121
Tecumseh 40, 42, 43, 56, 113
Tel Aviv 69, 74, 160, 191, 209, 211, 214, 293, 330, 342
TIFF (Toronto International Film Festival) 209, 210, 211, 214
Toronto 56, 60, 69, 129, 131–136, 139, 141, 148, 151–168, 172 –176, 179, 181, 190–194, 200, 202–205, 208–211, 214, 219, 220, 223, 230, 245, 246, 249, 250, 263, 274, 278, 312, 335, 338, 339, 342, 343, 353, 355–361
Toronto Star 174, 176, 191, 192, 246, 286, 291, 317, 329, 336, 344, 355–357
Ten mmCoandments (film) 96, 226
Terrorism 6, 5, 64, 76, 119, 158, 183, 191, 195, 200, 201, 202, 204, 205, 235
Thatcher, Margaret 198, 337, 351
Topham, Arthur 7, 236, 239, 240, 257–261, 266, 267, 271, 289, 355
Toronto 56, 60, 69, 129, 131–136, 139, 141, 148, 151–168, 172 –176, 179, 181, 190–194, 200, 202–205,

208–211, 214, 219, 220, 223, 230, 245, 246, 249, 250, 263, 274, 278, 312, 335, 338, 339, 342, 343, 353, 355–361
Toronto International Film Festival 209, 210, 211, 214
Torture 63, 126, 197, 205, 229, 313
Transjordan 22, 63, 103, 106
Treason 69, 322
Treaty, treaties 41, 49, 50, 51, 53, 55, 80, 111, 121, 177, 196, 228, 235, 295, 302, 317, 321
Trudeau, Justin 50–52 56, 69, 188, 205–208, 294–299, 301, 302, 321, 324, 326, 334, 335
Truman, Harry 186
Trump, Donald 13, 21, 55, 97, 100, 108, 118, 120, 191, 218, 285, 292, 295, 312, 324, 353, 357
Turkey 100, 111, 200, 202, 290, 304
Two state solution 63, 116, 344

U

United Church 10, 150, 151, 166–168, 170–172, 179, 186, 191, 335, 344, 356, 361
United Jewish Peoples' Order (UJPO) 157, 158, 343, 355
United Nations Declaration of Human Rights, 119,
United Nations Declaration of Indigenous Rights 51, 52, 119, 296
United Nations Educational, Scientific and Cultural Organization 206, 211–213
United Nations Relief and Works Agency 208
United Nations resolution 26
UN Security Council 196
UNDRIP (See UN Declaration of Indigenous Rights) 51, 52, 296, 299, 300, 315
University of Toronto 154, 159, 160, 179, 181, 278, 335, 338, 339, 358–361
UNESCO (See UN Educational,
Scientific and Cultural Organization 206, 211–213
UNWRA (See United Nations Relief and Works Agency) 208
Upper Canada 40, 42, 43, 54

V

Vatican 20, 67, 172
Verrall, Richard (See Richard E. Harwood) 245, 246, 250, 251, 253, 254
Vietnam 10, 24, 25, 98, 170, 191, 197, 238, 266
Vizier 87, 92, 193, 353

W

Wahhabi 199
Walsh, Bill72, 136, 138, 217, 332, 361
War, Six-Day (1967) 22, 174, 187
War, WWI 61,
War, WWII 25, 32, 142, 184, 229, 285, 289, 320, 333
War, Yom Kippur (1973) 333
War of Independence, Israeli (1948) 42, 147
War criminal 189, 263, 264, 289
Ward, The 139, 140, 167
Weinfeld, Morton 19, 177, 178, 180, 217, 218, 225,
Weizmann 23, 58, 59, 145, 177, 178, 253, 287,
West Bank 12, 29, 32, 78, 98, 121, 187, 190, 197, 206, 212–214, 226, 230, 265, 302–304
Wilde, Oscar 69
Wilson, Colin 93, 251, 252, 287,
Wikipedia 27, 33, 100, 251, 255, 285, 317, 328,
Wingate, Charles 31, 62
World Zionist Organization 58, 59, 177, 180
Wounded Knee 40, 43, 45, 114,
WZO (See World Zionist Organization) 58, 59, 177, 180

Y

Yad Vashem 25, 32, 80, 255
Yerida 68, 152, 226, 352
Yiddish 19, 89, 90, 93, 95, 97–99, 130, 132, 133, 137, 149, 154, 274
Yiddishkeit 85, 94, 95–99, 277, 347, 348, 352, 353
Yinon, Oded 78, 119,
York University 203, 210, 339, 340

Z

Zionism, anti- 24, 107, 281, 331–333, 335, 337, 339, 341, 343, 345– 349, 351–353, 357
Zionism, checkbook 226
Zionism, Christian 71
Zionism, liberal 100, 346, 348, 356
Zionism, neo- 22
Zionism, post- 23, 174, 175
Zionism, revionist 22, 23
Zionist Congress (1897) 261
Zochrot 215, 296
Zohan 98, 104
Zundel, Ernst 27, 161, 193, 223, 236, 239–241, 244–251, 254, 256–258, 260–267, 271, 275, 276, 286, 289, 297
Zyklon B 256